ROYAL HISTORICAL SOCIETY
STUDIES IN HISTORY
SERIES
No. 42

# THE *PARLEMENT* OF POITIERS

## War, Government and Politics in France 1418-1436

# Recent volumes published in this series include

For a complete list of the series please see pp. 249-51

# THE *PARLEMENT* OF POITIERS
## War, Government and Politics in France
## 1418-1436

Roger G. Little

LONDON: Royal Historical Society
NEW JERSEY: Humanities Press Inc.
1984

©Roger G. Little 1984
Watmoughs (City Print) Ltd ISBN: 0 901050 98 9
Humanities Press Inc ISBN: 0 391 03165 1

The Society records its gratitude to the following, whose generosity made possible the initiation of this series: The British Academy; The Pilgrim Trust; The Twenty-seven Foundation; The United States Embassy bicentennial Funds; The Wolfson Trust; several private donors.

First published in Great Britain in 1984 by Swift Printers (Publishing) Ltd, London EC1
for the Royal Historical Society
Printed in England by Watmoughs (City Print) Ltd, London EC1

To my Mother
and my Father

# CONTENTS

# PREFACE

In the course of preparing this book, I have incurred a number of debts both to individuals and to institutions which I would like to acknowledge here. My thanks are due to the French Government for the provision of a *bourse*, which enabled me to undertake original research, the basis of this study, in Paris. At the Archives Nationales I received much kindly assistance from the *équipe juridique*, and in particular from M. Henri Martin. I am also grateful to M. Jean Dujardin for kindly providing me with a copy of his unpublished work entitled *Les débuts de la carrière de Jeanne d'Arc*. Finally, I am grateful to the editorial board of *Studies in History*, for accepting my manuscript for publication in their series.

For additional assistance of a financial kind towards the research necessary for this book, I am indebted to the Trustees of the Bryce-Read Fund, the Arnold Fund and to members of the Graduate Studies Committee in the University of Oxford. Thanks are due, for the same reason, to the Trustees of the Pollard Fund in Wadham College, Oxford. Final preparation of the manuscript for publication was aided by a generous grant from the Trustees of the Twenty-Seven Foundation in the University of London.

For advice and guidance at various stages in the preparation of this work I am indebted to my research supervisor, Mr P.S. Lewis, to my examiners, Mr C.A.J. Armstrong and Dr C.T. Allmand; to Professor R. Favreau, Mme F. Autrand, Dr M.G.A. Vale and Dr P. Chaplais. My friend, Peter Gwyn, kindly read the typescript and Mrs J. Godden was ever helpful in seeing the book through the press.

R.G. Little

# ABBREVIATIONS

Wherever possible, the abbreviated forms of the titles of French journals and periodicals employed in this book conform to the style used by the *Bibliographie annuelle de l'histoire de France* (Paris, *Centre National de la Recherche Scientifique*). Titles not featured in the *Bibliographie* have (unless represented below) been kept sufficiently full as to be comprehensible without further expansion.

| | |
|---|---|
| *Arch. Frat. Pred.* | *Archivum Fratrum Praedicatorum* |
| *A.H.-G.* | *Archives départementales de la Haute-Garonne* |
| *Arch. hist. Poitou* | *Archives historiques du Poitou* |
| *AHSA* | *Archives Historiques de la Saintonge et de l'Aunis* |
| A.N. | Archives Nationales |
| *Beaucourt* | G. Du Fresne de Beaucourt, *Histoire de Charles VII,* 6 vols, Paris, 1881-91. |
| *BIHR* | *Bulletin of the Institute of Historical Research* |
| B.N. | Bibliothèque Nationale |
| —— MS.fr. | Manuscrit français |
| —— MS.lat | Manuscrit latin |
| —— Nouv. acq. | Nouvelles acquisitions |
| —— P.O. | Pièces Originales |
| *BSAO* | *Bulletin de la Société des Antiquaires de l'Ouest* |
| Chart. Univ. Paris | *Chartularium Universitatis Parisiensis* ed. H. Denifle and E. Chatelain. |
| Duparc, *Procès en nullité* | *Procès en nullité de la condamnation de Jeanne d'Arc,* ed. P. Duparc, 3 vols, *SHF,* Paris, 1977, 1978. |
| Favreau, *Poitiers* | R. Favreau, 'La ville de Poitiers à la fin du Moyen âge: une capitale régionale', *MSAO,* xiv-xv (1977-8), Poitiers, 1978. |
| *MSAO* | *Mémoires de la Société des Antiquaires de l'Ouest* |
| *Ordonnances* | *Ordonnances des roys de France de la troisième race,* 22 vols, Paris, 1723-1849. |

| | |
|---|---|
| Quicherat, *Procès* | *Procès de condamnation et de réhabilitation de Jeanne d'Arc, dite la Pucelle,* ed. J. Quicherat, 5 vols, *SHF,* Paris, 1841-9. |
| 'Rec. des docs' | 'Recueil des documents concernant le Poitou contenus dans les registres de la Chancellerie de France', ed. P. Guérin. |
| *Reg. consulaires* | *Registres consulaires de la ville de Lyon ou recueil des délibérations du conseil de la commune,* 2 vols, i (1416-1422), ii (1422-1450), ed. M.-C. and G. Guigue, Lyon, 1882-1926. |
| *R. Quest. Hist.* | *Revue des Questions Historiques* |
| Rymer, *Foedera* | *Foedera, conventiones, litterae, etc.,* ed. T. Rymer, 20 vols, London, 1704-35. |
| *SHF* | *Société de l'Histoire de France* |
| T./L., *Procès* | *Procès de condamnation de Jeanne d'Arc,* ed. P. Tisset and Y. Lanhers, 3 vols, *SHF,* Paris, 1960-71. |
| *TRHS* | *Transactions of the Royal Historical Society* |

## MONEY

| | |
|---|---|
| *l.p./t.* | *Livres parisis/tournois* |
| *s.p./t.* | *sous parisis/tournois* |
| *d.p./t.* | *deniers parisis/tournois* |

# INTRODUCTION

On 21 September 1418, four months after the Burgundian occupation of Paris, the Dauphin Charles in his capacity as lieutenant of Charles VI, ordered by virtue of the Ordinance of Niort the establishment at Poitiers of 'la court et juridiction sourveraine du royaume'.[1] From its foundation in 1418 until the death of Charles VI in 1422 the *Parlement* of Poitiers functioned not, primarily, as the Dauphin's representative but as the sole legitimate *Parlement* of Charles VI. In this sense – and the difference is important to grasp – the *Parlement* viewed itself not as an independent provincial creation but rather as the *Parlement* of Paris removed to Poitiers. It was only in 1422 with Charles VII's assumption of his father's title that the *Parlement* took, properly speaking, the status of an independent institution, faithful to Charles VII alone, and opposed to the work of its Anglo-Burgundian controlled counterpart in Paris. Yet despite this independence forced upon the Poitiers *Parlement* as a result of political events after 1418, it nevertheless continued, throughout its period of exile, to adhere faithfully to the style and organisation employed at Paris, with the result that between 1418 and 1436 France possessed, for the first time, two sovereign *Parlements* of identical status and organisation serving different rulers.

The archives of the *Parlement*, accumulated during its eighteen-year exile at Poitiers, have been considerably affected by the passage of time and today only a fraction of the original documentation exists.[2] Even so the residual material is of such great quantity that its complete evaluation would entail the assistance of a team of historians. This book attempts to use the surviving material to provide a reassessment, not only of the creation, organisation and function of the *Parlement* itself, but in a broader sense of the enigmatic early years of Charles VII's reign and the problems political, administrative and social underlying the period.

The *Parlement* of Poitiers has, until recently, received a consistently poor press from French historians writing on the period of the early fifteenth century. Voltaire, in his *Histoire du Parlement de Paris,* felt that: 'ce faible parlement resta longtems sans aucune autorité, et il n'eut guères d'autres fonctions que celle de casser inutilement les arrêts du Parlement de Paris, et de declarer Jeanne d'Arc pucelle.'[3] It was not until more than a century later that the

[1] The Ordinance of Niort is printed in *Ordonnances,* X, 477-80.

[2] On the extent of the Poitiers archives, see below, pp. 216ff.

[3] F.M.A. de Voltaire, *Histoire du Parlement de Paris* (London, 1773), 40.

2

naivety of Voltaire's remark was challenged[4] following the publication of Didier Neuville's 'Le Parlement royal à Poitiers (1418-1436)'.[5] However, while Neuville was able to produce an infinitely fuller account of the *Parlement*'s history, his conclusions, in broad terms, differed little from those of Voltaire. The *Parlement*, he concluded:

> faisait maigre figure avec son petit personnel . . . son ressort effectif. . . singulièrement réduit . . . sa compétence, quelque étendue qu'elle parût en théorie. . . bien diminuée en pratique par l'anarchie du royaume. Enfin, il était pauvre; à la longue, il devint même presque misérable.[6]

Neuville's views were echoed by Beaucourt in the pages devoted to the *Parlement* in his monumental *Histoire de Charles VII*[7], Beaucourt having drawn consistently upon Neuville's thesis in the composition of these pages.

Yet the views of Neuville and Beaucourt and indeed of many nineteenth-century French historians (views which have persisted in some circles until the present day) were deeply influenced by contemporary political events, and by the damagingly disproportionate interest displayed in Joan of Arc as a symbol of national regeneration. Interest in Joan of Arc, and the subsequent tendency by historians to portray Charles VII as the hapless foil for her achievements, meant that much historical material, rather than being evaluated in an objective manner, was employed, consciously or unconsciously, to support this view.[8] As a result, the more fundamental historical developments of the early years of Charles VII's reign have been reduced to near insignificance.

Some indication of the richness of the Poitiers archives was indicated in 1863 by Alphonse Grün.[9] Confirmation was provided in 1913 by Antoine Thomas, with his publication of extracts from the Poitiers archives concerning the *comté* of La Marche.[10] In 1914

[4]But see the notice by Alphonse Grün in E. Boutaric, ed., *Actes du Parlement de Paris* i (1863), ccxiii-ccxvi.

[5]*R. hist.* 6 (1878), 1-28, 272-314.

[6]Ibid., 21.

[7]Vol. ii (Paris, 1882), chap. XIII (*L'administration du roi de Bourges, 1422-1435*), passim.

[8]See, for example, the recent remarks by J. Harmand, 'Un document de 1435 concernant Houdan et la fin de l'occupation anglaise dans l'ouest de l'Île de France', in *B. Soc. Antiq. France* 1975, 207, n. 1.

[9]In Boutaric, ccxiii-ccxvi.

[10]*Documents relatifs au comté de La Marche extraits des archives du Parlement de Poitiers (1418-1436)*, Bibl. Éc. Hautes-Études 174 (Paris, 1910).

Thomas communicated more widely the existence of the first register of the *Conseil* of the Poitiers *Parlement,* covering the years 1418-31, whose 'loss' was regretted by Neuville.[11] The 'discovery' of this document and, more recently, the indication of a similar document in the *Archives départementales de la Haute-Garonne* (Toulouse),[12] has considerably increased our knowledge of the *Parlement*'s organisation and, in a broader sense, the effectiveness of Charles VII's government during the early years of his reign.

The weakness of Neuville's thesis, implicit in the works of Aubert[13] and Maugis,[14] has recently been further questioned by Professor Favreau,[15] and the forthcoming study of the Paris *parlementaires* by Madame Autrand[16] should revise our view of these years yet more dramatically. The function of this book will be to examine the question anew, in the light of the Poitiers documentation, and in so doing attempt to provide a more objective picture of Charles VII's government between 1418 and 1436.

[11] See A. Thomas, 'Le Parlement de Poitiers et l'Église de France', *Journal des Savants* 7 (1914), 315-17. (Cf. Neuville, 20-1.)

[12] A. Viala, *Le Parlement de Toulouse et l'administration royale laïque, 1420-1525 environ,* i (Albi, 1953), 10.

[13] F. Aubert, *Histoire du Parlement de Paris de l'origine à François I^er (1250-1515),* 2 vols (Paris, 1894).

[14] E. Maugis, *Histoire du Parlement de Paris,* 3 vols (Paris, 1913-16).

[15] See Favreau, *Poitiers,* 276-88.

[16] F. Autrand, *Naissance d'un grand corps d'État: les gens du Parlement de Paris, 1345-1454.* (Thèse d'État, Paris, 1978.)

# 1

# THE FOUNDATION AND EARLY ORGANISATION OF THE *PARLEMENT* OF POITIERS

## The Creation of an Alternative *Milieu* at Poitiers: Change and Continuity

The choice of Poitiers as the judicial capital of the 'kingdom of Bourges' was by no means an erratic one, for besides other important advantages the *Palais,* situated in the heart of the town, was uniquely qualified to meet the requirements of a sovereign *parlement.*[1] Earlier the residence of the counts of Poitou, the *Palais* became, during the thirteenth and fourteenth centuries, the administrative centre of the province of Aquitaine. In the last decades of the fourteenth century, an extensive programme of building and modification was initiated by Jean, duke of Berry, which as Favreau remarked, 'offrait de très larges possibilités d'accueil, dont le Dauphin Charles fera usage'.[2]

The extent to which this vast building catered for the requirements of the exiled *Parlement* is evidenced by the apparently small degree of structural alteration needed during the early years of its employment.[3] The first major modifications occurred in 1419 or early in the following year, when an existing chamber was refitted to accommodate the *Conseil* and a new chamber created to house the *enquêtes.*[4] Some years later, in December 1423, the *Parlement* authorised payment of 10*l.t.* to Antoine Mauloué, *greffier des présentations,* for 'reparacions et ouvrages . . . es tournelles de la salle du Palais de Poitiers pour mettre presentations de ladite court'.[5] The next major modification came early in 1426 when Charles VII ordered provision of 100*l.t.* to be made to Simon Macé, *maître des oeuvres du roi de charpenterie*

[1] On the appearance of the *Palais* see L. Magne, *Le Palais de justice de Poitiers. Étude sur l'art français au xiv^e siècles* (Paris, 1904), passim.

[2] R. Favreau, 'La Ville de Poitiers à la fin du Moyen âge. Une capitale régionale', *MSAO,* 4th Ser. 14-15 (1977-8), 216.

[3] See R. Favreau, 'Le Palais de Poitiers au Moyen âge. Étude historique', *BSAO,* 4th Ser. 11 (1971-2), 54-5, for the attempt to locate various chambers of the *Parlement* in their original positions within the *Palais.*

[4] Reference to the 'new' chamber of the *Conseil* occurs on 22 Apr. 1420 (*A.H.-G.* MS. 59, f.95ʳ); and to the new *Chambre des enquêtes* on 22 Aug. 1420 (ibid., f. 105ᵛ).

[5] *A.H.-G.* MS. 59, f. 190ᵛ (23 Dec. 1423).

in Poitou: 'estre convertie et employe a mestre appoint et appoinctier en nostre Palaiz de Poitiers une chambre pour y tenir la court et juridicion du fait des aides pour la guerre, et pour bancs, buffet et autres habillemens a ce necessaires.'[6]

Work of a minor nature undertaken on the *Palais* was financed from the *Recette des amendes et exploits* of the *Parlement,* though specific fines were occasionally employed for the general maintenance of the fabric of the building, and in particular of the *chapelle du Palais.* On 14 August 1427 Simon Felon, *procureur* in the *Parlement,* was ordered to pay 10*l.t.* towards work on the *chapelle* 'pour ce qu'il ne s'estoit appreste de dire et faire la cause d'appel de Guillaume Acton, du quel il estoit procureur'.[7] Work on the exterior of the *Palais* seems to have been prompted by general weathering on the roof of the building. On 12 January 1426 the *Parlement* paid Jean Baujart, *recouvreur de maisons,* of Poitiers, 6*l.t.* for re-covering part of the roof of the *Chambre des procès* during the preceding vacations.[8] Damage to the exterior of the *Palais* seems in turn to have engendered fears for the security of legal records, as on 22 February 1426 payment of 4*l.t.* was made to Guillaume Hucher for the manufacture of a special chest to contain the criminal processes.[9] A year later on 28 March 1427 a further 33*s.* 4*d.t.* was paid to Philippot Halier, mason of Poitiers, and a varlet, for five days spent at the *Parlement*'s command: 'pour estouper huisseries et fenestres, tant en l'Hostel du Palais de Poitiers que en la tour Maubregon joignant d'icelle . . . pour la seurte des proces de ladite court'.[10]

A symptom of the increasing litigation dealt with by the *Parlement* was the increase in numbers of prisoners detained in the prisons of the *Palais,* pending trial. The *Parlement*'s concern to increase the security of the prisons may have been aroused following the escape of Michelet Montléon, earlier brought for trial from Chinon, in February 1422.[11] On 21 June 1423 payments were accordingly made to Jean de May, of 33*s.* 4*d.t.* for the purchase, in December 1422, of 80lbs of iron

[6]'Documents sur les États généraux de Poitiers de 1424 et 1425', ed. R. Lacour (*Arch. hist. Poitou* 48 (1934), 116) (after B.N. MS. fr. 20583, no. 31).The *Cour des aides* was inaugurated on the 22 Oct. 1425 (B.N. MS. fr. 23878, f. 85ᵛ).

[7]A.N. X1ᵃ9198, f.306ᵛ. See also, *A. H.-G.* MS. 59, f.234ʳ(18 Apr. 1425). Care of the chapel was entrusted to a clerical *conseiller* (ibid., f.330ᵛ).

[8]*A.H.-G.* MS. 59. f.249ʳ.

[9]Ibid., fos.252ᵛ-253ʳ.

[10]Ibid., fos.289ᵛ-290ʳ.

[11]Ibid., fos. 153ᵛ-154ʳ. Following the incident the court 'fait voir le lieu par ou il est eschape (ibid., f.154ʳ). Montléon's accomplice, Girard Pasquier, was arrested simultaneously.

6

for the manufacture of 'quatre pareaux de fers a mectre prisonniers en la Conciergerie du Palais ... a Poictiers ... et ... un gros bareau de fer au travers de tres des fenestres des prisons du Pallais'; and to Jean de Villers, 50s. t., for the purchase of 'deux sommes de charbon', and the manufacture of the aforementioned irons.[12] In July 1423 further payment of 52l.t. was made through Adenet Sedile, *concierge du Palais,* 'pour certains ouvrages de prisons, cloisons de Paliz, et autres oeuvres necessaires de maconnerie et charpenterie faiz ou Palais du roy ... a Poictiers'.[13] The only other reference to work on the prisons occurs some years later on 4 April 1435 when a total of 1l. 10s. t. was paid to masons for moving the torture apparatus from its former site into a new chamber.[14] During the 1430s references to structural modifications to the *Palais* are scarce, an isolated example occurring in October 1434 when the *Procureur général du roi,* in response to a personal request by the ageing *premier Président,* Jean I de Vailly, consented to the construction of a special doorway in the wall of the *Chambre du Conseil* to facilitate the latter's easy passage between his house and the *Palais.*[15]

The hurried exit by the *parlementaires* from Paris during the summer of 1418 probably prevented the carriage of the heavy tapestries sewn with *fleurs-de-lis* which normally hung on the walls of the *Grand Chambre.* Thus from an early stage negotiations were begun to provide the court with furnishings appropriate to its sovereign status. On 4 December 1419 Naudain Vilain, *tapissier de haute lisse* living at Argenton, was paid 60s. t. for journeying to Poitiers and back to tender for two 'tapis de pers, semez et laurengiez a fleur-de-liz de couleur d'or pour le parement de la chambre de ladite cour'.[16] Vilain's tender was subsequently rejected, ostensibly because the price was too high; however, even at this stage the *Palais* was not without tapestries, for in September 1421 payment of 45l.t. was made to Perrot Negrer, *voiturier,* of Chardonchamp, near Poitiers, for carting the 'tapisseries, proces et autres abillemens de ladite cour, et des conseillers et officers d'icelle', from Poitiers to Châtellerault, situated

[12]Ibid., f.179[r-v].

[13]Ibid., fos.179[v]-180[r] (10 July 1423). Quittance delivered under the seal of Simon Macé, *maître des oeuvres du roi* in Poitou (ibid., f.180[r]).

[14]A.N. X2ª21, f.267[v].

[15]A.N. X1ª9194, fos.82[v]-83[r]. The construction of the door may not have been effected, as during the winter of 1434-5 some sessions of the *Conseil* were held in Vailly's house in Poitiers (A.N. X1ª9194, fos.82[v]ff.; A.N. X1ª9200, f.295[r]).

[16]*A.H.-G.* MS. 59, f.87[r-v]. (Negotiations for new tapestries may have been prompted by the murder of Jean Sans Peur at Montereau, in September 1419, and were probably begun on the *Parlement's* initiative).

to the north, where the court had recently moved to avoid the epidemic in Poitiers.[17] The carriage of the tapestries, perhaps already worn, may have caused further damage, as in March 1423 the *Parlement* was obliged to pay, on different occasions, sums of money to Huguet Naulin, *chasublier*, of Poitiers, for having 'appareille et repare aucunes fautes et rompture . . . es tapis de la chambre d'icelle court'.[18] The deteriorating condition of the tapestries may also have prompted the payment on 24 September 1423 of 20*l.t.* to the executors of the will of Simon de Cramaud, cardinal-archbishop of Reims, 'pour l'achapt de certain vielle tapisserie pour la chambre de ladite court'.[19]

Initiative for the replacement of the original tapestries by new ones appears to have come from Charles VII in person, and may have derived from his awareness of the need to maintain the status of the *Parlement* on a level with his recent assumption of the title of king, following the death of Charles VI in October 1422. On 16 September 1423 payment for new tapestries from Angers was made to Alain Dyonis.[20] This was followed on 14 November 1424 by a further payment of 100*s.t.* to Huet Le Roy, *varlet de chambre* of Charles VII, for 'la voiture que deux tapis a fleurs-de-liz ont couste . . . de la ville d'Amiens a celle de Poictiers'.[21] At the same date Huguet Noly, *chasublier* of Poitiers was paid 4*l.t.* for 'six aulnes de toille pour garnir et rubanner tout au tour desdites tapiz, comme pour sa peine et sallaire de avoir iceulx garniz et rubennez'.[22] Hence, within a very short period following its inauguration, the iconographical apparatus of the Poitiers *Parlement* was elevated to a level which could match its Parisian counterpart.

Provision for the smooth daily operation of the *Parlement* was made with careful regularity. Guard of the *Palais*, together with

[17]Ibid., f.141[r-v] (18 Sept. 1421). (On the family of Negrer, see Favreau, *Poitiers*, 257 n.756). Further payment of 44*l.t.* was made on 20 Dec. 1421 to Jean de Permillac and Ode Baudy, *voituriers et charetiers*, from Châtellerault, for bringing the tapestries back to Poitiers (ibid., f.151[r-v]).

[18]Ibid., fos. 170[v]-171[r] (17 Mar. 1423).

[19]Ibid., f.186[r] (the date is given incorrectly as 24 Sept. 1422).

[20]Ibid., f.184[r-v]. Dyonis was among those *liciers* who left Paris in 1418. For confiscation of property belonging to him by the Lancastrians, see A. Longnon, *Paris pendant la domination Anglaise, 1420-1436* (Paris, 1878), 71-3. During the occupation of Paris many other *liciers* were dispersed or ruined (P.A. Weigert, *La tapisserie française* (Paris, 1956) 39).

[21]*A.H.-G.* MS 59. f.200[v]. Interest in this purchase derives from the fact that the carriage of tapestries from Amiens to Poitiers could, presumably, only have been possible following the provision of a safe-conduct by the Burgundians.

[22]Ibid., fos.220[v]-221[r].

numerous other small services including the opening and shutting of the chambers between sessions and routine cleaning of their interiors, was assigned to the *concierge du Palais*.[23] In addition, from an early date, payments were made from the *Recette des amendes* to Guillaume Drapperie, *premier Huissier,* for the distribution of fresh grass and straw over the floors of the various chambers, including the *auditoire des requêtes de l'Hôtel*[24] (a device to promote cleanliness and freshness). At a later stage responsibility for the performance of these duties in the *auditoire des requêtes* appears to have been assigned to the *greffier des requêtes de l'Hôtel*.[25] Supervision of the prisons attached to the *Palais*, and responsibility for their security, as for the general well-being of prisoners, was entrusted to the *concierge du Palais*.[26] Items essential to the function of the *Parlement*, such as paper and other writing materials, were purchased in Poitiers, as evidenced by the payment on 15 November 1420 of 25*l.t.* to Guillaume de Baconcours, *épicier,* for the provision of 'quatre rames de papier pour la court de Parlement'.[27] The extent, in respect of this one commodity alone, to which the presence of the *Parlement* in Poitiers could enhance the economic life of the town is indicated by the further and considerable provision of 60*l.t.*, made to the *Procureur général du roi* on 3 January 1427, for the purchase of paper, parchment and other related necessities of his office.[28] The multiplication of this sum among the larger body of *parlementaires* could clearly entail a lucrative market for local merchants. Evidence for the local provision of foodstuffs to the *Parlement* is suggested by the payment of an annual wage of 6*d.t.* to the person in charge of the sale of fish in Poitiers.[29]

The advantages to be gained from the presence of a sovereign *parlement* at Poitiers might thus be considerable; early recognition of this fact was displayed by other towns loyal to the Dauphin.[30] The chief economic benefit derived from the demographic increase which

---

[23] Ibid., passim.

[24] Ibid., fos.225[r-v], 250[r-v] and passim.

[25] A.N. X1ª9194, f.10[r] (17 Mar. 1432).

[26] In particular see *A.H.-G.* MS. 59, fos.132[v]-133[v] and passim.

[27] Ibid., f.116[r].

[28] Ibid., f.279[r] (also ibid., f.297[r-v]).

[29] A.N. X1ª9194, f.12[r] (4 Apr. 1432).

[30] Notably at Lyon, whence on 19 Dec. 1418 Jean du Nièvre and Jean Caillé were dispatched to obtain concessions from the Dauphin including a 'parlement de droit escript' (*Reg. consulaires,* i, (Lyon, 1882), 143) (also, cf. ibid., 144-5 and ff., passim).

accompanied the installation of the *Parlement*. At Poitiers this initial augmentation was further enhanced by the increasing numbers of litigants coming to the town to present their cases before the *Parlement*; by the gradual expansion in numbers of ancillary royal officials permanently based at Poitiers; and, in addition, by the large numbers of refugees coming to the town, both from English-occupied Normandy, and, in the more immediate sense, from the vulnerable area within the environs of Poitiers.[31]

The rapid increase in population inevitably led to severe pressure on existing housing facilities in Poitiers, and many *parlementaires* experienced considerable difficulty in procuring suitable lodgings within the proximity of the *Palais*, at a reasonable price. As early as August 1422 Adam de Cambrai, *Président* in the *Parlement*, was involved in litigation with Henri Blandin for the possession of a house called *Les Arènes*, in Poitiers.[32] Cambrai's *avocat* stressed the importance of his client's office, and, as a corollary, the desirability of his possessing suitable accommodation with easy access to the *Palais*. In view of this, he argued, and the absence of alternative accommodation, 'et considere la difficulte de logis a Poictiers',[33] Cambrai should be awarded possession of the house. Despite the stress laid here upon the importance of Cambrai's office as a reason for preferential treatment in the matter of housing, the potential for exploitation of other *parlementaires* did not pass unnoticed by unscrupulous landlords in Poitiers. In March 1425 Charles VII was obliged to remind them that, since the publication of the Ordinance of Niort in September 1418 an agreement had been reached with local *bourgeois* to provide *parlementaires* with convenient lodgings at a reasonable rent. In spite of this agreement certain of the landlords: 'voians que iceulx noz conseillers et officiers n'ont pas hostels et maison en nostre dicte ville . . . ont depuis deux ou trois ans en ca excessivement encheri et encores plus encherissent . . . leurs dictes maisons'[34] – the aim being to exact higher rents from the vulnerable *parlementaires*. Moreover, he pointed out, the landlords, knowing this to be a time of strong currency, had refused to let houses except for payment in gold coin. The *parlementaires*, paid in 'white' money, could no longer afford the converted amounts. In view of the fact that many of them had lost both possessions and livelihoods in leaving Paris in 1418 and were subsequently forced to reside in Poitiers, and

[31] Favreau, *Poitiers*, 298-302 (and for the economic consequences, ibid., 305-9).

[32] A.N. X1ᵃ9194, f.126ʳ (see also, ibid., fos.139ʳ, 142ᵛ-143ʳ, 162ʳ).

[33] Ibid., f.142ᵛ (4 Sept. 1422).

[34] A.N. X1ᵃ8604, f.71ᵛ (6 Mar. 1425).

considering that Poitiers itself 'a este et est tres grandement honnoree enrichee et augmentee',[35] in future reasonable rents should be charged and payment made in 'white' money.

The king's personal intervention may have led to a substantial amelioration of the *parlementaires'* position, but it did not eliminate the possibility of arbitrary evacuation from lodgings. Some years later, in May 1432,[36] Jean d'Asnières, *greffier criminel* in the *Parlement,* complained of precisely this action by the abbot of La Réau, who, it appears, had attempted to repossess a house earlier let to Asnières in order to create lodgings for certain religious students at the new University of Poitiers. Asnières' *avocat* emphasised anew the importance of suitable accommodation for the *parlementaires*, if they were to be permitted to exercise their duties with maximum efficiency.

We can say little on the intellectual pursuits of the Poitiers *parlementaires* that would produce an analysis comparable to Mme Autrand's study of the Parisian *milieu* of a slightly earlier period.[37] Yet the Poitiers registers are not entirely mute on this subject. It is possible that certain of the *parlementaires* managed to bring personal possessions, including books, with them when they left Paris, particularly those who left in a more leisurely fashion after 1418. Some, clearly, began to purchase manuscripts at an early stage. Jean Budé, soon after his reception as a *notaire* in the *Parlement* on 20 November 1419, purchased a volume containing works by Isidore of Seville, Hincmar, Hilduin and Odon de Cluny, from the executors of the will of Guillaume de Ceries, bishop of Angoulême.[38] This volume later found its way into the library of Charles duke of Orléans. Some indication of the professional value of these objects is conveyed by litigation before the *Parlement* on 17 August 1422, following the death of clerical *conseiller* Guillaume de Marle.[39] Adam de Cambrai, *Président* in the *Parlement*, pointed out to the court that certain lawbooks loaned by him earlier to Marle were missing from the

---

[35] Ibid.

[36] On the conduct of this suit see A.N. X1ª9201, fos. 78ʳ and 78ᵛ (22 May 1432) and 84ʳ-86ʳ. For the location of lodgings of other *parlementaires* at Poitiers see A.N. X1ᶜ 145, no. 84; A.N. X2ª 21, f.3ʳ.

[37] F. Autrand, 'Les librairies des gens du Parlement au temps de Charles VI', *Annales* 28 (1973), 1219-44.

[38] G. Ouy, 'Histoire "visible" et histoire "cachée" d'un manuscrit'. *Moyen Age* 64 (1958), 115-38. For remarks on the identity of Jean Budé see G. Tessier and G. Ouy, 'Notaires et secrétaires du roi dans la première moitié du xvᵉ siècle d'après un document inédit', *B. philol.* 1963, 861-90.

[39] A.N. X1ª9197, f.145ᵛ.

inventory of the deceased *conseiller*.[40] The *Parlement* ordered Marle's executor to place before the court 'unes Decretales, une Institute et une Digeste vielle'.[41] The executor complied with this order, simultaneously denying possession of other books belonging to the deceased. Some evidence of the value attached to these items appears in 1434, when the *Parlement* ordered a *Breviary,* formerly the property of clerical *conseiller* Pierre Paumier, to be sent to Jean de Maine, called *de Blois, greffier civil,* for safekeeping.[42]

The Poitiers registers provide little information on the intellectual resources of the *Parlement* in general; though, again, as early as 11 December 1422, we have mention of a certain *maître* Robert, termed 'le libraire dudit Palais'.[43] This provides a poor basis for detailed analysis; however, the early purchase made by Jean Budé suggests that tendencies displayed at Paris before 1418 were maintained at Poitiers. The *Institute* (probably the *Institutiones* of Justinian), the *Digest* and the *Decretals* were, together with the *Breviary,* fundamental possessions of the practising magistrate during this period.[44]

The stress laid by Neuville upon the poverty of the Poitiers *parlementaires*[45] warrants considerable modification, particularly in its application to individual *conseillers* or their families. The constant rhetoric over the non-payment of wages by *parlementaires* should be viewed very carefully, for wages alone hardly represented a reliable index to the wealth of individuals. Concern for the regular payment of wages could be displayed, not so much because of the poverty of the *parlementaires*, but because the regular payment of wages was an important element in guaranteeing the continued stability of office.

Contemporary views on the financial situation of the Poitiers *parlementaires* differ sharply from those of Neuville. The author of the *Histoire de Charles VI, Roy de France* for instance, assures us that (at Poitiers): 'tous, par la grace de Dieu vivoient bien et honorablement.'[46] Others apparently agreed: in his testament, compiled

---

[40]The practice of lending books was commonplace among *parlementaires*, though many were apparently not returned to their original owners (Autrand, 1228 n.36).

[41]A.N. X1ª9197, f.145ᵛ.

[42]A.N. X2ª21, f.258ʳ (22 Sept. 1434).

[43]*A.H.-G.* MS. 59, f.119ʳ.

[44]Autrand, passim.

[45]D. Neuville, 'Le parlement royal à Poitiers (1418-1436)', *R. hist.* 6 (1878), 21 and passim.

[46]Jean Juvénal des Ursins, *Histoire de Charles VI, Roy de France,* ed. J.A.C. Buchon (Paris, 1838), 549.

in 1441, Guillaume II Le Tur, bishop of Chalon-sur-Saône and son of Guillaume I, late *Président* in the Poitiers *Parlement* and Jeanne Roze, recalled that:

> xxii ans a, ou environ, luy, monseigneur son pere, . . . sa mere, ses plusieurs parents et amis, pour les divisions qui lors estoient en ce royaume, avoient habandonne leurs pais pour leurs loyautes garder et soient venuz en ceste . . . ville, en laquelle ilz aient demoure continuellement, jusques a present, et y aient moult de biens et d'onneurs, especiallement ledit monseigneur, messir Guillaume.[47]

The fortunes of the Le Tur family increased rapidly in the years following the *Parlement*'s inauguration. The losses incurred by Guillaume I in the exit from Paris in 1418 did not go uncompensated: on 30 July 1418 the captive duke of Orléans ordered his treasurer, Pierre Renier, to make an immediate payment of 50*l.t.* to Le Tur: 'nostre ame et feal conseiller en parlement, . . . la quelle somme . . . nous . . . voulons lui estre baillee pour consideracion des services qu'il nous a faiz; et aussi pour consideraction de la necessite en quoy il est de la perte qu'il a faicte nagaires a Paris de tous ses biens.'[48]

During the 1420s the family's prestige continued to grow. Guillaume I, besides his dual charge of *avocat* at Poitiers for the Dauphin and for the duke of Orléans, was on 21 May 1421 additionally retained as *avocat* of the town of Lyon in the *Parlement*, with an annual pension of 10*l.t.*[49] These important functions were further supplemented by Guillaume's position as lieutenant-general or judge of the constable Buchan in *Parlement*.[50] Le Tur was finally elected third *Président* in 1427.[51] Guillaume's son, Guillaume II, was not slow to achieve individual distinction. Originally a clerical *conseiller* in the *Parlement*[52] he delivered the first lectures in civil law

[47] E. Audinet, 'Les origines de la Faculté de droit de l'Université de Poitiers', *BSAO*, 3rd Ser. 6 (1922-4), 41-2.

[48] B.N. MS. fr. 29380 (Le Tur), no. 6. (For the confiscation by the English of property in Paris belonging to other Poitiers *parlementaires*, see Longnon, passim.) The payment cf 50*l.t.* represented arrears on Le Tur's annual pension of 25*l.t.* as *avocat* of the duke of Orléans at Paris (ibid., loc. cit.; also ibid., nos. 8, 9). A quittance dated 4 Feb. 1421 styles Le Tur: 'licencie-en-loys, advocat et conseiller du roy. . . et de monseigneur le Regent. . . et conseiller de monseigneur le duc d'Orleans a Poictiers' (ibid., no. 8). Le Tur was still the *avocat* of Orléans in 1422 (ibid., no. 9).

[49] *Reg. consulaires,* i (Lyon, 1882), 240.

[50] A.N. X2ᵃ21, f.26ʳ (8 Jan. 1425).

[51] *A.H.-G.* MS. 59, f.308ʳ⁻ᵛ (20-1 Aug. 1427).

[52] Guillaume II's name appears on the roll of the *Parlement* for the first time on 12 Nov. 1423 (A.N. X1ᵃ9197, f.261ᵛ); he appears to have functioned prior to this date as a lay *maitre des requêtes de l'Hôtel* (A.N. X1ᵃ9197, f.1ʳ and *Reg. consulaires,* i (Lyon, 1882), 350).

at the newly-founded university of Poitiers.[53] Additionally a canon of Saint-Hilaire-le-Grand, Guillaume II remained at Poitiers until his promotion as bishop of Chalon-sur-Saône[54] in 1440.

## Early Recruitment to Office in the *Parlement*
### (1418-c. 1422)

The chronicle *Histoire de Charles VI* informs us that at Poitiers the *Parlement* adhered faithfully to the 'forme et maniere et stille qu'on gardoit . . . a Paris'.[55] The very nature of many of its members' exit from Paris in 1418 must have engendered fears of a possible dilution of their claim to be sole legitimate representatives of sovereign justice in France, the more so in view of their new provincial location. Similar fears accompanied the creation of a separate *parlement* to serve the Languedoc in 1420,[56] and calls were heard for a merger of the two institutions at Poitiers by 1426.[57] These considerations resulted in the determination to maintain at Poitiers,[58] and apparently also at Toulouse,[59] a predominantly Parisian *milieu* (this despite the practical problems posed by war, and the division of the kingdom, after 1418, into two hostile camps). Thus, in the years immediately after 1418 the

[53] P. Boissonnade, *Histoire de l'Université de Poitiers passé et présent (1432-1932)* (Poitiers, 1932), 138.

[54] Chalon was a Burgundian fief. Le Tur's predecessor as bishop was, according to Guérin (*Arch. hist. Poitou* 26 (1896), 374 n.3), Jean I Tudert, *maître des requêtes de l'Hôtel* of Charles VII, whose sphere of competence related largely to Burgundian affairs (Favreau, *Poitiers,* 286 n.961). Tudert died before his consecration as bishop, on 9 Dec. 1439.

[55] Jean Juvénal des Ursins, *Histoire de Charles VI, Roy de France,* ed. J.A.C. Buchon (Paris, 1838), 549.

[56] Created at Toulouse on 20 March 1420, the inaugural session took place on 29 May following (A. Viala, *Le Parlement de Toulouse et l'administration royale laique, 1420-1525 environ,* i (Albi, 1953), 54. The *Parlement* was transferred to Béziers in 1425, ostensibly to strengthen royal control in lower Languedoc following a rebellion at Béziers (Viala, i (Albi, 1953), 56).

[57] *A.H.-G.* MS. 59, f.260ʳ (29 May 1426). Lyon was mooted as a suitable venue for the merger of the *parlements.* On 24 Nov. 1426 Charles VII agreed to the reunion, but the Béziers *Parlement* ignored his directive (Viala, i (Albi, 1953), 58). Even after the formal reunion of the *parlements* at Poitiers on 7 Oct. 1428, the Béziers *Parlement* was still, for a time, operational (ibid., 59).

[58] Favreau, *Poitiers,* 279-80.

[59] Viala, i (Albi, 1953), 56 n.3. At Toulouse, as at Poitiers, the recruitment of *conseillers* was made primarily from Paris. Local recruitment was seen at the level of the ordinary *procureurs* and *avocats.* Viala suggests that the 'recruitement local des auxiliaires de la justice explique. . . leurs réticences à quitter Toulouse. Le mutisme des magistrats paraît avoir pour cause la disparition de l'élément toulousain à cette date' (ibid., 56).

14

recruitment of *parlementaires* at Poitiers, above the level of the ordinary *avocats* and *procureurs,* was governed by dynastic and Parisian considerations, to the detriment of Poitevin talent.[60]

## *Présidents* and *Conseillers*

Recruitment of *conseillers* following the small initial provision made by the Ordinance of Niort, in September 1418, was very rapid, and the complement indicated by the first existing register of *plaidoiries civiles,* beginning on 12 November 1421,[61] was probably reached during the period from late-1418 to mid-1421.

The function of *Procureur général* of the Dauphin was initially exercised by Benoît Pidalet. In a quittance dated 14 January 1419 he is styled: '*Procureur general de tres excellent et puissant prince, monseigneur le Regent, daulphin de Viennois.*'[62] It is possible that Pidalet's office was supplemented by the simultaneous function of a *Procureur général du roi,* which charge was exercised after 1418 by Pierre Cousinot.[63] The office of *Avocat du roi* and also *du Dauphin* was early confined to a single figure, Guillaume I Le Tur.[64]

Jean I de Vailly's presence in September 1418 as the sole *Président,* was supplemented by 11 January 1419 by the election of a second, Jean I Jouvenel, baron of Trainel.[65] A complement of three *Présidents* was achieved between 9 January and 11 August 1421 with the election of Adam de Cambrai,[66] earlier in competition for the office with Denis du Moulin,[67] *maître des requêtes de l'Hôtel,* and, for a brief period, also *Président* in the *Parlement* of Toulouse. Cambrai's election may have been made to compensate for the absence of Jean I Jouvenel, later detached as *Président* at Toulouse[68] following the

[60] Favreau, *Poitiers,* 179-80.

[61] A.N. X1ª9197, f.1ʳ, gives a total of 18 *conseillers* and 3 *Présidents,* some of whom were detached to function at Toulouse (cf. Viala, i (Albi, 1953), 61 n.2).

[62] B.N. *Clairambault,* no. 85, *pièce* 1955 (also A.N. X1ª9195, f.19ʳ).

[63] A.N. X1ª8604, f.66ᵛ (18 Aug. 1423), where Cousinot is confirmed as *Procureur général du roi,* an office he was acknowledged to have held since the *Parlement*'s inception.

[64] B.N. MS. fr. 29380 (Le Tur), nos. 6-9. A second *avocat du roi* did not function until 20 Dec. 1426 (*A.H.-G.* MS. 59, f.277ᵛ).

[65] *A.H.-G.* MS. 59, f.23ʳ (cf. E. Maugis, *Histoire du Parlement de Paris de l'avènement des rois Valois à la mort d'Henri IV,* iii (Paris, 1916), 72). Jouvenel's election came after 21 Sept. 1418 (B.N. Nouv. acq. lat. no. 1968, f.2ʳ).

[66] *A.H-G.* MS. 59, fos.120ʳ, 136ᵛ (11 Aug. 1421).

[67] Ibid., f.106ᵛ.

[68] Ibid., fos.99ᵛ-100ʳ (3 June 1420).

early exercise of that office by, successively, Simon de Nanterre and Denis du Moulin.[69] The total of three *Présidents* was maintained until August 1427 when a fourth, Guillaume I Le Tur, was elected.[70]

The small body of *conseillers* provided at Niort was also rapidly increased during the ensuing months: during 1418 by the addition of Guillaume I Le Tur,[71] mentioned earlier, Barthélemy Hamelin and Pierre d'Oger;[72] in 1419 by Hugues de Grimaud,[73] Jean Mauloué,[74] Guillaume Louvet[75] (in the *enquêtes*), Aynard de Bleterens[76] (also in the *enquêtes*), Charles de Vaudetar,[77] Guillaume de Laillier, Aimery Marchand, Philippe des Courtils, Mathieu Canu[78] and Geoffroy Vassal.[79] In addition to the individuals mentioned here, we can also affirm the presence during 1419 of Robert Honel (or Hoël),[80] *conseiller des enquêtes*, Pierre de Villars (Villers) and possibly Guillaume d'Aunay;[81] and finally in May 1421 of Guy Boulie.[82]

It is clear that in respect of the *conseillers*, as of the other offices within the *Parlement*, the tiny corpus of officials mentioned in the Ordinance of Niort was rapidly exceeded during the ensuing months. The extent of these numbers, which might include in addition a large body of ancillary staff, together with relatives and friends, communicates to a striking degree the scale of the migration of *parlementaires* from Paris in the wake of the Burgundian occupation.

[69] A.N. XI$^a$9808, f.374$^v$. Jean Juvénal des Ursins wrote that Jean I Jouvenel was sent to Toulouse 'a la charge d'aucuns trespassés' (*Écrits politiques de Jean Juvénal des Ursins*, ed. P.S. Lewis, i (*SHF*, Paris, 1978), 481. While true in the case of Simon de Nanterre, this seems to indicate, so far as Denis du Moulin is concerned, a rather euphemistic description of the reasons for Jean I Jouvenel's detachment to Toulouse (below, pp. 20-1). Simon de Nanterre's death must have occurred soon after the foundation of the *Parlement* of Toulouse (cf. 'Rec. des docs', *Arch. hist. Poitou* 26 (1896), 255 n.3).

[70] *A.H.-G.* MS. 59, f.308$^{r-v}$ (20-1 Aug. 1427).

[71] Cf. B.N. Nouv. acq. lat. no. 1968, f.2$^r$ and B.N. MS. fr. 29380 (Le Tur), no. 7.

[72] *A.H.-G.* MS. 59, f.19$^{r-v}$ (20 Dec. 1418).

[73] Ibid., f.23$^v$.

[74] A.N. X1$^a$9195, f.23$^r$.

[75] *A.H.-G.* MS. 59, f.44$^r$.

[76] Ibid., f.45$^{r-v}$.

[77] Ibid., f.91$^r$.

[78] Ibid.

[79] Ibid., f.101$^r$.

[80] Ibid., f.45$^{r-v}$. See also, Maugis, iii (Paris, 1916), 57.

[81] A.N. X1$^a$9195, f.2$^v$ (11 Jan. 1419). In addition see Maugis, iii (Paris, 1916), 37, 57.

[82] A.N. X1$^a$9195, f.122$^v$ (16 May 1421). Cf. also, Maugis, iii (Paris, 1916), 75.

## The *maîtres des requètes de l'Hôtel du Roi*

In the Poitiers *Parlement* the function of the *maîtres des requètes du Palais* was early incorporated within that of the *maîtres des requètes de l'Hôtel du Roi*,[83] the latter competence fulfilling both charges.

The Ordinance of Niort made provision for only three *maîtres des reqûetes de l'Hôtel* – Guillaume Thoreau, Arnaud de Marle and Bureau Boucher – all lay members.[84] These were to exercise an important supplementary function, namely: 'le fait de nostre Chancellerie soubz le scel par nous ordonne pour sceller les lettres de ladite court et juridicion souveraine.'[85] While no official designation was made at Niort of clerical *maîtres des requètes de l'Hôtel*, we find, at an early stage, individuals exercising this function: in 1419 Jean Tudert, dean of Paris;[86] probably before 19 April 1420 Guillaume Guérin, archdeacon of Embrun, and also a member of the *chancellerie* at Poitiers.[87] Before 12 November 1421 this initial complement was supplemented by the election of two more clerics – Robert de Rouvres, archdeacon of Blois and Denis du Moulin.[88] The death of Guérin in August 1421 provided, therefore, by November of the same year, a total of six *maîtres des requètes de l'Hôtel* in the *Parlement*, three lay and three cleric.[89] Certain features of their early judicial role are worthy of note. While the first register of *plaidoiries civiles*, commencing 12 November 1421, includes all three clerical *maîtres des requètes* within the official complement of the *Parlement*,[90] it appears that only one, Jean Tudert, performed a judicial function at Poitiers.[91] Robert de Rouvres and Denis du Moulin were, probably from the moment of their election, permanently detached from the court to function within the Dauphin's *conseil*.[92] In addition to his judicial role within the *Conseil*, Robert de Rouvres performed a highly important secondary function, that of *vice-Chancelier* of the

---

[83] Neuville, 11-13 (also F. Aubert, 'Les Requêtes du Palais (xiiie au xvie siècle). Style des Requêtes du Palais', *Bibl. Éc. Chartes* 69 (1908), 597).

[84] B.N. Nouv. acq. lat. no. 1968, f.2ʳ.

[85] A.N. X1ᵃ8604, f.28ᵛ.

[86] *A.H.-G.* MS. 59, f.56ʳ.

[87] A.N. X1ᵃ9195, f.86ʳ (19 Apr. 1420).

[88] A.N. X1ᵃ9197, f.1ʳ. Rouvres was a *maître des requêtes* before 1420 (B.N. MS fr. nos. 32137 and 32514).

[89] Ibid.

[90] Ibid.

[91] *A.H.-G.* MS. 59, passim.

[92] Neither receives any mention in the register of the *Conseil* prior to his appearance on the official roll of the *Parlement* on 12 Nov. 1421 (*A.H.-G.* MS. 59, passim).

Dauphin, *commis à la garde du sceau ordonné en l'absence du Grand.*[93] This function, of a transitory nature, would be exercised during the absence of the *Chancelier* and the *Grand Sceau* – a common occurrence in the years after 1418 owing to the frequent perambulations of the *Conseil.*

Yet this official number of six *maîtres des requêtes de l'Hôtel* is hardly indicative of the numerousness and variability of function of the *maîtres des requêtes.* In respect of the *Parlement,* not all those who functioned as *maîtres des requêtes de l'Hôtel* received this designation in its registers. Guillaume de Quiefdeville, for example, appears on 12 November 1421 among the ranks of the ordinary clerical *conseillers* in the *Parlement,*[94] yet he had exercised the function of *maître des requêtes de l'Hôtel* in a quasi-judicial capacity since 1418.[95] Other *conseillers* in the *Parlement* appear to have operated as *maîtres des requêtes,* again in quasi-judicial roles, before their formal election in the *Parlement.*[96] Others, again, though nominally *maîtres des requêtes de l'Hôtel,* appear to have had no formal attachment to the *Parlement,* working instead by rota in provincial locations on a variety of administrative and fiscal matters: individuals in this category include: before 1420 Jean Belart, dean of Le Mans;[97] before 1422 Simon Charles[98] and Nicole de La Barre.[99]

In addition to the function of 'invisible' *maîtres des requêtes de l'Hôtel* outside the *Parlement* it is clear that those who appear on the

[93] Beaucourt alluded to the presence of a *vice-Chancelier* as early as March-April 1420 (*Histoire de Charles VII,* i (Paris, 1881), 347 n.8). This office was occupied by Robert de Rouvres whose additional mention as *garde du sceau ordonné en l'absence du Grand* occurs in Feb. 1430 (A.N. X1ᵃ9199, f.239ᵛ) and Apr. 1433 (A.N. X1ᵃ9194, f.42ʳ) (cf. H.J. du Motey, *Jeanne d'Arc à Chinon et Robert de Rouvres* (Paris, 1927), 54, 62).

[94] A.N. X1ᵃ9197, f.1ʳ (12 Nov. 1421).

[95] On Quiefdeville's origins and career see P. le Verdier, 'Guillaume de Quiefdeville, ambassadeur de Charles VI et Charles VII. Notices nécrologiques', *Bull. Soc. Hist. Normandie* 15 (1931-9), 2-16.

[96] Jean Baubignon, for example, was elected *conseiller* lay in the *Parlement* on 7 Mar. 1429 (*A.H.-G.* MS.59, f.335ʳ); yet he was a *maître des requêtes de l'Hôtel* before this date (*Extraits des anciens registres aux délibérations des consaux de la ville de Tournai (1422-1430),* ed. H. Vandenbröek, *Mém. Soc. Hist. Litt. Tournai* 8, (1863), pp. 224-31, passim (Jan. - Feb. 1427). In January 1434 however the *Parlement* decided to elect another *conseiller* in Baubignon's place in view of the fact that he had recently been made a *maître des requêtes de l'Hôtel* (A.N. X1ᵃ9194, f.57ᵛ).

[97] Beaucourt, i (Paris, 1881), 111 n.7. Belart was designated *maître des requêtes de l'Hôtel du Dauphin* (ibid.).

[98] *Reg. consulaires,* i (Lyon, 1882), 322.

[99] See particularly A.N. X1ᵃ9197, fos. 144ʳ, 146ʳ⁻ᵛ, where La Barre is styled 'maistre des requestes de l'Ostel de monseigneur le Regent'.

official roll of the *Parlement* (probably after the traditional manner of the *requêtes du Palais*) i.e. by virtue of their judicial role, performed, from the outset, a variety of quasi-judicial functions.[100] The exercise of these functions, furthermore, took its initiative not from the *Parlement*, but from the Dauphin's *Conseil*. A final and highly important aspect of the early function of the *maîtres des requêtes de l'Hôtel* is indicated by the specific qualification of their title by the addition of *du Roi et de monseigneur le Regent*, or simply of *du Dauphin*. Certain of the *maîtres des requêtes* thus continued to operate after 1418 as the nominal representatives of Charles VI, and simultaneously of the Dauphin; others appear as officers of the Dauphin only – a measure presumably designed to provide a semblance of continuity of office, together with normality of function.

The placement of the *requêtes de l'Hôtel* in the *Parlement* and *Conseil* alike was made with a view to achieving maximum flexibility of function. Yet it is possible that in the pursuit of employment as *commissaires du roi* the judicial role of the *maîtres des requêtes de l'Hôtel* in the *Parlement* came to be viewed, increasingly, as a subsidiary one. The frequent, and often sustained, absence of the *maîtres des requêtes* from Poitiers appears, particularly during the 1430s, to have seriously affected the efficient operation of the tribunal.[101] Possibly designed as an *ad hoc* measure to offset the considerable distance between the Dauphin's *Conseil* and the *Parlement*, the replacement of the *requêtes du Palais* by the *requêtes de l'Hôtel*, while appearing to provide a closer rapport between the two institutions, may nevertheless have contributed in the long term to a significant decrease in the *Parlement*'s authority vis-a-vis the *Conseil*.

### The *maîtres des requètes de l'Hôtel* in *Parlement* and in the *Conseil*

An unusual feature of the early organisation of the *requêtes de l'Hôtel* in the Poitiers *Parlement* is that, while before 12 November 1422 they continue to be designated in the registers after the manner of the *requêtes du Palais*, certain of their number were nevertheless permanently delegated to functions within the Dauphin's *Conseil*. The exercise of judicial functions by *maîtres des requêtes de l'Hôtel* within the *Parlement* was thus confined, with the exception

---

[100]Neuville, 279ff.

[101]On 23 Feb. 1431 the *Parlement* decided, in view of the fact that Bureau Boucher was the only lay *maître des requètes* currently in Poitiers and thus unable to judge a suit pending in the *requêtes*, that the case would be evoked before its own competence (A.N. X2ª21, f.156ʳ).

of Jean Tudert, to lay members of the tribunal.[102] As in the case of the *Grande Chancellerie*,[103] this may indicate the embryonic development of the *Parlement* and *Conseil* alike into separate and independent jurisdictions. The presence of all six *maîtres des requêtes de l'Hôtel* on the official roll of the *Parlement* in 1421 and 1422[104] would thus at first sight seem to be erroneous, in view of the permanent location of certain of their number with the *Conseil*. While this may be merely a product of habit, the *greffier* simply deciding to list the names of the *maîtres des requêtes* in the traditional manner of the *requêtes du Palais*, it may also indicate either that the substitution of the *requêtes du Palais* by the *requêtes de l'Hôtel* was seen only as an *ad hoc* measure, and that a return to more conventional practice in the near future was thought likely; or, on the other hand, that before 1422 at least the idea of any clear distinction in the judicial function of the *maîtres des requêtes de l'Hôtel* within the *Parlement* or the *Conseil* is a premature one. Prior to the establishment of the *Conseil* at Bourges, and Charles VII's assumption of his father's title in 1422, it is possible to argue, in respect of the functions of the *requêtes de l'Hôtel*, for a nominally much closer relationship between the *Parlement* and the *Conseil*. In this respect it is interesting to note the disappearance of the names of the *maîtres des requêtes* from the official roll of the *Parlement* after 1422.[105] This may indicate the final abandoning of the idea of a revival of the *requêtes du Palais*, and the beginning of the gradual growth of *Parlement* and *Conseil* alike along individual lines.

This severance of the ostensibly close links between the *Parlement* and the *Conseil* seems to be reflected in the recruitment of *maîtres des requêtes* at Poitiers after 1422. Soon after this date Robert de Rouvres and Denis du Moulin, earlier nominally attached to the *Parlement* were replaced,[106] maintaining an overall complement of six *maîtres des requêtes*, three lay and three cleric, who, by permutation of their number, exercised their judicial functions predominantly within the

[102] See *A.H.-G.* MS. 59 (passim), for the presence of the *maîtres des requêtes* on the civil *Conseil* of the *Parlement*; and A.N. X2ᵃ21 (passim) for their representation on the criminal *Conseil*.

[103] See G. Tessier and G. Ouy, 'Notaires et secrétaires dans la première moitié du xvᵉ siècle d'après un document inédit', *B. philol.* 1963, 870-4. Also, 'Rec. des docs', *Arch. hist. Poitou* 26 (1896), xxxi, for the early annexation of the *Grand Chancellerie* to the *Parlement*.

[104] A.N. X1ᵃ9197, fos. 1ʳ, 148ᵛ.

[105] A.N. X1ᵃ9197, fos. 148ᵛff.

[106] *A.H.-G.* MS. 59 attests the presence of three new *maîtres des requêtes* during 1422-3: Guillaume de Charpaignes (f.178ᵛ), Jean de Montmorin (f.182ʳ) and Gérard Le Boursier (f.188ᵛ).

*Parlement.* This produced, perhaps for the first time since 1418, a clearer distinction between the judicial role of the *maîtres des requêtes* in the *Conseil* and in the *Parlement.*

A marked feature of the early careers of the *maîtres des requêtes de l'Hôtel,* and in particular of those who functioned permanently within the *Conseil,* was their immediate acquisition of high office and a concomitant accumulation of considerable wealth and prestige. Robert de Rouvres, probably from an early date *vice-Chancelier* of the Dauphin and *garde du sceau ordonné en l'absence du Grand,*[107] first appears as archdeacon of Blois.[108] Promotion to the bishopric of Sées in 1422-3[109] was followed in 1425-6 by Rouvres's translation to the see of Saint-Flour.[110] In 1433 he was again transferred, this time to the bishopric of Maguelonne (Montpellier),[111] which he retained until his death in *c.* 1453.[112] Rouvres's influence within the *Conseil* may be measured by the fact that from *c.* 1420 he was a counter-signatory to every important edict issued by the Dauphin, and the recipient of an annual pension of considerable (though apparently variable) proportions.[113] The career of Denis du Moulin, a native of Meaux, displayed a similar pattern. His name, like that of Rouvres's, appears at an early date upon official documents emanating from the *Conseil,* though his precise judicial function is difficult to determine. Early in 1420 he acquired the office of *Président* in the newly-created *Parlement* of Toulouse, apparently in succession to Simon de Nanterre.[114] However, the publication on 14 June 1420 of the first

[107] Above, p. 17.

[108] A.N. X1ᵃ9197, f.46ʳ (5 Mar. 1422). Rouvres was involved in litigation over the office in Aug. 1423 with Guillaume II Le Tur(ibid., f.244ʳ). He resigned as archdeacon before 1436 in favour of Jean Budé, a royal *notaire,* (A.N. X1ᵃ9193, f.183ᵛ).

[109] See C.T. Allmand, 'L'évêché de Sées sous la domination anglaise au quinzième siècle', *Annales de Normandie* 11 (1961), 302. Rouvres's election was ratified by Martin V on 15 Jan. 1423. Despite his absence from the see, then in English hands, Rouvres continued to administer his diocese through vicars (ibid.).

[110] See M.-D. Chaludet, 'Robert de Rouvres, évéque nommé de Saint-Flour', *Revue de la Haute-Auvergne* 7 (1905), 86-90.

[111] Elected 4 March 1433, Rouvres repaid his 'obligations' towards the Papacy with Medici credit on 8 July 1433 (Allmand, 302 n.11).

[112] Beaucourt, v (Paris, 1890), 82 (but cf. Du Motey, 133ff. and especially 138).

[113] In 1427, 1,000*l.t. p.a.,* paid on the *quart du sel* at Taillebourg (B.N. MS. fr.25970, no. 1139). After Rouvres's election to the see of Maguelonne (Montpellier) in 1433, his quittances for the pension carry the style 'Robert, par la permission Divine, évêque de Maguelonne' (B.N. MS. fr.25968, nos. 683-4, 689-91 (1433-1438)).

[114] A.N. XIᵃ9808, f.374ᵛ(17 Aug. 1423). Nanterre remained *Président* at Paris until at least 8 June 1418 (A.N. X1ᵃ1480, f.138ᵛ). Cf., also, *A.H.-G.* MS. 59, fos. 188ᵛ-189ʳ.

*arrêt criminel* of the *Parlement* which condemned a local cleric found guilty of blasphemy to have his tongue cut out, and later to be beheaded, aroused such strong opposition that Du Moulin was ultimately removed from the office of *Président*.[115] Only months after this incident Du Moulin presented letters of the Dauphin to the Poitiers *Parlement* in favour of his election as third *Président*, in opposition to Adam de Cambrai.[116] Du Moulin's claim was nevertheless rejected by the *Parlement* and the candidature of Cambrai upheld. Despite these setbacks in 1422 Du Moulin was eventually successful in gaining promotion to the archbishopric of Toulouse. Clearly, however, local ecclesiastial opposition to him was still strong, for on 5 August 1422 Jean Gentian, now *Président* at Toulouse in Du Moulin's place, led an inquiry into the 'griefs proposés par le chapitre metropolitain contre l'élection de Du Moulin'.[117] The resulting litigation between Du Moulin and the Chapter comprised the first major process to be heard before the new *Parlement*, with the decision being eventually awarded in Du Moulin's favour. Like Robert de Rouvres, Du Moulin was in receipt of regular, and frequently large, emoluments from Charles VII in return for his services in the *Conseil*,[118] and he undertook, as did Rouvres, a wide variety of quasi-judicial functions, notably in the realm of diplomatic and fiscal affairs.[119]

The careers of the *maîtres des requêtes de l'Hôtel* nominally attached to the *Parlement* were perhaps less spectacular, though they frequently performed lucrative functions for the *Conseil* in addition to their judicial role in the *Parlement*.[120] The hierarchical structure of the *requêtes de l'Hôtel* in the *Parlement* during the early years is difficult to perceive, though we have mention on 9 June 1421 of a gift of six boxes of *confitures* made at Lyon to Guillaume Thoreau, termed 'second President de Parlement'.[121] The probability that this title

[115]Viala, i (Albi, 1953), 55 n.1.

[116]*A.H.-G.* MS. 59, f.106ᵛ (24 Aug. 1420). For an additional comment on Du Moulin's rapacity see J.L. Gazzaniga, *L'Église du Midi à la fin du règne de Charles VII (1444-1461) d'après la jurisprudence du parlement de Toulouse* (Toulouse, 1973), 89, 124 n.73.

[117]Viala, i (Albi, 1953), 55 n.3.

[118]In 1436 200 *moutons d'or* (B.N. MS. fr. 25970, no. 1354); in 1438 500*l.t.* (ibid., no. 1355); and in 1434/7 375*l.t.* (ibid., no. 1356).

[119]Gazzaniga, 124 n. 73, for the influence of Du Moulin in Charles VII's *Conseil*.

[120]See, for instance, the payments made to Arnaud de Marle, *maître des requêtes de l'Hôtel* at Poitiers, during the period 1420-36, which ranged from 100*l.t.* to 1,500*l.t.* (B.N. MS. fr.28342 (Marle), nos. 36-49, passim.). In 1420 he was called 'maistre des requestes des Hostelz du Roy. . . et de monseigneur le Regent' (ibid., 36).

[121]*Reg. consulaires.*, i (Lyon, 1882), p. 306. See also, ibid., ii (Lyon, 1926), 315, for evidence of a payment in 1429-30 to 'moss. le Precedent, maistre des requestes'.

22

refs to Thoreau's status in the *requêtes de l'Hôtel* seems to be confirmed by Beaucourt, who suggests that in 1423 Thoreau occupied the position of *premier maître des requêtes*.[122]

### Ancillary officials of the *requêtes de l'Hôtel*

Conventional provision of ancillary officials for the *auditoire des requêtes de l'Hôtel* at Poitiers seems to have been made at an early date. The office of *greffier ou régisseur des requêtes de l'Hôtel* was exercised before 1422 by Simon de la Rue.[123] Following his death, and at a date somewhere before 27 February 1422,[124] La Rue was succeeded in this office by Antoine Chasteignier.

In addition to the office of *greffier*, we have a further mention on 27 February 1422 of Jean Gaultier, 'clerc et serviteur de maistre Anthoine Chastenier, greffier des requestes de l'Hostel du roy'.[125] At a slightly lower level we may also affirm the early presence of a number of *huissier-sergents* operating in the *auditoire des requêtes* independently of the ordinary *huissiers* in the *Parlement;* on 20 September 1420[126] Jacquet Guillemet, *huissier des requêtes de l'Hôtel du Roi*; in January 1428[127] a similar function is accorded to Jaymet de Rougemont; on 27 August 1429 Michel Guido is termed *huissier des requêtes de l'Hôtel*;[128] and finally on 29 July 1430 there is mention of Jean Potet, 'sergent ou huissier des requestes de l'Ostel du Roy'.[129]

### The *enquêtes*

Didier Neuville's confessed ignorance of the existence of a copy of the first register of the *Conseil* of the Poitiers *Parlement* led him to suggest

[122]Beaucourt, i (Paris, 1881), 616.

[123]*A.H.-G.* MS. 59, f. 167ʳ. La Rue was the father-in-law of lay *conseiller* Aimery Marchand (ibid.).

[124]A.N. X1ᵃ9197, f.42ᵛ. Chasteignier died between 17 Mar. 1433 (A.N. X1ᵃ9194, f.10ʳ) and 4 Aug. 1433 (a. Tessereau, *Histoire chronologique de la Grande Chancellerie de France* (Paris, 1676), 45).

[125]A.N. X1ᵃ9197, f.42ᵛ.

[126]*A.H.-G.* MS. 59, fos. 109ʳ, 182ʳ; A.N. X2ᵃ21, f.1ʳ.

[127]A.N. X1ᵃ9199, f.18ᵛ. It is possible that Rougemont, Gaultier (or Gautier) and Guillemet (or Guyonnet) were local recruits to the *Parlement* (cf. Favreau, *Poitiers,* index 669, 672, 705).

[128]A.N. Z1ᵃ8, f.18ᵛ, (cf. F. Aubert, *Histoire du Parlement de Paris de l'origine à François Iᵉʳ(1250-1515),* i (Paris, 1894), 38 n.4).

[129]A.N. X1ᵃ9192, f.194ʳ (also A.N. X2ᵃ21, f.100ʳ A.N. X1ᵃ9199, f.298). According to Aubert(Bibl. Éc. Chartes 69 (1908), 598), Laurent Râle was the *premier Huissier des requêtes de l'Hôtel* at Poitiers.

that no *Chambre des enquêtes* functioned at Poitiers until 1435.[130] However, provision for the *enquêtes* was clearly envisaged within the statutes which form a preamble to the first register of the *Conseil*.[131] On 28 March 1419 the *Parlement* received Guillaume Louvet: 'pour exercer son office aux enquetes *cum tempus affuerit*. . . cependant l'excercera en cette cour souveraine.'[132] At the moment of Louvet's reception the *Parlement* appears to have possessed only two *conseillers* to make the *enquêtes* (probably one lay and one cleric), as on 7 April 1419 Aynard de Bleterens was received lay *conseiller* in place of the deceased Robert Honel (or Hoël),[133] 'en la Chambre des enquestes, en lieu et temps convenable'.[134] The death of Guillaume Louvet was not, however, followed by any specific mention of his replacement in the *enquêtes*. Nevertheless, the creation of a new chamber to accommodate the *enquêtes* in August 1420[135] suggests that their function was maintained. In view of this, it is possible, as Favreau has suggested,[136] that the matter relating to the *enquêtes* which was discussed by the *Parlement* on 26 January 1435[137] concerned not their inauguration at Poitiers but a greater expansion in function and membership of the *Chambre*, after the manner observed at Paris, in order to speed up the business of judging the rapidly accumulating backlog of litigation before the *Parlement.* Whatever the truth of this assertion no evidence for the operation of this tribunal or of its membership occurs between 1420 and 1435. It is also certain that before 1435 its numbers were greatly inferior to that of its Parisian counterpart.[138]

## Huissiers

No immediate provision for the appointment of *huissiers* to the *Parlement* was made by the Ordinance of Niort in September 1418. However it is clear that the complement of eight *huissiers* recorded at

[130]D. Neuville, 'Le Parlement royal à Poiters(1418-1436)', *R. hist.* 6 (1878), 11, 15.

[131]*A.H.-G.* MS. 59, fos. 4ᵛ-6ʳ.

[132]Ibid., 44ʳ (also ibid., fos 45ʳ, 47ʳ). Louvet died *c.* 10 May 1419, and payment of arrears on his wages totalling 26*l.*17*s.* 6*d.p.* was made to his widow on 18 May 1419 (ibid., f.58ʳ).

[133]On Honel, see Maugis, iii (Paris, 1916), 57. There is no other reference to his presence at Poitiers.

[134]*A.H.-G.* MS. 59, f.45ʳ⁻ᵛ.

[135]Ibid., f.105ᵛ (22 Aug. 1420).

[136]Favreau, *Poitiers,* 279 n.895.

[137]A.N. X1ᵃ9194, f.88ᵛ.

[138]At its inauguration in July 1418 the Anglo-Burgundian *Parlement* had 2 *Présidents* and 31 *conseillers* to make the *enquêtes* (Maugis, i (Paris, 1913), 25).

the beginning of the 1421-2 session of the *Parlement*[139] was achieved soon after its inauguration. The early recruitment of *huissiers*, like that of other officers, seems to have been made from an exclusively Parisian *milieu*. As early as 20 March 1419 we have mention of *huissier* Pierre Belle, additionally 'commis a appeller au roolle'[140] – a function usually accorded to the *premier Huissier*. Belle does not, nevertheless, appear to have occupied this office, the first named *premier Huissier* being Guillaume Drapperie, on 30 September 1419.[141] On 20 April 1419 two more *huissiers*, Guillaume Taichier and Bertrand de Pontarcher, are mentioned;[142] and between May and July of the same year, a further four: Rogerin le Vavasseur, Aleaume Cachemarée, Jean Guillaume and Girard Maulin.[143] This known total of eight *huissiers* by late 1419 was supplemented, before 12 November 1421, by a further two: Philippot Duchesne and Philippe de Berlettes. With the disappearance of the aforementioned Belle[144] and Guillaume in the interim, this produced a total of eight *huissiers* by 12 November 1421.

## The *Greffiers*

The recruitment of royal *notaires* to specific offices within the *Parlement* is generally reflective of the gradual organisation of the *Parlement* in concert with the increasing amount of litigation dealt with in the early years of its existence. At the outset, in strictly *ad hoc* fashion, the *greffe* of the civil and criminal registers appears to have been confined to a single individual, probably the *greffier civil*. Yet no reference by name to the *greffier civil* on the official roll of the

---

[139] A.N. X1ª9197, f.1ʳ.

[140] *A.H.-G.* MS. 59, f.41ʳ.

[141] Ibid., f.84ʳ. But, see A.N. X1ª9200, f.11ᵛ, which indicates the presence of one Montalet, as *premier Huissier* before Guillaume Drapperie. Drapperie was given the office of *premier Huissier* by the Dauphin in May 1419, in succession to Montalet (ibid.).

[142] *A.H.-G.* MS. 59, fos.45ᵛ, 46ᵛ.

[143] Ibid., fos.50ᵛ, 66ʳ, 77ᵛ, 78ʳ. In Jan. 1420 Cachemarée opposed by *procureur* in the Paris *Parlement* Lambert Katelin's receipt of his old office of *huissier*, claiming that imprisonment at Poitiers had prevented his earlier return to Paris. This case provides evidence that during the temporary amnesty created by the treaty of Pouilly, in July 1419, many (including Cachemarée's relatives), who had earlier left Paris, returned (A.N. X1ª4792, fos. 171ʳ, 173ᵛ; A.N. X1ª1480, f.204ᵛ; cf., also, A.N. X1ª4793, fos. 73ʳ⁻ᵛ, 290ʳ⁻ᵛ).

[144] Belle returned to Paris after the treaty of Pouilly and was imprisoned in Nov. or Dec. 1419. Later released pending trial, Belle lost his old office to Renault le Clerc (A.N. X1ª1480, fos. 200ᵛ201ʳ).

*Parlement* appears until 12 November 1423.[145] Before 18 January 1419 the office of *greffier des présentations* was occupied by Guillaume Gruaud.[146] However on 20 November 1419 the *Parlement* decided that in view of the 'grant charge qu'a le greffier de la cour de ceans, la court a commis maistre Miles Chaligant a faire les registres et proces des causes criminelles'.[147] On the same day Chaligant, together with Jean Budé, had been received by the *Parlement* with orders that they should assist 'aux jours de plaidoieries et en la court comme nottaires, pour y exercer leurs offices et fair les lettres ainsi a Paris'.[148] In addition to these individuals we have mention on 20 March 1419 of Jean Morelon, appointed 'receveur des amendes et exploits de la court'.[149] By 12 November 1421 Morelon had relinquished this function to Miles Chaligant, who nevertheless continued as *greffier criminel*. Also, in the meantime, Guillaume Gruaud was superseded as *greffier des présentations* by Henri II Mauloué, and another *notaire* elected in Chaligant's place to assist Jean Budé in the office of *notaire* in the *Parlement*.[150] Between 1421 and 1423 the exercise of these offices attained its final form, with Chaligant relinquishing his earlier charge of *greffier criminel* to Jean d'Asnières, though nevertheless retaining his position as *receveur des amendes et exploits*. Jean de Maine, called *de Blois*, was additionally installed as *greffier civil*, leaving Antoine Mauloué confined to the single charge of *greffier des présentations* in place of his brother, Henri II Mauloué.[151]

## Clerks of the *Greffiers*

The first mention, by name, of the clerk of a particular *greffier* in the *Parlement* occurs on 27 February 1422 with a reference to Jean

[145] A.N. X1ª9197, f.261ᵛ. Jean de Blois, *greffier civil* before 24 Nov. 1422 (A.N. X1ª8604, f.59ʳ), was imprisoned in Paris in May 1418 (Clement de Fauquembergue, *Journal* (1417-1435), ed. A. Tuetey, i (*SHF*, Paris, 1903), 129), but was later freed. Tessier and Ouy's suggestion ('Notaires', 874), that in 1422 Blois managed both civil and criminal *greffes*, is, however erroneous, as the office of *greffier criminal* in 1422 was occupied by either Miles Chaligant (A.N. X1ª9197, f.1ʳ), or Jean d'Asnières (ibid., f.261ᵛ).

[146] *A.H.-G.* MS. 59, fos.27ᵛ and ff. (passim).

[147] Ibid., f.86ᵛ.

[148] Ibid., f.86ʳ.

[149] Ibid., fos.61ᵛ-62ʳ.

[150] A.N. X1ª9197, f.1ʳ.

[151] Ibid., Henri II Mauloué was the son of Henri I Mauloué, earlier *audiencier* in the *Grande Chancellerie* at Paris, and brother of Jean Mauloué, clerical *conseiller* at Poitiers and Antoine Mauloué, *notaire* in the *Parlement* in 1419 and later *greffier des présentations*. For an important note on the Maloués, see Tessier and Ouy, 'Notaires'. 866 n.2.

Gaultier, *clerc et serviteur* of Antoine Chasteignier, *greffier des requêtes de l'Hôtel du Roi*.[152] Further reference to these individuals is lacking until 6 February 1433 when we have mention of Robin Manay,[153] clerk of Jean d'Asnières, *greffier criminel*, Jean Cheneteau[154] and Jean Talort,[155] clerks of Jean de Maine, called *de Blois, greffier civil*, and Huguet Viniau,[156] who performed a similar function for Antoine Mauloué the *greffier des présentations*. The wages of the clerks were paid independently of the other *parlementaires*, by the way of a regular gift accorded by the king.[157] The *greffiers*, probably in respect of their dual functions as *notaires et secrétaires du roi*, appear to have been afforded a similar provision over and above their wages as *parlementaires*.[158]

## The Royal Chancery at Poitiers

The events of 1418 saw the *Grande Chancellerie*, along with the other monarchical institutions of France, split in two; a proportion of its complement of *notaires et secrétaires* henceforth elected to follow the Dauphin under a new *Chancelier*, Robert le Maçon. The additional provision, made by the Ordinance of Niort on 21 September 1418 for the creation of a sedentary *chancellerie* at Poitiers,[159] permitted for the first time, the simultaneous existence of two royal *chancelleries*. The first of these performed its functions in ambulatory fashion in the presence of the Dauphin and the *Chancelier*, and may be termed, by analogy, the *Grande Chancellerie*; its sedentary counterpart continued to function at Poitiers, being the prototype of the *Chancellerie du Palais* established at Paris after 1436, and

---

[152]Gaultier was taken prisoner in the *auditoire des requêtes* early in 1422 by Adenet Sedile, *concierge du Palais*, and Maurice Claveurier, *lieutenant-général de la sénéchaussée de Poitou*, following an assault upon the daughter of Herbert Guichard, *échevin* of Poitiers, by himself and a companion (A.N. X1ᵃ9197, fos. 42ᵛ, 254ᵛ). This incident was perhaps symptomatic (and productive) of tension between *parlementaires* and local families in Poitiers (cf. also, *A.H.-G.* MS.59, fos. 97ᵛ-98ʳ).

[153]A.N. X1ᵃ9194, f.35ᵛ. See also, ibid., f.53ʳ for reference to one Robin Moyron, likewise a clerk of Asnières's.

[154]Ibid., f.35ᵛ. Also, see A.N. X1ᵃ9200, f.42ᵛ and F. Aubert, *Histoire du Parlement de Paris de l'origine à François Iᵉʳ (1250-1515)* i(Paris, 1894), 231 n.1, 232, 233 n.1.

[155]A.N. X1ᵃ9194, f.35ᵛ.

[156]Ibid., Viniau was received as a *huissier* in the *Parlement* on 4 Dec. 1434 (A.N. X1ᵃ9194, f.55ʳ).

[157]*A.H.-G.* MS.59, f.328ʳ⁻ᵛ and passim. This sum, amounting to 60*l.p.*, was paid from the *amendes* of the court.

[158]Ibid., fos. 277ʳ⁻ᵛ, 278ʳ⁻ᵛ and 280ᵛ⁻281ʳ for 'gifts' of 60*l.p.* to each of the *greffiers* in the *Parlement*. For the wages of *greffiers* as *parlementaires*, see A.N. X1ᵃ8604, f.59ʳ (Nov. 1422).

[159]A.N. X1ᵃ8604, f.28ᵛ.

forerunner of the *petites chancelleries* later common in the provincial *parlements*.[160]

The precise division of personnel between the two institutions after 1418 is extremely difficult to quantify. This is particularly problematic in respect of two officers in the *Grande Chancellerie*, namely the *audiencier* and the *contrôleur de l'audience*. The survival of a memoir on the personnel of the *Grande Chancellerie*, compiled, probably in the 1440s, by Nicole Aymar,[161] does at least allow us to identify the individuals who occupied these offices after 1418. The function of *audiencier* is early accorded to Henri I Mauloué.[162] He was in turn succeeded as *audiencier* by his son, Henri II Mauloué.[163] The exact date of his succession is complicated by the fact that, despite his appearance in the memoir, Henri I appears not to have left Paris in 1418, remaining there until his death in c. 1420.[164] Henri II Mauloué appears for the first time in the Poitiers registers on 12 November 1421,[165] where he is termed *greffier des présentations*, which office he held in succession to Guillaume Gruaud, being replaced before 12 November 1423 by his brother Antoine Mauloué.[166] In the light of Henri I's remaining in Paris after 1418 it is thus possible that the charge of *audiencier* was occupied immediately after 1418 by Henri II Mauloué, the additional charge of *greffier des présentations* in the *Parlement* being coupled with that of *audiencier* on a temporary basis from c. 1420-c. 1423. After his death, c. 1435-6, Henri II Mauloué was in turn succeeded as *audiencier* by his brother, Antoine Mauloué.[167] After the return to Paris in 1436 Antoine Mauloué continued as *audiencier*, being finally succeeded in 1440 by Dreux Budé.[168] The office of *contrôleur*, we are told by Aymar, was exercised after 1418 by Jean Budé.[169] We know that a Jean Budé was received by the

[160]G. Tessier and G. Ouy, 'Notaires et secrétaires du rol dans la première moltié du xve siècle d' après un document inédit', *B. philol.* 1963, 870.

[161]B.N. MS. lat. 3208, fos. 6[r]-11[r] (transcribed by Tessier and Ouy, 'Notaires', 881-7).

[162]B.N. MS.lat. 3208, f.6[r].

[163]Ibid.

[164]Tessier and Ouy, 'Notaires', 866 n.2, 873. For confirmation of the fact that Henri I Mauloué remained in Paris after 1418 and, for a time at least, retained possession of the royal seals, see A.N. X1[a]9197, fos. 166[v], 194[v].

[165]A.N. X1[a]9197, f.1[r].

[166]A.N. X1[a]9197, f.261[v].

[167]A.N. X1[a]9194, f.155[v] (19 Oct. 1436). Also cf. A.N. X1[a]9200, f.285[v] (12 Nov. 1434), where Antoine is still termed *greffier des présentations*.

[168]Tessier and Ouy, 'Notaires', 863 n.1.

[169]B.N. MS. lat. 3208, f.8[r].

*Parlement* on 20 November 1419, together with Miles Chaligant, with orders to assist: 'aux jours de plaidoieries . . . et . . . en la court, comme nottaires, pour y exercer leurs offices et faire les lettres . . . ainsi . . . (qu') a Paris.'[170] This Jean Budé was still termed *notaire* in the list of officers in the *Parlement* of 12 November 1421.[171] But whether Jean Budé the *contrôleur* is synonymous with this individual is debatable.[172] Jean Budé was, nevertheless, succeeded as *contrôleur* by Jean de Sançoins.[173]

While the names of the individuals who occupied these charges are known to us, their location is not. Beaucourt pointed out the early existence, in the Dauphin's presence, and presumably in the presence of the *Chancelier*, of a hierarchy of 'simples secrétaires qui ont . . . un rôle actif et une sérieuse influence'.[174] But as Ouy and Tessier have remarked:

> On s'attendrait à trouver parmi eux l'audiencier et le contrôleur.[175]
> Or, certains indices donnent à penser que ces deux officiers auraient résidé à Poitiers, apparement contre toute logique, puisque le sceau dont étaient revêtus les actes expédiés par la chancellerie de Poitiers n'était pas le grand sceau.[176]

The suspicion that before 1422 at least the *audiencier* and the *contrôleur de l'audience* were both located at Poitiers might, however, be seen to be confirmed by the additional functions of Henri II Mauloué and Jean Budé within the *Parlement, c.* 1419-*c.* 1422.[177] If Henri II Mauloué was early obliged to couple the office of *audiencier* with that of *greffier des présentations*, and Jean Budé (if this is the Jean Budé intended by Aymar) was simultaneously *contrôleur* and *notaire* within the *Parlement*, it is difficult to see how they would be able to satisfactorily exercise these functions away from Poitiers.

---

[170] *A.H.-G.* MS.59, f.86[r].

[171] A.N. X1[a]9197, f.1[r].

[172] Tessier and Ouy, 'Notaires', 873 n.3, 874. Jean Budé is generally considered to be the great-grandfather of Guillaume Budé. Archdeacon of Blois before 1427 (Tessier and Ouy, 'Notaires', 873 n.3) in succession to Robert de Rouvres, *maîtres des requêtes de l'Hôtel* (A.N. X1[a]9193, f.183[v]), he resigned as archdeacon before 1434 in favour of Jean II de Villebresme, a royal secretary and student at the university of Orléans (A.N. X1[a]9196, fos. 101[v]-102[r], A.N. X1[a]9193, f.183[v]).

[173] Yet see Tessier and Ouy, 'Notaires', 863 n.2.

[174] Beaucourt, i (Paris, 1881), 118.

[175] Tessier and Ouy, 'Notaires', 873.

[176] Ibid.

[177] Above, pp. 27-8.

Difficulties about the existence of a *Grande Chancellerie* of the Dauphin before 1422 seem to derive from precisely the same objection as that raised by Tessier and Ouy against the location of the *audiencier* and the *contrôleur de l'audience* at Poitiers[178] – namely, that the seal employed in the expedition of its acts was not the *Grand Sceau*. In the years immediately after 1418 the *Grand Sceau* remained in Paris, the Dauphin employing, instead, a seal termed the '*scel du secret ordonne en l'absence du grant*'.[179] This would seem to provide little justification for locating the *audiencier* and the *contrôleur* with the Dauphin and the *Chancelier*, rather than at Poitiers.[180] It is possible however that in contradiction of Aymar's memoir, the functions of *audiencier* and *contrôleur* were not formally occupied until the Dauphin's accession as king – not that is, until 1422. Aymar's tendency to portray the occupation of these offices in continuous fashion from 1418 might be illustrative less of his willingness to comply with the facts, than of the more fundamental desire to maintain an unbroken succession to these offices which would compare with that exhibited by the *Grande Chancellerie* under the Anglo-Burgundians. Tessier and Ouy have remarked elsewhere[181] that the details of notarial and secretarial succession in Paris during the period 1418-36 had been carefully ignored by Aymar. If this should be the case we would need to see the structure of the Dauphin's *Grande Chancellerie* during the period 1418-22 as a highly provisional one, with its functions being carried out on the one hand by the *Chancelier* together with a small and variable group of royal *notaires et secrétaires*, and on the other by a commission of *parlementaires*, and possibly in the absence of either a *Grande* or *petite chancellerie* organised along independent lines. It is likely, however, that a formalisation of the functions of these ostensibly separate bodies took place after the Dauphin's *avènement* in 1422, and with this a much sharper delineation of organisation and personnel. This sort of development appears not to have been confined to the *Grande Chancellerie* alone; indeed, it is arguable that the events of 1422 witnessed the severance of the formerly close

[178]Tessier and Ouy, 'Notaires', 873.

[179]Beaucourt, i (Paris, 1881), 348 n.4.

[180]Further doubts about the existence, and certainly the status of the Dauphin's *Grande Chancellerie*, before 1422 at least, derive from the fact that when Robert le Maçon was replaced as *Chancelier* by Martin Gouge de Charpaignes, on 3 Feb. 1422, the office was deemed to have been vacant since the death of Henri de Marle. If (and this seems logical) the same principle applied to the offices of *audiencier* and *contrôleur*, the precise status of the *Grande Chancellerie* prior to this date is difficult to determine (Beaucourt, i (Paris, 1881), 348 nn.1-2).

[181]Tessier and Ouy, 'Notaires', 863, 869.

relationship between the *Parlement* on the one hand, and the Dauphin's personal administration on the other. Before this date the organisation of the *Grande Chancellerie* and the *requêtes de l'Hôtel*[182] display a certain similarity, in that they suggest a very fluid relationship between the royal *Conseil*, or *Grand Conseil*, and the *Parlement*. After 1422, both institutions appear to display increasing independence in terms of organisation and personnel. With the manufacture of a personal *Grand Sceau* by Charles VII in 1422, the *audiencier* and the *contrôleur* could fulfil their traditional functions within the *Grande Chancellerie*. It is particularly worthy of note that it was either late in that year or early in 1423[183] that Henri II Mauloué, whom Aymar designates as *audiencier*, relinquished his office of *greffier des présentations* in favour of his brother Antoine. In addition the name of Jean Budé disappears from the list of officials in the *Parlement*.[184] It is thus arguable that their relinquishing of function within the *Parlement* coincided with the commencement of their duties as *audiencier* and *contrôleur*.

If the year 1422 did mark the inauguration of a *Grande Chancellerie* organised along more independent lines then it is possible that the *petite chancellerie* at Poitiers achieved, simultaneously, a more distinct, though possibly considerably diminished, status compared with that originally accorded to it by the Ordinance of Niort. Very little is known about the Poitiers *chancellerie*, either before or after 1422. We know that the original commission for its formation was addressed to Jean I de Vailly, *premier Président*, Arnaud de Marle, Guillaume Thoreau and Bureau Boucher, *maîtres des requêtes de l'Hôtel*, Guillaume Guérin, archdeacon of Poitiers and Adam de Cambrai lay *conseiller*.[185] In January 1419, following the Dauphin's adoption of the title of Regent,[186] the *chancellerie* was provided with a new seal, manufactured by Gilet, *graveur des sceaux*, in Poitiers.[187] The seal was kept in a coffer covered in black leather and secured by two keys. Guard of the seal with its coffer was entrusted to Guérin, while the two keys were kept by Guillaume Thoreau and Pierre

---

[182]Below, pp. 54-5.

[183]A.N. X1ª9197, f.1ʳ (12 Nov. 1421), is the last reference to Henri II Mauloué.

[184]Ibid., for the final mention of Jean Budé as a *notaire*.

[185]A.N. X1ª8604, f.28ᵛ.

[186]Jean I de Vailly, *premier Président*, wrote to the *Parlement* from Tours, on 27 Dec. 1419, disclosing the Dauphin's intention to adopt the title of Regent (*A.H.-G.* MS.59, fos. 20ᵛ-21ʳ).

[187]This was not a completely new seal but the old one, subject to 'aucunes mutations, selon l'ordonnance de monsieur le Chancelier et du Conseil' (ibid. f.27ʳ), and presumably incorporating the new style of the Regent.

d'Oger, clerical *conseiller.*[188] In contradiction of M. Neuville's thesis,[189] the early foundation of a *chancellerie* at Poitiers was an event of the greatest importance,[190] both in respect of the more general development of the *Parlement,* and also with regard to the increasing autonomy, in judicial matters, which resulted from the emergence of a *petite chancellerie.* It has been remarked that 'les origines de la Chancellerie du Palais sont mal connues. Il est probable qu'elle s'est différenciée de la Grande Chancellerie dans le courant du xv^e siècle'.[191] While it is clear that the origins of the *Chancellerie du Palais* may be located in the terms of the Ordinance of Niort, its gradual emancipation from the *Grande Chancellerie* during the years 1418-36 is more difficult to follow.[192] It is however certain that by 1436 the process was sufficiently advanced to permit the establishment of a *Chancellerie du Palais* in the Paris *Parlement;*[193] it was, furthermore, an innovation important enough to guarantee its continued existence throughout the life of the *Parlement.*

While the stages in the growth of the *petite chancellerie* at Poitiers during our period are not clear, it is possible to offer a hypothetical picture of its development. I have argued earlier that the years 1418-22 evidenced close links between the *'Grande'* and the *'petite' chancelleries*, with neither institution, possibly, having a formal organisation. This situation was devised in an *ad hoc* manner to offset the frequent absence of the *Chancelier* from Poitiers, and to provide some sort of link between the separate parts of the *Grande Chancellerie.* I have also argued that it was possibly the Dauphin's assumption of his father's title in 1422,[194] and the subsequent manufacture of a

---

[188]Ibid., 28^{r-v}.

[189]D. Neuville, 'Le Parlement royal à Poitiers (1418-1436)', *R. hist.* 6 (1978), 13.

[190]Tessier and Ouy, 'Notaires', 870.

[191]'Guide des recherches dans les fonds judiciaires de l'Ancien Régime'. Pub. *Ministère de l'Éducation nationale,* Intr. C. Braibant (Paris, 1958), 136.

[192]G. Tessier, *Diplomatique royale française* (Paris, 1962), 170, suggests that the formal life of the *Chancellerie du Palais* began in 1436, but adds: on peut se demander si elle a existé avant la libération de Paris (ibid.).

[193]Ibid.

[194]Before 1422 the Poitiers *Parlement* saw itself as the legitimate representative not only of the Dauphin, but also, primarily, of Charles VI. This explains the simultaneous presence of a *Procureur du roi* and a *Procureur du Dauphin;* in addition, of a solitary *Avocat,* representative of Charles VI and the Dauphin alike; and of *maîtres des requètes* 'des Hostelz du Roi . . . et de monseigneur le Regent' (B.N. MS. fr.28342, (Marle) no. 36) or, simply, of the Dauphin-Regent alone (A.N. X1ª9197, f.144^r). If the same principle applied to the Dauphin's *Chancellerie,* it could be argued that the authority for letters issued immediately after 1418 was thought (by the Dauphin's supporters) to derive from the *Grand Sceau* of Charles VI, as it would under normal circumstances when the *Grand Sceau* was absent from Paris (O. Morel, *La Grande Chancellerie*

*Grand Sceau*, which simultaneously allowed both the *Grande* and *petite chancellerie* to assume a real and independent existence.[195] The likelihood that the Poitiers *chancellerie* obtained a new seal in 1422 is suggested by an order of the court dated 2 November 1436 and addressed to Adam de Cambrai, requiring the destruction of the 'seel et contreseel *du roy* qui estoit pardeca a Poictiers, *et dont a este tenue chancellerie long temps'*.[196] It is thus possible that the independent life of the *Chancellerie du Palais* began not in 1418 or 1436, but in 1422.

The emergence of the *petite chancellerie* as an independent body may have entailed a considerable modification of its role compared with that envisaged by the Ordinance of Niort, and a concentration upon matters relating predominantly to the *Parlement*. The little we know of its operation after 1422 seems to confirm this view. The distribution of personnel between the *Grande* and *petite chancelleries* is more problematic, and the existence of only a single *audiencier* and *contrôleur* in Aymar's memoir could mean that a clear distinction between the two institutions might be premature. On the other hand, it may merely indicate that Aymar's interest extended only to the *Grande Chancellerie*, and not to its counterpart at Poitiers. Clarification of these matters appears impossible, owing to the fact that no records of Charles VII's *Grande Chancellerie* survive; though it is perhaps going too far to suggest, as M. Guérin did, that they 'certainement n'ont pas été tenus jusqu' au retour de son gouvernement à Paris'.[197] The *petite chancellerie* certainly continued to function

*royale* (Paris, 1900), 119 n.2). Hence the *sceau du secret*, early employed by the Dauphin, might be seen as the legitimate delegate of the *Grand Sceau* of Charles VI, rather than the Dauphin's own seal. In the same manner the creation of the *petite chancellerie* at Poitiers may have been devised as a practical measure designed to offset the absence, not only of the Dauphin's seal (which was not the *Grand Sceau*), but also of the *Grand Sceau* of Charles VI. In either case the creation of a *petite chancellerie* may be seen as a practical response to a problem which had occupied the Paris *Parlement* long before 1418 (ibid., 201-3, 227-31). Such a view might argue further against the idea of a *Grande Chancellerie* proper to the Dauphin before 1422.

[195] The references to Robert du Rouvres in 1430 and 1433 as the *garde du sceau ordonné en l'absence du Grand* (A.N. X1ᵃ9199, f.239ᵛ; A.N. X1ᵃ9194, f.42ʳ) might suggest the presence of another seal *ordonné* at Poitiers (Tessier, 202-3) employed by the *petite chancellerie;* the destruction of the seal employed at Poitiers, in 1436 (X1ᵃ9194, f.156ᵛ), and the lack of documentation for the *petite chancellerie*, makes comparison with the device employed at Paris after 1436 impossible.

[196] A.N. X1ᵃ9194, f.156ᵛ (also, A.N. X2ᵃ21, f.136ᵛ). It is perhaps noteworthy that, after 1422, the *Parlement* adopted the style *Parlamentum regis* (Tessier and Ouy, 'Notaires', 869).

[197] Rec. des docs', *Arch. hist. Poitou* 26 (1896), xxxi.

during these years,[198] and it seems highly unlikely that a record of its proceedings would not have been kept.

How far, then, the creation of a *petite chancellerie* was envisaged as an *ad hoc* measure in the years before 1436, is uncertain. There are indications that certain of the *parlementaires* anticipated a return to more traditional forms of organisation after 1436. Certain innovations, however, survived the return; notable among these were the continued function of the *requêtes de l'Hôtel* in place of the *requêtes du Palais* and the maintenance of the *Chancellerie du Palais* itself. In other areas, notably the *enquêtes*, the prospect of the return to Paris may have prompted a deliberate return to traditional forms of organisation. The emergence of the *petite chancellerie* at Poitiers and its subsequent development at Paris provides a counter to the popular view of the weakness and disorganisation of the *Parlement* of Poitiers, and of Charles VII's early administration in general. Disorganisation could frequently lead to innovation, and it was the flexibility of Charles VII's government during the early years which provided the essential judicial framework for the 'recovery' of France.

## The *Cour des aides*

Despite its location in the *Palais de justice* with the other tribunals of the *Parlement,* the *Cour des aides* was, nevertheless, an independent sovereign court, dealing with a range of fiscal matters. At Poitiers, the early complement of the *Cour des aides* consisted of a single *Président,* Hugues de Combarel,[199] a bishop of Poitiers, and a fixed number of about five *généraux conseillers sur le fait des aides,* drawn from among the ordinary *conseillers* of the *Parlement.*[200] As with the *requêtes de l'Hôtel,* however, the ancillary staff of the *Cour* were both recruited apart from, and functioned separately from the *Parlement.* The title of *greffier de la Cour des aides* was accorded on 9 July 1431 to Jean Chasteignier,[201] probably a relative of Antoine Chasteignier, *greffier des requêtes de l'Hôtel.* In addition to

---

[198] See, for example, A.N. X2ª21, fos. 26ʳ, 136ᵛ, 172ᵛ, 214ʳ, 275ʳ. This might argue (*contra* Tessier, 170) for placing the origins of the *Chancellerie du Palais* prior to 1436, perhaps from 1422. The fact that the *chancellerie,* returned to Paris, had a new seal in 1436 (ibid.), might support less the idea of its actual creation at that date, than the simple fact of the need for a new seal following the destruction of the one formerly employed at Poitiers (A.N. X1ª9194, f.156ᵛ).

[199] Favreau, *Poitiers,* 289 n.982. By 1434 the *Cour* had a second *Président,* Guillaume I Le Tur (A.N. Z1ª8, f.122ᵛ).

[200] Ibid., 288.

[201] A.N. Z1ª8, f.45ʳ. Chasteignier was *greffier* from the inception of the *Cour* ('Rec. des docs', *Arch. hist. Poitou* 26 (1896), 408 n.1).

34

Chasteignier, the *Cour* included among its personnel a number of *huissiers* who carried the title *huissier de la chambre de la justice des aides*. Occupants of this office included: in September 1428 Yvonnet Petit;[202] in March 1432 Nicolas l'Escripvain;[203] in September 1432 Garnier de l'Esture;[204] and, finally, in February 1433, Colinet l'Escripvain,[205] possibly a relative of the aforementioned Nicolas. Recruitment of these officials, as with the other major tribunals of the *Parlement,* appears to have been governed by dynastic and Parisian considerations.

## The *Table de Marbre*

In addition to the major tribunals of the *Parlement* we may also affirm the presence at Poitiers of a *Table de Marbre,* tribunal of the constable of France, functioning independently of its Parisian counterpart. The only direct reference to the existence of the *Table* occurs on 27 July 1426 when litigation is mentioned before the 'constabulario Francie seu eius locumtenente ad *Tabulam Principalem,* aule seu palatii Pictavensis';[206] however, the presence of this tribunal at an earlier date is certain.

---

[202] A.N. Z1ᵃ8. f.1ᵛ and passim.

[203] Ibid., f.59ᵛ and passim.

[204] Ibid., f.71ʳ and passim.

[205] Ibid., fos.82ʳ and 82ᵛ.

[206] A.N. X1ᵃ9191, f.34ᵛ (cf. A.N. X2ᵃ21, f.36ʳ).

# 2

# RECRUITMENT, FUNCTIONS AND WEALTH OF THE *PARLEMENTAIRES* (c. 1422-1436)

## The *Huissiers* in the *Parlement*

By 12 November 1421[1] the *Parlement* had a complement of eight *huissiers*: Guillaume Drapperie, *premier Huissier,* Aleaume Cachemarée, Guillaume Taichier, Bertrand de Pontarcher, Philippot Duchesne, Philippe de Berlettes, Gerard Maulin and Rogerin Le Vavasseur. This number was maintained by 12 November 1423[2] with the addition of Jean de Montgobert and Guillaume Maignier in place of Maulin and Duchesne, the latter having resigned his office in the interim.[3] In 1424 the statutory figure of eight *huissiers* was exceeded by one, with the inclusion of Odinet du Breuil.[4] The death of Du Breuil in 1425,[5] together with that of Aleaume Cachemarée in 1426[6] nevertheless saw the number of *huissiers* remain at nine by 5 December 1426 with the election of Jean Le Clerc and Jean de Villy.[7] By 12 November

[1]A.N. X1ᵃ9197, f.1ʳ.

[2]Ibid., f.261ᵛ. Maignier's election was opposed by the other *huissiers* on 15 Nov. 1423. This opposition followed an earlier demand that their numbers should not exceed eight in all, a measure designed to prevent those who left Paris after 1422 from usurping the offices of others who had served the Dauphin since 1418 (A.N. X1ᵃ8604, f.64ʳ). Maignier was finally received to serve in an extraordinary capacity, without wages (A.N. X1ᵃ9197, f.262ʳ).

[3]For the circumstances of Duchesne's resignation see below, pp. 38-9.

[4]A.N. X1ᵃ9198, f.1ᵛ.

[5]See ibid., f.75ᵛ (9 June 1425), for the *Parlement*'s order to prepare an inventory of Du Breuil's possessions. Du Breuil had earlier been received in place of Philippot Duchesne, following the latter's resignation (ibid., f.94ᵛ). Shortly after Du Breuil's death Jean de Villy, *licencié-en-lois,* presented royal letters nominating him as the legitimate successor of the deceased (ibid.). Villy's claim was immediately contested by Guillaume Maignier, earlier received as an extraordinary *huissier.* Settlement of the dispute saw Maignier take the wages of Du Breuil, while Villy was received to serve in an extraordinary capacity (ibid., fos. 226ᵛ-227ʳ). Both are mentioned in the roll of *huissiers* on 2 Dec. 1426 (ibid., f.222ᵛ).

[6]Cachemarée died in May 1426 (A. Thomas, *Les États provinciaux de la France centrale sous Charles VII,* i (Paris, 1879), 300).

[7]Le Clerc's election was opposed by Jean de Villy, earlier received extraordinary *huissier* in competition with Guillaume Maignier (A.N. X1ᵃ9198, fos.223ʳff., passim), despite Le Clerc's possession of royal letters nominating him to the office formerly occupied by Aleaume Cachemarée. On 16 Dec. 1426 the established *huissiers* in the *Parlement* opposed the nominations of both Villy and Le Clerc (ibid., f.228ʳ⁻ᵛ), claiming that their reception would entail surpassing the statutory number of eight *huissiers,* fixed earlier by Charles VII (A.N. X1ᵃ8604, f.64ʳ). By 12 Nov. 1427 Villy had disappeared from the roll of *huissiers,* though Le Clerc was retained (A.N. X1ᵃ9199, f.1ᵛ).

1427[8] Villy was replaced by Philippon Guenet, though Guenet was himself replaced by Gilbert de La Grange before 13 November 1430.[9] The fusion during 1429 of the *Parlement* of Languedoc which had lately sat at Béziers with that of Poitiers saw the earlier number of nine *huissiers* increased by a further seven: Jean Arbalestre, Jean de Ruit, Jean Dessoye, Pierre Payen, Jean Poupon, Jean Duplessis and Maurice Barbier, making an overall total of sixteen *huissiers* by 13 November 1430;[10] though Poupon and Duplessis served without wages for the time being.[11] In the final existing roll of *huissiers* of 12 November 1434 this total was exceeded by one, and in the meantime Bertrand de Pontarcher had been elected *premier Huissier*[12] in place of the deceased Guillaume Drapperie.[13]

The pre-1429 number of eight *huissiers* was jealously guarded against enlargement by the established *huissiers*, in particular by those who came to Poitiers after 1418 and, more specifically, after the coronation of Charles VII in 1422. In May 1423[14] Charles VII was obliged to acquiesce with the demands of the established *huissiers* at Poitiers who complained that certain of those who had served the Anglo-Burgundian *Parlement* at Paris after 1418 had attempted to gain office at Poitiers, thereby prejudicing the positions of those *huissiers* who had worked for the Dauphin since 1418. Charles VII promised to maintain their number at eight only, with a further eight

---

[8]Ibid.

[9]A.N. X1ª9199, f.326ᵛ. La Grange had served earlier at Béziers with his relation, François de La Grange, lay *conseiller*.

[10]Ibid. Opposition to the reception of those *huissiers* who had earlier served at Béziers was formally brought by their counterparts at Poitiers on 31 Dec. 1429 (*A.H.-G.* MS.59, f.346ʳ⁻ᵛ. Cf. A.N. X1ª9199, f.222ʳ). Arbalestre, Ruit, Dessoye and Barbier were nevertheless received by the *Parlement* on 18 Jan. 1430 (*A.H.-G.* MS.59, f.353ʳ). Another *huissier* formerly at Béziers, Pierre Payen, who like Gilbert de La Grange did not figure in this confrontation was, like La Grange, allowed to take up office before 13 Nov. 1430 (A.N. X1ª9199, f.326ᵛ).

[11]Poupon and Duplessis were formally received by the *Parlement* on 8 Feb. 1430 (*A.H.-G.* MS.59, f.356ʳ). Another *huissier* formerly at Béziers, Ponce Le Roy, was received, also without wages, on 20 Aug. 1432 (A.N.X1ª9194, f.24ʳ). Also see A.N. X1ª9200, fos. 46ᵛff. (passim).) Le Roy was a native of Champagne (ibid., f.47ʳ).

[12]A.N. X1ª9200, f.285ᵛ; (but, see A.N. X1ª9196, f.92ᵛ).

[13]Ibid. In addition to Ponce Le Roy the list contains the names of a further three *huissiers* elected after Nov. 1430: Jean Dole, received 4 July 1433, in place of Jean Dessoye (A.N. X1ª9194, f.49ʳ); Huguet Viniau, received 4 Dec. 1433 to the office of Bertrand de Pontarcher and later elected *premier Huissier* in place of Guillaume Drapperie (ibid., f.55ʳ); and Guillaume d'Ayn, received before 1434 in place of Guillaume Maignier (on the date of Maignier's death, see A.N. X1ª9196, f.93ᵛ). The deaths of Dessoye, Drapperie and Maignier were probably caused by the severe epidemic in Poitou in the summer of 1433.

[14]See A.N. X1ª8604, f.64ʳ. (Also A.N. X1ª9198, f.228ʳ⁻ᵛ).

for the *Parlement* of Languedoc, which total of sixteen *huissiers* was simultaneously permitted to exceed the old Parisian complement by four. Subsequent receptions of individual *huissiers* in 1423,[15] 1425[16] and 1426-7,[17] were accompanied by organised opposition from the established *huissiers* and a recapitulation of the aforementioned edict. This course of action was taken even in respect of those *huissiers* who were obliged to serve at Poitiers following the union of the *Parlements* of Poitiers and Béziers in 1428.[18]

A notable example of the determination of the *huissiers* to safeguard their offices against those who had served the Anglo-Burgundian *Parlement* occurred in litigation before the *Parlement* in January 1432.[19] Opposition from the established *huissiers* followed the attempt by Pierre Dauvillier, formerly *premier Huissier* in the Paris *Parlement*,[20] to take up the office of *huissier* at Poitiers, with the additional proviso that he would be restored as *premier Huissier* when the *Parlement* returned to Paris. Dauvillier explained in his defence that he was:

> premier huissier de parlement quant seoit a Paris ... et que, sanz cause et sans le ouir, l'anti-parlement le debouta. Et depuis, quant le roy a este pardela la riviere de Seyne pour le recouvrement de sa seigneurie ... s'est mis en devoir, et a este de ceulx qui ont rendue l'obeissance; volst le roy qu'il retornast a son office, si est venu pardeca et a le roy voulu et ordonne en son Grant Conseil, et a la bonne relacion du conte de Clermont,[21] que, quant le Parlement sera a Paris, (Dauvillier) jouisse ... et ... qu'il use de l'office de simple huissier.[22]

Guillaume Drapperie, *premier Huissier* at Poitiers, together with the other *huissiers* of the *Parlement* and the *Procureur général du roi*, took exception to Dauvillier's claim. Jean Simon, the *huissiers'* *procureur*, pointed out[23] that Guillaume Drapperie was earlier

[15]A.N. X1ª9197, f.262ʳ.

[16]A.N. X1ª9198, fos. 75ᵛff., passim.

[17]A.N. X1ª9198, fos. 223ʳff., passim.

[18]*A.H.-G.* MS.59, fos. 346ʳff., passim. (Also A.N. X1ª9199, f.222ʳ).

[19]A.N. X1ª9200, fos. 10ʳ., passim, for what follows. Dauvillier (or Danvillier) first attempted to gain office at Poitiers on 15 March 1431 (*A.H.-G.* MS.59, f.414ᵛ).

[20]Dauvillier was made *premier Huissier* in the Anglo-Burgundian *Parlement* on 4 Aug. 1418 (F. Aubert, 'Les huissiers du Parlement de Paris (1300-1420)', in *Bibl. Éc. Chartes*, 47 (1886), 393, n.7).

[21]See A. Leguai, *Les Ducs de Bourbon pendant la crise monarchique de xvᵉ siècle* (Paris, 1962), 130-1.

[22]A.N. X1ª9200, f.10ʳ.

[23]Ibid., f.11ᵛ.

*examinateur du châtelet de Paris*, and, for some twenty years prior to this *Procureur du roi* at Troyes. In 1418 the Burgundians had taken him prisoner in the *châtelet* and murdered his wife and daughter; in leaving Paris to come to Poitiers he had, in addition, lost all his possessions. In May 1419 Drapperie had been created *premier Huissier* at Poitiers in succession to Montalet, and since then his position, as those of the other *huissiers* in the *Parlement*, had been confirmed by royal edict. This measure had proved effective in barring other claimants from gaining office at Poitiers in 1423 and 1427. Drapperie alleged, in addition, that Dauvillier had not been thrown out of office by the Anglo-Burgundians, but had instead sold it to Guillaume de Buymont[24] for his own profit. Dauvillier's additional claim to be *premier Huissier* when the *Parlement* returned to Paris was clearly prejudicial, not only to Drapperie, but also to the other *huissiers* who had served Charles VII at Poitiers. The *Parlement* finally rejected Dauvillier's claim, and, despite the offer of royal letters on 12 April 1432 in support of his case, he was not permitted to take office.

Many of those *huissiers* who left Paris immediately after 1418 were already in middle or late age, having had many years' experience at various levels of the royal administration under Charles VI. Drapperie's long career as a civil servant was matched by that of Aleaume Cachemarée, who died at Poitiers in May 1426. A native of Normandy, Cachemarée was formerly *tabellion* of the *vicomté* at Caen, then *Procureur du bailliage* (also at Caen). Transfer to Paris saw Cachemarée in 1389 promoted *clerc criminel du châtelet*, then in 1393 *huissier* in the *Parlement* of Paris.[25] The very considerable administrative experience of many of these early figures contrasts with that of the later recruits at Poitiers. Cachemarée's successor in the office of *huissier*, Jean de Villy, was a *licencié-en-lois* which suggests his comparative youth and inexperience.[26] The departure of entire families of *parlementaires* from Paris after 1418 may have introduced old enmities to the new Poitevin *milieu*. Such circumstances may have been responsible for the early resignation of one *huissier* in the Poitiers *Parlement* in 1423. On 30 July 1423[27] the *Parlement* was told that Guillaume Drapperie, *premier Huissier*, had been to the *Hôtel des Cordeliers* in Poitiers, where, in an adjacent chapel he

---

[24] See Aubert, 'Les huissiers', 377 n.2, on Buymont; ibid., 375, for resignations by *huissiers*.

[25] Thomas, *Les États*, i (Paris, 1879), 300.

[26] A.N. X1ᵃ9198, f.226ᵛ.

[27] See A.N. X2ᵃ21, fos. 1ᵛff., passim.

found Philippot Duchesne, also a *huissier* in the *Parlement*. Duchesne, with his wife and son, had recently been held prisoner in the *conciergerie du Palais* following an attack upon Marion, wife of Jacquet Guillement, *huissier des requêtes de l'Hôtel*, but had later escaped to the sanctuary of the Franciscan convent. However, the severity of the assault, which caused Marion to abort, saw the *Parlement* order Duchesne back to prison under threat of forfeiting his case and eviction from office. Duchesne's son, Jehannin, also involved in the assault, was, by virtue of being a cleric, handed over to the bishop of Poitiers for trial, and Duchesne and his wife were subsequently[28] fined 100*l.t.* and ordered to make a pilgrimage to Sainte-Catherine-de-Fierbois, 'nuz piez'. However the offer of letters of remission for the pair from Charles VII[29] and the infirmity of Duchesne's wife, Ysabeau, saw, in her case and in view of the 'guerres et perils des gens d'armes qui a present courent en ce royaume', the original demand for pilgrimage commuted to an additional fine of 40*l.t.*[30] The money was to be sent to Barthélemy Hamelin, *conseiller*, to be employed in 'euvres pitiables'.[31] As a result of the attack Duchesne was additionally obliged to resign his office of *huissier* in the *Parlement*.[32]

Other problems confronting the *huissiers* in their new *milieu* appear to have derived from their situation as aliens in Poitiers. This, coupled with their frequent absence from Poitiers on the business of the *Parlement*,[33] could make their houses convenient targets for local thieves. The not uncommon occurrence of larceny in the houses of *parlementaires* in general,[34] may be indicative of the wealth (or suspected wealth) accumulated by them during their stay at Poitiers. On 26 May 1436[35] Jean Briquet swore before the *Procureur général du roi* that he would employ the term of remission granted him to travel into the *Lyonnais* to try to find some of the money, in gold and

---

[28] *A.H.-G.* MS.59, fos. 181ᵛ-182ᵛ.

[29] A.N. X1ᵃ9197, f.243ʳ (12 Aug. 1423).

[30] A.N. X2ᵃ21, f.13ᵛ.

[31] Ibid.

[32] See A.N. X1ᵃ9197, f.261ᵛ.

[33] See *A.H.-G.* MS.59 (passim), for the frequency and duration of journeys made by *huissiers* outside Poitiers, on behalf of the *Parlement*.

[34] See, for instance, A.N. X2ᵃ21, f.37ʳ (31 July 1425) for the theft of a horse from Nicole de Grande-Rue, lay *conseiller*, by Guillaume l'Armurer (cf. Favreau, *Poitiers*, index, 677); A.N. X2ᵃ21, f.187ᵛ (7 Aug. 1432). for a robbery in the house of Mathieu Canu, clerical *conseiller*, ibid, fos. 285ff. (passim), for a robbery in the house of Mme Trainel, widow of Jean I Jouvenel, late *Président* in the *Parlement* (7 Dec. 1435).

[35] Ibid., f.302ʳ; (also, ibid., f.315ʳ, 13 Sept. 1436).

silver coin, which he had earlier stolen from the house of the late Philippe de Berlettes, formerly *huissier* in the *Parlement*, which would be transferred, by way of compensation, to Berlettes's widow, Beatrix. Some idea of the prosperity of individual *huissiers* is indicated by litigation before the *Parlement* in 1434[36] involving Philippe de Berlettes and Jacqueline de Mauny, the wife of Jean Cordoux, a prisoner in the *conciergerie*. Jacqueline, a native of Paris, alleged that she had earlier left the town to set up a business in 'marchandise et lingerie', at La Rochelle, her idea being that the 'plus honorables de la ville . . . lui bailloient leurs filles . . . a broder et aomrer de soye et lingerie'. However, she later met Berlettes, who eventually 'toucha de mariage', and persuaded Jacqueline to leave La Rochelle and go and live with him in Poitiers, which she subsequently did, 'longue pieca'. Berlettes later lent Jacqueline the considerable sum of 340 (old) *réaux d'or* to establish a new business venture selling wines. In the interim, however, their relationship ended and Berlettes had attempted to regain his original 'loan' of 340 *réaux*, demanding as part-compensation Jacqueline's house in Poitiers called *Le Coulombier*. The subsequent refusal by Jacqueline to pay an outstanding 190 *réaux* on the original sum lent by Berlettes, saw the latter eventually cite Jacqueline before the *Parlement*.

The *huissiers* occasionally had dynastic links with the *conseillers* of the *Parlement*, a notable case being that of Gilbert de La Grange *(huissier)* and François de La Grange (lay *conseiller*), both transferred from Béziers to Poitiers in 1429 following the union of the *Parlements*.[37] However, links of this kind at Poitiers were rare. Promotion above the rank of *huissier* was also infrequent, though the somewhat unusual circumstances under which recruitment was conducted at Poitiers appear to have led to the idiosyncratic placement of some *huissiers*. An example of this occurred in litigation before the *Parlement* on 27 June 1436 involving Jean de Ruit,[38] formerly a *huissier* at Béziers and Lancelot du Moncel, *greffier des requêtes de l'Hôtel* in 1433-4, in succession to Antoine Chasteignier.[39] The circumstances of the

---

[36] For what follows see A.N. X1ᵃ9200, fos. 345ᵛ-346ʳ.

[37] François died between 13 and 16 Aug. 1433, probably a victim, with other *parlementaires*, of the epidemic in Poitou during the summer of that year (A.N. X2ᵃ21, f.223ʳ).

[38] See *A.H.-G.* MS.59, f.353ʳ (18 Jan. 1430), for the reception of Ruit at Poitiers.

[39] Chasteignier died between 17 March 1433 (A.N. X1ᵃ9194, f.10ʳ) and 4 Aug. 1433 (A. Tessereau, *Histoire chronologique de la Grande Chancellerie de France*, (Paris, 1676), 45). Du Moncel, formerly a royal *notaire* (A.N. X1ᵃ9197, fos. 160ᵛff., passim), appeared as the *greffier des requêtes de l'Hôtel* in Dec. 1434 (A.N. X1ᵃ9200, f.295ʳ), though he probably took the office soon after Chasteignier's death.

dispute[40] originated in the expectation of both litigants that the return of the *Parlement* to Paris would see the automatic reinstatement of the *requêtes du Palais*, earlier absorbed into the *requêtes de l'Hôtel*.[41] Ruit, now a *huissier* at Poitiers, pointed out that, although the *requêtes du Palais* had been suspended at Poitiers: 'neantmoins speratur quod in brevi sera mis sus'. The office of *greffier des requêtes du Palais* had, he went on, been recently given to him by Charles VII, in anticipation of the impending return to Paris. Furthermore, since Du Moncel 'onques ne excerca que le greffe des requestes de l'Ostel, ne jamais ne excerca icelui du Palais, aussi ne povroit il eslire ne tenir deux offices, attendu le don de Ruit', then, in the event of the re-establishment of the *requêtes du Palais* at Paris, the office of greffier should be his. To Du Moncel's additional claim that he was a *huissier* and not, as would usually be the case with applicants for this office, a royal *notaire,* Ruit replied that:

> le Roy par ses lettres l'en a dispense . . . qu'il en use jusques sondit office de greffier doye et require exercice et lors est bien d'entencion . . . resigner es mains du Roy son dit office d'uissier pure et simplement. Le Roy la . . . peut tresbien faire *in suis officiis* car le pape *eciam* le fait chacun jour de deux de trois incompatibles.

Finally, he maintained, it was not necessary for those who exercised the *greffe des requêtes du Palais* to be royal *notaires,* 'senon que les juges comme la court de Parlement, les Requestes et generaulx'.[42]

The accumulation of considerable wealth and possessions, even at the level of the *huissiers,* may have been more commonplace than is normally envisaged. This could derive from the wide range of duties they were called upon to perform, not only as *parlementaires,* but, in the broader sense as members of the royal administration.[43] In the

[40]For what follows see A.N. X1ª9201, fos. 203ᵛ-204ʳ (27 June 1436).

[41]See F. Aubert, 'Les Requêtes de Palais (xiiiᵉ-xviᵉ siècle). Style des Requêtes du Palais', *Bibl. Éc. Chartes* 69 (1908), 597. In fact the separation of the *requêtes du Palais* from the *requêtes de l'Hôtel* did not take place until nearly twenty years after the return to Paris, at Montils-les Tours, in 1454 (ibid.).

[42]Ruit pursued his claim before the *Parlement,* now returned to Paris, on 4 March 1437. While it was prepared to acknowledge, in theory, the legitimacy of Ruit's complaint, the *Parlement* maintained that the election could only take practical effect when the *requêtes du Palais* were formally reconstituted (A.N. X1ª1482, f.11ʳ). The fact that this did not take place until 1454 meant the effective negation of Ruit's opposition to Du Moncel (cf. F. Aubert, *Histoire du Parlement de Paris de l'origine à François Iᵉʳ (1250-1515),* i (Paris, 1894), 36-7.

[43]See *A.H.-G.* MS.59, passim, and A.N. X1ª9194, passim, on the various functions of the *huissiers.* (For a study of their role at an earlier period, see F. Aubert, 'Les huissiers du Parlement de Paris (1300-1420)', *Bibl. Éc. Chartes,* 47 (1886), 370-93).

latter sense the basic wage levels of the *huissiers,* fixed by Charles VII in October 1422,[44] might represent only a rough guide to the real income of an individual *huissier.* Considerable differentation in wealth among the *huissiers* derived from seniority and status. Guillaume Draperie, *premier Huissier* from 1419-33, earned considerably more in basic terms than the other *huissiers.* This was further increased by regular payments for routine cleaning duties assigned to him within the various chambers of the *Parlement,* including the *auditoire des requètes de l'Hôtel.*[45] Drapperie was also, on occasion, the ambassador of both *Parlement* and king alike in negotiations with *seigneurs* or with town corporations. These could, on occasion, prove lucrative.[46] Similar responsibilities were delegated early, to an unknown degree, to other *huissiers.* In July 1420 Aleaume Cachemarée accompanied Guillaume de Laillier, lay *conseiller,* to a meeting of the Estates of the Auvergne to ask for 1,000 footsoldiers to serve in the Regent's army.[47] In 1425 Guillaume Taichier was sent by order of Charles VII, to levy a particular *aide* upon certain villages in the Limousin.[48] It was also a *huissier* in the *Parlement,* Bertrand de Pontarcher, who was delegated in 1431 to supervise the carriage of the registers and processes of the Béziers *Parlement* to Poitiers, following the union of the *Parlements* in 1428-29. The record of payment to Pontarcher for supervision of the operation records that 'en allant il fut detrousse'; despite this obstruction, Pontarcher managed to complete the task, and on 16 May 1431 he was paid 30*l.p.* from the *Recette des amendes* for the assault, and a further 148*l.p.* as wages for sixty-four days spent in the completion of the assignment.[49]

---

[44]See A.N. X1ᵃ8604, f.49ʳ (24 Nov. 1422) on the wages of the *huissiers* at Poitiers. Certain of the *huissiers* appear to have held subsidiary offices beside their duties in the *Parlement* (see, ibid., f.101ʳ⁻ᵛ).

[45]See *A.H.-G.* MS.59, fos. 225ʳ⁻ᵛ, 250ʳ⁻ᵛff., passim.

[46]See *Reg. consulaires,* ii (Lyon, 1926), 154, where in 1425 Drapperie is paid 2 *moutons d'or* by the consuls of Lyon for negotiating a particular *aide.*

[47]Thomas, 'Les États', i (Paris, 1879), 300 (cf. A.N. X1ᵃ9191, fos. 21ʳ-22ʳ).

[48]A.N. X1ᵃ9198, f.60ʳ. Like the *Présidents* and *conseillers* in the *Parlement* the *huissiers* appear to have played a prominent role in the imposition and levy of the *aides* (see, for example, A.N. X2ᵃ18, fos. 282ʳ-283ᵛ and A.N. Z1ᵃ8, fos. 125ᵛ-126ʳff., passim). The exercise of these and other administrative functions may have been responsible, by the 1430s, for the prolonged, and in some cases permanent, absence of some of the *huissiers* from Poitiers — a tendency also apparent during this period among the *conseillers* of the *Parlement* (cf. A.N. Z1ᵃ9194, fos. 123ᵛ and 124ʳ).

[49]See *A.H.-G.* MS.59, fos. 425ᵛ-426ᵛ.

## The *Greffiers* in the *Parlement*

Apart from the occasional exercise of a particular *greffe* by the clerk[50] of the *greffier* in question, or by a royal *notaire*,[51] the years 1422-36 witnessed few changes of personnel among the *greffiers*. Jean de Maine, called *de Blois*, remained in the office of *greffier civil* until the return to Paris in 1436. This was also the case with Miles Chaligant, *receveur des amendes et exploits* of the *Parlement*. Antoine Mauloué, *greffier des présentations*, remained in this office until *c.* October 1436[52] when he was promoted *audiencier du roi* in succession to his brother, Henri II Mauloué.[53] Antoine's former charge was filled before 1 December 1436 by Simon Compains.[54] Antoine Chasteignier was replaced as *greffier des requêtes de l'Hôtel* in 1433 by Lancelot du Moncel.[55]

The earlier careers of the *greffiers*, in terms of their experience in royal government, appear to have been quite varied. Miles Chaligant, *receveur des amendes et exploits*, had served in the royal *Chancellerie* for many years prior to his election to office at Poitiers.[56] Yet Jean d'Asnières, who took Chaligant's former charge of *greffier criminel* in 1423 had not taken his examination for the degree of *licencié-en-lois* when he arrived at Poitiers.[57] Asnières's career displayed a notable upturn after 1423; yet his stay at Poitiers began somewhat ignominiously. On 29 March 1424[58] he was involved in litigation before the *Parlement* with Adenet Sedile, *concierge du Palais*. Asnières alleged that he had earlier given Sedile 19 *moutons d'or* 'pour lui querir provisions de ble et de vin' (this possibly a measure against the severe famine in Poitou). Sedile took the money but

---

[50] See, for instance, A.N. X1ª9200, f.42ᵛ where Jean de Blois, *greffier civil,* is replaced by one of his clerks, Jean Cheneteau (5 May 1432).

[51] See A.N. Z1ª8, f.109ʳ, where Jean Chasteignier, *greffier* of the *Cour des aides,* is replaced by a royal *notaire* Nicole Savary (4 Jan. 1434).

[52] Royal letters of election as *greffier des présentations* were presented to the *Parlement* on 19 Oct. 1436 by Simon Compains (A.N. X1ª9194, f.155ᵛ). The court suspended final judgement on the matter until it had sufficient numbers to make a decision (cf. A.N. X1ª1482, f.1ᵛ) Mauloué was still 'prothonotaire et secretaire du roi et greffier des presentations' in 1435 (A.N. X1ª9201, f.180ᵛ).

[53] B.N. MS. lat., no. 3208, f.6ʳ.

[54] See A.N. X1ª1482, f.1ᵛ.

[55] Above, p. 40 n. 39.

[56] Favreau, *Poitiers,* 282.

[57] See A.N. X1ª9200, f.266ʳ.

[58] See A.N. X1ª9197, f.301ᵛ.

subsequently failed to buy provisions. In the resulting dispute between the pair, Asnières struck Sedile a blow in the face and the affair was subsequently brought before the *Parlement*.[59] In 1432 Asnières was again involved in litigation before the *Parlement*, this time with the abbot of La Réau.[60] Confrontation followed the attempt by the abbot to requisition Asnières's house, ostensibly in order to provide lodgings for certain of his religious students at the recently-created university of Poitiers, the act being perpetrated in the absence of Asnières, who had travelled to Châteauroux to attend his daughter's wedding.

The growing importance of Asnières's charge is emphasised by his decision to cite Huguenin d'Alon before the *Parlement* in July 1434[61] following the latter's refusal to entertain Asnières's presence on a commission of inquiry into a lawsuit in which he was involved. Authority to examine the suit had earlier been delegated to Asnières by Adam de Cambrai, *Président* in the *Parlement*. Not long after this incident on 5 May 1435[62] Asnières asked the *Parlement*'s permission: 'tenir et exercer le baillage des terres du seigneurie de Chasteauroux, pourveu qu'il ne sey occupe que a deux assises en l'an, l'une durant le Parlement, . . . l'autre es vacacions'. This function was probably to be exercised on behalf of his daughter and her husband whose marriage, mentioned earlier, took place at Châteauroux in 1432.[63] Finally in July 1436 we learn that Asnières, earlier 'commis a recevoir et faire venir ens les deniers des assignacions pour les gages de la court', was to be replaced 'durant l'empeschement qu'il a d'aler a Paris pour la commission a lui attribuee pour faire le greffe des commissaires ordonnez par le roy a pourveoir aux cas de souverainete et de ressort a Paris'.[64]

Of the career of Jean de Maine, called *de Blois, greffier civil* in the *Parlement*, relatively little is known. Imprisoned by the Burgundians in 1418, he was, nevertheless, later able to make his way to Poitiers, though the date of his reception as *greffier civil* remains uncertain, the first reference to him in this office occurring in November 1422.[65]

[59]Ibid.

[60]See A.N. X1ᵃ9201, fos. 78ʳ, 78ᵛ, 84ʳ-86ʳ.

[61]See A.N. X1ᵃ9200, fos.266ʳ, 271ᵛ-272ᵛ. The *greffiers* were only occasionally delegated to this function by the *Parlement* (cf. A.N. X1ᵃ9195, fos.208ʳ, 216ʳ⁻ᵛ, 276ᵛ-277ʳ).

[62]A.N. X1ᵃ9194, f.99ʳ⁻ᵛ.

[63]Above.

[64]A.N. X1ᵃ9194, f.142ᵛ.

[65]A.N. X1ᵃ8604, f.59ʳ

During the 1430s Blois was involved in litigation before the *Parlement*, initially with Jean de Beloisel, *maître de la Chambre aux deniers du roi*, for the dignity of canon and *maître d'école* of Saint-Hilaire-le-Grand in Poitiers.[66]

## Royal *Notaires et Secrétaires*

The steady drift of *parlementaires* from Paris after 1418 and, to a less marked extent, following the death of Charles VI in October 1422 was accompanied by a similar tendency on the part of those *notaires et sécrétaires* who had formerly served in the *Grande Chancellerie* of Charles VI.[67] Yet it appears that the *ad hoc* nature of the Dauphin's government during the years immediately after 1418 witnessed the dispersal of *notaires et secrétaires* over a very wide range of administrative functions.[68] The importance of these individuals, particularly in the realm of finance, remains to be properly evaluated, though some indication is provided in a recent study by Tessier and Ouy.[69] On a hypothetical level, it is possible to argue that the years 1418-36 witnessed a considerable decline in the autonomy of the various institutions of royal government, vis-à-vis the royal administration more generally speaking. This may have entailed, for individuals serving in these institutions, undertaking a far wider range of functions than their official titles would suggest.

The difficulties of the political situation between 1418 and 1422 made the problem of the reception of *notaires* who had remained in Paris for some time after the Burgundian invasion difficult to envisage in terms of any immutable law. This situation was further complicated by the Dauphin's desire to encourage defections from the Anglo-Burgundians, and, in a more specific sense, by the pressure created in favour of reception of an individual by influential relatives or patrons within the various institutions of government, particularly the *Grand Conseil* where most nominations to office seem to have originated.[70]

[66]See A.N. X1ª9201, f.36ᵛ; A.N. X2ª18, fos. 327ᵛff.; A.N. X2ª20, fos. 77ᵛ-78ᵛ, 88ʳ-90ᵛ.

[67]See G. Tessier and G. Ouy, 'Notaires et secrétaires du roi dans la première moitié du xvᵉsiècle d'après un document inédit', *B. philol.* 1963, 867ff.

[68]Ibid., 878-9.

[69]Ibid., 878.

[70]See, particularly, A.N. X1ª9197, fos. 297ʳff. (29 Feb. 1424) for a dispute over the succession to the office of a royal *notaire et secrétaire*, Pierre Ferron, deriving from separate nominations within the *Grand Conseil* (cf. P. Robin, *La Compagnie des secrétaires du roi (1351-1791)* (Paris, 1933), 67 n.2).

These complex problems are amply illustrated by litigation before the *Parlement* in December 1422,[71] involving royal *notaire* Lancelot du Moncel, and Jean Thoreau, brother of Guillaume Thoreau, *premier maître des requêtes de l'Hôtel du Roi*, who had left Paris to seek election to the office of royal *notaire* some years after the establishment of the *Parlement* at Poitiers. Moncel alleged[72] that, following the creation of a sovereign *Parlement* at Poitiers, the Dauphin had ordered 'tous ceulx qui tenoient le party desdits ennemis estre privez de tout offices royaulx'. In addition, he claimed that Thoreau had willingly served the Anglo-Burgundian administration since 1418, being among those responsible for the death of the suspected 'Armagnac' Jean de Bris. On one occasion Thoreau took royal seals allegedly 'found'[73] by him to the house of Henri I Mauloué, formerly *audiencier* in the *Grande Chancellerie* of Charles VI, demanding 30 *écus* d'or from Mauloué for their return. Other crimes allegedly committed by Thoreau included riding in the company of the Veau de Bar, wearing the cross of St. André; and the theft of a horse and other possessions belonging to Du Moncel. To try and recoup some of these losses Du Moncel alleged that following the signing of the treaty of Pouilly he returned to Paris and asked Thoreau to return his property. Evidently Thoreau would only comply in return for Du Moncel's letters of office, claiming that the office of *notaire* had originally belonged to him and was therefore his by right. Now, some years after these events, Thoreau had come to Poitiers to attempt to regain the office of *notaire* currently occupied by Du Moncel, ostensibly for reason of the 'chierte des vivres qui estoit a Paris'.

In the face of these allegations Thoreau claimed[74] that he had defected purely out of loyalty for the Dauphin's cause. In the course of the Burgundian occupation of Paris he had, he alleged, suffered considerably, being twice imprisoned by the Veau de Bar on suspicion of being an 'Armagnac' sympathiser. On the second occasion he was ordered, under pain of death, to pay a large ransom. Only the personal intermission of a certain 'jeune fille' on Thoreau's behalf saved him from certain death. Not long after these events, while in the company of the Veau de Bar on a journey to Rouen, Thoreau heard news of further massacres in Paris; at Vernon, however, he fell ill, and, using

---

[71] Details of this affair may be found on A.N. X1ª9197. fos. 160ᵛ, 166ʳ, 166ᵛ, 192ᵛ, 194ʳ-195ʳ, 197ᵛff. Du Moncel was later received *greffier des requêtes de l'Hôtel.*

[72] For this and what follows, see ibid., f.194ʳ.

[73] Du Moncel claimed that these had been stolen by a third party in league with Thoreau.

[74] See ibid., fos. 194ʳff.

this as a pretext to return to Paris, left instead for Chinon, where he finally arrived at Christmas in the year of the Burgundian occupation (1418). Thoreau claimed that the persistence of his illness compelled him to remain for some months at Chinon. Following his recovery, however, and the subsequent announcement by the Dauphin, in contradiction of his earlier pronouncement, that all those who came over to his cause would be maintained in office, Thoreau was received to exercise the office of royal *notaire*.

The difficulty of determining the veracity of these accounts, let alone pronouncing in favour of either claimant, is emphasised by the cryptic pronouncement of Guillaume I Le Tur, who, speaking for the *Procureur général du roi* in the *Parlement*, declared that: 'il . . . ne s'entend faire partie, *quia solum queritur de officio et non de excessibus.* '[75] The great difficulties raised by this case, in view of the Dauphin's changed attitude to the reception of defectors, provided an early example of the sort of problem faced by the *Parlement* after the return to Paris in 1436, when confronted with the claims to property and possessions by those who had formerly supported the Anglo-Burgundian regime.[76] In the event, the attitude adopted by the *Parlement* to the dispute between Thoreau and Du Moncel derived from the same pragmatic considerations which would predominate over strictly legal attitudes in the matter of determining lawful ownership of property in Paris after 1436.[77] Thoreau's election was allowed to stand, and both he and Du Moncel were allowed to continue as *notaires*.

Some idea of the competition for royal notarial office during our period is evidenced by litigation before the *Parlement* in March 1433.[78] Here an established *notaire*, Regnault Filleul, demanded reinstatement to office in the face of opposition by Charles Chaligant,[79] the son of Miles Chaligant, *receveur des amendes et exploits* in the *Parlement*. The circumstances of the dispute were no less extraordinary than those between Thoreau and Du Moncel. Filleul alleged that he had occupied the office of *notaire* since 1426.[80] In 1429 he journeyed,

---

[75]Ibid., f.198ᵛ.

[76]On this problem see A. Bossuat, 'The Re-Establishment of Peace in Society during the Reign of Charles VII'. (In *The Recovery of France in the Fifteenth Century*, ed. P.S. Lewis, (London, 1971)), 60-81, especially 62 n. 5.

[77]Ibid., 70ff.

[78]See A.N. X1ᵃ9200, fos. 132ʳ⁻ᵛ, 154ᵛ-155ᵛ.

[79]See *A.H.-G.* MS.59, f.180ʳ⁻ᵛ (10 July 1423) for a payment made by the *Parlement* to Charlet Chaligant for having 'double ou coppie . . . certain proces'.

[80]A.N. X1ᵃ9200, f.132ʳ. (But see also, Tessier and Ouy, 'Notaires', 887).

in the company of many others, to Reims to witness the coronation of Charles VII. During the course of the journey, however: 'icelui . . . Regnaut prinst, si firent autres, de grans froidures, dont lui revenu il en cher en grant maladie, en laquele ses amis et . . . sa femme[81] comme . . . Anthoine Mauloué, Guillaume Taichier[82] et autres le visitoient.'[83] Concern for Filleul's deteriorating health appears to have prompted his friends to persuade him to sell his letters of office as royal *notaire*. Filleul apparently complied with this advice, and his office was given to Charles Chaligant. However, Filleul survived, and subsequently demanded to be restored to his old office.[84]

Jean Barbin, replying[85] for the Chaligants, explained that Charles's father, Miles, was a notable man:[86] 'et . . . deu plusieurs beaux estaz . . et a belle ligne, et que maistre Charles Chaligant est bien cognu et ame a la court du roy ou il a longuement servi soubz maistre Jehan Le Picart.'[87] Filleul, he went on, had earlier been dangerously ill, and during the course of his illness had asked friends for their opinion as to his estate, 'et comment pourroit avoir finance'. Their advice was that 'plus promptement n'en povoient avoir que de vendre son office de notaire a bourses et gages, la quelle fut ainsi exposee en vente'. However, Chaligant was willing to pay only 200 *réaux* d'or for the office, while another contender, the *clerc du trésorier de la Reine*, offered 300 *réaux*. Yet some time after Chaligant's offer was made Antoine Mauloué approached Charles's father, Miles, informing him that Filleul had now changed his mind and wished to relinquish his office to Miles's son, and to no other. The transaction was finally completed for the sum of 300 *réaux* in the presence of Henri II Mauloué, *audiencier* in the *Grande Chancellerie*,[88] and additionally both relative and attorney of Regnault. The decision was approved by Charles VII, and Filleul handed over the 'coffret ou estoient les lettres des bourses' to Miles Chaligant. Despite this, Filleul later adjourned the Chaligants before the *maîtres des requêtes de l'Hôtel* at Poitiers,

[81] Filleul was married to Katherine Nicolase, niece of Pierre de Tuillières lay *conseiller* in the *Parlement*. Following Katherine's death Filleul was involved in litigation with Tuillières over the partition of her inheritance (A.N. X1ª9200, fos. 200ᵛff., 245ᵛff., passim; also, A.N. X1ª9195, f.107ʳ (1434)).

[82] Guillaume Taichier was a *huissier* in the *Parlement*.

[83] A.N. X1ª9200, f.132ʳ.

[84] Ibid.

[85] For what follows see ibid., fos. 154ᵛff.

[86] On Miles Chaligant, see Favreau, *Poitiers*, 282.

[87] On the career of Le Picart see Tessier and Ouy, 'Notaires', 872.

[88] See ibid., 873.

demanding restitution to office. Finally, Barbin, speaking for the *Procureur général du roi* in *Parlement*, declared that: 'les offices de notaire du roi . . . ne sont venales pour doubte de concussion.'[89] The transaction was consequently declared null and void and on 19 December 1433 the *Parlement* ordered Miles Chaligant to compel his son to relinquish 'les bourses du notaire du roy'. Filleul was to take up office again one month after restoration of the 100 *écus d'or* already paid by Charles Chaligant in respect of the transaction.[90]

The dynastic links which underlay both these cases were strongly exhibited by other notarial families in the service of Charles VII. Like the Mauloués, the Thoreaus, the Chaligants or the Bouchers[91] they could extend upward into the hierarchy of the *Parlement*; or, in the case of the Budés[92] and others, horizontally within the ranks of the *notaires et secrétaires* alone.

Something of the importance of the *notaires et secrétaires* within the whole complex of the royal administration has been indicated earlier. An idea of the influence and prestige accumulated by certain individuals is indicated by litigation before the *Parlement* in 1431, involving Jean Budé, *contrôleur de l'audience* after 1418.[93] In February of that year Jehannequin Choisel, *écuyer de cuisine* of the Dauphin Louis, demanded from Marion Renarde, widow of Jean I de Villebresme, royal *notaire*, and Jean Budé, *guardian* of Villebresme's children,[94] the restitution of a certain sum of money which Choisel claimed to have lent to the Villebresme family to facilitate their earlier escape from Paris. Budé's defence stressed his client's importance as

[89]On the problem of venality in respect of notarial offices see ibid., 879.

[90]A.N. X1ᵃ9194, f.55ᵛ.

[91]Pierre Boucher, a relative of Bureau Boucher, lay *maître des requètes de l'Hôtel*, was *Procureur du Collège des notaires* in 1431 (A.N. X2ᵃ21, f.160ʳ). Further reference to the *Procureur* of the *Collège* occurs in 1426 (A.N. X1ᵃ9198, f.204ʳ), though not by name.

[92]For important remarks on the Budé family, see G. Ouy, 'Histoire "Visible" et histoire "cachée" d'un manuscrit', *Moyen Age* 64 (1958), 115-38. Also, Tessier and Ouy, 'Notaires', passim.

[93]See A.N. X1ᵃ9199, fos. 359ʳff., for what follows.

[94]The links between Jean Budé and the Villebresme family were very close. Following the death of Jean I de Villebresme, in 1430, (Tessier and Ouy, 'Notaires', 872), Budé was the tutor of his sons, Jean II and Guillaume. Archdeacon of Blois before 1427 (Tessier and Ouy, 'Notaires', 873 n. 3), in succession to Robert de Rouvres, *maître des requètes de l'Hôtel* (A.N. X1ᵃ9193, f. 183ᵛ), Budé resigned as archdeacon before 1434 in favour of Jean II de Villebresme, then a student at the university of Orléans (A.N. X1ᵃ9194, f.61ʳ; A.N. X1ᵃ9196, fos. 101ᵛ-102ʳ), following his own promotion as archdeacon of Angoulême (A.N. X1ᵃ9201, f.186ʳ). After the return to Paris, in 1436, Budé resigned his wages as *notaire et secrétaire* in favour of Villebresme's second son, Guillaume (Tessier and Ouy, 'Notaires', 872).

one of the most eminent royal *notaires*, who, 'l'annee passe ... fut dela la riviere de Sayne avecques monseigneur le Chancellier de France et fut ordonne a venir d'envers le Roy pour le fait de certain traicte'.[95]

In addition to their functions with the *Grande Chancellerie* of Charles VII, the *notaires* played an important, and as yet undocumented role in the royal fiscal administration.[96] Diligence in performing these functions for the king could on occasion bring serious confrontation with *parlementaires* involved in similar activities. An example of this came before the *Parlement* in February 1432.[97] The case involved Jean Vousy, royal *notaire* and collector of a particular *aide* in Poitou, and Léon Guérinet,[98] canon of the church of Poitiers and relative of Jean Rabateau, *Avocat général criminel* in the *Parlement*.[99] At root the affair may have originated in the uneasy relationship between certain members of the *Grand Conseil* and *parlementaires* who were simultaneously members of that institution.

Vousy explained that he was formerly clerk to Guillaume I Le Tur, now *Président* in the *Parlement*,[100] then royal *secrétaire* and keeper of the *contre-rôle de la Chambre aux deniers*.[101] Lately he had 'grant charge de plusieurs des finances du roy ainsi ... de monseigneur de La Tremoille'. Established at Poitiers for the execution of his duties, Vousy had supervised payment of 'v a vi mille francs ... deuz pour raison de la despense du roy et de la royne'. On 28 February 1432, at about three o'clock in the afternoon, Vousy entered the 'sale de ceans' where he found in conversation near the *auditoire des requêtes*, Jean Rabateau, *Avocat criminel,* Maurice Claveurier, *lieutenant-général* of the *sénéchaussée* of Poitou, and Pasquier, receiver of the aforementioned *aide* in Poitou. Rabateau motioned Vousy to join them, then challenged him about the matter of the payment of 200*l. t.* which was owed to Rabateau for his part in the levy of the *aide* and promised to him earlier by Charles VII at Chinon. Vousy

[95] A.N. X1ª9199, f.359ʳ.

[96] For their participation in the collection of the *aides* see, for example, A.N. Z1ª8, fos.6ᵛ, 9ʳff., 24ʳff., 28ᵛ, 39ʳff., 49ʳ, etc.

[97] For details of this affair see A.N. X2ª21, fos. 174ᵛ (27 Feb. 1432) and ff.; A.N. X1ª9201, fos. 81ᵛ (27 May 1432) and ff.

[98] On the family of Guérinet see Favreau, *Poitiers,* index, 596.

[99] For comments on Rabateau's influence in the *Grand Conseil* of Charles VII see below, pp. 75-7. A study of Rabateau's career is provided by H. Daniel-Lacombe (*R. Bas-Poitou* 4 (1891), 48-66; 5 (1892), 22-51, 297-328; 6 (1893), 158-87; 7 (1894), 272-98).

[100] For confirmation of this see *A.H.-G.* MS.59, fos. 202ʳ-203ᵛ.

[101] For what follows see A.N. X1ª9201, fos. 81ᵛff.

denied responsibility for the payment and a heated argument developed between him and Rabateau. At this point, Guérinet, who had been observing events, suddenly intervened and delivered Vousy 'deux ou iii gros cops ... par le visage, et lui arracha des cheveux'. Rabateau's retreat before the *Parquet* of the *Procureur du roi* saw the irate Vousy in hot pursuit; however, Guérinet, determined to restrain him, administered Vousy another 'gros cop par derriere, et le saisy au corps', this before a chamber crowded with onlookers.[102] Guérinet, in defending his action, alleged that Vousy 'n'est parcil a Rabateau, qui est du *Grant Conseil* du roy'. Vousy, he went on, had had the temerity to accuse Rabateau of corruption before an assembled chamber, and, apart from Guérinet's relationship with Rabateau, such behaviour was hardly diplomatic, considering Rabateau's position as one of Charles VII's most respected civil servants. Soon after the incident,[103] Rabateau was allowed to communicate the details of his case to the *Grand Conseil* of Charles VII; Vousy immediately demanded that he be allowed to see the letters, fearing a likely bias on Guérinet's behalf. This led the court to the extraordinary step of imprisoning Rabateau while the letters were examined. In the meantime a tug-of-war developed between the jurisdictions of the bishop of Poitiers and the chapter of Saint-Pierre for Guérinet, who explained that he was 'licencié en ------[104] et l'eut bien par un an et demy l'ordinaire pour son docteur'. Rabateau continued to resist the authority of the court in the judgement of his case, preferring that of the *Grand Conseil*; he was eventually released on bail of 4,000 *réaux d'or,* provided by Maurice Claveurier,[105] *lieutenant-général* of the *sénéchaussee* of Poitou, and Etienne Gillier, bourgeois of Poitiers and brother-in-law of the *premier Président,* Jean de Vailly. Guérinet was, in the meantime, also released into the household of Guillaume Gouge de Charpaignes, *maître des requêtes de l'hôtel,* on bail of 2,000 *réaux,* provided by Jean l'Archier, *échevin* and sometime mayor of Poitiers.

Rabateau's considerable links with the *échevins* of Poitiers are illustrated by the fact that on Monday 3 March 1432 'le maire et plusieurs bourgeois de Poitiers sont venuz en la court requerir ... qu'il plaise ... elargir Rabateau'. Soon after this, letters close arrived from Charles VII 'par lesquelles le Roy evocque la cause ... d'entre Vousy

---

[102]Cf. F. Aubert, *Histoire du Parlement de Paris de l'origine à François I<sup>er</sup> (1250-1515),* i (Paris, 1894), 92 n.2 and 93 n.2.

[103]For what follows see A.N. X2ª21, fos. 174ᵛff.

[104]Sic. (See A.N. X1ª9201, f.82ʳ).

[105]Claveurier was, like Rabateau, an important member of the royal fiscal administration in Poitou and, additionally, a member of Charles VII's *Grand Conseil.*

et Rabateau devant lui en son Grant Conseil'. After a short delay Rabateau was released to go before the king, and ultimately both he and Guérinet received royal pardons for their part in the affair.

Evidence of the wealth of notarial families is offered by litigation before the *Parlement* in January 1435 involving Dreux Budé, relation of the aforementioned Jean.[106] Dreux had complained to the court that before the siege of Orléans in 1428 he had sent a quantity of 'biens meubles de la valeur de mil et v$^c$ escus d'or' to the safekeeping of Macé Sabart, treasurer *ordinaire* at Carcassonne.[107] In return Macé had forwarded his cedule to acknowledge receipt of the goods. After the successful lifting of the siege Dreux demanded the return of his possessions; however, Macé Sabart had died in the interim and his brother Jean denied all responsibility for the goods, or any knowledge of the contract made by his father. As a result of this, Budé cited Sabart before the *maîtres des requêtes de l'Hôtel* at Poitiers. In July 1436 the *Parlement* awarded Budé compensation to the extent of 500 *écus d'or*, this representing the value of three houses belonging formerly to Macé Sabart, of which two were situated at Blois and another at Meung-sur-Loire.[108]

A similar action, this time in respect of a loan, was taken before the *Parlement* in July 1430 by another royal *notaire*, Pierre Tarenne.[109] Tarenne had cited before the court, in absentia, the duke of Orléans, 'pour raison de xli$^m$ livres en quoy est tenu monseigneur d'Orleans audit Tarenne et ses freres'. The money had been lent some years earlier by Jean I Tarenne, Pierre's father, who died at Paris during the Burgundian massacres, at the time of the count of Angoulême's visit to England as a hostage of the duke of Orléans. In return for the loan the latter had obliged the duchies of Orléans and Valois, the county of Beaumont and numerous other lordships. The Tarennes, heirs of their father, now demanded that the duke repay the outstanding amount.[110]

[106] Dreux Budé was the son of Jean I Budé, *contrôleur de l'audience*. Among the most influential of the group of *notaires et secrétaires* around Charles VII, Dreux was promoted *audiencier* in the *Grande Chancellerie* in 1440 (Tessier and Ouy, 'Notaires', 863, n.1). Like his father, Jean I, Dreux appears to have had particularly close links with the house of Orléans.

[107] See A.N. X1$^a$9200, f.298$^r$ (19 Jan. 1435). The contract with Sabart was signed on 15 Feb. 1427 (n.st.) (cf. A.N. X1$^c$152, nos. 7 and ff.).

[108] A.N. X1$^c$152, nos. 7 and ff.

[109] On Pierre Tarenne (alais Tharenne) see Tessier and Ouy, 'Notaires', 884 (after B.N. MS. lat. 3208, f.8$^v$). One of Tarenne's brothers, Guillaume, was a *greffier* in the *Parlement* of the Languedoc which had earlier sat at Béziers (A.N. X1$^a$9196, f.112$^v$).

[110] A.N. X1$^a$9199, f.311$^v$ (27 July 1430). See also A.N. X1$^a$9201, fos. 101$^v$ff. (passim); A.N. X1$^a$9200, f.267$^r$; A.N. X1$^a$9193, fos. 32$^v$-33$^r$. On 14 Aug. 1431 Pierre Tarenne and his brothers cited Étienne l'Amirault before the *Parlement*, about a

The various privileges and immunities enjoyed by royal *notaires* were jealously guarded against infringement by outsiders. Corporate protection in such cases was afforded by the legal representative of the *Collège des notaires*. An example of the protection afforded by this community occurred on 8 August 1426 when the *Procureur du Collège des notaires* joined with Anthoine Chasteignier, *greffier des requêtes de l'Hôtel du roi*, in condemning the action of Guiot Motart, '*garde du seel aux contraz a Poitiers*', who had attempted to constrain Chasteignier, 'notaire du roy . . . a payer emolument du seel pour le seelle d'une lettre seellee dudit seel aux contraz, qui . . . est contre le privilege et franchise des notaires'.[111] Again, on 16 April 1431, these privileges were emphasised by Pierre Boucher, '*Procureur du College des notaires du roy*', in opposing the reception of Michel du Tillay as a royal *notaire*.[112]

## The *Maîtres des Requêtes de L'Hôtel du Roi*[113]

Together with other important offices in the *Parlement*, notably those of the *Procureur général du roi* and the *Avocat du roi*, the style of the *maîtres des requêtes de l'Hôtel du Roi* between 1418 and 1422 seems to reflect the intention of the Dauphin's government to portray itself as the sole legitimate representative of royal authority in France, that is, as the representative of the Dauphin, and also, primarily, of Charles VI. Hence during the period before 1422 we have *maîtres des requêtes de l'Hôtel* styled *du Roi*, or *du Roi et de monseigneur le*

quantity of salt stored in the *grenier* at Orléans, the property of their father, Pierre I (A.N. X1ª9192, f.251ʳ (cf. A.N. X1ª9201, f.152ʳ)). However in 1433 Pierre was himself cited before the *Parlement* by Pierre Raguier, over a 'certaine somme d'or' loaned to him by Raguier soon after the Burgundian entry into Paris, to enable him to journey to Paris 'pour savoir l'estat de son pere' (A.N. X1ª9201, f.101ᵛ).

[111]See A.N. X1ª9198, f.204ʳ (contd. ibid., f.217ʳ⁻ᵛ). On the *Collège* generally, see P. Robin, *La Compagnie des secrétaires du roi (1351-1791)* (Paris, 1933).

[112]A.N. X2ª21, f.160ʳ. Opposition to the reception of Du Tillay was brought on behalf of Jean de Maine, called *de Blois*, *greffier civil* in the *Parlement* .

[113]A comprehensive study of the *maîtres des requêtes* for the fifteenth century is still lacking. Useful material can be found in A. Guillois, *Recherches sur les Maîtres des Requêtes de l'Hôtel des origines à 1350* (Paris, 1909); G. Bailhache, 'Les Maîtres des Requêtes de l'Hotel du Roi depuis l'avènement de Jean le Bon jusqu' à l'édit de Compiègne (1350-1553)', in *École nationale des Chartes. Positions des thèses soutenues par les élèves de la promotion de 1924 . . .* , (Paris, 1924), 27-32. Also helpful is G. Dupont-Ferrier's 'Le rôle des commissaires royaux dans le governement de la France, spécialement du xivᵉ au xviᵉ siècle', in *Mélanges R. Fournier* (1929), 171-84. A list of the names of *maîtres des requêtes* to 1575 is given by F. Blanchard, *Les généalogies des Maîtres des Requestes ordinaires de l'Hostel du Roy* (Paris, 1670).

*Regent*,[114] and others styled simply *du Regent* or *du Dauphin*.[115] The former qualification appears to have been applied exclusively to those *maîtres des requêtes de l'Hôtel* nominally attached to the *Parlement*, while the latter was confined to individuals working under the direction of the Dauphin's *Conseil* in a variety of provincial locations, who receive no specific mention in the records of the *Parlement*.

## The *maîtres des requêtes de l'Hôtel* in the *Parlement*

The register of *plaidoiries civiles* of 1421 and 1422 carries the names of six *maîtres des requêtes de l'Hôtel* nominally attached to the *Parlement*.[116] In style this recalls the manner of the representation of the *requêtes du Palais* in the *Parlement* of Paris before 1418. In practice, however, the function of the *requêtes du Palais* had been earlier absorbed into that of the *requêtes de l'Hôtel*[117] and only a fraction of the six represented performed a judicial function in the *Parlement* – Guillaume Thoreau, early *Président* of the *maîtres des requêtes de l'Hôtel*, Bureau Boucher, Arnaud de Marle (all lay members) and Jean Tudert (cleric).[118] These individuals performed their judicial function by rotation and never as a result of their permanent corporate presence at Poitiers. The loss of the proceedings of the *requêtes* for this period makes it impossible to determine how many among them were needed to staff a working tribunal, or, within this, the proportion of lay and clerical members present at any given time. However the fact that the *requêtes* possessed a mixed competence suggests that they could be present in any proportion above a given minimum complement. From an early date both lay and clerical *maîtres des requêtes de l'Hôtel* sat upon both the civil and criminal *Conseils* of the *Parlement*, usually being a maximum of two or three in number. Guillaume II Le Tur, who is designated among the official complement of the *requêtes de l'Hôtel* in November 1421[119] does not, nevertheless, appear to have presided in any permanent judicial capacity, and his appointment seems to have been only a temporary

[114]See above, p. 31n. 194.

[115]See for instance, A.N. X1ª9197, f.144ʳ (5 Sept. 1422), referring to Nicole de la Barre.

[116]Ibid., fos. 1ʳ, 148ᵛ.

[117]Above, p. 16 n. 83.

[118]See *A.H.-G.* MS.59 (passim) for the presence of these individuals at Poitiers, on the *Conseil* of the *Parlement*.

[119]See A.N. X1ª9197, f.1ʳ. This may refer to Guillaume I Le Tur, as it is the office of lay *maître des requêtes* which is indicated. But see *Reg. consulaires,* i (Lyon, 1882), 350.

one. After 12 November 1422[120] the designation of the *maîtres des requêtes de l'Hôtel* in the *Parlement* after the earlier manner of the *requêtes du Palais* ceases altogether, this being merely a belated recognition of the loss of function of the latter competence to the former.[121] The *requêtes du Palais* were not formally re-established until 1454.

Despite the fluidity of function of the *maîtres des requêtes de l'Hôtel* between their judicial role in the *Parlement*, and their broader duties as royal administrators, the 'pool' of *maîtres des requêtes de l'Hôtel* at Poitiers seems to have been maintained at about six, or, in other words, at a figure close to the old complement of the *requêtes du Palais*.[122] The permanent exercise of function away from Poitiers by Robert de Rouvres and Denis du Moulin saw the appearance on the *Conseil* of the *Parlement* on 22 November 1422 of Guillaume Gouge de Charpaignes, *maîtres des requêtes de l'Hôtel* in succession to Nicole Fraillon;[123] of Jean de Montmorin in August 1423;[124] and Gérard Le Boursier in December of the same year.[125] The presence of these individuals brought the clerical 'pool' of *maîtres des requêtes de l'Hôtel* at Poitiers to a total of four. The number of lay members, diminished to two by the death of Guillaume Thoreau *c.* 1423, was maintained at three in March 1425 with the appearance of Girard Blanchet.[126] On 20 March 1425[127] a total of *six maîtres des requêtes* appear on the *Conseil* – Gérard Le Boursier, Guillaume Gouge de Charpaignes and Jean Tudert (clerics); Bureau Boucher, Arnaud de

---

[120]See A.N. X1ª9197, fos. 148ᵛff.

[121]Above, p. 16 n. 83.

[122]See, for example, *A.H.-G.* MS.59, f.229ʳ (20 March 1425), and ibid. (passim).

[123]'Rec. des docs', *Arch. hist. Poitou* 29 (1898), 116 n.1. Charpaignes appears among the ordinary *conseillers* in the *Parlement* in Nov. 1423 (A.N. X1ª9197, f.261ᵛ). The accumulation of the office of *conseiller* in the *Parlement* with that of *maître des requêtes* was not an uncommon occurrence (Bailhache, 29). Cf. D. Neuville, 'Le Parlement royal à Poitiers (1418-1436)', *R. hist.* 6 (1878), 287.

[124]*A.H.-G.* MS.59, f.182ʳ. Montmorin was received as a *maître des requêtes* in 1421 (Neuville, 286). Doctor *utroque* before 1431 (A.N. X1ª9196, f.37ʳ⁻ᵛ), Montmorin was later promoted bishop of Agde (Neuville, 286).

[125]*A.H.-G.* MS.59, f.188ᵛ (11 Dec. 1423). Gérard le Boursier became a *maître des requêtes* in 1422 (Neuville, 287), operating frequently in Saintonge and the Île de Ré. He was involved in litigation before the *Parlement* in 1426 for the living of the parish church of Saint-Martin, in the Ile de Ré (A.N. X1ª9195, f.246ʳ).

[126]*A.H.-G.* MS.59, f.229ʳ (20 March 1425). A native of Champagne, Blanchet became a *maître des requêtes* in 1422 (A. Thomas, *Les États provinciaux de la France centrale sous Charles VII,* i (Paris, 1879), 287. For remarks on Blanchet's career see ibid., 287-91.

[127]*A.H.-G.* MS.59, f.229ʳ.

Marle and Girard Blanchet (lay). None of these appearances was preceded by formal reception to the office of *maître des requêtes* at Poitiers.[128] The only recorded reception of this type occurred on 10 April 1434[129] when Jean Bernard, protégé of the House of Anjou,[130] was formally received *maîtres des requêtes de l'Hôtel* in the office of cleric, and gave the accustomed oath. There is, however, no indication that Bernard subsequently presided in a judicial capacity at Poitiers. A similar case is offered by Jean Baubignon, elected lay *conseiller* at Poitiers in March 1429[131] (though he had certainly functioned as a *maître des requêtes* prior to this date),[132] and later replaced following his election as a *maître des requêtes de l'Hôtel*.[133] Baubignon did not remain permanently at Poitiers after his reception as a *conseiller*.[134]

Certain of the ordinary *conseillers* in the *Parlement* carried the title of *maître des requêtes* to enable them to undertake quasi-judical missions of importance for Charles VII, notable examples being Guillaume de Quiefdeville and Guillaume Gouge de Charpaignes. Conversely, a number of individuals received as ordinary *conseillers* in the *Parlement*, had earlier functioned – in an 'extraordinary' fashion – as *maîtres des requêtes de l'Hôtel,* among them Guillaume II Le Tur, Jean Baubignon and Nicole Géhée.[135]

[128]Bailhache (28) advised that the taking up of functions by a *maître des requêtes* entailed, from the beginning of the fifteenth century, a double reception by the *Chancelier* and the *Parlement*. But he added (ibid., 29) that 'l'investiture du Chancelier est nécessaire et suffisante, sauf exception très rare, pour exercer comme extraordinaire. Mais la réception en Parlement donne seul son caractère complet au maître des Requêtes.'

[129]A.N. X1ª9194, f.65ᵛ. (On the significance of this reception see the preceding note).

[130]For an important note on Jean Bernard see B. Chevalier, *Tours: Ville royale (1356-1520)* (Paris/Louvair, 1975) 478-9.

[131]*A.H.-G.* MS.59, f.334ᵛ.

[132]See for instances, *Extraits des anciens registres aux dèliberations des consaux de la ville de Tournai (1422-1430),* ed. H. Vandenbröeck, *Mèm. Soc. Hist. Litt. de Tournai* 8 (1863), 224, 230-1.

[133]A.N. X1ª9194, f.57ᵛ.

[134]Baubignon's disappearance from the ranks of the *conseillers* at Poitiers may have followed his resignation of that office. Others, such as Guillaume de Quiefdeville, continued in their dual roles as *conseillers* in the *Parlement* and *maîtres des requêtes*. (See, especially, Neuville, 290 n.5.).

[135]As I have argued (above, p. 55 n. 123). The tendency to combine the office of *maître des requêtes* with that of *conseiller* in the *Parlement* was frequently practised at Poitiers, though in such cases the office of *maître des requêtes* would probably have been held in an extraordinary capacity. Of those *maîtres des requêtes* created after 1418, only the reception of Jean Bernard, mentioned earlier, possessed a complete character of the kind outlined by Bailhache (29).

Implicit here is the great benefit, in terms of flexibility of function, which could accrue to Charles VII in substituting the *requêtes du Palais* by the *requêtes de l'Hôtel*. In the disorganised *milieu* of the 'kingdom of Bourges' the *maîtres des requêtes de l'Hôtel* could provide a wide range of expertise of a judicial, fiscal and diplomatic kind, while at the same time fulfilling more specific functions within the various institutions of government. The constant interchange of functions of the *maîtres des requêtes* between the *Conseil* and the *Parlement* could also serve to maintain a constant rapport between these institutions – an important factor considering their geographical separateness.

## *Maîtres des requêtes* on the *Conseil du Roi*

The absence, during our period, of comprehensive lists of participants on the *Grand Conseil*, or any of the more amorphous *Conseils* of Charles VII, makes the question of the regular representation of the *maîtres des requêtes de l'Hôtel* on these bodies difficult to define in precise quantitative terms. From *c.* 1420 onwards, the only *maître des requêtes* whose name appears consistently among the members of the *Conseil* is Robert de Rouvres, early archdeacon of Blois, then in 1422 bishop of Sées.[136] Additionally *vice-Chancelier* of the Dauphin, and, probably from an early date, *garde du sceau ordonné en l'absence du Grand*, Rouvres was a signatory to every edict of importance issued by Charles VII after 1422. The presence of other *maîtres des requêtes* on the *Conseil*, and, in addition to this, the frequency of their apeparance, is more difficult to ascertain. Rouvres's most frequent companion, judging by the documents we possess, was Denis du Moulin, archbishop of Toulouse.[137]

Where any proportion of those individuals who participated at sessions of the *Conseil* is indicated by name it is rare to find among them more than two or three *maîtres des requêtes de l'Hôtel*.[138]

---

[136]The elections of Rouvres as bishop of Sées, and Denis du Moulin as archbishop of Toulouse, in 1422, were unusual in that both were allowed to retain their offices as *maîtres des requêtes*. During the fourteenth century, promotion to an episcopal dignity entailed the resignation of the office of *maître des requêtes* (Guillois, 73). It was not until the sixteenth century that the practice of combining both offices became widespread (Bailhache, 29).

[137]On the early career of Du Moulin, see above, pp. 20-1. One of the most influential and rapacious members of Charles VII's *Conseil*, Du Moulin became bishop of Paris in 1439.

[138]Some indication of the representation of the *maîtres des requêtes* on sessions of the *Conseil* and *Grand Conseil* of Charles VII can be found in A.N. X1ᵃ8604 (passim). A comprehensive list of members of the royal *Conseil* for Charles VII's reign is only

However it is clear that the number of different *maîtres des requêtes* who sat on the *Conseil*, or took their directives from that body, was considerable.

## Representation of the *maîtres des requêtes de l'Hôtel* in the *Conseil du Roi* on the *Conseil* of the *Parlement*

On occasion, and this is apparent particularly during the 1430s, those *maîtres des requêtes de l'Hôtel* normally located with the *Conseil* or *Grand Conseil* sat, together with other important members of those bodies, on the civil and criminal *Conseils* of the *Parlement* at Poitiers. Conversely those *maîtres des requêtes de l'Hôtel* who performed a judicial function at Poitiers were frequently numbered among the members of the *Conseil* or *Grand Conseil*.[139] The representation of the *Conseil* of the *Parlement* of *maîtres des requêtes de l'Hôtel* normally serving within the *Conseil* or *Grand Conseil*, and other members of these institutions, normally carried a double significance; first, that Charles VII was actually present at Poitiers; second, and by way of qualification of the first signification, the presence of the king, together with members of the *Conseil* or *Grand Conseil* at Poitiers usually coincided with meetings of the general Estates of the Languedoil held in the town, or at locations not far distant.[140]

Robert de Rouvres, *vice-Chancelier* and *garde du sceau ordonné en l'absence du Grand*, was, among those *maîtres des requêtes* in the *Conseil*, the most frequent visitor to Poitiers. We find his name on the list of *conseillers* in the *Parlement* in July 1425,[141] May 1426[142] and on 7 March 1429[143] (additionally a fact of importance with regard to

---

available for the period post-1455 (N. Valois, *Le Conseil du roi au xiv<sup>e</sup>, xv<sup>e</sup> et xvi<sup>e</sup> siècles* (Paris, 1888), 231-323), a fact which inhibits any reliable assessment of the *Conseil*'s composition prior to this period.

[139]For remarks on the interchange of personnel between the royal *Conseil* and the *Parlement*, see N. Valois, *Étude historique sur le Conseil du roi* (Paris, 1886), ixff.

[140]French historians of the nineteenth century were concerned to stress the 'apathetic' nature of Charles VII's kingship during the early years — a view designed less to give an accurate picture of events than to stress the 'miraculous' recovery of French fortunes following the appearance of Joan of Arc. In fact the period 1418-36 marked a dynamic phase of Charles's reign, characterised by ceaseless journeying. Neither was this constant perambulation without a practical motive, for a study of Charles VII's movements after 1422 suggests that his itineraries were prepared chiefly to coincide with his personal attendance at assemblies of the general Estates of the Languedoil or the Languedoc.

[141]*A.H.-G.* MS.59, f.238<sup>r</sup> (meeting of the general Estates of the Languedoil at Poitiers, Oct. 1425).

[142]Ibid., f.256<sup>v</sup>

[143]Ibid., f.334<sup>v</sup>.

Joan of Arc's stay at Poitiers preparatory to the siege of Orléans).[144] Following the coronation at Reims in July 1429, we can attest the presence of Rouvres, together with other members of the *Conseil,* at Poitiers in March 1431,[145] November 1434, February 1435[146] and March 1436. In addition to Robert de Rouvres, Denis du Moulin, another of those *maîtres des requêtes de l'Hôtel* who sat regularly upon sessions of Charles VII's *Conseil,* was numbered among members of the *Conseil* at Poitiers in March 1436.[147]

The frequency of representation of the *maîtres des requêtes de l'Hôtel* who performed a judicial function at Poitiers, upon the *Conseil* or *Grand Conseil* of Charles VII, is difficult to assess with any accuracy due to lack of documentation.[148] However it is clear that, so far as these individuals are concerned, their judicial role at Poitiers constituted only a small proportion of their duties as royal administrative agents. The disproportionate nature of these functions is indicated both by the very long periods of absence of the *maîtres des requêtes* from Poitiers in the fulfilment of various royal commissions, and by the often great contrast between their wages as *parlementaires* and the gratifications accorded by Charles VII as a result of the commissions undertaken by them.[149]

**Members of the *requêtes de l'Hôtel* performing functions of a quasi-judicial kind**[150]

The numbers of *maîtres des requêtes* who performed functions of a judicial nature was supplemented by others whose duties appear to have been of a predominantly quasi-judicial kind.[151] Among these we may attest the presence of, from *c.*1420, Nicole de La Barre and Jean

[144]See below, pp. 94ff.

[145]*A.H.-G.* MS.59, f.420$^r$ (meeting of the general Estates of the Languedoil at Poitiers, March-April 1431).

[146]A.N. X1$^a$9194, fos.83$^v$, 90$^r$ (meeting of the general Estates of the Languedoil at Poitiers, Jan. 1435).

[147]Ibid.

[148]For remarks on the representation of the *maîtres des requêtes de l'Hôtel* in the *Conseil* at a later date, see Valois, *Étude historique,* cxvi-cxix.

[149]See below, pp. 72-3.

[150]For a brief description of the range of functions see Bailhache, 31.

[151]These were the *maîtres des requêtes 'extraordinaires'.* Those who performed functions of a predominantly judicial nature in the *Parlement* or *Conseil* were called *maîtres des requêtes 'ordinaires'.*

Baubignon;[152] from c.1421 Simon Charles[153] and Jean Girard;[154] in 1422 Guillaume II Le Tur;[155] and after 1434, Jean Bernard.[156] Hence while the 'visible' numbers of maîtres des requêtes in the royal Conseil or the Parlement may appear modest, their combination with the 'invisibles', who functioned as maîtres des requêtes, but are not formally designated as such within the registers of the Parlement, and others who though permanently exercising this office only rarely receive mention in the records of the Conseil or the Parlement, could nevertheless constitute a large and flexible 'pool' of expertise to which the king could delegate a variety of important matters. Certain features of the quasi-judicial activity of the maîtres des requêtes are worthy of note. In the first place it seems important to emphasise the very great degree of authority invested in these individuals to enable them to negotiate various matters on the king's behalf. The quasi-independent function of the maîtres des requêtes was in part owing to the often great distances separating their sphere of operations from the royal Conseil or Grand Conseil. A second feature of importance may be seen in the fact that, in the execution of their quasi-judicial duties, the maîtres des requêtes appear to have had designated to them particular areas of geographical expertise[157] (Jean Tudert having particularly close relations with Burgundy,[158] Jean Girard with the Dauphiné,[159] Guillaume de Quiefdeville with Castile,[160] Gérard le Boursier with Saintonge[161]) to which they were frequently sent to conduct negotiations, fiscal or diplomatic, on the king's behalf. As in the case of the judicial functions, the maîtres des requêtes

[152]See for instance, A.N. X1ª9197, fos. 144ʳff. For additional notes on Baubignon, Jean Bernard and Simon Charles, mentioned below, see H. Gilles, 'Autorité royale et résistances urbaines, un exemple Languedocien: l'échec de la réformation générale de 1434-1435', in B. philol. 1961, 120-1.

[153]See Reg. consulaires, i (Lyon, 1882), 322ff (passim). Charles was styled 'clerc des comptes de monseigneur et nostres' on 9 June 1421 (L. Caillet, Étude sur les relations de la commune de Lyon avec Charles VII et Louis XI (1417-1483), (Lyon, 1909).

[154]See Neuville, 281ff. Doctor utroque, Girard was promoted bishop of Embrun in 1433, then in 1444, archbishop of Vienne, in succession to Geoffroy Vassal.

[155]Reg. consulaires, i (Lyon, 1882), 350ff. Le Tur was promoted bishop of Chalon-sur-Saône in 1440, in succession to Jean Tudert, maître des requêtes.

[156]See above, p. 56. Bernard was promoted archbishop of Tours in 1442 (Chevalier, 479).

[157]See Favreau, Poitiers, 186.

[158]Ibid., 286 n.961.

[159]Neuville, 282.

[160]Favreau, Poitiers, 286 n. 960.

[161]Neuville, 287. See also, A.N. X1ª9200, fos. 88ᵛff., 192ᵛ. A.N. X1ª9195, f.246ʳ.

appear to have undertaken quasi-judicial duties by rotation among their number, though some, by virtue of the fact that they appear to have had relatively little contact either with the royal *Conseil,* or the *Parlement* at Poitiers, were more or less permanently located within their particular sphere of operations.

The assiduousness of the *maîtres des requêtes*, recognised by the often considerable sums given to them by the king, supported an administrative network which underpinned the structure – fiscal, judicial and diplomatic – of that part of France loyal to Charles VII.

### General fiscal duties of the *maîtres des requêtes*

One of the most important quasi-judicial functions of the *maîtres des requêtes* who exercised a judicial charge at Poitiers was, by virtue of their additional roles as *commissaires généraux* of royal finances, their frequent appearance as the king's representatives at meetings of the Estates, and in particular their supervision of the imposition and levy of *aides* imposed upon these gatherings, or, in a secondary sense, upon towns contributing specific portions of the *aides.* In addition they could provide an important link between the *Conseil* and the Estates, or individual corporations, in negotiations resulting from the imposition of a particular *aide.*

In 1419 Jean Tudert, *maître des requêtes de l'Hôtel,* was sent with Jean I Jouvenel, *Président* in the *Parlement,* as the Dauphin's representative to an assembly of prelates at Clermont.[162] In June 1421 we find Guillaume Thoreau, *premier maître des requêtes* at Poitiers, at Lyon,[163] sent by the Dauphin to review the fortifications of the town. Here it is already possible to discern the measures taken by the consuls to employ the important strategic position of Lyon as a means of ameliorating fiscal obligations. Thoreau was gilded with six boxes of 'confitures' in order that he should 'plus recommander icelle envers monseigneur le Regent . . . afin d'avoir de lui plus legierement aucun aide pour la fortiffier'.[164] In January 1422 another of the *maîtres des requêtes,* Guillaume II Le Tur, was at Lyon[165] to ask for the provision of 150 men-at-arms for the Dauphin, together with sufficient finance to sustain them in combat for six months – a measure

---

[162]*A.H.-G.* MS.59, f.74ʳ⁻ᵛ (3 July 1419).

[163]*Reg. consulaires,* i (Lyon, 1882), 306-7.

[164]Ibid., 307.

[165]Ibid., 349ff.

taken in anticipation of a renewed military offensive by the English early in 1422. The consuls initially agreed to provide 150 men, without the desired financial provision, 'pour ce que aucuns le despendent autrement que au prouffit dudit seigneur'.[166] It is difficult to gauge to what extent this initial refusal represented a genuine complaint on the part of the consuls, as opposed to a deliberate attempt to avoid the obligations placed upon them. In the event, the full provision appears nevertheless to have been made.[167]

The element of 'backstairs negotiation' met earlier by Guillaume Thoreau was encountered again in August 1425[168] by Girard Blanchet, *maître des requêtes*, charged by Charles VII with the levy of Lyon's portion of an aide of 120,00*l.t.* accorded by the Estates at Poitiers in July 1425. Blanchet, *commissaire du roi,* was presented by the consuls with 'un gobellet d'argent... pesant ix onces et dyme... lequel gobellet l'on a donne a maistre Girard... pour ce qu'il amondre la somme de ladicte ville'.[169] Blanchet was once again at Lyon in November 1426[170] for the levy of an 'eleventh' accorded to Charles VII by the general Estates of Languedoil at Poitiers in October 1425. Blanchet was, on this occasion, offered 100*l.t.* by the consuls in the event of his being prepared to forestall the levy until a delegation from the town had had the opportunity to plead amelioration of Lyon's portion of the *aide* with the king.[171]

On 2 November 1428 we encounter Arnaud de Marle in the capacity of *commissaire* 'sur le fait de la visitacion et reparacion generalle des chiefs d'ostel et bellegues du pais de Languedoc'. Marle was involved in the execution of this commission from 1 to 15 June 1427, from 3 November 1427 to 19 May 1428, and from 5 August to 31 October 1428. Payment at the rate of 100*s.t.* per day gave him the considerable return of 1,500*l.t.*[172] In 1431 Girard Blanchet[173] was delegated together with Guillaume I Le Tur, *Président* in the

---

[166]Ibid., 351

[167]Ibid., 352.

[168]*Reg. consulaires,* ii (Lyon, 1926) 145ff.

[169]Ibid., 146.

[170]Ibid., 200ff.

[171]Ibid., 201.

[172]B.N. MS. fr.28342, (Marle), nos. 44-5. For earlier commissions of a fiscal kind undertaken by Marle see Neuville, 179-80. A *maître des requêtes* since 1414 Marle was later a *Président* in the Paris *Parlement* (ibid., 179).

[173]For what follows on Blanchet see Thomas, *Les États provinciaux de la France centrale sous Charles VII,* i (Paris, 1879), 289.

*Parlement,* to act as the king's representative at a meeting of the regional Estates of Auvergne. Fulfilment of a similar mission in January 1432, this time with Jacques de Canlers, saw Blanchet receive gifts of 200*l.t.* from the Estates and a further 100*l.t.* from the prelates and barons of Basse-Auvergne, for his part in the negotiation of the aide. In late January of the same year Blanchet was sent to Lyon by Charles VII to obtain a contribution of 1,500 *réaux d'or* towards La Hire's ransom. Later in 1432 another commission took Blanchet yet further afield, this time to the Dauphiné, for the supervision of the levy of a one-*florin* hearth-tax. This resulted in the payment of a further 300 *florins* to Blanchet. Finally, in September 1432, Blanchet's attendance at a meeting of the general Estates of Auvergne brought him a further 'gift' of 400*l.t.* from the representatives of Basse-Auvergne. The considerable wealth resulting from this assiduousness enabled Blanchet to lend Charles VII's treasury 1,000 *réaux d'or* in 1433 to finance a military expedition by Dunois into Champagne.[174] In December 1433 Arnaud de Marle, mentioned earlier, was at Lyon in the company of Guillaume Jouvenel, lay *conseiller* at Poitiers,[175] for the levy of a particular *aide* imposed by the general Estates of Longuedoil meeting at Tours in September-October 1433. Not long after this in 1434-5 Marle figured among the members of a commission including other *maîtres des requêtes*, Jean Bernard, Jean Baubignon and Simon Charles, sent into the Languedoc to inquire into the abuse of royal fiscal prerogatives.[176]

Fiscal charges of an elevated order were delegated to another of the *maîtres des requêtes* at Poitiers, Jean Tudert. As early as 1423 Tudert received a large gratification from Charles VII for the levy of certain *aides* at Blois and Orléans.[177] In 1429 he was given the administration of royal finances 'par deca la riviere de Seine'.[178] In addition to his frequent employment by the royal *Conseil* and the *Parlement* in matters of a fiscal kind, Tudert also presided, together with other members of the *requêtes de l'Hôtel*, at sessions of the *Chambre des comptes* at Bourges.[179]

---

[174]See B.N. MS. fr.25968, no. 689 (18 Apr. 1437).

[175]*Reg. consulaires,* ii (Lyon, 1926), 356ff.

[176]See Gilles, 115-146. Marle had undertaken another important fiscal commission in the Auvergne in 1432 (D. Neuville, 'Le Parlement royal à Poitiers (1418-1436)', *R. hist.,* 6 (1878), 279-80).

[177]Ibid., 281.

[178]Ibid.

[179]See B.N. Nouv. acq. fr. 7626, fos. 414ʳff.

## Diplomatic activity of the maîtres des requêtes

On occasion those maîtres des requêtes who performed a judicial function at Poitiers were employed by Charles VII in diplomatic negotiations of the highest order, with members of the nobility, with princes and with foreign powers. Prominent in this ambassadorial capacity was, again, Jean Tudert, dean of Paris. A participant in the negotiations which led to the publication of the treaty of Saint-Maur-les-Fossés in September 1419, Tudert was again employed as the Dauphin's political agent between December 1418 and January 1419 in negotiations with Henry V of England.[180] Tudert's main sphere of diplomatic expertise was, in the ensuing years, concerned with Burgundian affairs, and he was closely involved in negotiations with Philippe le Bon at Arras in 1429, at Auxerre in 1432 and finally at Arras once more in 1435.[181] Only four years after the formulation of a Franco-Burgundian settlement at Arras Tudert received promotion to the bishopric of Chalon-sur-Saône, situated in Burgundian territory.[182] Tudert's importance was paralleled by that of Girard Blanchet.[183] Blanchet was early employed on diplomatic missions of great importance, being in 1422 among the members of a deputation including Tudert sent by the Dauphin to treat with Amadeus VIII, duke of Savoy on the matter of peace with Burgundy. In the following year, Blanchet accompanied the prévôt of Paris, Tanguy du Chastel, to treat with the representatives of Jean V, duke of Brittany. In March 1424 Blanchet once again journeyed to meet Jean V at Nantes, this time accompanied by Arnaud de Marle, and the Chancelier of France. In recompense for a voyage which saw Marle journey from Poitiers to Angers, then on to Nantes and finally, via Bourges, to rejoin Charles VII at Espaly near Le Puy, he received 400l.t.[184]

Negotiations conducted by the maîtres des requêtes frequently obliged them to travel outside France. In March 1428 Girard Blanchet left Amboise for a meeting with Jean I, count of Foix, later travelling on to conduct negotiations with the Aragonese court. Blanchet did not finally return to France until September 1428 and he received a gift of 500l.t. from Charles VII for his services, paid from a sum granted by the Estates of Languedoil at Chinon on 1 October 1428. Blanchet undertook further embassies to the count of Foix late

[180]Beaucourt, i (Paris, 1881), 287ff.

[181]Favreau, Poitiers, 286 n.961.

[182]Neuville, 281. Tudert was earlier a canon of Sainte-Radegone of Poitiers (ibid., 334), source, after 1418, of strong pro-Burgundian sympathies.

[183]For what follows on Blanchet see Thomas, Les États, i (Paris, 1879), 287ff.

[184]B.N. MS. fr.28342 (Marle), nos. 37ff. (passim),

in 1428, and again in 1429. Yet perhaps the best example of sustained diplomatic activity was displayed by Guillaume de Quiefdeville,[185] who combined the office of *maître des requêtes* with that of clerical *conseiller* in the *Parlement*. Between periods of service in the *Parlement* Quiefdeville undertook no fewer than eight different missions for Charles VII to Castile and Scotland. The frequency and duration of his visits to Castile were so great that Quiefdeville, a native of Normandy, was eventually made a naturalised subject of that country.[186] The first of Quiefdeville's visits to Castile, early in 1419, was responsible for securing an assurance of Castilian naval support for the Scots army raised by the Dauphin.[187] In January 1420 the Castilian fleet, under the command of the admiral Braquemont, inflicted a heavy defeat on English forces off La Rochelle. The last of Quiefdeville's embassies to Castile, in late 1428, was financed by a loan of 300 *écus d'or* from Georges de La Trémoille.[188] Quiefdeville died in Spain in the course of this mission and the execution of his will was supervised by the *Parlement* in 1430.[189]

## Judicial function of the *maîtres des requêtes* in the *Conseil* and *Grand Conseil*

In the absence of any comprehensive record, one of the most problematic areas of the judicial function of the *maîtres des requêtes* during our period is their participation, and numerical representation, on the *Conseil* and *Grand Conseil* of Charles VII, and beyond this their role in the evolution of a judicial *Grand Conseil*, which had appeared by the 1450s.[190]

---

[185]On the diplomatic career of Quiefdeville (or Quiesdeville) see above, p. 17 n. 95.

[186]Favreau, *Poitiers*, 286 n.960.

[187]Beaucourt, i (Paris, 1881), 308ff.

[188]See A.N. IAP 171, no. 47 (29 Oct. 1428), where from a sum of 11,107 *écus d'or* lent to Charles VII's treasury Quiefdeville, 'qui va en embaxade en Espaigne', was allocated 300 *écus d'or* expenses.

[189]Following the death of Quiefdeville in Spain (A.N. X2ª21, f.134ʳ), Jean de Quiefdeville, claiming to be Guillaume's heir, appeared before the *Parlement* to obtain possession of the latter's possessions, left in the safekeeping of Jean de Blois. The *Parlement* subsequently relinquished Guillaume's possessions, with the exception of a 'petit coffret de noyer, fermant a clef, et ce qui est dedans, que on dit appartenir a maistres Jehan du Pont, chanoine de Nerbonne' (ibid., f.134ᵛ, 1 June 1430). (Cf. Favreau, *Poitiers*, 286 n.960.).

[190]For remarks on the evolution of the judicial *Grand Conseil* see Valois, *Etude historique*, xxvff.

That the *maîtres des requêtes* did play an important judicial role in the royal *Conseil* is evident as early as 16 June 1424 when the consuls of Lyon rewarded Jean Girard, *maître des requêtes de l'Hôtel,* with 20 *moutons d'or,* representing 'les especes du proces qui estoit devant lui', concerning the attempt by the consuls to avoid the imposition of a tax of 3*d.t. per livre* on salt, recently decreed by the *Conseil.*[191] Refusal by the consuls to consent to the imposition of the tax had presumably resulted in their adjournment before the *Conseil.* In April 1426 certain of the consuls were adjourned before the king by Jean Rascart, *huissier d'armes*, this time for reason of the non-payment of part of an *aide* accorded by the general Estates of Languedoil in October 1425.[192] On 17 May 1426 the consuls paid Rascart 10 *francs* 'pour avoir revoque l'adjornement personnel . . . par devant le Roy contre lesdits conseillers'.[193] While there is no evidence during our period to support the existence of a judicial *Grand Conseil* of the type which appeared later in Charles VII's reign, it is clear that the *Grand Conseil* had in part a judicial function.[194] Certain of the *maîtres des requêtes de l'Hôtel* would have been present at judicial sessions of the *Grand Conseil*, though the extent of their representation and precise function is unknown.[195]

The jurisdictions of the *Parlement* and the *Grand Conseil* were occasionally in confrontation over the matter of precedence in the right to entertain particular cases.[196] Confrontation usually followed the request, ostensibly by Charles VII, that the exercise of justice in respect of certain individuals should be referred to the *Grand Conseil*; examples of this initiative by the king may be seen in 1426,[197] 1427,[198]

[191]*Reg. consulaires,* ii (Lyon, 1926), 101.

[192]Ibid., 180ff.

[193]Ibid., 185.

[194]The amount of litigation before the *Grand Conseil* appears to have steadily increased during Charles VII's reign (Valois, *Etude historique,* xxvii-xxviii). One of the major reasons for the emergence of a judicial *Grand Conseil* in the 1450s seems to have been the inability of the *Grand Conseil,* essentially a political body, to deal with this litigation in view of its primary preoccupation with political matters (see, ibid., xxvii n.6).

[195]See ibid., cxvi ff., on the problem of the relationship of the *maîtres des requêtes* to the *Grand Conseil.*

[196]For the putative attempts by Charles VII to restrict the judicial authority of the *Grand Conseil* vis-à-vis the *Parlement* see ibid., xxviii.

[197]A.N. X2ª21, f.46ʳ.

[198]Ibid., f.86ʳ.

1432[199] and 1436.[200] On 28 July 1432[201] in the course of litigation before the *Parlement* between Jean Aimeric and Jean Le Fèvre, called *Mareschal*, the plaintiff requested the *Procureur général du roi* 'que certaine cause d'appel pendant ceans entre eulx (*i.e.* between him and Le Fèvre) soit renvoiee pardevant les gens du Grant Conseil du roy, ainsi que le Roy l'a mande par ses lettres patentes a la court'. On this occasion the *Parlement* agreed to Charles VII's directive and the case was duly referred to the *Grand Conseil*. On other occasions, however, the *Parlement* was less readily disposed to comply with the king's demand. On 20 May 1433[202] the *Parlement* received letters from Charles VII evoking 'a soy et a son Grant Conseil les causes pendans ceans entre son Procureur, demandeur, et Leonart et Jehan de Janoillac', together with Jean Pradeau, tutor and guardian of the children of the late Marcial Vidal. However on this occasion litigation had already commenced in the *Parlement* between the *Procureur général du roi* and the aforesaid, defendants, together with certain other bourgeois of Poitiers, accused, together with Leonard Janoilhac, earlier *maître particulier de la monnaie* at Poitiers, of serious embezzlement of the revenues of the royal mint located in the town. Despite Charles VII's insistence, the *Parlement* appears successfully to have prevented the case being sent back before the *Grand Conseil*.

## Quasi-judicial functions of the *maîtres des requêes* in the royal *Conseil*

Among those *maîtres des requêtes* who operated predominantly within the orbit of the *Conseil* or *Grand Conseil* the exercise of a permanent judicial function within these bodies appears to have been undertaken only by Robert de Rouvres, bishop of Sées. As *vice-Chancelier* of Charles VII and *garde du sceau ordonné en l'absence du Grand*,[203] Rouvres's position was of great importance and

---

[199] Ibid., f.186[v] (cf. A.N. X2[a]18, f.330[v]); also A.N. X2[a]21, f.177[r].

[200] Ibid., f.312[r]. For evidence of another case before the *Grand Conseil*, in 1433, see A.N. X2[a]21, f.204[r-v].

[201] Ibid., f.330[v], for what follows.

[202] A.N. X1[a]9194, fos. 44[v]ff.

[203] On the attributions of this seal, see O. Morel, *La Grande Chancellerie royale* (Paris, 1900), 219-20. Tessier (*Diplomatique royale française* (Paris, 1962), 202), has remarked that during the reign of Charles VII, 'vont se differencier deux sceaux ordonnés. Le premier en dignité, si l'on peut dire, parce qu'appelé à valider des actes de Grande Chancellerie, est utilisé par le roi soit à Paris soit en province, en l'absence de son chancelier, et confié à un personnage "commis à la garde du scel ordonné en l'absence du grand" .' The creation of this seal almost certainly dates from 1422, and

commensurate influence, as evidenced by his considerable income. The office of *maître des requêtes* during our period was evidently not a stipendiary one; however in November 1422[204] Rouvres's wage, after the manner of the *requêtes du Palais,* was paid together with the wages of the other *conseillers.* Certain of the *maîtres des requêtes* who performed a judicial function at Poitiers also appear to have been provided with a fixed wage together with other *parlementaires,*[205] this being paid in addition to ad hoc sums received from the king for undertaking quasi-judicial missions. After 1422 Rouvres was in receipt of an annual pension of considerable proportions: in 1426-7, 1,000*l.t.* paid on the revenue of the *quart de sel* at Taillebourg (near Saintes).[206] Further payments towards Rouvres's pension (now as bishop of Montpellier), may be found in 1433-4, 250*l.t.*; in 1434-5, 400*l.t.*; in 1435-6, 300*l.t.*; finally, in 1437-8, 300*l.t.*[207] In addition to his pension, Rouvres was, together with other members of the royal *Conseil,* frequently the recipient of liberalities from Charles VII in return for his services.[208]

Like the members of the *requêtes de l'Hôtel* at Poitiers, Rouvres was not confined to judicial functions. In January 1422 he formed part of a commission sent by the Dauphin to Tours to supervise the levy of a certain *aide.*[209] In June 1423 he accompanied Girard Blanchet, also a *maître des requêtes*, and Tanguy du Chastel, on an embassy to Jean V, duke of Brittany, at Nantes.[210] In June 1426 he was a signatory, together with Denis du Moulin, to letters of Charles VII revoking all donations made by the treasury under the direction of the *Président de Provence*, Jean Louvet.[211] In February or March 1429 Robert de Rouvres was among those 'theologians' delegated by Charles VII to interrogate Joan of Arc following his conversation with the Maid after her arrival.[212] On 30 March 1430 he was a signatory to letters given at

Robert de Rouvres appears as keeper of the seal 'ordonné', in the 1430s (cf. Morel, 235).

[204]A.N. X1ᵃ8604, f.59ʳ (24 Nov. 1422).

[205]See *A.H.-G.* MS.59 (passim) for payment of the wages of the *maîtres des requêtes.*

[206]B.N. MS. fr.25970, no. 1139.

[207]B.N. MS. fr. 25968, nos. 683, 684, 687, 689 (cf. nos. 688, 690, 691) Rouvres's quittances are styled 'Robert, par la parmission Divine, evesque de Maguelonne'.

[208]See B.N. MS. fr.25968, no. 686. B.N. MS. fr.27177 (Chartres) no. 71.

[209]Beaucourt, i (Paris, 1881), 363 n.3.

[210]Ibid., ii (Paris, 1882), 72 n.1.

[211]See A.N. X1ᵃ8604, f.83ʳ⁻ᵛ. Denis du Moulin was also a signatory.

[212]Below, pp. 94ff.

Sully, introducing Charles of Anjou to the *Grand Conseil*.[213] On 5
December of that year he was again signatory to a new treaty with the
duke of Brittany.[214] In 1433 he was among the petitioners for the
release of Charles of Orléans from captivity. In short Robert de
Rouvres was probably the most important civil-servant bishop among
the members of Charles VII's *Conseil*.[215]

Like Robert de Rouvres, Denis du Moulin, archbishop of Toulouse
and a *maître des requêtes de l'Hôtel du Roi*, was a long-standing
member of the *Conseil*.[216] While no record exists, as in the case of
Rouvres, of his receipt of a regular pension, he was perpetually the
recipient of large sums distributed by Charles VII to regular members
of his *Conseil*.[217] Like Rouvres he was also a signatory to many of the
most important edicts of Charles VII, and, in addition, carried out
numerous other functions for the *Conseil*. As early as 20 January
1420 Du Moulin was at Lyon, charged by the king to negotiate the
matter of annual fairs held by the town.[218] On 31 December 1422[219]
he was once again at Lyon where the consuls offered him, in company
of the *Chancelier,* the sum of 50 *écus d'or* conditional on passing: 'la
remission de la transgression des monnoyes; item la confirmation des
privileges de la sauvegarde non-violee; item et donner licence
d'amener du sel de l'Empire jusques a iiiᶜ sommes.'[220] Similar
liberalities accompanied Du Moulin's visit to Lyon in August 1423,
this time in the company of Jean Girard, *maître des requêtes de
l'Hôtel,* for the imposition of a new salt tax of 3 *deniers per livre*.[221]
Du Moulin was once again at Lyon in December 1423 to supervise
the imposition of a particular contribution in place of the *aides*. Early
in February 1424 he was at Lyon again, for negotiations concerning
the aforementioned tax on salt.[222]

The *maîtres des requêtes de l'Hôtel* could, on occasion, occupy
important offices of a fiscal kind within the royal court. Jean Bernard,

[213]Beaucourt, ii (Paris, 1882), 267 n.1.

[214]Ibid., 272 n.3.

[215]On the origins and career of Rouvres see H.J. du Motey, *Jeanne d'Arc à Chinon et
Robert de Rouvres* (Paris, 1927).

[216]On Du Moulin's early career see above, pp. 16-21.

[217]See for instance, B.N. MS. fr. 25970, nos. 1354, 1355 and 1356.

[218]*Reg. consulaires,* i (Lyon, 1882), 220ff.

[219]Ibid., ii (Lyon, 1926), 31.

[220]Ibid.

[221]Ibid., 60ff.

[222]Ibid., 85.

received as a maître des requêtes in the *Parlement* on 10 April 1434,[223] never exercised a judicial function there. In a quittance dated 15 July 1434, he is styled: '*conseiller et maistre des requetes de l'Ostel du Roy, et tresorier general de toutes . . . finances de la Royne et de monseigneur le Dauphin de Viennoiz*'.[224] Fulfilment of this function provided him with an annual income of 150*l.t.* Another of the *maîtres des requêtes de l'Hôtel*, Girard Blanchet, may be seen in August 1432 providing something in the manner of a private banking service for the then current 'favourite' of Charles VII, Georges de La Trémoïlle.[225]

### Quasi-judicial functions of the *maîtres des requêtes* in the general orbit of the royal *Conseil*

The complicated pattern of diplomatic, fiscal and administrative expertise woven by the *maîtres des requêtes* who performed judicial functions at Poitiers, or within the *Conseil*, was extended still further by others having no judicial attachment to these bodies, operating rather within the general supervision and direction of the royal *Conseil* on a variety of quasi-judicial matters. Hence, in addition to the diplomatic relations established by the *maîtres des requêtes* at Poitiers, or in the royal *Conseil*, with Aragon, Castile, Savoy, Burgundy, Brittany and Scotland, we may affirm the presence of another of the *maîtres des requêtes*, Simon Charles, at Tournai in 1423, 1424, 1425 and 1426.[226] In late 1428 and early 1429 Charles was sent on embassy to Venice in an attempt to procure finance for Charles VII's military campaigns.[227] Some years later on 30 April 1436 Charles, termed 'chevallier de l'Ostel du Roi', was at Lyon,[228] having visited the town on earlier occasions.[229] The consuls presented him with:

> 22 ducats d'or employes en quatre asnes d'esquarlete fine,

[223]For a note on Bernard's reception see above, p. 56.

[224]B.N. Nouv. acq. fr.21291, no. 69. (Cf. A.N. K63, no. 28, for Bernard's election to this office).

[225]A.N. 1AP 172B, no. 22, where the sum of 7,100 *réaux d'or* is given to Blanchet by La Trémoïlle for safekeeping.

[226]See *Extraits des anciens registres aux délibérations des consaux de la ville Tournai (1422-1430),* ed. H. Vandenbröeck, *Mém. Soc. Hist. Litt. de Tournai* 8 (1863) (passim).

[227]See A. Morosini, *Chronique,* ed. G. Lefèvre-Pontalis, ii (*SHF,* Paris, 1899), 339 n.1.

[228]For what follows see *Reg. consulaires,* ii (Lyon, 1926), 458.

[229]Ibid., i (Lyon, 1882), 322ff.

donnee oudit maistre Symon Charles afin que plus diligemment
et de meilleur cuer il procure que la Saint Concile qui est a Bale...
s'en viegne lougier en ceste ville de Lion,[230] comme le roy ... a
chargie expressement ... l'arcevesque de Vienne et Symon
Charles.

In addition to Simon Charles's diplomatic excursions another of the
*maîtres des requêtes*, Jean Girard, formed a permanent liaison
between the independent government of the Dauphiné and the
*Conseil* of Charles VII.[231]

The activities of Charles, Girard and others were frequently
diverted to negotiations with the Estates. Yet in addition to these more
grandiose tasks certain of the *maîtres des requêtes* were confined to a
permanent provincial location or area, in which they seem to have
operated more or less permanently, fulfilling a range of predominantly
fiscal duties. The pursuit of these duties might on occasion bring about
confrontation with the *Parlement.* An instance of this sort of conflict
appeared before the *Parlement* in September 1422[232] involving
Nicole de La Barre,[233] here styled '*maistre des requestes de l'Ostel de
monsieur le Regent*', and later, in November 1424, *bailli* of Meaux.[234]
La Barre explained that the Regent was aware that for a long time and
from day to day, there had been a considerable accumulation of
unclaimed objects both along the coastline of Saintonge and Poitou,
and elsewhere inland, none of which had accrued to his personal
profit. Hence, in consultation with the *Grand Conseil,* he had
delegated La Barre and Jean Baubignon 'de telz espaves et confiscations
prendre, reveu et faire venir ens au proufit de monseigneur le Regent'.
In his diligent execution of this brief, La Barre seized the property of
Jean Turel, a recently deceased royal sergeant. Turel, Barre claimed,
was formerly a native of Valois, and had no legitimate heirs in that
part of France loyal to the Regent; under the general rubric of his
commission, therefore, his possessions automatically escheated to
the Regent. This action was contested by the executors of Turel's will
together with the *Procureur général du roi* in the *Parlement.*

---

[230]On the attempt to transfer the Council of Basle to Lyon see M.J. Vaesen, 'Un
project de translation du Concile de Bale à Lyon en 1436', in *R. Quest. Hist.* 30 (1881),
561-8.

[231]See Neuville, 282. Also A. Thomas, *Les États provinciaux de la France centrale
sous Charles VII,* i (Paris, 1879), 329-30.

[232]For what follows see A.N. X1ª9197, fos. 144rff.

[233]On La Barre's career see the notice in Thomas, *Les États,* i (Paris, 1879), 278-9.

[234]The office of *bailli* was frequently coupled with that of *maître des requêtes*
(Bailhache, 29).

Exception was also taken to the general terminology of the Regent's directive to Nicole de La Barre, by Maurice Claveurier, mayor of Poitiers, and Herbert Taunay, *lieutenant-général* of the *sénéchaussée* of Poitou and *Avocat fiscal du roi* in Poitou. The reason for this multiple opposition was explained by Guillaume I Le Tur, speaking for the plaintiffs.

The directive, he explained, indicated that the Regent was:

> informe du mauvais gouvernement de ses offices de Poictou, en ce que ont fait nulle ou petite diligence de recueiller les espaves, confiscations et biens, de par ou pour lui escheut, telement que riens n'en vient a cognoissance...; et que aucuns les enboursent. Dit que c'est mal fait de ainsi parler ne rentrer au poinct en termes generaulx, et que du coste desdits Claveurier et Tannay n' y a eu faulte.

Furthermore the recently-deceased receiver for Poitou had kept scrupulous records of these matters, where they came to his knowledge.

For the *Procureur général du roi* and Turel's executors, Le Tur maintained that La Barre's commission: 'n'est en forme de justice, car, soubz couleur et par la couleur d'icelui, on pourra prendre les biens de qui bon sembleront, sanz condemnacion; et ne se doit tele commission autrement execut.' With regard to the specific execution on the goods of Turel Le Tur explained: 'attendu que Turel est l'officier du roy... et qu'il a, ou peut avoir, des heriters, qui leur droit ont a soustenir, et qu'il a fait son testament', then the execution of the will lay properly with the *Parlement*, and Turel's possessions should remain with his legitimate heirs. The *Parlement* subsequently ordered Turel's goods to be taken into custody pending further litigation.

## Wealth of the *maîtres des requêtes*

The great importance of the various tasks undertaken by the *maîtres des requêtes de l'Hôtel* was reflected in the large sums afforded by the king for their successful undertaking. The reliance, by the latter, on the constancy and diligence of the *maîtres des requêtes* is also reflected by the lavish provision made for them in a private, or domestic sense.

It was commonplace for members of the *requêtes* to marry into families of financiers faithful to Charles VII; this is seen in the cases of Arnaud de Marle, Bureau Boucher, Guillaume Thoreau and Girard Blanchet. On his marriage to Isabeau de Champeaux, sister of Guillaume de Champeaux, bishop of Laon, and sister-in-law of Macé

Heron, treasurer-general of the Regent, the Regent gave Blanchet 500 *moutons d'or* 'pour monter son hotel'.[235] Such displays of *largesse* could extend even to the relatives of the *maîtres des requêtes*; hence, on 28 February 1436 Arnaud de Marle, a *maître des requêtes* '*ordinaire*', acknowledged receipt, on behalf of his mother, Mahauld Barbière, widow of the late Henri de Marle, killed by the Burgundians in 1418, of the sum of 66*l*. 13*s*. 4*d.t.* paid on the treasurer at Toulouse, representing part of a larger sum of 200 *l.t.* given by Charles VII to Henri de Marle's widow for each year of her life.[236] Even in the absence of royal *largesse,* a carefully contrived marriage alliance might lay the foundations of considerable fortunes for the *maîtres des requêtes*. In October 1436 Arnaud de Marle, by way of his marriage to Martine Boucher, daughter of Bureau Boucher, also a *maître des requêtes de l'Hôtel* and himself married to Gilet Raguier,[237] daughter of Raymon Raguier, claimed provision on the will of Raymon of 4,000 *écus d'or*, and a further 400 *écus d'or* annual rent; this by virtue of an agreement made earlier between himself and Michel Raguier, brother of Gilet.[238]

The wealth and possessions accumulated by the *maîtres des requêtes*, seen on occasion during the partition of their wills by the *Parlement,* appears in vast disproportion to their wages within the *Parlement.*[239] Indeed, on occasion, the *maîtres des requêtes* could display a certain contempt for the provision made for the wages of the *conseillers* in general, by going to the source of a particular assignation and taking their share before the greater sum reached the *Parlement.*[240] Yet this fixed wage, while small (and this should be borne in mind with regard to the constant rhetoric of the *parlementaires* over non-payment of wages), signified both an important element in the *permanency* of their position as civil-servants, and, beyond this, the possibility of access to much larger occasional payments.

[235]Thomas, *Les États,* i (Paris, 1879), 288. See Neuville (287), for a similar gift of 200*l.t.* by Charles VII to Gerard le Boursier, in 1423.

[236]B.N. MS. fr.28342 (Marle), no. 49.

[237]See A.N. X1ᶜ152, no. 69.

[238]Ibid., no. 70. (See, also, ibid., nos. 67, 71).

[239]See A.N. X1ᵃ8604, f.59ʳ and *A. H.-G.* MS.59 (passim) on the levels of wages of the *requêtes.*

[240]See below, p. 200.

**Later ancillary personnel of the *auditoire des requêtes de l'Hôtel* at Poitiers**

We have already dealt with the early personnel of the *auditoire des requêtes de l'Hôtel* at Poitiers. Some changes may be discerned during the 1430s, notably the election of Lancelot du Moncel to the office of *greffier des requêtes de l'Hôtel* in 1433, following the death of Antoine Chasteignier.[241] We may also affirm, in addition, the presence of a number of *huissier-sergens* in the *auditoire*; in February 1433 Jean Marly;[242] in April 1433 Jacques de Rubemonte;[243] in April 1436 Jacques Bouverel,[244] and finally, on 31 August 1436, Jean de Sexaulx.[245]

**The *Procureur General du Roi* and the *Avocats du Roi***

We noticed earlier the possible simultaneous function of a *Procureur général* both *du roi* and also *du Dauphin* at Poitiers after 1418.[246] This is a feature of considerable importance because it suggests that in the years before 1422 the Poitiers *Parlement* saw itself as the legitimate representative not primarily of the Dauphin but of Charles VI.[247] Despite the fact that the murder of Jean Sans Peur and the Treaty of Troyes in 1420 forced a *de facto* independence upon the *Parlement*, it was only with the death of Charles VI in October 1422 and Charles VII's assumption of his title in the same month, that the *Parlement* became properly-speaking sole representative of the latter. Hence in 1423 Pierre Cousinot was confirmed in the charge of *Procureur général du roi* by Charles VII – a position which he had nevertheless occupied since 1418.[248]

---

[241]Above, p. 40 n. 39.

[242]A.N. X1ª9200, f.118ᵛ. (Cf. A.N. X1ª9194, f.40ᵛ).

[243]A.N. X1ª9192, f.320ʳ (referring to 1431).

[244]A.N. X1ª21, f.298ʳ.

[245]A.N. X1ª9101, f.221ʳ (possibly *Septaulx* (see Gilles, 120 n.7. and F. Aubert, *Histoire du Parlement de Paris de l'origine à François Iᵉʳ (1250-1515)*, i (Paris, 1894), 16, n.2, 50)).

[246]Above, p. 31 n. 194.

[247]On 19 July 1419 Charles VI, by virtue of the treaty of Pouilly, signed eight days earlier, confirmed the *arrêts* of the *Parlement* and the acts of the *chancellerie* at Poitiers while simultaneously ending the life of these institutions. The murder of Jean Sans Peur in September following this announcement saw the negation of this edict and the continued function of the *Parlement* (Favreau, *Poitiers*, 278).

[248]A.N. X1ª8604, f.66ᵛ (18 Aug. 1423).

Before 1426 the office of *Avocat du roi* and *du Dauphin*, and substitute of the *Procureur général du roi*, was exercised by Guillaume I Le Tur.[249] However on 20 December 1426 Jean Juvénal des Ursins, doctor *utroque*, was received in an 'extraordinary' capacity in place of André Cotin.[250] Juvénal was permitted to adopt the title and function of *Avocat du Roi*, but his election was not formalised until 1429.[251] The election of Guillaume I Le Tur as fourth *Président* in August 1427[252] saw his position taken by Jean Rabateau, termed *Avocat général criminel*.[253] On 2 June 1429[254] the formal reception of Jean Juvénal, now dean of Avranches, increased the official number of *Avocats du roi* to two; this figure was maintained following Juvénal's election to the bishopric of Beauvais in 1432, by the election of Jean Barbin.[255] This total of two *Avocats* was maintained until the promotion of Jean Rabateau as *Président* of the *Chambre des comptes* in 1433.

The importance of the charge of *Avocat du roi* brought with it the prospects of clientage from princes, nobles and corporations. Guillaume I Le Tur, between 1418 and 1422 at least, coupled the charge of *Avocat du roi* with that of *avocat* of the duke of Orléans and of the town of Lyon.[256] After Le Tur's promotion as fourth *Président* in 1427 his replacement, Jean Rabateau,[257] probably took over as representative of the duke of Orléans in the *Parlement* ; a quittance dated 5 August 1430 styles him 'conseiller en icelle court de monsieur le duc d'Orleans'.[258] The pension of 10*l.t. per annum* which Rabateau

---

[249]Above, p. 14.

[250]*A.H.-G.* MS.59, fos. 277ᵛ-278ʳ. Cotin almost certainly never exercised office at Poitiers (E. Maugis, *Histoire du Parlement de Paris de l'avènement des rois Valois à la mort d'Henri IV,* iii (Paris, 1916), 332, 339). He was received as a lay *conseiller* in the Paris *Parlement c.* 1442.

[251]Ibid., f.335ᵛ.

[252]Ibid., f.308ʳᵛ (20-21 Aug. 1427).

[253]Ibid., fos. 308ᵛ-309ʳ (22 Aug. 1427).

[254]Ibid., f.335ᵛ. On 29 Dec. 1429, Jean d'Açy, *Avocat du Roi* in the *Parlement* of the Languedoc since *c.* 1420, sought reception in this office at Poitiers. Açy was received 'au serment d'advocat general' (ibid., f.343ʳ) on the same day, though he appears not to have served at Poitiers after his reception (A. Viala, *Le Parlement de Toulouse et l'administration royale laïque, 1420-1525 environ,* ii (Albi, 1953), 472).

[255]A.N. X1ᵃ9194, fos. 11ᵛ, 13ʳ (Apr. 1432). (Cf. Maugis, i (Paris, 1913), 52).

[256]Above, p. 12 n. 48.

[257]On the career of Rabateau see H. Daniel-Lacombe, 'L'Hôte de Jeanne d'Arc à Poitiers: maître Jean Rabateau, Président du Parlement de Paris', in *R. Bas-Poitou* 4 (1891), 48-66; 5 (1892), 22-51 and 297-328; 6 (1893), 158-187; 7 (1894), 272-298.

[258]B.N. MS. fr. 26053, no. 1390. Besides Rabateau and Le Tur, Orléans's legal representatives at Poitiers included, in the 1430s, Jean Juvénal des Ursins (*Écrits politiques de Jean Juvénal des Ursins,* ed. P.S. Lewis, i (*SHF* Paris, 1978), 324 n.1).

received for this charge might be small in comparison with the incidental benefits from the '*éspices*' accorded by a wealthy client to his legal representative. Rabateau began as an ordinary *avocat* in the *Parlement;* though from an early stage he was also closely involved in supervising the levy of royal finances in Poitou. On 19 June 1425 he received 100*l. t.* 'que monseigneur l'evesque de Poitiers, le vicomte de Thouars et le maitre des arbalestriers . . . commissars en ceste partie . . . ont ordonnes estre paiee et delivree', for his part in the imposition of an *aide* accorded by the Estates of Languedoil.[259] In March 1429 Rabateau was host to Joan of Arc at Poitiers, and by 20 January 1430[260] he achieved promotion to the *Grand Conseil* of Charles VII, perhaps in recognition of his role in her 'Mission'. In the years after 1429 Rabateau appears to have been prominent among those members of the *Grand Conseil* keen to reach a permanent political settlement with Burgundy.[261]

On 30 May 1431 Rabateau and Maurice Claveurier, then mayor of Poitiers, received a gift of 500*l. t.* from Charles VII: 'pour nostre part et porcion de la somme de 9,400 livres tournois . . . donne et octroye a messires de son Grant Conseil et a nous.'[262] Again, in 1431, Rabateau and Claveurier were charged with the levy of an *aide* of 10,000 *francs*: 'pour la recouvrance d'aucuns places de nouvel prises et occuppees en icellui nostre pais par aucuns Bretons et autres, rotiers.'[263] On 12 February 1432 the pair are termed 'generaulx refformateurs commis par le roy sur la reparacion des abus commis en ce royaume en fait des Monnaies du roy et transportz de billon'.[264] Later, on 22 December 1432, Rabateau received a further 200 *florins* together with others of Charles VII's *Grand Conseil,* 'sur noz pensions et voyages'.[265] Further promotion was to follow this activity of a predominantly fiscal kind: in 1433 Rabateau was elected *Président* in the *Chambre des comptes* and on 15 June 1434 he received 100 *réaux d'or* for having: 'nagairez . . . ordonne noz (*i.e.*

---

[259] B.N. P.O., no. 2419 (Rabateau), no.2.

[260] *A.H.-G.* MS.59, f.354ᵛ (*contra* Daniel-Lacombe, 5 (1892), 301-3). During the 1430s Rabateau's frequent absence from Poitiers led to complaints by the other *conseillers* (ibid., 6 (1893), 166).

[261] See ibid., 5 (1893), 305ff.

[262] B.N. P.O., no. 2419 (Rabateau), no. 4.

[263] B.N. Nouv. acq. fr. no. 7627, fos. 322ʳff.

[264] A.N. X2ª18, f.282ʳ. Both Claveurier and Rabateau were *génèraux conseillers* in the *Cour des aides* (see A.N. Z1ª8 (passim) for their presence in the *Cour*). In 1428 they are additionally termed: 'generaulx commissars sur le fait de toutes Monnaies en Languedoc' (A.N. X2ª21, f.91ʳ).

[265] B.N. P.O., no. 693 (Chartres), no. 71.

Charles VII's) droiz et finances a nous appartenans a cause des acquisicions faites par non-nobles de nobles, et . . . par gens d'eglise non-amorties, estre cueillie et levee en nostre obeyssance por nous aider en noz affaires.'[266] In 1436 Rabateau was elected fourth *Président* at Poitiers, in succession to Jean I de Vailly,[267] and had also, in the meantime, become *seigneur* of La Caiullière, near Fontenay-le-Comte (by 1430),[268] and of Auzance (?Auzances/ Auxances) (by 1438-9).[269]

Hence, despite the *Parlement*'s unwillingness to recruit from Poitevin sources, it is clear that some of its members could forge very close links with the notables of Poitiers, themselves also frequently *commissaires du roi*, thus blurring the division between 'town' and 'gown'.

The career of Jean Barbin[270], elected *Avocat du roi* in April 1432, at the age of only twenty-six, displayed a similar development. Barbin was the son of Nicolas Barbin, *seigneur* of Touteville and captain of Montsoreau, and Jeanne Baranger. In March 1429 he acquired the *seigneuries* of La Tour Sybile and Grange-Hocquet in the parish of Sepmes, near Loches, from Marguérite de Craon.[271] On 28 December 1432 Barbin made a lucrative marriage to Françoise Gillier, whose father, Étienne, *échevin* of Poitiers, was also brother of Jeanne Gillier, wife of *premier Président* Jean de Vailly.[272] In the ten years following his election Barbin accumulated considerable landed wealth in Poitou and Touraine and great prestige in the *Parlement* of Paris, being simultaneously *pensionnaire* of René d'Anjou, Charles d'Anjou and of the town of Poitiers.[273] Barbin was also among those who testified in favour of Joan of Arc[274] at the Rehabilitation proceedings in the 1450s.[275]

[266] B.N. P.O., no. 2419 (Rabateau), no. 5.

[267] A.N. X1ᵃ9194, f.124ᵛ (20 Feb. 1436).

[268] See A.N. X1ᵃ9196, f.29ʳ (1 Sept. 1430).

[269] See B.N. P.O., no. 2419 (Rabateau), no. 8.

[270] See P. Souty, 'Jean Barbin, riche et influent seigneur de Touraine et Poitou sous Charles VII', in *Bull. Soc. Archéol. de Touraine* 37 (1974), 383-7, for details of the career of Barbin.

[271] Ibid., 383.

[272] Ibid., 384. Vailly's marriage to Jeanne Gillier took place also in 1432 ('Rec. des docs', *Arch. hist. Poitou* 29 (1898), 27 n.4).

[273] See Souty, passim, and Favreau, *Poitiers*, 334.

[274] Favreau, *Poitiers*, 334.

[275] In addition to his participation in the Rehabilitation of Joan of Arc, Barbin played an important part in the political trials conducted by Charles VII in the 1450s.

## The *Présidents* in the *Parlement*

The election of Guillaume I Le Tur to the office of *Président* in the *Parlement* on 20-1 August 1427[276] provided a total, at that date, of four *Présidents*.[277] By December 1429, the incorporation of Junien Le Fèvre, lately *premier Président* at Béziers in succession to Jean Gencian, within the Poitiers complement, brought the total to five.[278] The arrival of Le Fèvre saw, in addition, a protracted battle develop between himself and the recently-elected Le Tur over the matter of precedence within the presidential hierarchy.[279] The issue was finally decided early in March 1430, with Le Tur being placed fourth *Président* and Le Fèvre fifth.[280] The death of Jean I Jouvenel, second *Président* and baron of Trainel in 1431[281] saw the numbers of *Présidents* once again reduced to a total of four. This was diminished still further in March 1435 with the death of Jean de Vailly, *premier Président*.[282] His position as *premier Président* was taken by Adam de Cambrai[283] and the vacant position of fourth *Président* filled on 20 February 1436[284] by the election of Jean Rabateau, since 1433 *Président* in the *Chambre des comptes* at Bourges.

There is little evidence, in respect of the *Présidents* at Poitiers, that the often severe losses incurred in the exits from Paris in 1418 resulted in enduring hardship. The case of the Jouvenel family provides

---

[276]*A.H.-G.* MS.59, f.308$^{r-v}$.

[277]Jean I de Vailly, *premier Président*, Jean I Jouvenel, Adam de Cambrai and Guillaume I Le Tur.

[278]Le Fèvre asked to be received *Président* by the *Parlement* on 14 Nov. 1429 (*A.H.-G.* MS.59, f.339$^{r-v}$). From 10 December he was received to sit in an extraordinary capacity, on the *Conseil* of the *Parlement*, pending a decision on his reception (ibid., fos. 340$^{v}$ff).

[279]For details of this affair see ibid., fos. 346$^{v}$ff (4 Jan. 1430).

[280]Ibid., f.362$^{r}$ (4 March 1430).

[281]Jean I Jouvenel probably died in late March or April 1431. His last appearance on the *Conseil* of the *Parlement* was on 27 March 1431 (ibid., f.421$^{r}$). Maugis's view (*Histoire du Parlement de Paris de l'avènement des rois Valois à la mort d'Henri IV*, iii (Paris, 1916), 72), that Jouvenel was replaced as *Président* on 13 Nov. 1430 by Junien Le Fèvre is clearly erroneous.

[282]Vailly died on 9 March and was buried on 12 March 1435 ('Rec. des docs'. *Arch. hist. Poitou* 29 (1898), 27 n.4). On 12 March the *Parlement* wrote to Charles VII asking him not to increase the remaining number of three *Présidents* — though this plea went unheeded.

[283]The registers of the *Parlement* contain no details of Cambrai's reception. He is first mentioned as *premier Président* on 20 Aug. 1436 (A.N. X1$^{a}$9194, f.146$^{r}$).

[284]A.N. X1$^{a}$9194, f.124$^{v}$. Rabateau's reception at Poitiers was witnessed by Regnault de Chartres, *Chancelier*, Raoul de Gaucourt and Robert le Maçon, members of Charles VII's *Conseil* (ibid.).

a good illustration of this point. Jean Juvénal des Ursins's graphic picture of the reduction of his father's fortunes[285] carries perhaps a touch of rhetoric. As early as 22 April 1423 Jean I Jouvenel cited Hugues de Chalon, *comte* of Tonnerre, before the *Parlement,* demanding payment of 200 *écus d'or* in arrears accumulated on property valued at 2,000 *écus d'or* rented earlier by Hugues and his late father.[286] Payment was not finally made until 6 August 1427.[287]

A further case of Jean I Jouvenel's accumulation of landed wealth was seen before the *Parlement* in February 1432, not long after his death.[288] Here Michele de Vitry, his widow, together with Jean Juvénal, *Avocat du roi,* Guillaume Jouvenel,[289] lay *conseiller,* Jacques Jouvenel *avocat* in the *Parlement* and Jehannette and Michelet, children of the deceased, cited Guillaume d'Argenton, *seigneur* of Villentrois before the court for infringement of their rights in succession to their father, *seigneur* of Valençay. The plaintiffs explained that Jean I Jouvenel was lately *seigneur* of Valençay, where he had, in addition, seven or eight leagues of land called the forest of La Gâtine. Jean Jouvenel's heirs explained that they were entitled to hold:

> court et jurisdicion a cause de ladite forest, et des cas touchans le fait d'icelle, audit lieu de Villantras, et de y faire convenir et adiourner les delinquancs et autres tenuz a cacher de ladite forest, cognoistre et decider et faire execucion et exploiz de justice et faire crier ses assises en quelque lieu que ... plaist, de la terre de Villantras, sans supplier ... ou requierir le seigneur de Villantras, et sans ce que ledit seigneur ... leur puisse donner empeschement

In his lifetime Jean I Jouvenel had regularly held his assizes at Villentrois 'et y avoit juge, greffier et sergent'. Lately, however, the captain of Villentrois had visited the assizes and imprisoned the sergeant and *greffier,* tearing up the records of the latter in the process. The plaintiffs hence demanded that the defendant acknowledge their rights and restore the assizes.

---

[285] Jean Juvénal des Ursins, *Histoire de Charles VI, Roy de France,* ed. J.A.C. Buchon (Paris, 1838), 549.

[286] A.N. X1ᵃ9197, f.189ʳ⁻ᵛ (cf. ibid., fos. 236ʳff., passim).

[287] A.N. X1ᵃ9198, f.264ᵛ.

[288] For what follows see A.N. X1ᵃ9200, f.22ᵛ.

[289] The use of the form *Juvénal des Ursins* by a member of the Jouvenel family appears in the Poitiers registers for the first time in February 1435, in respect of Guillaume Jouvenel (A.N. X1ᵃ9196, fos. 118ᵛff., passim).

Further evidence of the considerable wealth of Jean I Jouvenel was seen before the *Parlement* in December 1435. Here, one Thomasse Regnaude was found guilty of a robbery in the house of Jouvenel's widow, in Poitiers, which involved the theft of 80 pieces of gold in *écus* and (old) *moutons d'or*.[290] Following the incident Adam de Cambrai, *premier Président* in the *Parlement*, instructed locksmiths living in Poitiers that in future they should fashion no more keys for houses without the specific consent of the owners.[291] For Thomasse, perpetrator of the crime, the penalty was severe; she was to be: 'fustignee par trois Samedis par les quarrefours et places . . . devant Nostre Dame La Grant a Poictiers, de la regracerie et du Pilory, et apres estre pilorisee par chacun desdits Samediz et a avoir en l'une des foiz les cheveulx brulez ou pilory'. In addition, Thomasse was to be retained prisoner in the tower of the *prévôté*, and afterwards banished in perpetuity from the kingdom.[292]

The fortune of Jean I de Vailly, *premier Président*, was made in a slightly different manner. Although the *Parlement* took considerable care to prevent overmuch penetration of its ranks by local candidates, this did not prevent members of the *Parlement* from securing lucrative marriage alliances with eminent *échevin* families in Poitiers. In 1432 Vailly contrived a second marriage to Jeanne Gillier, daughter of Denis Gillier, *échevin* of Poitiers.[293] Jeanne was, in turn, via her mother, Jeanne Taunay, also related to the Taunay family, again *échevins*, having as uncle Herbert Taunay, on occasion both *Avocat fiscal du roi* and mayor of Poitiers. In addition, and in more conventional fashion, Vailly's daughter Jeanne was married to Nicole de La Barre, *maître des requêtes de l'Hôtel du Roi*. On 5 May 1432 Vailly, as heir of his deceased daughter, claimed a portion of the sum of 500 *livres* outstanding on the wages of her deceased husband,

[290]A.N. X2ª21, f.285ᵛ (7 Dec. 1435). On 10 Dec. 1435 (ibid., f.286ʳ) Jacques Jouvenel demanded the much larger sum of 380 *écus d'or* outstanding from a total of 500 *écus* allegedly stolen by Thomasse from his mother's house.

[291]Ibid., f.285ᵛ.

[292]Ibid. Thomasse was finally released on 19 June 1436 (ibid., f.304ᵛ), pending payment of the money stolen.

[293]See 'Rec. des docs', *Arch. hist. Poitou* 29 (1898), 27 n.4. Jeanne's sister, Françoise, married another of the *parlementaires*, Jean Barbin, *Avocat du roi* in the same year. Following Vailly's death in 1435 litigation ensued, between his wife and Vailly's heirs over the partition of the former *Président*'s possessions, including a house situated near the Franciscan convent earlier purchased from Jean Le Bourgeois (A.N. X1ᶜ149, no. 67, i, ii and iii). The purchase of property in Poitiers may also be seen in the case of Junien Le Fèvre, *Président*, in 1430 ('Rec. des docs', *Arch. hist. Poitou* 29 (1898), 28 n.1).

granted by the king on the Estates of Limousin, contributors to a larger aide accorded by the Estates of Languedoil at Chinon in 1428.[294]

Jean de Vailly's position as *premier Président* from the inauguration of the *Parlement* was a highly prestigious one. Like the other *Présidents*, he had a considerable retinue of clerks and domestic servants, and towards the end of his life considerable concession was made by the *Parlement* to accommodate his presence in the *Grand' Chambre*. By 1434 Vailly's health had deteriorated to such an extent that, as explained, he was no longer able to travel any great distance, either by foot or on horseback.[295] From late 1434 important sessions of the *Conseil* took place in Vailly's house near the *Palais*. Finally, in response to a personal plea from the *premier Président*, a special door was constructed in the wall of the *Palais* in order that he might come and go between sessions more easily.[296] Vailly's importance as *premier Président* was measured not only in respect of his position in the *Parlement;* he was also, like the other *Présidents,* frequently ambassador of the king at meetings of the Estates, or in diplomatic negotiations with internal and foreign powers. From a very early date he was present at meetings of the Dauphin's *Conseil,* and probably figured closely in the organisation of the *Parlement* together with the then *Chancelier*, Robert Le Maçon.[297]

The considerable wealth accumulated by Guillaume I Le Tur was founded upon the multiplicity of charges which he occupied earlier, in addition to that of *Avocat du roi*.[298] Elected fourth *Président* in 1427, Le Tur was, in addition, before 1434, lay *Président* in the *Court des aides*.[299] Service of a fiscal nature could bring an individual more closely within the orbit of the royal *Conseil* – the most important source of both financial gain and of advancement in terms of one's career. Access of this kind tended to be largely, though not exclusively, confined to the higher echelons of the *Parlement,* and promotion to high office tended to be both dynastic and hierarchical. The proclivity of the Jouvenels to high office is well enough documented. A similar case may be made for the Vaillys and the Le Turs, while the Cambrais

[294]See A.N. Z1ᵃ8, 62ʳff., passim.

[295]See A.N. X1ᵃ9194, f.82ᵛ.

[296]Ibid., f.83ʳ.

[297]For details of the importance of the role of Robert le Maçon, *Chancelier* from 1418-22, in the early organisation of the Dauphin's administration see especially, A.N. X1ᵃ9198, f.19ʳ (23 Jan. 1424).

[298]See above, p. 12.

[299]? (See A.N. Z1ᵃ8, fos. 122ᵛff. passim).

were seemingly represented both in the *Parlement* and the *Chambre des comptes*.

The fiscal advantage to be gained by the *Présidents* as the king's representatives at meetings of the Estates is well displayed by Le Tur. On 17 July 1427, styled '*Président en Parlement*' (though he was not formally elected into that office until 20-1 August following), he received 20 *livres* from the receiver for Haute-Auvergne of the portion of an *aide* accorded by the Estates of Languedoïl at Montluçon in 1426, for 'd'avoir este present a l'octroye et assiette dudit aide'.[300] Again in 1430, Le Tur was *commissaire du roi* in the county of Poitou for the *aide* accorded by the Estates of Languedoil assembled at Chinon in September 1430, for which he received 200 *livres*.[301] Later, in 1431, he accompanied Girard Blanchet, *maître des requêtes de l'Hôtel*, to preside over a meeting of the Estates of Auvergne.[302] Considerably later again, in December 1438, Le Tur received 300 *florins* from the Estates of the Dauphiné 'delivree en pur et liberal don, de par l'universite dudit pais, de et sur la somme de 2,000 florins a eulx ordonnee des deniers dudit aide'.[303] Such gifts could greatly implement wages afforded by a purely judicial function within the *Parlement*.

### The ordinary *Conseillers* in the *Parlement*[304]

In the years after 1418 the numbers of ordinary *conseillers* in the Poitiers *Parlement* continued to increase in striking contrast with the steadily declining complement of its Parisian counterpart.[305] By 1422 the register of *plaidoiries* indicates the presence of eighteen *conseillers*, excluding the *Présidents* and *maîtres des requêtes de l'Hôtel*.[306] At this stage the only great disproportion with the numbers of Paris was noticeable in respect of the *enquêtes*;[307] recruitment to

[300] B.N. MS. fr.29380 (Le Tur), no. 10.

[301] Ibid., no.11.

[302] A. Thomas, *Les États provinciaux de la France centrale sous Charles VII,* i (Paris, 1879), 289.

[303] B.N. MS. fr. 29380 (Le Tur), no. 12.

[304] A list of the Poitiers *parlementaires* is furnished by Maugis (iii (Paris, 1916), 72-8) but this contains a number of omissions and many inaccuracies (cf. Favreau, *Poitiers,* 280 n.909).

[305] See Favreau, *Poitiers,* 283-4

[306] A.N. X1ᵃ9197, f.1ʳ (12 Nov. 1422).

[307] It is worthy of note that at Paris too, the numbers of *conseillers* in the *enquêtes* declined rapidly after 1418 (F. Aubert, *Histoire du Parlement de Paris de l'origine à François Iᵉʳ (1250-1515),* i (Paris, 1894), 25).

this function at Poitiers appears to have been very small at the outset, and it is possible that after 1421 or 1422 the function of the *enquêtes* was absorbed within the more general sphere of competence of the *conseillers,* not being fully reinstated until January 1435.[308]

The union of the *Parlement* of the Languedoc with that of Poitiers in 1428 saw the numbers of ordinary *conseillers* increase still further, to a total of twenty-nine by 13 November 1430.[309] In respect of the overall numbers of the *Parlement,* Poitiers now matched its Parisian rival. However, by 12 November 1434,[310] with the number of ordinary *conseillers* at Poitiers increased still further, to a total of thirty-three, the overall Parisian total was finally exceeded. A notable feature of the complement of the Poitiers *Parlement* was the perpetual predominance of clerics over lay members. By 12 November 1423,[311] the proportion of clerics outnumbered the lay *conseillers* by almost two to one. However, following the union of the two *Parlements* the preponderance of clerics was somewhat diminished, and the final recorded complement on 12 November 1434,[312] of thirty-three, gives nineteen clerics and fourteen lay *conseillers.*

It appears impossible to make generalisations about the 'poverty' of ordinary *conseillers* in the *Parlement* purely in respect of their judicial preoccupations. The *ad hoc* fiscal administration of the 'kingdom of Bourges' provided numerous opportunities for *commissaires du roi,* delegates to supervise the levy of various *aides* accorded by the Estates, to acquire considerable wealth and prestige. Conveniently placed in this respect were the *généraux conseillers sur le fait de la justice des aides,* operating from the *Cour des aides* in the *Parlement.*[313]

The career of Geoffroy Vassal, clerical *conseiller,* is not altogether untypical of the lot of the enterprising *conseiller* in the *Cour des aides.* Early a canon of the church of Poitiers, Vassal must have been a frequent absentee from Poitiers. In 1427 he was at Lyon to negotiate the levy of a certain sum of money accorded by the Estates

[308]See above, p. 23. Also, Favreau, *Poitiers,* 279 n.895.

[309]A.N. X1ª9199, f.326ᵛ.

[310]A.N. X1ª9200, f.285ᵛ.

[311]A.N. X1ª9197, f.261ᵛ.

[312]A.N. X1ª9200, f.285ᵛ. See A.N. X1ª9194, f.54ᵛ (1433), for an appeal by the *Parlement* to Charles VII to increase the numbers of lay *conseillers* at Poitiers.

[313]Despite the physical situation of the *Cour des aides* in the *Parlement* 'son activité fut bien celle d'une cour souveraine' (Favreau, *Poitiers,* 289). The *généraux conseillers* in the *Cour* were, for the most part, drawn from the larger body of *parlementaires* (ibid., 288-9).

of Languedoil at Montluçon in the previous year.[314] In August 1430 we find him in litigation before the *Parlement* with Macé Mouette for the office of dean of the church of Poitiers. On 25 November 1430, however, Vassal suddenly withdrew his opposition to Mouette by agreement made 'en la galerie de l'ostel ou demoure ledit monseigneur, President a Poitiers'.[315] Despite this setback Vassal's career continued on the ascendant: in 1432 he was termed 'du Grant Conseil du roy'.[316] In July 1435 Charles VII gave him 300 *moutons d'or* in recognition of the 'bons et agreables services qu'il nous a faiz, tant en assistant en noz consaulz que autrement'.[317] In October 1435 Vassal numbered among those who had 'fort travaillie envers le roy', in employing a certain aide contributed by the Estates of *Haut* and Bas Limousin in order to obtain the deliverance of Domme and Mareul, and the *'vuidance'* of Courbeffin.[318] On 19 March 1436 he received a further 100 *l.t.* from Jean Vousy, receiver in Poitou of an *aide* accorded by the Estates of Languedoil in January 1436, given by 'ceulx dudit pays de Poitou. . . avecques autres messires du conseil dudit seigneur. . . oultre. . . le principal dudit aide'.[319] Service in the *Grand Conseil* brought in turn even greater rewards; after the return to Paris Vassal was promoted archbishop first of Vienne, then, in 1444, of Lyon.[320]

It is difficult, in the absence of detailed evidence, to assess how far Vassal's career was typical of that of the average *conseiller* at Poitiers. An office in the *Cour des aides* could provide certain advantages in the respect that it provided a greater opportunity for undertaking a range of royal fiscal commissions,[321] and also brought the individual *conseiller* into closer contact with the royal *Conseil* and thus with sources of political patronage. However, even in the case of the ordinary *conseillers* in the *Parlement*, such evidence as we possess suggests that during our period some had begun to acquire

[314]*Reg. consulaires,* ii (Lyon, 1926), 228ff., passim.

[315]A.N. X1ᵃ9199, f.322ᵛ. Following litigation for the priory of Mirabeau in 1420 (A.N. X1ᶜ119, no. 27, i and ii) Vassal later forged close links with the church of Poitiers, being canon (A.N. X1ᵃ9193, f.306ᵛ (1432)) and, in 1435, precentor in the cathedral chapter (Favreau, *Poitiers,* 282 n.923). Vassal's clerk, Jean Garnier, was also a native of Poitiers, member of an eminent *échevin* family (A.N. X1ᶜ145, no.71).

[316]See A.N. X2ᵃ18, f.328ʳ.

[317]B.N. MS. fr.29416 (Vassal), no. 4.

[318]Thomas, *Les États,* ii (Paris, 1879), 67 no. 19.

[319]B.N. MS. fr.29416 (Vassal), no. 3.

[320]'Rec. des docs', *Arch. hist. Poitou* 29 (1898), 152 n.2.

[321]See B.N. MS. fr.29516 (Vitry) for commissions undertaken by Thibaud de Vitry, also a *général conseiller* in the *Cour des aides*.

both land and property[322] — certainly, any generalised view of the 'poverty' of the *parlementaires* would be extremely difficult to sustain.

## 'Town and Gown'

The perpetual conflict between the jurisdictions of the major towns of the 'kingdom of Bourges' and their local royal counterparts was a characteristic feature of our period. Yet at Poitiers several factors could combine significantly to moderate the extent of this conflict, apart from the presence of the *Parlement* in the midst of the town. While recruitment of *parlementaires* among notable *échevin* families might be strictly limited, marital and dynastic links between the *parlementaires* and local families appear to have become, at least by the later years of the *Parlement*'s stay in Poitiers, numerous and complex.[323] Such links could do much to diminish the traditional conflict between *parlementaires* and the *échevins* of Poitiers.

Of those *parlementaires* mentioned in the Ordinance of Niort only three — Guillaume Gúerin, Jean Tudert and Nicolas Eschalart — appear to have had close links with Poitiers: even then, their formation was essentially Parisian.[324] However, in the years following the *Parlement*'s foundation, links with the local bourgeoisie were formed at practically every stage of the *Parlement*'s hierarchy. We saw earlier the case of Jean I de Vailly, *premier Président,* who married into the Gillier-Taunay dynasty.[325] In addition to this, Nicolas Eschalart, *conseiller,* who died in March 1422, was both son of a Poitiers *bourgeois* and, at the same time, the son-in-law of second

---

[322]Pierre de Tuillières, a lay *conseiller,* was *seigneur* of La Rochebacon, in Poitou, in 1434; Philippe des Courtils, also a lay *conseiller,* acquired two houses in Poitiers in 1434 (A.N. X1ª9193, f.6$^{r-v}$) and Hélie d'Alée, a lay *conseiller,* had acquired seigneurial status by the 1430s (A.N. X1$^c$149, nos. 113, 115. A.N. 1AP175, no. 47).

[323]It is interesting to speculate to what extent, in the event of the *Parlement* having been forced to remain at Poitiers for a protracted period after 1436, the symbiosis between 'town' and 'gown' in Poitiers might have contributed to an erosion of the 'Parisian' formation of the court. Given time local recruitment of personnel might have been accelerated by the foundation of the university of Poitiers, for in Sept. 1432 we have a mention of Jean Baçonnet, of local origin, as a student at Poitiers and ordinary *avocat* in the *Parlement* (A.N. X2ª21, fos. 192$^v$-193$^r$).

[324]Favreau, *Poitiers,* 280.

[325]Above, p. 80. Soon after his marriage to Jeanne Gillier Vailly was involved in litigation with Étienne and Jean Gillier, brother of Jeanne, over the partition of the inheritance of Herbert Taunay, lately *Avocat du roi in Poitou* and sometime mayor of Poitiers (A.N. X1ª9200, fos. 167$^r$ff., passim, A.N. X1ª9194, fos. 48$^v$ff., passim). (Cf. Rec. des docs', *Arch. hist. Poitou* 26 (1896), 397 n.1).

*Président,* Jean I Jouvenel.[326] Eschalart's niece, Louise, was later third wife of Maurice Claveurier, lieutenant-général of the *sénéchaussée* of Poitou, and sometime mayor of Poitiers.[327] Junien Le Fèvre, fourth *Président* after 1430, was the son of a notary of Poitiers.[328] Finally, Guillaume II Le Tur, son of Guillaume I, *Président* in the *Parlement,* was among those who developed enduring links with Poitiers, being from 1432-40 Professor of Civil Law in the newly-created University of Poitiers.[329]

Among the *Avocats du roi,* Jean Rabateau, elected *Avocat général criminel* in 1427, besides his considerable landed interests in the county of Poitou, was also related to Léon Guérinet,[330] clerical *conseiller* of *bourgeois* issue, and had other close ties of a professional kind with notable *échevins,* in particular Maurice Claveurier. Jean Barbin, *Avocat du roi* in 1432 had, like Rabateau, numerous landed interests in Poitou,[331] and was, like *premier Président* Jean de Vailly, also linked by marriage to the Gillier-Taunay dynasties.[332]

Of the *conseillers,* Léon Guérinet,[333] though his formation in a professional sense was essentially Parisian, was, as we have seen, also of local *bourgeois* issue, and by virtue of his brother's marriage to Guillemine Turpin related both to that family and the Merichons.[334] Nicholas Géhée, also a clerical *conseiller,* elected in 1429, was the son of Pierre Géhée and Louise de Parthenay and further related, by his sister's marriage, to Hugues Giraud, sometime *Procureur ducal* in Poitou, and mayor of Poitiers.[335] Guillaume de Laillier, originally of Auvergnat *bourgeois* issue, was also related to the Bernards of Poitiers, an important *échevin* family, and to Pierre de Tuillières their

[326]E. Maugis, *Histoire du Parlement de Paris de l'avènement des rois Valois à la mort d'Henri IV,* iii (Paris 1916), 74.

[327]Favreau, *Poitiers,* 599.

[328]Maugis, iii (Paris, 1916), 72.

[329]Above, p. 13.

[330]Above, p. 50.

[331]P. Souty, 'Jean Barbin riche et influent seigneur de Touraine et Poitou sous Charles VII', *Bull. Trimest. Soc. Archéol. de Touraine* 37 (1974), 383-7, passim.

[332]Above, p. 80 n. 293.

[333]Guérinet's election as a *conseiller* was originally solicited at Poitiers by Robert de Rouvres and Jean Girard, *maîtres des requêtes* and members of Charles VII's *Conseil* (*A.H.-G.* MS.59, f.299[r-v]). The *Parlement* resisted these overtures and Guérinet was not received until 1433. He became bishop of Poitiers in 1457.

[334]Favreau, *Poitiers,* 596.

[335]Ibid., 598.

'affin'. Finally, a similar case may be put for Jean Colas, lay *conseiller* in 1433.[336]

At the level of the *huissiers*[337] and the *greffiers* of the *Parlement,* dynastic or marital ties with local families are hard to discern, but even here evidence is not completely lacking; however, it is unlikely that, in respect of these offices, links would be formed at a very exalted level. In respect of the *procureurs*[338] in the *Parlement,* some form of local association might be offered for Guillaume Gendrault — one Jean Gendrault being earlier *principal fournier de la ville*[339] — and Guillaume Garnier.[340] In addition to these dynastic links, further infiltration by the *parlementaires* into the general *milieu* of the town came with their acquisition of benefices, both in the notable churches in Poitiers, and in the immediate environs of the town.[341] Mitigation of local conflict with inferior jurisdictions could also occur through close surveillance by the *Parlement* of their prerogatives. One of the most important of these and, in other towns, often the source of friction between both royal officials and town corporations, was the court of the bishop of Poitiers. The early election of Hugues de Combarel[342] as bishop of Poitiers solved the problem to some degree, as Combarel was simultaneously both member of Charles VII's *Conseil, conseiller* in the *Parlement,* and early *Président* of the *Cour des aides.* This did not, however, prevent the *Parlement* from placing frequent injunctions upon the episcopal court to restrain its authority.

At a very early stage the *Parlement* also took steps to limit the authority of the court of the *sénéchal* of Poitou,[343] which had attempted to retain authority at the expense of the *Parlement.* Policing of the town was also carried out in close liaison with the mayor and *échevins,*[344] and, in addition, rights of visitation of the

---

[336]Ibid., 280.

[337]Centain of the *huissier-sergens* in the *auditoire des requêtes de l'Hôtel* were local recruits from *échevin* families. There is no evidence of a similar origin for any of the ordinary *huissiers,* nor for the *greffiers* in the *Parlement.*

[338]See A.N. X1ª9200, f.42ʳ; A.N. X1ª9194, f.16ᵛ.

[339]See Favreau, *Poitiers,* 242 n.648.

[340]See ibid., 669. A Jean Garnier was additionally clerk to Geoffroy Vassal, *conseiller* in *Parlement* (A.N. X1ª145, no.7).

[341]Favreau, *Poitiers,* 282 n.923.

[342]For remarks on the career of Hugues de Combarel, see 'Rec. des docs', *Arch. hist. Poitou* 29 (1898), 54 n.2; and Favreau, *Poitiers,* 313 n.1143.

[343]See *A.H.-G.* MS.59, f.173ʳ (23 March 1423).

[344]See ibid., fos. 356ᵛff., passim (14 Feb. 1430). The delegation by the *Parlement* of certain *conseillers* to policing duties in Poitiers appears to have coincided with a period of widespread political unrest within Poitou generally (below, pp. 203ff.).

prisons of the bishop and the *prévôt* were constantly maintained,[345] and appointment to important positions within the town hierarchy, notably that of mayor,[346] similarly closely supervised. In the latter case, both the mayor and *échevins* of Poitiers were obliged to perform an annual oath of fealty to the *Parlement*.

A final and important respect in which conflict between the *Parlement* and the town might be diminished was seen in the tendency for the greater proportion of the *échevins* to be recruited among those notables who simultaneously functioned as royal officers.[347] This was most noticeable in the appointment of the mayors of Poitiers during our period. Maurice I Claveurier, who served in this capacity during 1421-2, 1424-6, 1431-2 and 1434-7, was in addition *lieutenant-général* of the *Sénéchaussée* of Poitou, fiscal agent of great importance of Charles VII in Poitou generally, and also an important member of the royal *Conseil*. Herbert Taunay, mayor during 1418-19, 1422-3 and 1430-1, was similarly a royal councillor and *Avocat fiscal* in Poitou from 1418-29. In addition, like Claveurier, he was a former servant of the duke of Berry.[348] In addition to this predilection for royal officers, the office of mayor was, between the years 1414-37, the preserve of only five *échevin* dynasties — Claveurier, Taunay, Larcher, Guichard and Mourraut. In addition to this the recruitment of the *échevins* was increasingly made not only among those already legists and royal officials but also in an increasingly dynastic fashion. From 1420 to 1428 only one merchant family was represented among the *échevins;* all the others 'ont exercé quelque office royal ou charge rattachée à l'administration royal'.[349] Naturally, this evolution was considerably to the advantage of the *Parlement* and made the problem of control considerably easier, and these factors combined to harden a social tendency already under way during the administration of Jean, duke of Berry.[350] In the more immediate sense, this phenomenon, together with the other links, marital, dynastic and judicial forged by the *Parlement* with local institutions could afford, at an exalted level,

---

[345]A.N. X2ᵃ21, fos. 4ᵛ, 63ʳ, 223ᵛ.

[346]See, for instance, A.N. X1ᵃ9199, f.322ʳ (22 Aug. 1430) and A.N. X1ᵃ9194, f.21ʳ. Similar visitation over the election of the mayor was exercised by the *Parlement* at Niort (A.N. X1ᵃ9194, fos. 10ᵛff., passim).

[347]See Favreau, *Poitiers,* 315-16.

[348]R. Favreau, 'La condition sociale des maires de Poitiers au xvᵉ siècle', in *B. philol.* 1961, 170.

[349]Favreau, *Poitiers,* 317.

[350]Ibid., 223ff. (especially 226-7 and 230).

considerable interaction between 'town' and 'gown'; yet at the same time the *Parlement* could still fiercely defend itself against any threat of encroachment by the authorities which, in other respects, it was glad to embrace.

[351]Ibid., 280-2.

# 3

# THE *PARLEMENT*, THE SIEGE OF ORLÉANS
# AND JOAN OF ARC (*c.* 1429-1431)

Some concern (albeit occupational) for the vulnerability of the town of Orléans on the part of the Poitiers magistrates was indicated by litigation before the *Parlement* on 11 July 1427.[1] Here Guillaume 1 Le Tur, speaking for the *Procureur général du roi* and the town of Orléans, could presuppose: 'comment la ville d'Orleans, assise en la frontiere des ennemis et adversaires, a plus de necessitez, *temporibus modernis,* que n'eut onques; et... chacun de la ville doit contribuer... en tel necessitez.'[2]

The situation was evidently serious enough to prompt some to evacuate their possessions to a safer place. Early in 1428 Dreux Budé, royal *notaire et secrétaire,* sent 'biens meubles de la valeur de mil et vᶜ escus d'or' to the safekeeping of Macé Sabart, treasurer *ordinaire* at Carcassonne.[3] Action of this kind was probably initially confined to those having possessions in Orléans itself,[4] or in the immediate environs.

In the summer of 1428 the decision by the English to abandon the projected invasion of Anjou in favour of a direct thrust into the 'kingdom of Bourges', through Orléans, must have confirmed the worst fears of those with property and goods in the immediate hinterland of the town. The *Parlement*'s concern was exemplified by its desire to obtain the immediate removal of the *Parlement* of Languedoc from its current situation at Béziers into a single unit at Poitiers.[5] Such a desire was by no means new — similar complaints

---

[1]See A.N. X1ª9198, fos.289ʳff., for what follows.

[2]Jean Juvénal des Ursins, replying for the minters of Orléans, refusing to contribute to a certain *aide,* 'a ce que la necessite estoit a Orleans plus que onques, dit que non, et que c'estoit [*i.e.,* the *aide*] a faire dons et plaisirs'.

[3]A.N. X1ª9200, f.298ʳ (10 Jan., 1435) (cf. A.N. X1ᶜ152, nos. 7-9, 13).

[4]From 1427 onwards varying degrees of concern for the safety of Orléans were displayed by towns in close proximity (see. for instance, A. le Roux de Lincy, *La Bibliothèque de Charles d'Orléans à son château de Blois en 1427* (Paris, 1843), passim; Favreau, *Poitiers,* 265, nn. 795-6; B. Chevalier, 'The Policy of Louis XI', in *The Recovery of France in the Fifteenth Century,* ed. P.S. Lewis (London, 1971), 277 n.22. By 1428-9 concern had spread to Lyon (*Reg. Consulaires,* ii (Lyon, 1926), 297ff.).

[5]For confirmation that it was predominantly the *Parlement*'s concern to reunite two institutions, see Favreau, *Poitiers,* 278 n.890.

had been heard since 1426[6] — but it was evident that evacuation from Poitiers in the event of English success at Orléans could invite the odious prospect of the absorption of the *Parlement* into its satellite at Béziers, and with it the possibility of loss of office.[7] Hence on 14 October 1428 the *Parlement* ordered Miles Chaligant, *receveur des amendes et exploits,* to forward 'ce qu'il conviendra pour le chevaucheur qui ira devers le roy pour faire sceller les lettres de l'union des parlemens, et de la publication des jours de Languedoc'.[8] By 11 December 1428 the king had agreed to this request; henceforth a single *Parlement* would sit at Poitiers 'jusques autre lieu plus convenable soit advise par le roy'.[9]

The commencement of the siege of Orléans in October 1428 was followed on 15 November, by a request to the *Parlement* by the Chancellor, Regnault de Chartres, who, on the king's behalf, asked that all 'deposts. . . devers la court et ailleurs a Poictiers. . . en deniers d'or et d'argent ou en vaisselle', be surrendered to him to provide finance for the king.[10] Somewhat earlier the *Parlement* had received another plea for help, this time from the inhabitants of Blois; the *Parlement* decided to respond by writing individually to the constable Richemont, and to the counts of Clermont and Pardiac, to seek their support.[11] But it is anachronistic to view the matter of concern for the situation at Orléans as a simple manifestation of latent patriotism. Individual attitudes to the 'crisis' might be affected by numerous, more pragmatic concerns. The response of the consuls of Lyon to royal letters received on 3 December 1428[12] demanding help for the Orléanais was mildly encouraging; after some debate the town decided to send 'deux quintaulx de salpetre, six ballons d'acier, trois quintaulx

[6]See *A.H.-G.* MS.59, fos.251$^v$-252$^r$ (Feb. 1426). Here Lyon was mooted as a suitable venue for the merger (cf. also. ibid., f.260$^r$ (May 1426)).

[7]Relations between the *Parlements* of Poitiers and the Languedoc between 1420 and 1428 were never particularly cordial (C. Devic and J. Vaissètte, *Histoire générale de Languedoc,* ix (Toulouse, 1885), 1099 n.3 and x (Toulouse, 1885), cols 2021-30). Opposition to the creation of provincial *parlements* was maintained by the *Parlement* of Paris after 1436.

[8]A.N. X1$^a$9199, f.104$^v$.

[9]Ibid., f.107$^r$. The ordinance confirming the union was proclaimed at Chinon on 7 Oct. 1428 (*Ordonnances,* xiii, 140) but the Béziers *Parlement,* reluctant to comply, remained operational for a time, and *arrêts* on cases transferred to Poitiers only appeared in May 1431 (A.N. X1$^a$9192, fos. 231$^r$ff, passim).

[10]A.N. X1$^a$9199, f.106$^v$.

[11]*A.H.-G.* MS.59, f.330$^v$.

[12]*Reg. consulaires,* ii (Lyon, 1926), 297.

de soffre, et le demourant de trait jusques a six charges',[13] to the besieged. Sympathy for the Richemont-Clermont-Pardiac coalition was, however, tainted by the fact that during the last months of 1428 Lyon had been plagued by the presence of *routiers* Vallete, Rodrigo de Villandrando and other 'soy-disans au conte de Pardiach'.[14] Furthermore, distance from Orléans appears to have considerably diminished concern for the town's plight.[15] Concern for Orléans was, at the outset, probably a localised matter confined largely to those interests in the immediate proximity of the town; however, as we shall see, the series of events following the relief of the place could in turn provide a cover for other, more ambitious interests.

The early months of 1429 witnessed some form of deadlock in the pattern of the siege. French confidence was not helped by the heavy defeat at Rouvray at the hands of an English force on 12 February.[16] However, while it was by no means certain that the besieged town would not have been able to hold out for a long period it was perhaps evident that unless some means was found to break the deadlock, the Anglo-Burgundian assault force might succeed by sheer attrition. This fact, and the need for remedy of the situation was, it seems, recognised by some at Poitiers. Jean Juvénal des Ursins later recalled that, while he was at Poitiers (during March 1429):

> ou le roy estoit. . . il vint ung compaignon raporter en ma presence a ung de ceulx qui avoient lors plus grant puissance prez du roy, et lequel me appella, et luy dit une maniere de destruire les Anglois, qui estoit vraye, se il eust mis a execucion ce qui il disoit; mais ledit seigneur et moy ne feusmes mye d'oppinion que il en fist riens, car la maniere estoit chose non accoustumee et tres deshonneste, et si croy que il ne l'eust peu faire.[17]

---

[13] Ibid., 298. On 22 February, not long after the French defeat at Rouvray, the consuls served 'torches' and 'confitures' to Jean I de Vailly, *premier Président* and Guillaume I Le Tur, also *Président* at Poitiers sent to the town possibly to secure further aid for the town of Orléans (ibid., 308).

[14] Ibid., 288ff.

[15] Aid was sought by the besieged Orléanais from several towns in the Midi but, if the response of Toulouse was typical, the reaction appears to have been at best lukewarm (see A. Thomas, 'Le Siège d'Orléans. Jeanne d'Arc et les capitouls de Toulouse', in *A. Midi* 1 (1889), 232-7).

[16] For the importance of the Rouvray defeat as the galvanising force upon Charles VII's *Conseil* in the attempt to provide a solution to the problem of Orléans, see C. Desama, 'Jeanne d'Arc et la diplomatie de Charles VII: l'ambassade française auprès de Philippe le Bon en 1429' (*A. Bourgogne* 40 (1968), 290ff. also Y. Lacaze, 'Philippe le Bon et le problème hussite: Un projet de croisade bourguignon en 1428-1429' (*R. hist.* 241 (1969), 93).

[17] *Écrits politiques de Jean Juvénal des Ursins,* ed. P.S. Lewis, i (*SHF,* Paris, 1978), 460.

A practical means of diminishing the power of the English investing force, both materially and psychologically, might be the attempt to detach their Burgundian allies from the siege. Shortly after Rouvray,[18] a small deputation left Orléans to treat with Burgundy, having at its head Poton de Saintrailles, *premier écuyer de l'Écurie* of Charles VII and an old ally of Philippe le Bon. The embassy's objective was to put certain proposals to Philippe regarding the position of the town, namely that: 'il. . . fit lever le siege. . . sous. . . condition que lui, au nom de son cousin d'Orleans y mettrait les gouverneurs, que la moitie des revenus serait au roy d'Angleterre et l'autre moitie au duc d'Orleans pour son entretien.'[19] In addition, the English could come and go as they wished within the town and the inhabitants would contribute 10,000 *écus d'or* annually towards the Lancastrian war budget in northern France.[20]

Failure by the Lancastrians to entertain these proposals represented a major diplomatic blunder which in the short term was directly responsible for the withdrawal of Burgundian forces from the besieging army before Orléans and the collapse of the residual English morale. In the longer term, the blatant unwillingness of the Lancastrian Council to entertain the notion of genuine power-sharing with Burgundy saw Philippe le Bon move into a closer alliance with Charles VII, a development which was to lead, in the face of continued English intransigence, to the Treaty of Arras in 1435. Yet while it is possible to view the split between the English and Burgundians over the proposals put by the Orléanais as merely the accidental outcome of a desperate attempt by the latter to break the deadlock in the siege and thus provide immediate relief for the town, it is equally plausible, as Desama has suggested, that initiative for the embassy's departure, together with an awareness of the effect of its proposals upon the Anglo-Burgundian alliance derived not, as is habitually assumed, from the Orléanais themselves, but from Charles VII's *Conseil*.[21] Desama further argues that it is within the much broader, and considerably anterior, perspective of both the build-up of arms and provisions to relieve Orléans, and the deliberate attempt by Charles VII's *Conseil* to detach Burgundian power from the allied

[18]See Desama, 'Jeanne d'Arc et la diplomatie de Charles VII', 290-1, for a discussion of the date of the embassy's departure.

[19]*La Chronique d'Antonio Morosini,* ed. G. Lefèvre-Pontalis, iii (*SHF,* Paris, 1901), 19.

[20]Ibid.

[21]Desama, 'Jeanne d'Arc et la diplomatie de Charles VII', 295-6.

force before the town, that the employment of Joan of Arc should properly be viewed.[22]

If Desama's view is correct, we would need to see Joan's 'Mission' not as the prime motivating force behind the movement to lift the siege of Orléans, but as merely a single, and perhaps relatively insignificant element within a much more ambitious political scheme.[23]

## The Chronology of Joan of Arc's stay at Chinon and Poitiers

The precise date of Joan of Arc's arrival at Chinon, and beyond this the chronology of her stay at Poitiers, judicial capital of the 'kingdom of Bourges', has been much debated by historians. With regard to Joan's arrival at Chinon, following the testimony of the *greffier de l'hôtel de ville de la Rochelle,* who wrote some months after the event, the date of 23 February has been generally accepted as a reliable one.[24] More recently however, Desama, relying on independent calcuations, has put Joan's arrival 'de preférence dans les derniers jours de février ou les premiers de mars, avec comme *terminus ad quem* le jeudi 3 mars'.[25]

Fresh light on this seemingly intractable problem is offered by the first register of the *Conseil* of the Poitiers *Parlement,* covering the years 1418-31.[26] At the date of Monday 7 March 1429[27] is recorded a session of the *Conseil.* The list of participants includes the names of three individuals whose presence at Poitiers was a comparatively rare occurrence: Regnault de Chartres, *Chancelier* of Charles VII and archbishop of Reims; Robert le Maçon, *seigneur* of Trèves in Anjou and formerly *Chancelier* (1418-22); finally, Robert de Rouvres, *vice-chancelier* of Charles VII, *maître des requêtes de l'Hôtel du Roi*

---

[22]Ibid., 296ff.

[23]Any objective assessment of the role played by Joan of Arc in Charles VII's military successes at Orléans and in the ensuing months appears impossible in view of what M. Harmand has called 'l'influence déplorable de la légende Johannique' ('Un document de 1435 concernant Houdan et la fin de l'occupation Anglaise dans l'ouest de l'Île de France', in *B. Soc. Antiq. France* 1975, 207 n.1) Desama's suspicion that the relief of Orléans may have derived from more rational forces than Joan of Arc's appearance ('Jeanne d'Arc et la diplomatie de Charles VII', 290-9), is equally applicable to events following the lifting of the siege.

[24]See T./L., *Procès,* ii, 55 n.3, for a discussion of the problem of the arrival date.

[25]C. Desama, 'La Première Entrevue de Jeanne d'Arc et de Charles VII à Chinon (mars 1429)', in *Analecta bollandiana,* 84 (1966), 117.

[26]*Archives départementales de la Haute-Garonne,* MS.59 (F. 49) (copy of the first register of the *Conseil* of the Poitiers Parlement covering the years 1418-31).

[27]See ibid., f.334ᵛ.

and bishop of Sèes. How can the presence of these men, normally in the company of the king and his *Conseil,* be explained at Poitiers?

Let us first examine the problem in respect of Robert de Rouvres. Rouvres was, first of all and beyond reasonable doubt, among those who had interrogated Joan at Chinon following her initial meeting with Charles VII; this is confirmed by Alençon's deposition at the Rehabilitation proceedings:

> postmodum [that is, following Charles VII's meeting with Joan] vero rex conclusit quod ipsa Johanna examinaretur per gentes Ecclesie; et fuerunt deputati episcopi Castrensis, confessor regis; Silvanectensis, Maglonensis et Pictavensis; magister Petrus *de Versailles,* postmodum episcopus Meldensis, et magister Jordanus *Morin* et quam plures alii, de quorum nominibus non recolit, qui eamdem Johannam interrogaverunt in ipsius loquentis presentia.[28]

It is the identity of *Maglonensis* which concerns us here. Vallet de Viriville saw the man intended by Alençon as being the 1429 occupant of the see, or, in other words, the incumbent at the time of the interrogations.[29] Quicherat offered no interpretation,[30] though his confusion over the matter led him to suggest *Silvanectensis,* another of those who participated in the interrogations, was the incumbent at the time that Alençon was speaking.[31] In fact Alençon intended neither of these interpretations: he referred to each man in terms of the office he occupied at the time of his death (*tempore sui obitus*). The same procedure was used by the other Rehabilitation witnesses. In the light of this fact, we can clearly identify Alençon's *episcopus Maglonensis* (Maguelonne) as none other than Robert de Rouvres himself,[32] Rouvres being bishop of Maguelonne from 1433 until his death, *c.* 1453.[33]

---

[28]Duparc, *Procès en nullité,* i, 381-2.

[29]See A. Vallet de Viriville, 'Charles VII roi de France et ses conseillers', in *L'Investigateur* 8 (1858), 17. It is difficult to see how this contention could apply to *Silvanectensis* (Senlis), for in Feb.-March 1429 the town was English-occupied, falling to Charles VII only in the following August.

[30]Quicherat, *Procès,* iii, 92 n.2.

[31]Ibid., 92 n.1.

[32]See, additionally, H.J. du Motey, *Jeanne d'Arc à Chinon et Robert de Rouvres* (Paris, 1927), 25 n.3.

[33]As a *maître des requêtes de l'Hôtel du Roi* and *vice-chancelier* of Charles VII, Rouvres's presence at Poitiers with the king and other members of the *Conseil* was perfectly logical. It is worthy of note that, despite his close involvement in the vetting of Joan of Arc, and the fact that he did not die until *c.* 1453, Rouvres was not called to give evidence at the Rehabilitation proceedings.

In view of this evidence, the presence of Rouvres at Poitiers so soon after the initial interrogations by 'theologians' at Chinon is most logically accounted for by the fact that he had recently travelled from Chinon in the company of Charles VII, Joan of Arc and other members of the *Conseil*, preparatory to beginning the second round of interrogations ordered by the king to be conducted at Poitiers. The presence of Regnault de Chartres and Robert le Maçon is most convincingly explained in the same fashion, for they were, like Rouvres, also members of Charles VII's *Conseil*.

This allows us to conclude beyond reasonable doubt that Joan of Arc was present with Charles VII at Poitiers on 7 March 1429. More important, is the date of 7 March equatable with the date of Joan's arrival at Poitiers? Difficulty in confirming this point derives from the fact that we have no reliable date, either for Joan's initial arrival at Chinon, or, apparently, for the termination of her stay at Poitiers. Let us examine the latter problem first. In the course of her trial at Rouen Joan explained that, following the termination of the interrogations at Poitiers, she was led once more to Chinon for a second interview with Charles VII.[34] She was, furthermore, able to attest that this interview took place 'in mense aprilis vel marcii, prout ei videtur. Dixitque: in proximo mense aprilis aut in presenti mense marcii essent duo anni elapsi, et. . . fuit post Pascha.'[35]

The fact that the interview took place unequivocally *after* Easter 1429 is extremely important. In the first place it allows a clear distinction between this encounter and the first meeting between Charles VII and Joan in late February 1429. I shall argue that it was at this second meeting that the interview of the 'sign' took place. More important for our immediate purpose is the fact that Joan's statement confirms that the second interview took place sometime *after* 27 March 1429 (this being Easter Day). Desama suggests that Joan's hesitation in dating the interview with conviction was probably due to it occurring so close to the juncture of March and April; he therefore suggested a date for Joan's return to Chinon for the second interview of somewhere between 27 March and 3 April 1429.[36] The very fact of

---

[34] A convincing argument in favour of placing the interview of the 'sign' after the termination of the interrogation at Poitiers is offered by C. Desama, 'Jeanne d'Arc et Charles VII: l'entrevue du signe (mars-avril 1429)', in *R. hist. Religions* 169-70 (1966), 29-46. On the distinction between this encounter and the earlier meeting between Charles VII and Joan of Arc, see Desama's 'La Première Entrevue', 113-26. Despite their being the most important recent contributions to the study of Joan of Arc's early career, these studies have been neglected by historians (see T./L., *Procès*, i-iii, passim).

[35] T./L., *Procès*, i, 135.

[36] Desama, 'Jeanne d'Arc et Charles VII', 38.

Charles VII's presence at Chinon in early April with Joan (which is additionally confirmed by independent evidence offered by Beaucourt)[37] immediately contradicts Boissonnade's view that Joan remained continuously with Charles VII at Poitiers for a total of six weeks. It also has an important bearing on the interpretation of certain aspects of the so-called *Résumé* document published by Quicherat[38]

In addition to this evidence of Joan's departure for Chinon once again late in March 1429, we are told by Joan's judges at Rouen that she was examined by certain religious during the space of one month, by others during the space of three weeks.[39] This suggests that certain of the 'theologians' had interrogated Joan both at Chinon and at Poitiers within the context of a stay of one month at the two places; others had simply participated at Poitiers only, during an overall stay of three weeks. This is adequately confirmed by Rehabilitation witnesses: Dunois, alluding to events at Chinon and Poitiers, attested that: 'transacto autem trium hebdomadarum aut unius mensis spatio, quo pendente tempore rex jusserat dictam Puellam examinari par clericos prelatos et doctores theologie.'[40] Raoul de Gaucourt similarly testified that Joan was visited 'spatio et tempore trium septimanarum et amplius, tam Pictavis quam Caynone'.[41] Finally Garinel, who was clearly referring to events at Poitiers alone, indicated a duration of 'quasi trium septimanarum'.[42] In view of these separate testimonies it seems reasonable to conclude that Joan's stay at Chinon and Poitiers amounted to periods of one week and three weeks respectively. However, and this will be apparent with a study of the '*Résumé*' document, this does not automatically mean that during these periods Joan was interrogated continuously, or by 'theologians' alone. Indeed, it seems perfectly clear from Alençon's account of events at Chinon,[43] that so far as the 'theologians' are concerned, interrogation 'during the space of one week' was reconcilable with a single visitation only, conducted within the context of an overall stay of one week. I shall argue later that certain factors suggest that this may have been the case at Poitiers, and that interrogation 'during the space of three weeks' may be, in reality, reconcilable with a single

[37]Ibid., 39 n.3.
[38]See Quicherat, *Procès,* iii, 391-2 (cf., also, ibid., v, 471-3).
[39]See T./L., *Procès,* i, passim.
[40]Duparc, *Procès en nullité,* i, 312.
[41]Ibid., 326.
[42]Ibid., 328.
[43]Ibid., 381-2.

visitation, conducted, as at Chinon, within the context of an overall stay of three weeks.

However, if we now compare our original date for Joan's arrival at Poitiers, 7 March 1429, with these separate pieces of evidence, we obtain a perfectly satisfactory agreement. A period of three weeks from 7 March would provide a date for the termination of Joan's stay at Poitiers of 28 March 1429. Therefore the return to Chinon in preparation for the second interview with Charles VII would have been accomplished by either the last days of March, or by the latest at the beginning of April. This is perfectly compatible with the independent suggestion of Desama;[44] more important, however, it tallies perfectly with Joan's own attestation.[45] If we now employ the date of 7 March in a retrospective manner to try to obtain the date of Joan's original arrival at Chinon, it is possible to argue, in the light of Joan's stay at Chinon lasting one week, the addition of two days for the journey to Poitiers[46] would provide us with the date of 27 February 1429. Once again this agrees with the tendency by Desama to place the event in the last days of February 1429. In conclusion, there is a strong case for adopting 7 March 1429 as the beginning of Joan's stay at Poitiers. At the least it is clear that the formerly popular date of 6 March for Joan's arrival at Chinon is completely untenable,[47] as those members of Charles VII's *Conseil* recorded in the session of the *Parlement* on 7 March 1429 would clearly, if they were to have interrogated Joan, have had to be in two places at the same time.

In the light of our earlier calculation, it is possible that Joan of Arc made her entry at Poitiers on Sunday 6 March 1429. Her appearance may have been deliberately anticipated through the medium of popular preaching.[48]

On 1 March 1429, according to my calculations some two days after Joan's arrival at Chinon, three of those theologians later ordered

[44]Desama, 'Jeanne d'Arc et Charles VII', 37-9.

[45]T./L., *Procès*, i, p. 135.

[46]See P. Boissonade, 'Une Étape capitale de la mission de Jeanne d'Arc: le séjour de la Pucelle à Poitiers, la quadruple enquête et ses résultats (1er mars - 10 avril 1429)', *R. Quest. Hist.* 113 (1930), 22.

[47]This date has been generally discounted by historians (see T./L., *Procès*, ii, p. 55 n.3), though on rather uncertain grounds.

[48]The importance of open-air preaching as a means of spreading news of political events (and possibly political propaganda) has been little studied for the fifteenth century, yet see B. Chevalier '*Tours: ville royale*' (Paris/Louvain, 1975), 198-202. With particular reference to Joan's victory at Orléans, see also M. Hardy, 'La Mission de Jeanne de'Arc prêchée à Perigueux en 1429', *B. Soc. Hist. et Archéol. du Perigord* 14 (1887), 50-5.

to interrogate Joan at Poitiers — Guillaume Aimery, Dominican and probably at the time Inquisitor of the Faith for that part of France loyal to Charles VII, Jean Lambert, another Dominican and member of the convent of that denomination in Poitiers, and Pierre Seguin, Carmelite — received payment from the mayor and *échevins* of Poitiers for preaching unspecified sermons to the community during Lent.[49] We know nothing of the content of these sermons, but it is perhaps not impossible that it was by this means that the news of Joan's coming and of her 'mission' was initially broadcast to those at Poitiers.

## The Theologians at Poitiers

The fundamental study of the Poitiers interrogations was prepared by M. Prosper Boissonnade to coincide with the quincentenary of Joan of Arc's visit to the town.[50] The effect of this study, whether deliberately intended or not, was to produce a dual distortion of the true picture afforded by the evidence at our disposal.[51] In the first place Boissonnade attempted to provide for the Poitiers interrogations a regularity of procedure and personnel comparable to those employed by the English at Rouen;[52] in fact our evidence does not permit such an interpretation. Secondly, Boissonnade's desire to see the work of the theologians assembled at Poitiers as the principal cause of the final sanction afforded for the Maid's 'mission', had the incidental effect of diminishing the earlier events at Chinon to a position of relative insignificance;[53] again, there appears to be no justification for this assumption.[54]

Let us examine the former contention first. Boissonnade's computation of the numbers of theologians assembled at Poitiers to interrogate Joan derived from a simple addition of those known to have interrogated Joan earlier at Chinon to those who are mentioned only in respect of events at Poitiers. This provided him with a total of

[49] Boissonnade, 36 n.1 and 37 nn. 1, 7.

[50] Ibid., 12-67.

[51] Severe criticism of Boissonnade's study is given by J. Dujardin, 'Les Débuts de la carrière de Jeanne d'Arc', *Séminaire d'Histoire Moderne, Université de Liège* (Liège, 1962). Besides its criticism of Boissonnade's work, Dujardin's study (still unpublished) is a perceptive analysis of events at Chinon and Poitiers, again largely ignored by historians of Joan of Arc.

[52] See Boissonnade, 42, 48.

[53] Ibid., passim.

[54] See Dujardin, 6ff.

100

seventeen or eighteen ecclesiastics.[55] However, contrary to his assumption, there is no evidence that Hugues de Combarel, bishop of Poitiers, Jean Raffanel, later bishop of Senlis, or Robert de Rouvres, later bishop of Maguelonne (Montpellier) took *any part in the interrogations whatever.*[56] In addition to this a further two religious, Regnault de Chartres, archbishop of Reims, and Gérard Machet, Confessor of Charles VII and later bishop of Castres, whose presence at Poitiers is indicated by the Rehabilitation proceedings, similarly cannot be proved to have taken an active part in the business of actually interrogating Joan.[57] Hence of Boissonnade's original total of seventeen to eighteen theologians we may safely attest an active number of only twelve:[58] Pierre de Versailles, abbot of Talmont and Jourdan Morin, members of the earlier Chinon group indicated by Alençon; plus Guillaume Aimery, Jean Lambert, Guillame Seguin and Pierre Turelure (all Dominicans); Pierre Seguin (Carmelite), Mathieu Menage, Guillaume le Marié, Jean de Mâcon, Jean Hérault and Jacques Maledon, whom our evidence indicates were present at Poitiers alone.[59] Similar doubts can be posed about the regularity of the proceedings at Poitiers. Boissonnade provided the 'commission' with a 'head', in the shape of Regnault de Chartres; failing him a 'deputy', Hugues de Combarel, bishop of Poitiers.[60] Yet, once again, our evidence provides no apparent justification for the assumption of any comparable formality. Finally, on the question of the regularity of the visitations by the theologians, it is impossible, in the absence of any formal record of the proceedings, to confirm the existence of a formal ecclesiastical tribunal at work.[61] At Rouen Joan alluded more than once to the presence of a formal register of

[55]Boissonnade, 27.

[56]See Duparc, *Procès en nullité*, i, passim.

[57]Where the names of Machet and Regnault de Chartres appear in relation to the business of interrogating Joan their role is an active one only in the sense that they order others of the theologians to this end (Duparc, *Procès en nullité*, i, 368, 471). In the case of Chartres, furthermore, this initiative derived not from his position as 'head' of the 'tribunal' but from his capacity as member of Charles VII's *Conseil* (ibid., p. 471). This suggests that the motive for the interrogation was not primarily doctrinal but political.

[58]See Duparc, *Procès en nullité*, i, 328, 334, 368, 375, 389 and 471.

[59]On the early careers of these individuals see Boissonnade, 32-40 (the most reliable part of his work, though nevertheless containing numerous analytical and factual errors).

[60]Ibid., 29.

[61]On Boissonnade's tendentious reconstruction of the Poitiers 'tribunal' see the critical analysis by Dujardin (23ff.). It may be preferable to view the Poitiers 'tribunal' simply as an *ad hoc* assembly put to the task of interrogating Joan (primarily for political motives) by Charles VII and his *Conseil*.

proceedings,[62] presumably compiled by the Poitiers theologians; but the very great discrepancies which must have occurred between a formal document of this nature, and the so-called *résumé* of the deliberations published by Quicherat, which we will examine later,[63] makes the inevitable existence of such a document a matter for speculation.

The evidence of the Rehabilitation proceedings provided reliable evidence of two independent visitations, attested by witnesses who had actually participated in them. Of these, the deposition of Thibault appears to militate strongly, when coupled with our evidence for the chronology of Joan's stay at Poitiers, against Boissonnade's view of a series of interrogations by theologians conducted continuously over a period of three weeks. Thibault recalled that: 'ipsa Johanna fuit in villa Pictavensi interrogata et examinata per defunctum magistrum Petrum de Versailles. . . et per magistrum Johannem Erault. . . cum quibus ipse loquens, de mandato defuncti domini Castrensis episcopi'.[64] Certain features of this statement are worthy of note. It was at this visitation, conducted on 22 March 1429, that Joan dictated her famous letter to the English captains. The fact that she was able to take this initiative suggests that by now all reasonable doubts about her faith had been overcome.[65] Yet if we have calculated the date of her arrival at Poitiers right,[66] the issue of this letter, and, implicit in it, the sanction by Charles VII's theologians of Joan's 'mission', came only two weeks after her initial appearance at Poitiers. This implies that the 'interrogations' at Poitiers could not have endured for a period of three weeks.

In the light of this contention, let us now consider the deposition of another eye-witness, Guillaume Seguin. Seguin attested that he was ordered 'ex parte regis',[67] by Regnault de Chartres and others of Charles VII's *Conseil*, together with other clerics, to interrogate Joan in the house of Jean Rabateau, *Avocat fiscal général* in the *Parlement*. Seguin assured that they were given additional instructions, namely: 'referendum consilio regis quid sibi de ea videretur'.[68] This

[62]See T./L., *Procès*, i, 71, 73 and 93.
[63]Below, pp. 108ff.
[64]Duparc, *Procès en nullité*, i, 368.
[65]As much is conceded by Boissonnade (42).
[66]Above, pp. 94ff.
[67]Duparc, *Procès en nullité*, i, 471.
[68]Ibid.

directive was duly followed, and the religious consequently reported to the *Conseil* that: 'fuerunt opinionis quod attenta necessitate eminenti et periculo in quo erat villa Aurelianensis, rex poterat de ea se juvare et eam mittere Aurelianis.'[69] Here a number of features are perfectly clear. First, that the initiative for this interrogation, supplied ostensibly by Regnault de Chartres, came not from a religious tribunal but from Charles VII's *Conseil.* The motive for the interrogation was not, therefore, doctrinal, but political. This is further stressed by Seguin's affirmation (and this is echoed in the *'Résumé'* document) that the primary purpose of the interrogation was not the question of Joan's faith, but rather the more pressing question of her political employment in the relief of Orléans.

A second point of importance is that, in the light of Seguin's desposition, the 'commission' reported its findings to Charles VII's *Conseil* on the strength of a single sitting only.[70] This would appear strange if Joan was to be the subject of a rigorous doctrinal inquiry conducted along formal lines over a period of three weeks. Neither here nor elsewhere in the Rehabilitation proceedings is there conclusive evidence for a continuous series of interrogations at the hands of theologians alone. This, together with the fact that, as we have argued, the matter of Joan's faith was resolved by 22 March, only two weeks after her arrival at Poitiers, gives rise to strong suspicion that at Poitiers, as at Chinon,[71] the conclusions of the theologians may have been arrived at in the course of a single visitation. In the light of this argument let us now examine the composition of the Chinon group delegated by Charles VII to interrogate Joan after their initial meeting. It is first of all by no means clear that their role in the sanction of Joan's 'mission' was any less important than that of the Poitiers 'commission', for without their initial approval, and Charles VII's subsequent satisfaction, events clearly might never have proceeded as far as Poitiers. Attempts to distinguish between the relative importance of the groups in terms of numbers alone (the procedure adopted by Boissonnade) are equally futile; indeed we have no means of proving that either of the groups had any numerical preponderance. Alençon attested the presence of six *gentes ecclesie* at Chinon, but added that there were 'quam plures alii, de quorum nominibus non recolit'.[72] The

[69]Ibid., 473

[70]See, for example, the *Chronique de la Pucelle,* ed. A. Vallet de Viriville (Paris, 1859), 275, which states that the theologians 'y furent (i.e., in Rabateau's house) plus de deux heures'. No mention is made of a further interrogation.

[71]Above, pp. 97-8.

[72]Duparc, *Procès en nullité,* i, 382.

difficulty in comparing the size of the groups is emphasised by the knowledge that Boissonnade certainly exaggerated the numbers of those present at Poitiers. Hence attempts to distinguish between the groups in terms purely of their relative importance in Joan's sanction may introduce distinctions of a kind that contemporaries at least were unaware of.

Yet at the same time it is possible to argue that a certain distinction between the work of the two groups may be found in respect of the *type* of sanction afforded to Joan's enterprise. At least one witness at the Rehabilitation proceeding suggests that before Joan left Chinon she was subject to an examination for virginity.[73] This is of considerable importance because, together with the interrogation by 'theologians' at Chinon, the early sanction afforded Joan resembled that given at Poitiers in the sense that it was of a complete kind. Yet, if this was so, it could be argued that such a sanction would immediately have negated the need for duplicate proceedings at Poitiers. It may thus be more pertinent to ask precisely what form of sanction was afforded Joan at Chinon, and in what way did it differ from that provided at Poitiers? The answer to this question may lie in the composition of the Chinon group (so far as it is known to us). First, two among those known to have interrogated Joan at Chinon, namely Hugues de Combarel, bishop of Poitiers[74] and Robert de Rouvres,[75] *maître des requètes de l'Hôtel du Roi* and *vice-Chancelier* of Charles VII, cannot be termed theologians in any sense of the word: they were lawyers of eminence and habitual members of Charles VII's *Conseil*. The application of the term 'theologian' in its strictest sense is equally difficult in respect of Gérard Machet,[76] Charles VII's Confessor, and Pierre de Versailles,[77] then abbot of Talmont; for both were additionally politicians of considerable status who almost certainly figured from time to time among the members of the royal *Conseil*. The same can probably be said for Jean Raffanel, later bishop of

---

[73]Ibid., 389 (*dép.* Pasquerel).

[74]For remarks on Combarel's career see 'Rec. des docs', *Arch. hist. Poitou* 29 (1898), 54 n.2. Also Favreau, *Poitiers,* 288 n.979 and 291 n.990.

[75]Robert de Rouvres's importance with the royal *Conseil* has already been discussed at length (above, passim).

[76]Machet had, earlier, close links with the House of Orleáns. On 13 May 1416 the duke of Orléans ordered his treasurer, Pierre Renier, to pay Machet 100l.t.: 'employer en certaines besongnes au concille general touchans notre bien honneur et prouffit' (B.N. P.O., 1787 (Machet), nos. 2-3).

[77]On the early political career of Versailles see A. Coville, 'Pierre de Versailles (1380?-1446)', in *Bibl. Éc. Chartes* 93 (1932), 210ff.

Senlis, and Jourdan Morin; and both display, additionally, a strong attachment to the Angevin faction at Charles VII's court.[78]

The presence of this group at Chinon at the time of Joan of Arc's arrival is best explained by the fact that they were already present in the town together with other member of the *Conseil,* Charles VII having been resident at Chinon since the winter of 1428-9. It is thus possible to view the group of 'theologians' who subjected Joan to her initial interrogation as simply a clerical portion of the overall complement of the *Conseil.* If this should be the case, we would need to view Joan's initial sanction as primarily a political act, a view which in turn gives events at Poitiers not so much a predominant role in Joan's sanction, but rather the appearance of a political *fait accompli.*

A study of the composition of the Poitiers 'commission' invites marked comparison with those known to have been present at Chinon. Here there is little evidence for any close relationship with Charles VII's *Conseil,* or for any marked political or administrative pre-occupation.[79] Like the *parlementaires* who left Paris after 1418 most were of Parisian origin, being former students and teachers of theology at the University of Paris. Since 1418 furthermore, the majority had been resident at Poitiers and were actively engaged in the study and teaching of theology within the town. Recourse to their more properly 'doctrinal' opinion was perhaps politic if Charles VII was to proceed in his employment of the Maid. Depending upon which side of the political fence one sat, their sanction might be considered tantamount (or, perhaps, under the circumstances, the only opinion readily comparable) to that of the university of Paris itself.

In this respect it is notable that, in terms of their intellectual formation, and, as a partial concomitant of this, their broader political attachments, the merger of the two groups produced a striking similitude. Of those permanently located at Poitiers, the majority had studied at the university of Paris. Certain among them, notably Guillaume Le Marié, Jean Lambert and Guillaume Seguin, comprised, together with Pierre de Versailles, Jourdan Morin and Gérard Machet, a more intimate circle linked by common intellectual and political sympathies.[80] In addition to this, a number, including Pierre

[78] See Boissonnade, 31 (on Raffanel), and S. Luce, *Jeanne d'Arc à Domrémy* (Paris, 1886), (*Preuves*), n. 1xix n.1. (on Morin).

[79] See Boissonnade, 34-40, and Favreau, *Poitiers,* 291-3.

[80] The figurehead of this group appears to have been Machet himself (see *Chart. Univ. Paris.,* iv, under *Machet*).

de Versailles, Jourdan Morin, Jean Lambert, Jean de Mâcon and Gérard Machet had, with Jean Gerson, participated in different sessions of the Council of Faith.[81] The nucleus of those assembled at Poitiers had therefore been intimately involved in the debate upon Jean Petit's justification of the murder of Louis of Orléans by Burgundian henchmen. Their almost uniform flight from Paris in the summer of 1418,[82] allied to the new threat of Anglo-Burgundian domination at Orléans, could thus mean that, like those assembled to try Joan at Rouen,[83] their attitude to the Maid might be dominated first and foremost by political considerations.[84]

### The Chronology and Significance of the Interview of the 'Sign' (March-April 1429)

After the termination of her stay in Poitiers Joan was led once again to Chinon for a second meeting with Charles VII. Evidence for this meeting is conveyed both by Joan's personal testimony at Rouen[85] and by the deposition of at least one Rehabilitation witness.[86] I argued earlier that this meeting took place either in late March or early April 1429.[87] Furthermore, certain logical factors suggest that it was then, and not as is habitually contended, during the first meeting between Charles VII and Joan of Arc at Chinon in late February, that the interview of the 'sign' took place.

In the first place it is clear that an event designed to display the sanctity of Joan's 'mission' could hardly have taken place before she had received the formal approbation of Charles VII's theologians. Indeed, had Joan displayed such a 'sign', as is often contended, during her first encounter with Charles VII, then the work of the theologians, both at Chinon and Poitiers, would have immediately become otiose;

[81]See ibid., 269ff.; also A. Coville, *Jean Petit: la question du tyrannicide au commencement du xv siècle* (Paris, 1932), chap. xiv (passim).

[82]See *Chart. Univ. Paris.*, iv, no. 2104, where the flight of six of those who interrogated Joan at Chinon and Poitiers: Machet, Versailles, Morin, Lambert, Aimery and Raffanel, is mentioned in 1418.

[83]See the recent study by P. Wolff, 'Le théologien Pierre Cauchon de sinistre mémoire', in *Mélanges. . . Edouard Perroy* (Paris, 1973), 553-70.

[84]Political rather than doctrinal considerations may have provided the impetus for Gerson's declaration in favour of the Maid (see G. Ouy, 'In Search of the Earliest traces of French Humanism: the Evidence from Codicology', *The Library Chronicle*, Univ. of Pennsylvania, 43 (no. 1), 1987, 13-14 and n. 24.

[85]T./L., *Procès*, i, 135.

[86]Duparc, *Procès en nullité*, i, 389 (*dép.* Pasquerel).

[87]Above, pp. 96-7.

it was precisely their function to affirm the sanctity of her 'mission'. The most plausible explanation of the significance of the interview of the 'sign' is, bearing this consideration in mind, offered by Desama,[88] who suggests that the first meeting between Charles VII and Joan saw the former venture his support for the Maid, conditional upon the satisfactory outcome of the interrogations by his theologians. The interview of the 'sign' thus appears as a logical consequence of the earlier meeting where Joan, having by now gained the approval of the theologians, could offer explicit proof of the sanctity of her 'mission'. Through the medium of a simple ceremony Charles VII could reciprocate by affirming his personal support for the venture. It is clear, however, that Charles VII's personal sanction in the matter was not designed merely to allow Joan's immediate departure for Orléans; for, if, as we have suggested, this exchange of faith took place late in March or early in April 1429, then fully two weeks were to pass before Joan was allowed to depart with an armed force for Blois. How may this delay be explained, give the 'perilous' situation of Orléans? A traditional explanation is merely that this delay was necessary in view of the need to assemble sufficient men and munitions to effect the raising of the siege. However an alternative view is offered by Desama,[89] who suggests that the real reason for the delay was the need to know the outcome of the negotiations with Burgundy begun much earlier, ostensibly by the Orléanais, concerning the possible transfer of Orléans into Burgundian hands. It was only on 21 April 1429, four days after the return of the deputation to Orléans carrying news of Burgundy's decision to withdraw its troops from the siege, that Joan was allowed by the *Conseil* to depart for Blois in preparation for the accomplishment of her 'mission'.[90]

Certain evidence suggests, however (and this quite apart from the rational supposition that the preparation of a force of sufficient proportions to relieve Orléans could hardly have been accomplished in two weeks) that the small force led by Joan by no means represented the entirety of the relieving army: rather, it was joined to a much larger body of men and munitions which had been accumulating over a much longer period, possibly since the original French defeat at Rouvray on 12 February 1429.[91] If this is an accurate projection of events, then it is possible that the appearance of this force, coupled to

---

[88]Desama, 'Jeanne d'Arc et Charles VII', 43ff., for what follows.

[89]C. Desama, 'Jeanne d'Arc et la diplomatie de Charles VII: l'ambassade française auprès de Philippe le Bon en 1429', *A Bourgogne* 40 (1968), 296-9.

[90]Ibid., 299.

[91]Ibid., 297 n.6.

the psychological effect of the withdrawal of Burgundian troops upon the residual English complement, would have been sufficient to relieve Orléans quite independently of Joan of Arc.

Another, and quite different explanation for the delay between the interview of the 'sign' and Joan's departure for Orléans, turns more specifically upon the question of why the interview of the 'sign' ever took place at all. Beyond this, what was its significance in relation to the so-called *Résumé* document compiled only a few days later?

On 10 March 1431 at Rouen Joan was asked: 'quando signum venit ad regem suum, qualem reverenciam ipsa fecit sibi, et utrum illud venerit ex parte Dei.' She replied: 'quod ipsa regraciata fuit Deo de hoc quod liberavit eam a pena que sibi fiebat per clericos de illa parte qui arguebant contra ipsam. . . Dicit, ultra, quod clerici cessaverunt arguere eam quando habuerunt signum predictum.'[92] This revelation invites comment, particularly in view of the fact that, as I have argued,[93] the interrogations at Poitiers, whose purpose was to banish all doubts about Joan's faith, had officially terminated, apparently on a favourable note, several days before the interview of the 'sign' took place at Chinon. In fact Joan's statement seems to indicate a serious residue of doubt[94] on the part of the theologians, which had endured even beyond the termination of the formal examination at Poitiers. The additional fact that this opposition was apparently silenced in the aftermath of the interview of the 'sign', might suggest that the event was contrived deliberately with this end in view. This would, if true, necessitate a review of Charles VII's role in the affair. Far from appearing as the passive instrument of Joan's personal ambition, Charles could become, through his employment of the interview of the 'sign', an active determinant in the employment of the Maid for political ends.

The interpretation of the interview of the 'sign' as predominantly a political device to stifle opposition towards Joan assumes an enhanced significance when considered in conjunction with the so-called *résumé* document. One of the most noticeable features of this document is the very broad, even nebulous, terms of its support for Joan's enterprise, couched in cautious and negative language.[95] This

---

[92]T./L., *Procès,* i, 117. Joan's statement seems to provide conclusive proof that the interview of the sign took place *after* the interrogations by theologians.

[93]Above, pp. 96ff.

[94]This element of doubt, not to say derision, was apparently not confined to the theologians (Desama, 'Jeanne d'Arc et Charles VII', 43-5).

[95]See below, pp. 110ff., for a discussion of this aspect of the *'Résumé'* document.

again would appear strange if it were really the product of a rigorous doctrinal examination conducted over a period of three weeks by Charles VII's most eminent theologians. In fact, as I shall argue, it may be nothing of the sort. In the first place, the terminology of the document is suggestive less of complete confidence in the Maid, than of a lingering scepticism; scepticism which is overcome, as it was earlier in the interrogations at Poitiers, by shifting the emphasis away from the more specific matter of Joan's spiritual credibility and onto the question of Charles VII's immediate political necessity.[96] It is perhaps to this undercurrent of scepticism that we should look for the real reason for the compilation of the 'Résumé' document.

It is possible, as I have argued earlier,[97] that, in the light of Joan's statement at Rouen, the interrogations by theologians at Poitiers, far from providing a satisfactory doctrinal sanction for her employment, may have initiated opposition to her on precisely these grounds. If, as we have suggested, the interview of the 'sign' was deliberately contrived to suppress this opposition, then it is plausible to suggest that the issue of the 'Résumé' document was in some senses complementary to this act, its object being to provide broad political justification for Joan's employment in the face of more specific doctrinal opposition. In this light certain features of the document, notably the cautious terms of its assent, the clear lack of reference to any regular doctrinal examination, and, also, its apparently wide dissemination, become more comprehensible. It is perhaps correctly viewed not as the résumé of a doctrinal enquiry, but, rather, as an instrument of royal propaganda intended to vindicate Charles VII's employment of the Maid for political purposes, in the face of opposition provoked by the inquiry itself.

### The 'Résumé' document published by Quicherat

In the third volume of his *Procès de condamnation et de réhabilitation de Jeanne d'Arc,* Quicherat published the document (discovered earlier by Buchon) which he entitled the 'Résumé des conclusions données par les docteurs réunis à Poitiers (mars-avril 1429)'.[98] This document has since received little critical scrutiny, yet it reveals much of importance in relation to our understanding of the early

---

[96] See below, pp. 113n. 120.

[97] See above, p. 107.

[98] Printed in Quicherat, *Procès,* iii, 391-2. My analysis of this document owes much to the penetrating study by J. Dujardin ('Les Débuts de la carrière de Jeanne d'Arc', *Séminaire d'Histoire Moderne, Université de Liège* (Liège, 1962), 20ff.).

stages of Joan of Arc's career. Not the least remarkable feature of the document was its very wide distribution. This was recognised by Quicherat, who wrote that the '*Résumé*' 'paraît avoir été repandu par le gouvernement de Charles VII à un grand nombre d'examplaires'.[99] He added, however, that 'notre texte français n'a toutefois rien d'officiel'.[100] Quicherat's projection was confirmed later by Lefèvre-Pontalis, who pointed out the presence of similar specimens in different chronicles relating to the Dauphiné, Tournai, Scotland and various German towns.[101] The existence of these other exemplars, similar to that published by Quicherat, appears to militate against the view that Quicherat's document need necessarily represent the archetypal *Résumé* document. It may be preferable to view it, along with the other examples, as merely a local copy[102] of an official circular or propaganda sheet (now probably lost) emanating from a central source, possibly the *Conseil* of Charles VII.

A point of additional importance in relation to the '*Résumé*' document may be seen in the fact that where it has been incorporated in the works of chroniclers it is usually accompanied by other pieces relating to Joan of Arc's career — most notably the letter to the English captains, reputedly dictated by the Maid during the course of her stay at Poitiers.[103] Writing in relation to their incorporation in the work of the German chronicler, Windecke, Lefèvre-Pontalis suggested that these documents represented, in reality, 'actes de source pareille, émanés très vraisemblablement de la cour de Charles VII'.[104] If this should be the case the '*Résumé*' document and Joan's letter to the English captains appear rather less as disinterested and unconnected statements on the part of their compilers, rather more as instruments of royal propaganda, issued deliberately with a view to publicising news of Joan's 'mission' to a wider audience. Successive stages of the Maid's career were, apparently, accompanied by similar bulletins

[99]Ibid., v, 472.

[100]Ibid., 473.

[101]See *La Chronique d'Antonio Morosini*, ed. G. Lefèvre-Pontalis, iii (*SHF*, Paris, 1901), 98 n.4. Also, by the same author, *Les sources allemandes de l'histoire de Jeanne d'Arc. Eberhard Windecke* (Paris, 1903), 32-4.

[102]The fact that Quicherat's version was merely a copy of an official document would explain why, in his own words, it 'n' a toutefois rien d'official'.

[103]Lefèvre-Pontalis, *Les Sources,* 142. This important study has received little attention from historians, yet it contributes much to our understanding of the way in which royal propaganda could play an important part in arousing enthusiasm for Joan of Arc's 'mission'.

[104]Ibid., 50.

having a French provenance.[105] The careful preservation of these documents by a number of independent chroniclers offers, perhaps 'preuve... de la circulation, non seulement à travers la France, mais à travers l'Europe, de documents spéciaux, quasi officiels, relatifs à Jeanne d'Arc et aux phases successives de sa prodigieuse action'.[106]

M. Lefèvre-Pontalis remarked many years ago on the importance of 'l'émission et la transmission, à cette époque... de Bulletins officiels contenant exposé, ou... narration complète, des événéments les plus importants'.[107] This advice has been largely ignored in relation to the early stages of Joan of Arc's career but it is nevertheless arguable that it has an important bearing upon the correct interpretation of the 'Résumé' document, and, beyond this, the real reason for its compilation.

Bearing this in mind, if we turn our attention to the 'Résumé' document itself, two questions predominate: first, can the document be seen as a genuine résumé of conclusions presented by a regular ecclesiastical tribunal? Second, if this is not the case, how should the document be interpreted? The date of issue of the document is, first of all, lacking. Yet it affirms that at the time of its compilation Joan of Arc had been in Charles VII's company 'bien par l'espace de six sepmaines'.[108] Difficulty in interpreting this statement stems from the fac that it is not clear whether the period of six weeks indicated runs from the time of Joan's arrival at Chinon, or from the beginning of her stay at Poitiers. A period of six weeks from both dates[109] would, however, give a date for the issue of the document of c. 9 – c. 18 April 1429. This means that the issue of the document came two or three weeks after the end of the Poitiers interrogation, and one or two weeks after the interview of the 'sign'. At first sight this might appear curious, in view of the fact that it was precisely the function of these events to

[105] Ibid., 142-3 and passim.

[106] Ibid., 139. News of Joan's exploits, possibly conveyed by quasi-official bulletins similar to the 'Résumé' document, had reached Rome early in 1429, being incorporated in the *Collectarium Historiarum* of Jean Dupuy, bishop of Cahors, who was resident in Rome when Orléans was relieved. The appendix to Dupuy's work, devoted to Joan's victories, contains detailed reference to Joan's interrogation by theologians at Chinon and Poitiers but deliberately omits aspects of the interrogations which were doctrinally dangerous (A. Dondaine, 'Le Frère Prêcheur Jean Dupuy, évêque de Cahors et son témoinage sur Jeanne d'Arc', *Arch. Frat. Pred.* 12 (1942), 118-84. However, two other versions of the *Collectarium* found by Dondaine in Spain contain those parts omitted in the Rome version, and in a greatly-expanded form (see *Arch. Frat. Pred.* 38 (1968), 31-41).

[107] Lefèvre-Pontalis, 'Les sources', 140.

[108] Quicherat, *Procès*, iii, 392, 11. 4-5.

[109] 26 February and 7 March respectively (above, pp. 94ff.).

affirm the sanctity of Joan's 'mission'. This, together with the broad and numerous dissemination of the document, suggests that it was by no means preaching to the already (in a *de facto* manner at least) converted. In this sense it appears, rather, as a broad political justification for Joan's employment, prepared, perhaps, for consumption by a wider, and possibly less immediately interested audience.[110] In addition the '*Résumé*' document affords no preference, in terms of the approbation accorded to the Maid, either to the visitation by theologians at Poitiers, or even to events at Poitiers alone. Indeed any specific reference to events at Chinon or Poitiers is omitted: rather it is indicated that approbation was given, in a cumulative manner, 'par prudence humaine, en enquerant de sa vie, ses meurs et de son entencion. . . et par devote oroison'.[111] The fact, furthermore, that these observations were conducted 'depuis la venue de laditte Pucelle', [112] may mean (if it is the arrival at Chinon which is intended) that events at Chinon and Poitiers were viewed as a whole. Certainly there are no grounds for assuming that the document refers to events at Poitiers alone; and we have argued earlier that to distinguish between events at the two places in terms of the importance of their role in the Maid's sanction is unwarranted.[113]

In this sense it may be unwise to view the document as the product of an inquiry conducted solely at Poitiers. In respect of its being the product of a regular doctrinal inquiry it is, furthermore, apparent that in the terms of the document the inquiry by theologians represented only a small contribution to the overall matter of Joan's sanction. We are told that during her stay with Charles VII (again, possibly at Chinon and Poitiers) Joan received the approval (in the negative manner that 'en elle on ne trouve point de mal')[114] of 'toutes gens. . . soyent clers, gens d'eglise, gens de devocion, gens d'armes, femmes, veufves et autres'.[115] Here no precedence is afforded to the 'theologians' in the matter of Joan's sanction above that of the 'gens d'armes,

---

[110]The production of this document at a point between 9 Apr. (arrival at Chinon envisaged) and 18 Apr. (arrival at Poitiers envisaged) 1429 would mean that it had begun to be circulated 3 to 12 days before Joan's departure from Chinon in preparation for the siege. The date of 18 Apr. is particularly compelling, since in this case the issue of the document would have come just one day after Joan's final sanction by the *Conseil,* and one day after the return of the Orléanist deputation to Orléans carrying news of Burgundy's withdrawal from the siege.

[111]Quicherat, *Procès,* iii, 391, 11. 8-11.

[112]Ibid., 1. 17.

[113]Above, pp. 99ff.

[114]Quicherat, *Procès,* iii, 392, 1. 17.

[115]Ibid., 11.5-7.

femmes, veufves et autres': rather their work is viewed as an ensemble.

Finally the contribution of a regular ecclesiastical tribunal to this document is highly questionable. We have no mention of the terms 'Commission', 'Tribunal', 'Inquiry', 'Judges', or even 'theologians'. Furthermore the wording of the document counsels strongly against such a regular source: we have the guarded words: 'Le Roy, attendue (la) necessite de luy et de son royaulme, et considere les continues prieres de son povre peuple envers Dieu. . . ne doit deboutter ne dejetter la Pucelle, qui se dit estre envoyee de par Dieu pour luy donner secours, non abstant que ces promesses soyent euvres humaines; ne aussy ne doit croire en lui tantost et legierement.'[116] The juxtaposition of 'ne point deboutter ne dejetter' with the immediate proviso 'ne aussy ne doit croire en lui tantost et legierement' is suggestive less of confidence in the Maid than of a marked residual doubt on the part of those who compiled the document. How could scepticism of the Maid endure in the aftermath of a prolonged doctrinal examination? In a different sense, if complete confidence in the Maid had been afforded by the examination by theologians, why should the production of this document, coming as it did some weeks after the interrogations, be necessary at all? In the light of our earlier discussion on the distribution of this document it is perhaps advisable to view it not as a *résumé* of the conclusions reached by theologians, but as a form of broad political justification for the Maid's employment at Orléans, including as a single (and by no means predominant) element the favourable opinion of the theologians themselves. Such a view naturally raises problems in respect of the 'register' supposedly compiled by the theologians at Poitiers during the course of their interrogations. While it may be going too far to suggest that no record of proceedings was kept,[117] it seems impossible to view the document published by Quicherat as a *résumé* of those proceedings.

Why was the document issued, and what were its consequences for Joan's career? Hence, two different interpretations could be equally valid. As I argued earlier, certain indications suggest that opinions towards Joan, both among the theologians and within Charles VII's

---

[116]Ibid., 391, 11.1-7.

[117]Joan alluded at Rouen to the presence of a register of proceedings (T./L.; *Procès,* i, 71, 73 and 93) but Dujardin ('Les Débuts de la carrière de Jeanne d'Arc', *Séminaire d'Histoire Moderne, Université de Liège* (Liège, 1962), 32 n.129) rightly remarks that the absence of this document is 'surtout troublant. . . dans le procès de réhabilitation où il n'apparaît pas que ce texte, pourtant capital, ait été recherché; jamais on n' a posé la question à un témoin, et jamais il n'en a parlé.'

*Conseil* generally, were sharply divided from the moment of her arrival at Chinon.[118] It is possible that opposition to her employment was accumulating throughout her stay at Chinon and Poitiers, and that Charles VII's removal of Joan once again to Chinon, and the ensuing interview of the 'sign', was a device to quieten opinion against her. In this sense the *'Résumé'* document could be viewed as a double-edged device both to stifle more specific objections to Joan's employment nearer home while at the same time accumulating support for the Maid further afield. If this is an accurate interpretation, then it might be further suggested that motivation for Joan's political employment despite this opposition, derived predominantly from a certain faction or factions within Charles VII's *Conseil.* Another seemingly equally valid interpretation of the document's function may be, following the suggestions of Lefèvre-Pontalis, that it is simply one of a number of pieces of royal propaganda issued in support of Joan of Arc's 'mission', whose general purpose may have been to initiate enthusiasm for the venture. Such a view would clearly mean that the support aroused for the Maid could owe as much to the effectiveness of royal propaganda as to Joan's personal charisma. It would in turn afford Charles VII a more active role in her employment than has previously been afforded.

Whichever is the correct interpretation, the strongly political tone of the *'Résumé'* document is evident in the final clause: 'Le roy, attendu la probacion faicte de ladicte Pucelle. . . et considere sa responce, qui est de demonstrer signe divin devant Orleans. . . ne la doit point empescher d'aler a Orleans,. . . mais la doit faire conduire honnestement.'[119] Final proof of the Maid's divine agency was to be the lifting of the siege: a partisan stipulation indeed in view of the circumstances.[120]

### The Coronation at Reims

Only a matter of days after Joan of Arc's appearance at Orléans, the siege, which had by now lasted several months, was successfully raised. It is impossible to gauge realistically the part played by the Maid in what was perhaps, at root, a triumph of royal diplomacy and royal propaganda. However the inspiration provided by this victory

[118]See especially, C. Desama, 'Jeanne d'Arc et Charles VII', 43-5.

[119]Quicherat, *Procès,* iii, 392, 11. 16-22.

[120]More important is the fact that this provision once again shifts the burden of responsibility in the matter of Joan's agency away from the theologians and on to her own success or failure at Orléans.

was perhaps the primary motivation for the attempt to have Charles VII crowned at Reims, long the traditional anointing-place of French kings. At the same time it is perhaps unwise to assume that the march to Reims was necessarily an inevitable result of the victory at Orléans, or that the venture received the wholehearted support of all of Charles VII's nobility. Indeed it is impossible to assess at exactly what point the enterprise was envisaged as a practical objective. The turnout of Charles VII's nobility at the coronation, which by all accounts appears to have been considerable, may well have owed rather less to the charismatic influence of Joan of Arc than to well-tried political methods of persuasion.

Partisans of Joan's cause were keen to portray noble support for the venture as a form of spontaneous recognition of her 'mission'. In his *Chronique d'Alençon*, Perceval de Cagny related that 'touz chevaliers et escuiers et autres gens de guerre (furent) tres bien contens de servir le roi en sa compagnie, combien qu'ilz furent petitement souldoyez'.[121] Another unashamed patriot, Jean Chartier, wrote that 'par le moyen de. . . Jehanne la Pucelle venaient tant de gens de toutes parts devers le roy pour le servir a leurs despens'.[122] A rather more prosaic (yet no less effective) interpretation of events is offered by a deliberation of the *Conseil* of the Poitiers *Parlement* on 30 December 1429.[123] The debate followed the receipt of:

> certaines lettres royaux presentees ou bailees a la court par maistre Jacques Hamelin, lieutenant-general du baily des ressorts et exemptions de Touraine, Anjou et le Maine, a ce qu'elles feussent leues et publiees, et par lesquelles lettres le roy mandoit et commetoit audit bailly, audit maistre Jacques Hamelin, son lieutenant et a maistre Jacques Dreux, procureur du roy, la cognoissance de reformer les vassaux qui n'avoient este au mandement ou armee du roy faite pour aller a son couronnement et sacre a Reims, et les punir, etc., non obstant appellations et oppositions, etc.

After deliberating upon their content, the *Parlement* decided 'icelles lettres veues, . . . que point ne seront leues ne publiees en cette court ne ailleurs de par icelle; mais avant que on die ceste deliberation audit Hamelin, elles seront monstrees aux advocats et procureur du roy pour scavoir s'ilz vouldront riens dire sur ce'.[124]

---

[121]Cit. by P. Contamine, *Guerre, Etat et Société à la fin du Moyen âge*, (Paris, 1972), 247 n. 73.

[122]Ibid., n.74.

[123]For what follows, see *A.H.-G.* MS.59, fos. 343ᵛ-344ʳ.

[124]Ibid., f.344ʳ.

The publication of letters which might indicate less than universal support for Charles VII's coronation was perhaps viewed by the *Parlement* as an irresponsible step and, despite the clarity of the king's directive, no attempt appears to have made to carry it out. Similar responsibility for Charles VII's 'needs' was displayed by the *Parlement* during the course of Joan of Arc's trial at Rouen.[125]

Some indication of the underlying reason for the issue of this directive by Charles VII, and with it a more realistic explanation of the support for the Reims coronation, appears in litigation before the *Parlement* on 10 January 1430. The plaintiff, Louis de La Tour, argued that: 'il a este et est notoire que le roy a fait son mandement pour le voyage de son couronnement a Reims, et que chacun tenans en fief et arriere fief y alast sur peine de confiscacion de corps et de biens.'[126] La Tour, who had obeyed the directive and travelled to Reims, had apparently employed the non-appearance of Breton *seigneurs* Jean Angier and Jean de Malestroit as a pretext for the seizure of the latters' property, situated in Anjou. Somewhat later, on 28 January 1432, Pierre de La Halete reiterated La Tour's claim that 'le roy, pour aler a son sacre et couronnement a Reims fist son arriere ban, que touz tenans en fief et arriere fief de lui y alassent soubz penie de confiscacion'.[127] In this case, La Halete had employed the edict as a pretext for the confiscation of Hugués Catus's fief of Saint-Generoux, in Anjou, despite the fact that Catus claimed that he had sent his son mounted and armed to Reims, and, in response to a similar edict issued by Charles VII at Sens, had sent one Jean Bertran equipped with five or six horses. In addition to indicating that support for the march to Reims was by no means universally displayed by Charles VII's nobility our evidence suggests that, for those who did make the journey, the convocation of the *ban et arrière-ban*, and with it the threat of loss of noble status allied to seizure of person and goods, might have played a more important part in their appearance than the mere presence of Joan of Arc.[128]

News of the coronation was joyfully received by the *Parlement* at Poitiers on 28 July 1429:

> ce jour, ainsi que on vouloit appeler advocaz pour plaider, vindront les nouvelles comment le xvij jour de ce mois le roy

[125]Below, pp. 119ff.

[126]A.N. X1ᵃ9199, f.216ʳ (cf. A.N. X1ᵃ9192, fos. 310ᵛff. and A.N. X1ᵃ9193, fos. 56ʳff.).

[127]A.N. X1ᵃ9200, f.17ᵛ (cf. ibid., fos. 81ᵛff.).

[128]For comments on the increasingly severe measures taken by Charles VII before 1429 to compel his nobility to fulfil their military obligations, see Contamine, 256-7.

nostre seigneur, Charles vij^me avait este sacrez et couronnez a Reims. Et pour (ce) a este sursus de plaider ce jour et les nouvelles notifier a ceulx de la ville, ou a este assemble a l'eglise cathedral de Poitiers; et ille a este chante *Te Deum Laudamus* et la messe du Saint Esprit celebrer tressolement.[129]

For the *parlementaires*, exiled at Poitiers since 1418, knowledge of the coronation must have engendered hopes of a return to Paris. Excessive preoccupation with such thoughts caused Jean d'Asnières, *greffier criminel* at Poitiers, to write at the beginning of the 1430-1 session of the *Parlement*: 'ce jour, apres que la messe du Saint Esperit fut chantee solemnelement en la chapelle du Palais royal a *Paris*, messeigneurs les Presidens et conseillers s'en entrerent en la chambre de Parlement.'[130] In the event, these expectations were not to be finally fulfilled for a further seven years.

Support for the coronation of Charles VII, though perhaps less spontaneous and more overtly political than the chroniclers would have us believe, was by all accounts very considerable indeed. It is also arguable that this event, contrasted with the subdued manner in which Charles VII had adopted his father's title nearly seven years earlier, and considering also Henry VI's minority, was of great psychological importance for all parties involved in the war. In the short term, at Compiègne, it had the effect of drawing Burgundy into a closer alliance with Charles VII; in the slightly longer term the English, stung to retaliation through the medium of Henry VI's counter-coronation in Paris and the trial of Joan of Arc at Rouen, were forced to increase their financial commitment to the war at a time when enthusiasm at home was waning.[131]

Yet despite the impact of the coronation another six years were to lapse before a final settlement was reached with Burgundy at Arras, another twenty-four before the English were finally driven from France. The real reasons for this 'delay' lay not so much in the 'treacherous' abandonment of Joan of Arc as in the complicated pattern of individual political interests which had developed throughout the years of Lancastrian occupation and alliance with Burgundy. It will be argued later that to introduce nationalistic overtones into a conflict which was nevertheless, at root, merely a phase in the attempt by the French crown to subdue the individual ambitions of its more powerful vassals is an anachronistic view of events.

[129]A.N. X1^a9199, f.186^r.

[130]A.N. X2^a18, at the date of 13 November 1430.

[131]See M.H. Keen, *England in the Later Middle Ages* (London, 1975), 391-2, 418-23.

Partisans of Charles VII's cause certainly felt that the coronation and the succession of military victories which followed it, culminating in the victory over the English at Patay, should have provided the basis for 'recovery' of the kingdom and the expulsion of the enemy. Jean Juvénal des Ursins later complained: 'se la chose eust este bien conduite, vous aviez, sans difficulte, recouvre toute vostre seignourie. Lesquelles obeissances a vous faictes sont retournes comme a leur totale destruccion et perdicion.'[132] Jean Chartier agreed wholeheartedly, but was simultaneously more specific about the reason for the failure to employ the initiative gained at Orléans against the English:

> disoient plusiers que, si ledit sire de la Trimouille et autres du Conseil du roy eussent lors voulu recueiller tous ceux qui venoient au service du roy, . . ils eussent peu facilement recouvrer tout ce que les Anglois usurpoient dans le royaume. Mais on n'ozoit parler. . . contre ledit sire de la Trimouille, combien que chacun voyoit clairement que la faute venoit de lui.[133]

Nineteenth-century French historians generally endorsed Chartier's view and held the individual ambitions of La Trémoïlle responsible, both for the 'treacherous' abandonment of Joan of Arc, and, in a broader sense, the failure of Charles VII to capitalise upon the advantage won at Orléans and Reims. Yet the ink spilt on Joan of Arc would have been better employed evaluating the individual ambitions of those members of Charles VII's nobility embroiled in the affair. A warlord such as Jean II duke of Alençon, whose lands lay in English hands, might be understandably keen to lend his support to Joan of Arc's activities; yet his motive for doing so might be no more 'patriotic', no less self-interested, than those of La Trémoïlle, who, having relatives in both the English and the Burgundian camps, might understandably be keener to restore the political *status quo ante* with Burgundy and thus preserve the interests of his family as a whole.

In the weeks following the coronation this war of differing personal ambitions was waged within Charles VII's *Conseil.* Ultimately those in favour of negotiation with Burgundy won the day. For them the way of peace might clearly be more profitable than the way of war. Among the members of the *Conseil,* La Trémoïlle appears to have been predominant among those in favour of negotiation with Burgundy. This strategy was, however, not without its opponents: the *Chronique*

---

[132]*Écrits politiques de Jean Juvénal des Ursins,* ed. P.S. Lewis, i (*SHF,* Paris, 1978), 321.

[133]Jean Chartier, *Histoire de Charles VII,* ed. D. Godefroy (Paris, 1661), 28.

*de la Pucelle* relates that 'il y avoit aucuns en la compaignee du roy qui avoient grand desir qu' il (*ie.*, Charles VII) retournast vers la riviere de Loire, et lui conseillerent fort; auquel conseil il adhera fort. Et estoit de leur opinion.'[134] The retreat across the Seine was to take place at Bray, which had a good firm bridge. The occupation of the place by Lancastrian forces, however, meant that the passage was temporarily prevented. At this, the *Chronique* assures:

> les ducs d'Alencon, de Bourbon et de Bar, et les contes de Vendosme et de Laval, et tous les capitaines furent bien joyeux et contents, pour ce que ladite conclusion de passer fut contre leur gre et volonte. Et estoient d'opinion que le roy devoit passer oultre pour tous jours conquester, veue la puissance qu'il avoit et que ses ennemis ne l'avoient ose combattre.[135]

Yet the decision to retreat below the Loire meant, in the longer term, that the immediate scenario for the satisfaction of the individual ambitions of Charles VII's nobility was to be the 'kingdom of Bourges' itself. Among those areas most seriously affected was Poitou, where the rival ambitions of Alençon, Richemont and La Trémoïlle engendered a conflict of crippling proportions which was not resolved until Charles VII's forceful subjugation of the rebel magnates in the 1440s. The need to reach a firm political settlement with Burgundy in 1435 might thus be motivated by considerations other than simply the war with the English.

It is within this sphere of conflicting ambitions among Charles VII's nobility that the military career of Joan of Arc after Reims should be viewed. She became a pawn in the hands of those keen to mount an offensive in Normandy. The extent to which 'concern' for her might derive from individual political considerations is conveyed by Guillaume Gruel, Richemont's (admittedly partisan) biographer. On one occasion, he wrote, Alençon, La Hire and others asked Joan to disclose her strategy. Joan replied, allegedly, that she wished to take up arms against Richemont. At this, the chronicler reported: 'ils lui respondirent que si elle alloit . . . elle trouveroit bien a qui parler; et qu'il en avoit en la compaignie qui plutost seroient a lui que a elle; et qu'ilz ameroient mieulx lui et sa compaignie que toutes les pucelles du royaume de France.'[136]

---

[134]*Chronique de la Pucelle,* ed. A. Vallet de Viriville (Paris, 1859), 325.

[135]Ibid.

[136]Guillaume Gruel, *Chronique d'Arthur de Richemont,* ed. A. Le Vavasseur (*SHF,* Paris, 1890), 71.

The Treaty of Compiègne, in August 1429, signified the effective end of official support for Joan of Arc's activities. Yet the decision to abandon the Maid provided the English with the opportunity to employ her earlier association with Charles VII deliberately to discredit the latter, and to diminish the advantage won by the Reims coronation. The fact that the coronation of Henry VI in Paris 1431 appears to have been arranged in conjunction with events at Rouen might suggest that this was the underlying motive of the trial.

Once again, therefore, Joan of Arc was to be put to the test for predominantly political reasons. It was, in addition, the determination of the Lancastrians to identify her with Charles VII's successes, rather than any realistic part she may have played, which may have been primarily responsible for the creation of the Joan of Arc legend. If the trial at Rouen represented, at root, an attempt by the Lancastrians to discredit Charles VII by way of his association with the Maid, then from the moment that proceedings were put in motion it may have been clear to many at Poitiers — not least those theologians who some two years previously had given their active sanction to Joan's 'mission' — that any expression of concern with events at Rouen should be deliberately suppressed. This feeling was perhaps enhanced by the fact that Charles VII's arrival at Poitiers was anticipated early in 1431. On 23 January the *Parlement* announced that:

> quand le roy vendra prochainement a Poitiers la cour ira audevant luy faire la reverence, attendu qu'il n'y fut depuis son couronnement. Et est messire Jean de Vaily, President, chargie de parler luy recommander justice et qu'il plaise garder l'Eglise et le Domaine d'icelle, et luy remonstrera le fait des pilleries. Et parlera de la non-residence des seneschaux et baillis et aussy de l'assignation que la cour a sur la traicte.[137]

Charles did not finally arrive at Poitiers until 24 March 1431,[138] the official purpose of his visit being the convocation of the general Estates of the Languedoïl. On 27 March 1431[139] Regnault de Chartres, *Chancelier,* Robert de Rouvres, *vice-Chancelier* and *maître des requêtes de l'Hôtel,* Robert le Maçon, *seigneur* of Trèves and others of the royal *Conseil,* joined with the *Conseil* of the *Parlement* to witness the election of Guillaume Bellier as *bailli* of Troyes. By the time of Charles's arrival, events at Rouen were already

[137] *A.H.-G.* MS.59, f.407[r].
[138] Ibid., f.421[r].
[139] Ibid.

under way. He remained at Poitiers, furthermore, for several weeks, during which time Joan of Arc was condemned and burnt at the stake. It is difficult to know whether Charles VII's decision to remain at Poitiers was in any way conditioned by knowledge of the developments at Rouen; but if any official concern were to be displayed on Joan's behalf, it would surely have been most appropriately voiced from Poitiers, home of the tribunal. In the event, no move whatever was made to support the Maid.

This does not mean, however, that news of developments at Rouen had not filtered through to Poitiers. Indeed, certain evidence suggests that a reaction to the trial had begun only a short time after the initiation of proceedings. On 5 February 1431, barely a month after the beginning of the trial, the *Conseil* of the Poitiers *Parlement* convened to discuss complaints against Pierre Genet (or Gilier), Franciscan and *bachelier* in the convent of that denomination at Poitiers, situated not far from the *Palais*. According to certain witnesses 'dignes de foy', Genet had, apparently, 'aucunement preschie ou dit paroles en plain sermon, malsonnans et scandaleuses, et aussi avoit parle autrement que a point de certain notable sermon que avoit fait messire Pierre de Versailles le jour de la Chandeleur (Candlemas) en l'eglise de Poictiers'.[140] Unfortunately we know nothing of the content of Versailles' sermon, nor, again, of Genet's objections. Yet the affair is not without interest considering events at Rouen. We have seen earlier[141] that Versailles played an important part in the interrogation of the Maid both at Chinon and at Poitiers. Despite his participation, however, Versailles appears to have been among those more sceptical of the Maid's employment,[142] and the coincidence of his sermon, preached some three weeks after the beginning of events at Rouen, and objected to so vociferously by Genet, may well have been related to proceedings there.

The reaction of the *Parlement* to Genet's own sermons may also indicate that Genet was aware of the Maid's plight, and had openly spoken on her behalf. With the arrival of Charles VII anticipated in the near future it was perhaps clear that the *Parlement* should act promptly on his behalf to prevent any expression of sympathy for Joan which might in turn implicate him in the affair. The *Parlement* subsequently ordered Genet, in the presence of brother Jean Guerreau, also a member of the Franciscan convent at Poitiers, that in the name

[140]Ibid., f.410$^{r-v}$.

[141]Above, pp. 95, 100.

[142]See, for instance, Duparc, *Procès en nullité*, i, 376.

of king and Court he should leave Poitiers immediately and live elsewhere.[143] The following day Gilier (sic) appealed against the decision, complaining that he was: 'chargie de respondre des questions en l'hostel des Freres Mineurs de Poictiers a ce prochain Caresme prenant. Et de faire certains sermons en Caresme',[144] because of this it was necessary for him to continue to reside in Poitiers. However, the *Parlement* immediately quashed Genet's appeal, and ordered him to leave the town immediately, 'jusques a Quasimodo' (Low Sunday).[145] The speed, as the severity, of this action by the *Parlement* appears to underline the seriousness of Genet's offence.

Not long after this incident on 23 March 1431[146] the *Parlement* was called upon to review a similar case, this time involving a certain brother Richard, like Genet also a member of the Franciscan order, whose earlier career had been closely involved with the 'mission' of Joan of Arc. On 10 May 1429 Richard, adherent of the cult of Jesus, had been expelled from Paris by the English for the potentially subversive nature of his preaching. In Lent 1430 huge crowds had flocked to hear him preach at Orléans, apparently without opposition from Charles VII's government;[147] however the situation of Rouen in 1431 could drastically alter attitudes towards Richard's preaching. Clearly an untimely display of enthusiasm on Joan's behalf by Richard at this point, perhaps following his recent arrival at Poitiers, could have embarrassing consequences not only for the king, but also for those theologians and *parlementaires* earlier called to sanction Charles VII's political employment of the Maid.

In the light of these factors it is interesting to note the presence among those who reviewed Richard's case on the *conseil* of the *Parlement*, of a number of new individuals: Pierre de Versailles, lately promoted abbot of Saint Martial of Limoges; Guillaume Aimery, here formally termed Inquisitor of the Faith; Seguin Cousin; the bishops of Saintes and Le Puy; finally, Jean de La Marche, Jean d'Étampes and Itier Marchon, vicars and representatives of Hugues de Combarel, bishop of Poitiers.[148] No fewer than four of those

[143]*A.H.-G.* MS.59, f.410ᵛ.

[144]Ibid., fos. 410ᵛ-411ʳ (6 Feb. 1431).

[145]Ibid., f.411ʳ.

[146]See ibid., fos. 419ᵛff.

[147]J. de La Martinière, 'Frère Richard et Jeanne d'Arc à Orléans, mars-juillet 1430', *Moyen Age* 44 (1934), 190-1.

[148]*A.H.-G.* MS.59, f.419ʳ⁻ᵛ.

represented here (and possibly others) had been among those who had provided doctrinal sanction for the Maid's 'mission', either at Chinon or at Poitiers.[149] Their apparent determination to prevent the preaching of brother Richard, bearing in mind his earlier connection with Joan of Arc, was perhaps provoked by the knowledge that, with the fate of the latter undecided at Rouen, and Charles VII's presence anticipated in Poitiers, any potentially incriminating sympathy for the Maid from Charles's camp, and particularly from Poitiers, where Joan had been formally interrogated, should be prematurely suppressed. The nature, or indeed the actual *fact* of Richard's preaching was not even specified. Indeed, the wording of the supplication addressed to the *Parlement* regarding Richard, by Hugues de Combarel, bishop of Poitiers and Guillaume Aimery, Inquisitor of the Faith 'pour faire deffenses a frere Richard de l'ordre des Freres Mineurs qu'il ne face quelque fait de predication, jusques a ce que par eux autrement en soit ordonne, et qui'il soit arreste en l'Hostel du couvent dudit ordre a Poictiers'[150] suggests that active preaching need not yet have occurred. It is possible that Richard had recently arrived in Poitiers and the supplicants, aware of his earlier association with Joan, and with the additional knowledge of Pierre Genet's outburst against Pierre de Versailles, had decided that it would be expedient, in view of the events taking place at Rouen, and also of their earlier involvement in Joan's interrogation, to take prompt measures to prevent Richard speaking out on Joan's behalf.

The *Parlement,* as in the earlier case of Genet, was quick to take action in upholding the supplicants' order. In view of their request,

> et aussi pour ce que iceluy frere Richart n'est venu devers la court qui l'avoit mande, icelle court a ordonne qu'apres ladite deffences ou arrets faits par lesdits de l'eglise audit frere Richart, et en confortant iceux, ... luy soit deffendu de par la court qu'il ne face fait de predication et qu'il ne parte dudit couvent mais y tienne arrest jusques a ce que autrement en soit ordonne. *Et super hoc tradita est commissio* a Guillaume Taichier, huissier de Parlement.[151]

On Saturday 24 March 1431 the *Parlement* ordered Philippe des Courtils and Pierre de Tuillières, *conseillers,* to act with Maurice Claveurier, *lieutenant général de la sénéchaussée* of Poitou and

---

[149]Above, pp. 95, 100. For an additional note on La Marche and Étampes, see Favreau, *Poitiers,* 291 n.990. On Itier Marchon, see ibid., 460.

[150]*A.H.-G.* MS.59, fos. 419v-420r.

[151]Ibid., f.420r.

Guillaume Taichier, *huissier,* and bring Richard before the court, 'et le contraindre, se mestier est, iceluy prendre *etiam in loco sacro'.* Richard was duly found and handed over to the Inquisitor of the Faith and the representatives of the bishop of Poitiers as they had demanded.[152] On the same day, Charles VII made his formal entry into Poitiers.

[152]Ibid., f.420^v.

# 4

# THE *PARLEMENT*, SOCIETY AND THE ECONOMY

## Merchants and Merchandise

The mercantile resources of the 'kingdom of Bourges', though affected by war and by the Anglo-Burgundian occupation of Paris and large areas of northern France, were by no means derisory. The years after 1418 probably witnessed a considerable re-orientation of commercial activity away from the manufacturing centres of Flanders, Normandy and to a lesser extent, England,[1] towards the ports of Italy and Spain. An important economic consequence of this shift was the intensification of trading activity through the major *entrepôts* remaining loyal to Charles VII: via Avignon, Montpellier, Marseille and Béziers with the great Italian manufacturing centres, with Sardinia, eastern Spain and beyond this with the Orient; via La Rochelle on the west coast with northern and western Spain, Italy, Brittany, Flanders, Germany and Scotland; and finally via Lyon with Geneva, the Empire and north-eastern Italy.

Commercial links between the court of Charles VII at Bourges and the Italian peninsula were naturally facilitated by the already close political relations with the Peninsula, of the House of Anjou. In the years after 1418 Bourges, its population swollen by large numbers of immigrants from northern France, by royal officials working in the *Chambre des Comptes* and that of the *monnaies,* and by large numbers of courtiers and *conseillers,* rapidly developed into a commercial centre of considerable importance, attracting a highly cosmopolitan retinue of merchants and craftsmen supplying a range of predominantly luxury goods.[2] Some idea of the scale of the demographic growth of

[1] Trade links between the 'kingdom of Bourges' and the Flemish and Norman manufacturing centres were by no means completely eroded by the war. After 1418 cloth from Flanders and Normandy was imported through La Rochelle (Favreau, *Poitiers,* 308); Norman and English cloth was openly sold at Tours, probably being introduced overland, through Brittany (B. Chevalier, *Tours: ville royale (1356-1520)* (Paris/Louvain, 1975), 154 n.176. More distant towns such as Toulouse continued to trade with the English (P. Wolff, *Commerces et marchands de Toulouse* (Paris, 1954), 236 n.26). The possibility of direct English trade with La Rochelle after 1418 is suggested by the *échevins'* allusion to a demand made by Georges de La Trémoïlle for payment of 500 *réaux d'or,* for a certain 'saufconduit qu'il disoit... avoir eu et obtenu dudit feu roy Charles, en l'an 1431, pour tous Angloys venante marchandement en ladite ville de La Rochelle, durant certain temps... estre declaire audit saufconduit' (A.N. 1AP 176, no. 15 (i).

[2] On the choice of Bourges for the location of Charles VII's quasi-permanent residence, and its subsequent development as a commercial centre, see Chevalier,

the town during this period may be inferred by comparison with Poitiers, home of the *Parlement* M. Favreau writes that here, 'paradoxalement, dumoins en apparence, ces jours si sombres représentent un des temps les plus forts de l'histoire de la ville'.[3] Such evidence as we possess for the other major towns of the 'kingdom of Bourges' suggests that the occupation of northern France and the resulting drift of very large numbers of immigrants, including craftsmen, south of the Loire, produced in each case symptoms of rapid demographic expansion similar to that exhibited at Poitiers.[4]

The reception given to the immigrants, particularly craftsmen, was often far from friendly. The exercise of particular trades, notably that of butchery, was in many cases jealously guarded by native craftsmen precisely at the time when the demand for their products was greatest. This, allied to the problem of the devastation by war of arable land outside the towns, may have placed severe demands on existing food supplies. Yet in other respects, notably that of the propagation and growth of new industries, or the rapid expansion of existing ones, the long-term economic effects of these migrations may have been of a highly beneficial kind, particularly for the larger towns.[5]

The supply of merchandise to Charles VII's court was frequently met by recourse to the great manufacturing centres of Italy. On 8 January 1425 Charles paid Étienne Filleul, Avignonese merchant, 4,000 *l.t.* for silk and woollen cloth, 30 measures of black satin, 19 measures of scarlet (of which 4 measures were given to 'un femme du pays d'Ecosse'), 12 measures of velvet ('poil de Lyon et fleur de peschier'), 18 measures of black Belveau and six measures of 'drap bleu' (given to the husband of the aforementioned Scotswoman).[6]

214-19; also, G. Dodu, 'Le roi de Bourges ou dix-neuf ans de la vie de Charles VII', *R. hist.* 94 (1928), 52-4.

[3] See Favreau, *Poitiers,* 261. Favreau stresses the problems engendered by the rapid rise in population (ibid., 298-303); yet the economic benefits appear to have been considerable (ibid., 305-9).

[4] The registers of the Poitiers *Parlement* disclose signs of a significant rise in population at Orléans (which provided refuge for large numbers of Parisians), Bourges, Blois, Tours, Chinon and Angers, in addition to the well-documented case of Poitiers. A similar case may be put for La Rochelle, where numbers of refugees from the north were augmented by merchant families. Against the economic benefits of this expansion must be set the frequent devastation of surrounding countryside and the dramatic fall in population of many smaller towns (see Favreau, *Poitiers,* 301-2).

[5] See for instance, Favreau, *Poitiers,* 300-1. Also, in respect of the tapestry industry at Angers, above, p. 7 n. 20.

[6] B.N. Nouv. acq. fr. 7626, fos. 443[r]ff.

Regular demand for such items is suggested by the frequently large sums allocated to Marie by Charles VII for the maintenance of her estate and that of her ladies-in-waiting: for example, 12,000*l.t.* in 1426,[7] and a further 6,750*l.t.* in 1427.[8] The continuing resort to Florence for materials of high quality is further indicated by payments made by Marie of Anjou personally: on 6 March 1431[9] to Jean Cavaillon, Avignonese merchant, 162*l.* 10*s.t.*, in lieu of 100 *florins* papal money, for 'ung veloux bleu plain', given to a lady-in-waiting on her marriage; a further 536*l.* 5*s.t.*, in lieu of 330 *florins* papal money, for a certain rich cloth 'd'or, viole cramoysi a hault et bas poil' employed as a wrap for Radegonde, daughter of Marie and Charles VII, on the day of her birth.[10] In addition, Géry de Guerardin, a Florentine merchant, was earlier assigned 6,000*l.t.* on the royal mint at Angers as payment for cloth of gold on silk supplied to the court.[11] Provisioning the court was not, however, the sole prerogative of Italian merchants. On 29 June 1426 Grard Hagne, a German merchant, asked on the king's behalf provision of 1,000 *couronnes* from the consuls of Tournai, 'pour acater toilles, haguenees, et autres coses dont ladite Madame la Royne de France a Mestier'.[12]

The liquid wealth of Italian merchants frequently provided a convenient recourse for Charles VII in his constant need for ready capital. On 10 July 1427 Dino Boche, a Luccese merchant living at Montpellier, received 1,000*l.t.* compensation from Charles VII for losses incurred in the repayment of an original loan of 12,000*l.t.* in 'weak' currency.[13] On 22 February 1434 the Florentine merchant Francesco Martelly was paid interest of 250 *réaux d'or* on an earlier loan of 2,000 *réaux* made to Charles VII 'pour le paiement des

[7]B.N. MS. fr.20417, no.3; ibid., no. 4 for a payment of 10,000*l.t.* to Yolande of Aragon it Feb. 1426, for expenses incurred in bringing 'nostre treschier et tresame frere le roy de Sicile' to meet Charles VII for certain purposes.

[8]Ibid., no. 12 (cf., also, no. 13).

[9]B.N. MS. fr.26054, no. 1517.

[10]Ibid., no. 1518 (6 March, 1431) (cf. Beaucourt, ii (Paris, 1882), 187).

[11]Chevalier, 219, no. 27. The pattern of Italian commercial operations within the kingdom of Bourges is uncertain. Apart from Bourges itself, Italian mercantile presence was marked at La Souterraine (*Documents relatifs au comté de La Marche extraits des archives du Parlement de Poitiers (1418-1436)*, ed. A. Thomas, *Bibl. Éc. Hautes Études* 174 (Paris, 1910), xiii, n.1); and at La Rochelle (Favreau, *Poitiers,* 308 n.1110).

[12]*Extraits des anciens registres aux délibérations des consaux de la ville de Tournai (1422-1430)*, ed. H. Vandenbröeck, *Mém. Soc. Hist. Litt. de Tournai* 8 (1863), 209.

[13]A.N. K62, no. 35. Charles had recourse for loans to Italian merchants at Montpellier (ibid., no. 33) and particularly at Avignon (Chevalier, 219 n. 27).

Ecossois ordonnez pour la garde du corps de cellui seigneur', which Martelly had, apparently, carried 'a ses perils et fortunes audit seigneur es villes de Blois, Ambois et Bourges'.[14] Chief marts for the trade with the western Italian states were the ports of Avignon and Montpellier, which during this period must have witnessed economic activity of a degree little inferior to that displayed during the residence of the papacy at Avignon during the fourteenth century.[15]

In addition to material goods and finance the Italian states also provided supplies of gunpowder and munitions both for the armies of Charles VII and for the towns remaining faithful to his cause. Italian arms and armour[16] and, by way of the numbers of Italian mercenaries who served in Charles VII's armies,[17] some of the techniques of Italian warfare, also found their way into France through the ports of southern Languedoc.

Litigation before the *Parlement* shows both its awareness of the desirability of maintaining mercantile operations in the Mediterranean, between France and the major ports of Italy and Spain, and, within this, the need to safeguard merchants of French, or naturalised French provenance, trading with these areas. The accomplishment of this objective inevitably brought the *Parlement* into conflict with both internal and foreign powers. The increase in trade within the Mediterranean may have produced an increase in the frequency of acts of piracy committed against unarmed merchant ships. The difficulty of bringing legal action against the pirates stemmed largely from a general lack of precision in the terms which divided a deliberate act of piracy from the frequent practice of raiding ships during the course of war at sea.[18]

In September 1430[19] the *Parlement* heard the complaint by Jean Almodene, a native of Catalonia and naturalised subject of Charles VII operating from Béziers, that in 1425 he had sent a number of

[14]B.N. MS. fr.26057, no. 2237.

[15]For a note on the importance of Avignon during this period see Chevalier, 218 n.23.

[16]For the presence of Italian armourers in the service of Charles VII and of Charles d'Anjou see ibid., 231-2 and passim.

[17]See for instance, P. Contamine, *Guerre, État et Société à la fin du Moyen âge* (Paris, 1972), 253-5.

[18]For a discussion of this problem see M. Mollat, 'De la Piraterie sauvage à la course réglementée (xive-xve siècle)', *Mél. Ecole franç. Rome. Moyen Âge, Temps modernes* 87 (1975), 7ff.

[19]For what follows see A.N. X1ᵃ9196, fos. 25ᵛ-26ᵛ. (Further details of the affair may be found on ibid., f.31ʳ⁻ᵛ; A.N. X1ᵃ9192, fos.238ᵛ-239ᵛ and A.N. X1ᶜ140, nos. 72 (i-ii) and 73).

merchant ships on a trading mission to the port of Oristano on the west coast of Sardinia. On their passage through the Mediterranean the ships were confronted by a Genoese pirate force led by Pierre d'Aurie. Almodene complained that as a result of the confrontation valuable merchandise was 'prins, ostez et raviz par force et violence' by Aurie. The *Parlement* was quick to uphold Almodene's complaint, dispatching Adam de Cambrai, *Président*, to the port of La Rochelle with the order to seize the goods of Genoese merchants living there to the value of 6,000 *réaux d'or*.[20] Cambrai subsequently ordered the sequestration of the goods of Bernado Castaing, Daniel Pinel, Meraut de Grille, Termen Herbieon, Baptiste de Marin, Berthome Marille, Anthoine de Claveau and Ambroy Lomelin.[21] This action met with an immediate rebuff from the mayor and *échevins,* who claimed that they had:

> priviliges, franchises et libertes par lesquelx touz marchans, de quelque pays, terre ou nation. . . venans et affluans. . . par mer comme par terre a. . . La Rochelle avecques leurs biens, . . . sont ou saufconduit especial du roy, et ne peuvent ou doyvent estre executez en ladite ville pour quelque cas. . . que ce soit.

The frustration engendered by this refusal appears to have caused Almodene to resort to force in an attempt to exact compensation from the Genoese at La Rochelle. The *Parlement,* mindful of the need to maintain good relations with the *échevins,* was obliged to prevent Almodene's action and recognise the *échevins'* privileges. By way of compensation Almodene was permitted to take reprisals against other Genoese merchants and their property located in France other than at La Rochelle.

A similar case appeared before the *Parlement* on 23 December 1435,[22] this time on appeal from the jurisdiction of the governor of Montpellier. Litigation stemmed from a complaint by the mercantile consortium of Durand operating out of Montpellier, against certain 'Florentinos seu. . . piratus de Florencia', who had earlier seized a merchant ship belonging to them. It appears that the consortium had

---

[20] For this and what follows see A.N. X1ᶜ140, nos. 72 (i-ii) and 73.

[21] After 1418 Genoese merchant ships provided one of the means of sustaining an apparently vigorous sea-trade between La Rochelle and Flanders (R. Doehard and C. Kerremarns, ed., *Les relations commercials entre Gênes, la Belgique et l'Outremont d'après les archives notariales gènoises,* iv (1400-1440), (Brussels, 1952), 336 (no. 302) ff., passim. On two occasions Genoese ships carried merchandise from La Rochelle to English ports (ibid., 505 no. 660 (Nov. 1430) and 563 no. 748 (Oct. 1432)).

[22] For what follows see A.N. X1ᵃ9193, f.119ʳ.

initially wished to compensate for its losses in the manner sanctioned by *Parlement* earlier on behalf of Jean Almodene. The governor of Montpellier apparently consented to this action, ordering reprisals against Florentine merchants based at Montpellier.[23] However, the governor's commissioners, rather than following this directive in its strictest terms, took specific reprisals against Bernardo Venture. The resulting appeal by Venture saw the affair come before the Poitiers *Parlement*. However, the *Parlement* ultimately rejected Venture's appeal and the case was returned to the governor's jurisdiction. This general protection afforded by the *Parlement* against arbitrary acts of piracy, and its willingness to permit reprisals against the subjects of foreign powers, could, on occasion, allow similar recourse in the event of losses incurred in overland trading in other countries: on 9 April 1435 the *Parlement* upheld the claim for 'marque et reprisaille' against the king of Aragon and his subjects by Jean de Laon, a merchant operating out of Béziers, following the seizure of a quantity of saffron belonging to him by Aragonese officials in the course of a trading mission to Aragon and Catalonia in 1425. Compensation to the extent of 200 *réaux d'or* was afforded Laon by the *Parlement*, to be taken from a larger fine imposed on certain Aragonese by virtue of an *arrêt* dated 13 September 1431.[24]

Against the more distant outlets of the Languedocian coast the port of La Rochelle remained, during the years 1418-36, the sole maritime link for the landlocked 'kingdom of Bourges'.[25] The loyalty of the mayor and *échevins* to Charles VII's cause was thus a matter of the utmost concern, and the locating of the *Parlement* in close proximity to the town may be seen to have been a fortuitous step. Like many other large towns in the 'kingdom of Bourges', the war provided La Rochelle with the means to employ its important strategic situation to enhance its judicial and economic independence, and the years after 1418 witnessed persistent attempts by the *Parlement* to maintain a measure of control over the frequently recalcitrant jurisdiction of the *échevins*.

The heavy mercantile traffic out of La Rochelle inevitably afforded, as in the case of the Mediterranean trade routes, opportunities

---

[23] The Durands' complaint may have been responsible for the seizure of goods belonging to Petro and Alberto Aldobrandini, Florentine merchants based at Montpellier (A.N. X1ª9196, fos. 24ᵛ-25ʳ).

[24] A.N. X1ª9193, fos. 98ʳ-90ᵛ (also A.N. X1ª9194, f.96ᵛ).

[25] For evidence of the cosmopolitanism of La Rochelle after 1418 see E. Trocmé and M. Delafosse, *Le commerce rochelais de la fin du xvᵉ siècle au début du xviiᵉ siècle* (Paris, 1952), 73, 76.

for acts of piracy. The *Parlement*'s difficulty in dealing with this problem is indicated by litigation on 11 August 1430.[26] Here Pierre Vinages, a Spanish pirate, had seized merchandise belonging to a Breton merchant, Olivier Hamon. Vinages had allegedly openly sold the plundered goods at La Rochelle but Hamon's attempted reprisal against Vinages was thwarted by the *échevins* of La Rochelle. Jean V instantly retaliated by ordering the seizure of the goods of other Rochelois merchants in Brittany; in addition the imposition of a new tax on merchandise leaving the duchy was devised to offset Hamon's losses. The subsequent refusal by certain varlets of Pierre Bragier, merchant of La Rochelle, to pay the new tax saw them imprisoned by Breton officials. Bragier's appeal to the *Parlement* merely enhanced the difficulty of objective judgement in a matter which might affect diplomatic relations with Jean V.

The growth of a large immigrant population at La Rochelle meant that on occasion the *Parlement* was forced to entertain the complaints of foreign merchants and tradesmen who had settled there, against French subjects. An example of this occurred on 12 April 1421[27] following the demand by Martin Martinez, a Castilian merchant, against Guillaume l'Évêque, called *de Montfort,* of La Rochelle, for the restitution of 200*l. t.* together with a silver cup and other valuables held in safekeeping by the latter. L'Évêque's appeal was rejected by the *Parlement* and the case retained within its jurisdiction. On 31 July 1423[28] another claim by Castilian merchants[29] with the king of Castile was heard before the *Parlement*; in this case the issue of an *arrêt* permitting them recourse to the inheritance of the late André de Berneville met with a counter demand by Jean Cochet, *bourgeois* of La Rochelle, who claimed that by virtue of an *arrêt* delivered in his favour by the *Parlement* of Paris in April 1418, the Castilians owed *him* 180*l. t.* Cochet's demand was upheld by the *Parlement*.

The influx of foreign merchants at La Rochelle could, on occasion, result in serious confrontation between the *Parlement* and the jurisdiction of the town governors. An example occurred before the *Parlement* on 1 March 1428[30] when the *Procureur du roi* clashed with the jurisdiction of the *échevins* over the execution of the will of a

---

[26] For details of this case see A.N. X1ª9201, fos. 21ʳ-22ʳ; A.N. X1ª9199, fos. 335ᵛ-337ᵛ.

[27] See A.N. X1ª9190, f.151ʳ⁻ᵛ.

[28] Ibid., fos. 247ʳ-248ʳ.

[29] Martin Perez, Luis Martin, and Gonsalve, Jean and Gilles Salvador.

[30] For what follows see A.N. X1ª9199, fos. 32ʳff.

German merchant. The merchant in question, Clard Lamboynd, had earlier arrived at La Rochelle by sea on a trading mission with a larger party of Flemings and Germans. During the course of his stay in the town he was suddenly taken ill and died in the house of Jean Quenaut, *bourgeois* of La Rochelle. Quenaut claimed that before his death Lamboynd had appointed him as his executor, and as a result he had proceeded with the accomplishment of this duty. For the *Procureur du roi*, Jean Rabateau claimed, to the contrary, that by virtue of the fact that Lamboynd was an alien, and that as the king disposed of supreme powers of justice and lordship at La Rochelle, the goods of the deceased automatically escheated to the crown. This was countered by the *échevins* who maintained that by virtue of the safeconduct issued by Charles VII in 1425 to foreign merchants visiting the town, the matter remained outside the *Parlement*'s jurisdiction. Despite the opposition of the *échevins,* the *Parlement* upheld the action of royal authorities at La Rochelle who had originally opposed Quenaut's claim to be the executor, and rejected the appeal of the *échevins* in support of him. The *Parlement* ordered Quenaut to restore to the court 125 *écus d'or* taken from the inheritance of the deceased, and demanded that his inventory of Lamboynd's possessions be checked and made anew.[31]

The *Parlement* was also aware of the need to provide protection for foreign merchants buying and selling in the vicinity of La Rochelle under royal safeguard. Such individuals could easily be exposed to arbitrary acts of violence or dispossession. On 19 February 1431[32] André de Bessandolles and Job Felix, Flemish merchants, complained to the *Parlement* that under the protection of a royal safeconduct they had earlier come to La Rochelle to buy wine,[33] in the town itself and in the immediate environs. In the course of their business they were encountered by Heliot de Jambes who, in contravention of the safeconduct, imprisoned the merchants at Fouras and demanded a ransom payment. Gérard Le Boursier, *maître des requêtes de l'Hôtel,* was informed of the affair and Jambes was subsequently brought before the *Parlement* to answer charges. Despite Jambes's claim that he had 'bien servi le roy, et fut a son couronnement armes et en chevaulx', and that as captain of Fouras he had the duty of guarding

---

[31] See A.N. X1ᵃ9194, fos. 30ᵛ-31ʳ (19 Nov. 1432) (also, A.N. X1ᵃ9196, fos. 78ᵛ-79ʳ (23 Dec. 1432)).

[32] For what follows see A.N. X2ᵃ18, f.284ʳ⁻ᵛ.

[33] La Rochelle had long been an important centre for the export of wines (Favreau, *Poitiers,* 309 n. 1113). Further evidence of the export of wine to Flanders may be found on A.N. X1ᵃ9198, f.182ʳ (1426) and A.N. X1ᵃ9201, f. 61ʳ. After 1418 Flemish cloth continued to be sold at La Rochelle and at Poitiers (Favreau, *Poitiers,* 308 n. 1110).

coastal areas against the enemy, the *Procureur du roi,* for the Flemings, reminded Jambes that in breaking the safeconduct he had committed the crime of *lèse-majesté.* This case provides some indication of the difficulties promoted by the economic and political situation of the 'kingdom of Bourges' which constantly prevented the adoption of a partisan stance by the *Parlement* in favour of its more 'loyal' subjects. Yet, while the *Parlement* might be willing to afford some degree of protection for merchants of foreign provenance whose activities were directly advantageous to the king, it was equally quick to take action to the contrary in instances involving activity prejudicial to his person or estate.

It was possibly treatment of the kind experienced earlier by Felix and Bessandolles which ultimately resulted in the appearance of Hennequin Bize, merchant of Bruges, before the *Parlement* on 22 December 1431.[34] One of a family of eleven children, Bize explained that his father, Jacob, *bourgeois* of Bruges, maintained a constant rapport with those merchants operating south of the Loire. Some of his children had been sent to France to learn the language and to acquire the skills of merchandising. Hennequin claimed that he had earlier travelled to Rennes, in Brittany, to avoid the plague at Bruges, but also: 'pour aprandre a parler Francoiz et faisoit merchandises'. Soon after his arrival in Brittany in 1429 Bize was imprisoned, first in the garrison at Durestal, near Rennes, then, following his release by virtue of royal letters of safeconduct, a second time by the baron of Coulans on 1 May 1429. The latter attempted to exact a ransom from Bize under the pretext that both he and his father had openly supported the Burgundian cause. Whether as a result of this alleged partiality for the Burgundians, or as a result of Bize's frustration with his circumstances, and the long term of prison he had been forced to endure, he had at some point openly declared in favour of Burgundy, maintaining that he was: 'bon et loyal et. . . bon chevalier (which) ne deust faire, car le roy avoit faire tuer son pere en traison.'

Jean Barbin, for the *Procureur du roi,* reminded Bize that, both on account of his remarks against the king's honour, and, by virtue of his open favouring of the Burgundian cause, he was guilty of the crime of *lèse-majesté.* Barbin demanded that on account of this the unfortunate Bize be 'pilorise, fleschy ou front et ait la langue pertee *ut ceteris';* and, in addition, that his goods be seized into the court's hands, prior to his eventual banishment from the kingdom. Clearly the line drawn by the

---

[34] See A.N. X2ª18, fos. 308ʳ-309ʳ for what follows. The affair was introduced before the *Parlement* on 22 Dec. 1431 (A.N. X2ª21, fos. 171ᵛ, 178ᵛ, 179ʳ). See also, A.N. X2ª20, fos. 46ᵛ-47ʳ.

*Parlement* between respectable trading and support of the enemy cause was at times a tenuous one — the more so if one is to believe Bize's claim that witnesses supporting Coulans's case amounted to 'une fillette publique. . . chamberiere de l'une de ses parents. . . et. . . ceux de la garnison de Durestal, qui devoient participer en sa recon'.[35]

On occasion action taken by Flemish authorities against the *échevins* of La Rochelle, in respect of merchandise, led to the latters' appearance before the *Parlement* . Failure to pay for merchandise brought to La Rochelle by the Flemish merchant Guillaume du Busson saw Colas Regnaudin and Pierre Lucas called to Bruges to answer for the town. Their reluctance to pay the resulting fine of 1,500 *écus d'or* imposed on them by the Flemish authorities led to the arbitrary seizure of the goods of other Rochelois merchants trading with Flanders. Among the victims was Guillaume Moulin, who suffered the loss of 160 tuns of wine; hence, on 25 June 1426 Moulin promptly adjourned the *échevins* of La Rochelle before the *Parlement* demanding restitution of the value of his goods.[36]

Like their Italian and Languedocian counterparts, French merchants operating by sea out of La Rochelle could on occasion render valuable services for Charles VII's war effort. An example of this type of co-operation is provided by litigation before the *Parlement* on 1 June 1434.[37] Here, Colin Langlois explained that some years earlier he had provided Charles VII with a number of merchant ships for the transport of Spanish troops to France.[38] The debt for this service amounted to 12,000 *francs* which, Langlois explained, was compensated by his receiving 'la ferme de la Prevoste de La Rochelle. . . pour et en paiment de vj$^m$ iij$^c$ livres jusques a neuf ans. . . et fut a deux fois', to finish on Ascension day 1434. Despite the fact that he was still owed 3,334*l.* 15*s. t.,* for which he had been sent the farm for a further four years, Langlois complained that Jean Rabateau, *Président* in the *Chambre des comptes,* had seized the farm under the pretext of the non-payment of his wages as *Président.* A deeper motive underlay

---

[35] A.N. X2$^a$18, f.308$^v$.

[36] A.N. X1$^a$9198, f.182$^r$. The dispute, which began in 1423, was still not resolved in 1430 (A.N. X1$^a$9192, fos. 208$^r$-209$^r$).

[37] See A.N. X1$^a$9200, fos. 244$^v$-245$^v$. Langlois was a native of Harfleur.

[38] Foreign merchant ships were frequently contracted by Charles VII to bring troops to La Rochelle. In 1423 Scottish soliders were brought from Dumbarton by Perruche de La Sau, master of the *Santa Maria* ('Documents relatifs à l'histoire maritime du xv$^e$ siècle', ed. P. Marchegay, *R. Soc. Savantes,* 6th Ser., 2 (1875), 160). In 1433 Flemish and Spanish ships were deployed for the attack on English-held Mornac (A. Barbot, 'Histoire de La Rochelle', ed. D. Joly d'Aussy, *AHSA* 14 (1886), 300).

this appropriation, for in the aftermath of the incident the *Chambre des comptes* refused to restore the farm to Langlois until his accounts had been thoroughly checked. The suspicion that Langlois was embezzling the revenues was shared by the *Procureur du roi* at La Rochelle, who had Langlois cited before the jurisdiction of the governor. Langlois's appeal to Poitiers was eventually met by opposition from the *Procureur du roi* in the *Parlement.*

About the time of his initial receipt of the farm of the *prévôté*, on 9 August 1423,[39] Langlois was involved in a further case of fraudulent dealing, this time in respect of a certain ransom payment. The plaintiff in this instance, Jean de Villeneuve, also a merchant of La Rochelle, explained that during November-December 1422 he had taken a quantity of merchandise to Le Crotoy, where he heard that a friend of his, Regnault Girart, had been taken prisoner by the English at Calais and ransomed for 500 *écus d'or*. Wishing to obtain Girart's release, Villeneuve approached Langlois, then *maître particulier de la Monnaie royale* at Le Crotoy, for the loan of the necessary finance. Having no gold coin, Langlois gave Villeneuve a quantity of 'black' money, consisting of 'doubles de deux deniers' of Tournai, assuring him that he would be able to convert them into gold coinage at Boulogne. On arriving at Boulogne, Villeneuve claimed 'ceulx d'icelle ville tenans le parti adversaire du roy lui dient que c'estoit faulse monnoie'; as a result he was imprisoned, and only obtained his release through a further payment of 200 *l.t.* On regaining Le Crotoy, Villeneuve was confronted once more by Langlois, who demanded the repayment of his original loan under threat of imprisonment. The appeal by the unfortunate Villeneuve was eventually quashed and he was ordered to make restitution of the original 500 *écus d'or* to Langlois.

On occasion the fines exacted by the *Parlement* from Rochelois merchants could be aimed at highly practical ends, this being the case in March 1436,[40] when by virtue of an *arrêt* against Robert Compain, *conseiller des élus de La Rochelle,* Compain was ordered to provide large quantities of wine and grain for the French forces currently besieging Harfleur.

During the early years of exile from Paris, persistent attempts were made to restrict trade with English-occupied areas, which might inadvertently fuel the enemy's campaign. On 23 September 1419[41]

[39] See A.N. X1ª9197, f.240ʳ for what follows.
[40] A.N. X1ª9194, fos. 128ʳff. (cf. A.N. X2ª21, fos. 295ʳ, 296ᵛ).
[41] A.N. X1ª8604, fos. 28ᵛ-29ʳ.

the Regent issued an edict prohibiting the transport of grain and wine outside the 'kingdom of Bourges' 'pour resister a l'enterprise et dampnable voulente des Anglois'. On 27 September[42] the order was repeated, this time with the incentive that anyone reporting the offence would receive one quarter of the goods confiscated upon the culprits. Practical difficulties caused by the severity of the bouts of famine which affected Poitou and the surrounding areas during the years 1419-22 meant, however, that some form of external resort was inevitable if dwindling supplies of foodstuffs were to be replenished. Hence on 19 November 1419[43] the Regent was forced to grant permission for the inhabitants of the Île de Ré and La Rochelle to import wine and grain from outside Poitou; given the strategic importance of these places, it was perhaps inevitable that some concessions should be made for fear that they might otherwise be won over to the enemy. The ambiguity arising out of the practical implementation of these edicts provided numerous loopholes for less scrupulous merchants; on 13 April 1420[44] the Regent again complained that 'soubz umbre de certains saufconduits, baillez et octroyes ausdiz adversaires par aucuns capitaines et autres de ce royaume, et soubz umbre de certaines lettres de licence baillees par lesdiz capitaines ou autres a plusieurs marchans dudit royaume', the traffic in illegal merchandise had continued largely unabated, notably at Talmont, La Rochelle and elsewhere on the coastal marches of Poitou.

Simultaneously with these prohibitions on trading with the enemy, commissioners were appointed to confiscate the goods of Burgundians, or of Burgundian sympathisers. The *Parlement* was active at an early stage in judging litigation arising from this type of action. The great difficulty involved in resolving, to any accurate degree, the positive guilt of those so accused, stemmed partly from the fact that many merchants who had left Normandy early, in the face of the English invasion, and in particular those who moved across the border into Brittany, continually ran the risk of arbitrary seizure of their property by unscrupulous commissioners on the pretext that they were of Norman origin. An early example of this sort of complaint was made before the *Parlement* in April 1419.[45] The

[42] Ibid., fos. 29$^v$-30$^r$.

[43] Ibid., fos. 30$^v$-31$^r$. A similar provision was made for the Île de Ré on 14/22 Dec. 1419 (ibid., f.31$^r$).

[44] Ibid., f.32$^r$ (cf. A.N. X2$^a$18, f.21$^v$ (9 May 1424), where Gervaise Le Musnier was held prisoner by the *Parlement* 'pour. . . d'avoir favorise les Anglois et leur porte vivres').

[45] See A.N. X1$^a$9190, fos. 16$^r$-17$^v$. On the migration of Norman merchants to Blois and Saumur see ibid., f.22$^r$ and A.N. X1$^a$9200, f.22$^r$.

136

plaintiffs, Jean I and Jean II Courroucié, natives of St. Lô, and Geoffroy Cornu, native of Hambuye, explained that they had left Normandy to take up residence at Fougères. Cloth merchants, in August 1418 they had departed from Fougères on a trading mission to Berry and the Auvergne. They were arrested at Romorantin by officers of the duke of Orléans and their merchandise impounded on the pretext that they were English sympathisers. In this instance, the merchants' appeal was upheld by the *Parlement*, and the case retained within its jurisdiction. On 8 May 1419[46] a similar appeal by Jean Suau, Merchant of Tours, accused of witholding goods belonging to a Burgundian sympathiser was rejected by the *Parlement.* This was followed on 12 July 1421[47] by the appeal of Collette Baudete, wife of Étienne Billard, a refugee at Bourges following the Burgundian capture of Melun. On the pretext that her husband had remained at Melun, Collette's possessions had been seized by Jean Pidoe, *'commissarium et reformatorem super facto bonorum per Burgundos adversarios nostros confiscatorum',* despite her protest that her husband had remained at Melun only because he had been forcefully detained by the Burgundians. Once again the appeal was upheld by the *Parlement,* Clearly the judicious review of these cases was of the utmost importance if sympathy for the Regent's cause was to be maintained.

Despite the occupation of Normandy by the English after 1418 and the Burgundian control of the Flemish manufacturing centres, a flow of trade was maintained by merchants with these areas, presumably by the provision of safe-conducts from the enemy. La Rochelle remained an important centre for the import of cloth from Saint Lô, Bruxelles and Ypres, and received, possibly, in the 1420s, imports of Spanish wool together with linen cloth from Brittany.[48] Mercantile relations with Brittany were possibly intensified during this period given the impossibility of wider travel within Normandy; overland into Poitou came quantities of cloth, linen and serge; notable among exports from Poitou and Saintonge into Brittany were large quantities of local wine.[49] Wine passing overland through Les Ponts de Cé into Brittany was subject to royal taxation, the enforcement of this duty being supervised by a *commissaire* drawn from the

[46] A.N. X1ª9190, fos. 58ʳ-59ʳ. On the status of Suau, a merchant-draper, at Tours, see B. Chevalier, *Tours: ville royale (1356-1520)* (Paris/Louvain, 1975), 191, 431.

[47] See A.N. X1ª9190, fos. 162ʳ-163ʳ.

[48] See Favreau, *Poitiers,* 308 nn. 1110-11. Also Chevalier, 154 n. 176.

[49] See Favreau, *Poitiers,* 309 n. 1113.

*conseillers* in the *Parlement.*[50] A similar levy was imposed on wine exported to Brittany by sea.

Funds for the purchase of large quantities of merchandise frequently derived from the formation of large consortia; occasionally disputes between their members were heard before the *Parlement.* But the business of buying and selling represented at times only one aspect of the wealth and influence of merchants. Many played important secondary roles in the realm of finance, acting as supervisors of the mints run by large town corporations or as receivers for individual *seigneurs* — this in addition to their frequent prominence in the governments of individual towns. The great wealth accumulated in the course of these manifold functions provided a convenient recourse both for the king and members of the nobility. The employment of this *ad hoc* finance by individuals met various needs: on 11 January 1425 the merchants of the Loire complained to the *Parlement* that they had earlier loaned the sum of 3,000 *réaux d'or* to a member of the family of Jean de Craon, *seigneur* of La Suse, to effect a ransom payment.[51] On 12 December 1429[52] Jean Caillerot, a merchant, accused by the *Procureur du roi* in *Parlement* of the embezzlement of royal mints at La Rochelle, Niort and Fontenay-le-Comte[53] to the extent of 20-30,000 *écus d'or* claimed, in a somewhat desperate defence, that he had lent numerous sums to the king; for the siege of Meulant 1,000 *francs,* then a further 200 *écus d'or;* for the first voyage into Scotland 1,000 old *écus d'or;* and on another occasion, when Charles was still Dauphin, 1,000 *écus d'or.* In addition Caillerot claimed that he had sent his brother mounted and armed to the siege of Gallardon, and further 'qu'il a este en la compaignie du roy a son couronnement accompaignie d'un homme d'arme' (this was becoming by now something of a *sine qua non* for the exercise of partisan behaviour). Again, on 29 November 1430,[54] Jean Benoyn, plaintiff before the *Cour des aides,* claimed to have lent Charles VII 100 *écus d'or* 'pour le faicte de Beaugency'. This was followed on 18 February 1434[55] by

---

[50] See A.N. X1ª9199, f.144ᵛ. Also ibid., fos. 147ᵛff.

[51] See A.N. X1ª9198, fos. 14ᵛff., passim.

[52] See A.N. X2ª18, f.179ʳff. for what follows (also A.N. X2ª21, fos. 113ᵛ, 149ᵛ; A.N. X1ª9199, f.190ʳ).

[53] The registers of the Poitiers *Parlement* contain many references to the embezzlement of royal mints and to the corruption of mint officials in the towns of the 'kingdom of Bourges', notably Orléans, Tours, Poitiers, Niort, Fontenay-le-Comte and La Rochelle.

[54] A.N. Z1ª8, f.34ᵛ.

[55] Ibid., f.113ʳ⁻ᵛ.

a similar claim by Jacques Hamelin, *juge* of Touraine, to the effect that he had provided 1,000 or 1,100 *écus d'or* of his own money at the request of Yolande of Aragon and Charles VII in order to evacuate the English, who had come to the very gates of Tours and Chinon, from a nearby *château*. Clearly the people of Chinon did not share Hamelin's patriotic urge, for in the aftermath of the event they had refused to contribute to an *aide* intended to recompense his original outlay.

Litigation before the *Parlement* only indicates the barest outlines of the mercantile wealth which underlay the 'kingdom of Bourges'. Future studies of the commerce of the major ports remaining loyal to Charles VII during this period — Montpellier, Béziers, Avignon and La Rochelle — will add much in detail. Deeper study, in particular of the trading relations with Italian cities, might in turn reveal something of the transference of cultural influences between France and Italy during this period, for these years witnessed, arguably, the development of a cosmopolitanism in the 'kingdom of Bourges' more marked than at any other time.

### Migration and Settlement in the 'Kingdom of Bourges'

#### By refugees arriving from northern France

The Lancastrian settlement of Normandy, and, more particularly, the occupation of Paris by Burgundian forces in 1418, resulted in the drift of large numbers of refugees away from the occupied areas into the major towns of the 'kingdom of Bourges'.[56] The social and economic consequences of migration on such a large scale were highly complex, and merit serious study.

It is first of all clear that whether or not the motivation for the original departure of the refugees derived from some sort of vague patriotic urge, the various problems engendered by their reception meant that their sentiments were often not shared by towns burdened with the problem of accommodating, and above all, feeding them. Reactions to the arrival of the refugees probably varied greatly from town to town, and from emotive,[57] or purely pragmatic considerations. At Poitiers, for instance, M. Favreau has warned that the influx of refugees could not have been viewed by the town simply in terms of

[56] On the scale of the migrations, especially at Poitiers, see Favreau, *Poitiers*, 299-302.

[57] See for instance, B. Chevalier, *Tours: ville royale (1356-1520)* (Paris/Louvain, 1975), 179 n.16.

economic gain. With many of the smaller neighbouring towns significantly depopulated as a result of the war, and much arable land abandoned or uncultivated, the business of feeding a swollen population could clearly produce problems. Allied to the question of food supply the density of population naturally facilitated the spread of disease — a fact evidenced by the growth of almonries and cemeteries in Poitiers — and made the upkeep of roads and buildings both difficult and expensive.[58]

The difficulty experienced by many of the towns receiving the refugees in maintaining adequate food supplies, raises the matter of the sufficiency of the diet of individuals living within them. In practically every major town for which evidence is forthcoming, the period after 1418 witnessed the rapid creation of new butcheries to cope with the increased demand for meat. The very creation of new stalls, and, in some cases the extension of permitted slaughtering hours, allied to the apparently comparatively low price of meat throughout our period, suggests that a plentiful supply was forthcoming At Tours, M. Chevalier suggests that 'il n'était. . . pas impossible, même aux petites gens, de manger de la viande au moins deux ou trois fois par semaine'.[59] The maintenance of supplies of cereals is also evidenced in some areas by the creation of new mills, or the enlargement and renovation of old ones. Throughout these years and beyond, the price of corn and its derivative products remained, certainly in relation to meat, relatively high,[60] a fact which suggests erratic and generally diminished production. In addition to meat and cereals, the continuing export of wines, notably in Poitou and Saintonge, suggests that a certain amount was available for home consumption.[61] While one should be careful not to exaggerate the importance of these statistics it is reasonable to assume that since the production of meat, cereals and wine depended on the maintenance of a certain degree of agricultural production, evidence for the wholesale destruction of the French countryside by war might be equally difficult to sustain. Given the present state of research on this problem it is impossible to generalise; future studies may show that, so far as agricultural production is concerned, the effects of war may have varied greatly from region to region, from year to year.

[58] See Favreau, *Poitiers,* 301ff.

[59] Chevalier, 130

[60] Ibid., 126-31. Also, A.N. X1ª9198, f.109 ʳ·

[61] On the increase in the consumption of wine at Poitiers during this period see Favreau, *Poitiers,* 301.

In considering the difficulties and disadvantages created for the towns by their reception of large numbers of refugees, it might be equally pertinent to ask to what extent their presence resulted in long or short-term economic benefits. Statistical evidence on this matter is, again, greatly lacking, and it is furthermore probable that benefits would vary greatly from town to town. M. Favreau has recently demonstrated that, in respect of Poitou, the advent of Norman craftsmen in the region had an important effect in initiating certain manufacturing industries and significantly expanding others.[62] It is highly likely that this pattern of growth was repeated elsewhere in the 'kingdom of Bourges'.[63] Also, quite apart from their participation in the creation and growth of new industries, the enhanced demand created by the refugees for manufactured goods, and particularly for a range of foodstuffs, could result in the rapid growth of indigenous trades supplying these commodities.

The rapid demographic expansion experienced by the major towns of the 'kingdom of Bourges' is most clearly indicated by the greatly increased demand for domestic commodities, notably food. Yet it must be emphasised that the increased demand for these products came not solely from immigrants; a large proportion derived from those who had moved to the safety of the towns from more vulnerable areas in the immediate neighbourhood. If the creation of new butcheries represents a reliable index of an increasing population, we may employ their presence to tell us something of the distribution of immigrants among the major towns of the 'kingdom of Bourges'. At Poitiers, home of the *Parlement,* the period from 1421-36 witnessed the creation of three new butcheries to cope with the demand for meat from the town's rapidly increasing population.[64] There was a similar situation at Tours, where in 1434 it was decided, in addition, to allow the butchers to sell their products on Saturdays, and, further, to slaughter after midnight and butcher the carcasses on Sundays after ten o'clock.[65] Such demand must have considerably enhanced the economic well-being of the indigenous butchers. But litigation before the Poitiers *Parlement* suggests that they were hardly prepared to adopt a patriotic attitude towards the attempts by immigrant craftsmen to benefit from the increased demand by erecting stalls of their own. As early as January 1420 the archbishop of Tours and the established

---

[62] Ibid., 300-1.

[63] In the case of Tours see Chevalier, 139 n. 109.

[64] Favreau, *Poitiers,* 305-6.

[65] Chevalier, 130.

butchers of Chinon opposed the attempt by Jean de La Mote to set up a butchery stall in Chinon, despite the fact that La Mote claimed that the Dauphin had given him express permission to do so.[66] On 1 April 1420[67] a similar complaint was lodged by the master butchers of Bourges, this time against Pierre l'Enfant, who had attempted to set up a stall in the great butchery situated near the *Porte Gordaine*. In this case the *Parlement* upheld the complaint by the established butchers. The attempt to create a new butchery at Bourges was the source of further litigation before the *Parlement* on 7 August 1427.[68] On this occasion, certain of the indigenous 'butchers' alleged that: 'aucuns forains. . . sont venuz demoure a Bourges. . . et se sont efforcez d'empetrer, et par moien d'aucuns de la court du roy ont de fait empetre, que peussent vendre et detailler chair par les carrefours et ailleurs, ou bon sembleroit.' Though simple enough in appearance this opposition was not without a more selfish motive. The defendants, Jean and Naudain Forez and Guillaume Miton alleged, to the contrary, that 'plusieurs sont retraiz a Bourges pour la guerre'. In view of this, they went on, provision had been made at Poitiers and Tours and elsewhere in the 'kingdom of Bourges', for the creation of new butcheries to cope with the increased demands of a population swollen by large numbers of immigrants. In addition, they pointed out that: 'est a noter l'affluence du peuple es bonnes villes, et que de present au plat pays, obstant la guerre, cesse tout fait de boucherie, et se pourvoit tout a la bonne ville.' Despite the provision made by Charles VII for the creation of new butcheries at Bourges, it appears that ten or twelve individuals had continued to monopolise the sale of meat within the town, with the result that the price of this commodity had risen sharply,[69] the absence of competition preventing, at the same time, any effective amelioration of the situation. More important, in view of this allegation, was the defendants' allegation that Bastart (lieutenant of the *bailli* of Bourges) and Alabat (*Procurerur du roi* at Bourges), responsible for the opposition, were not butchers at all, but royal officials who, in collaboration with a small number of resident butchers, were attempting to preserve a monopoly on the sale of meat. Profit for both parties could be drawn both in the form of high prices

---

[66] A.N. X1ª9190, f.79^{r-v} (31 Jan. 1420).

[67] Ibid., f.92^v.

[68] For what follows see A.N. X1ª9198, fos. 303^r-304^r (contd. on A.N. X1ª9199, fos. 82^vff., passim; A.N. X1ª9191, fos. 87^r-88^r; A.N. X1ª9192, fos. 240^r-241^v).

[69] 'le marchie de la char est meilleurez de la moitie *vel quasi*, et si sont bien de xx a xxx forains, bouchers, qui en recueillent leur vie; et aussi plusieurs de monseigneur le roy et autres s'en doloient; et sont plusieurs qui y ont interestz que les adiournez' (ibid., f.303^v).

demanded as a result of the monopoly, and from the vastly inflated rents charges by the butchers for the existing stalls. Activity of this kind, it was pointed out, appeared particularly odious at a time when so many people obliged to seek refuge at Bourges by virtue of the war desired meat at a reasonable price.

So far as Bourges was concerned, this form of protectionist activity on the part of indigenous craftsmen was by no means confined to the butchers alone; for on 3 July 1428 the *Parlement* heard a complaint by certain 'maitres fonsores' alleging opposition from the oligarchy of Bourges to their attempt to set up a trade in woollen goods.[70]

Opposition to immigrant craftsmen by indigenous guilds appears to have endured throughout the years 1418-36. On 3 March 1429 the *Parlement* reviewed another complaint against the established butchers of Chinon, once again by other craftsmen wishing to establish stalls and slaughterhouses within the town.[71] Yet again, on 3 May 1436, the practice of monopolies was the source of litigation. On this occasion the butchers 'jurez' of Angers protested about the attempt by Jean I and II Beautort and others, natives of Le Mans and Mortagne, to practise their craft within the town. In this instance the (perhaps dubious) allegation by the established butchers that the defendants were in reality 'texiers et marreschaulx', and had openly sold 'dead' beef (*i.e.* from animals which had died from causes other than slaughtering, and which would normally be considered unfit for human consumption), was nevertheless supported by the *Procureur général du roi* in the *Parlement.*[72]

With regard to trades other than butchery it appears that in some cases the creation of monopolies by indigenous craftsmen resulted, in the face of the increased demand, in a serious shortage of manufactured goods. The great influx of immigrants, including a large number of Parisians, to Orléans after 1418 witnessed a deliberate attempt by the established guilds to increase their members' production. Evidence of this strategy appears in litigation before the *Parlement* in April 1422.[73] Here it is apparent that the major guilds of the town were fully

[70] A. N. X1ª9191, f.100ʳ.

[71] A.N. X1ª9199, f.135ʳ⁻ᵛ. Similar situation at La Rochelle in 1430 (A.N. X1ª9199, fos. 246ᵛ-247ᵛ).

[72] A.N. X1ª9201, fos. 198ᵛ-199ʳ (cf. A.N. X1ᶜ147, nos. 47-8).

[73] For what follows see A.N. X1ª9197, fos. 70ᵛff. (contd. A.N. X1ª9191, fos. 148ᵛ-149ᵛ (10 Sept. 1429)). For opposition to alien tanners and bakers establishing their businesses at Orléans see A.N. X1ª9199, fos. 330ʳ-331ʳ, 367ᵛff.; A.N. X1ª9200, fos. 70ᵛff.

aware of the economic potential deriving from the greatly increased demand for manufactured goods. Yet rather than attempting to satisfy demand and to keep prices stable by permitting the creation of new manufacturing centres, certain guilds appear to have been more concerned to maintain a monopoly of production to the exclusion of external competition.

Not long after the occupation of Paris by Burgundian forces some of the more powerful guilds at Orléans, including carpenters, shoemakers, barrelmakers and others, gained permission from Guillaume Cousinot, Chancellor of Orléans, to allow their members to carry on production into the night, both, apparently, as a means of meeting the increased demand for their products, and, at the same time of diminishing the likelihood of resort to alternative sources of production. Despite the issue of this provision, its renewal in December 1422 nevertheless appears to have been accompanied by a considerable rise in the price of certain commodities. Opposition to the monopoly was displayed by Pierre Piquelin, *maître des cordonniers de la ville et faubourg d'Orléans,* soon after the renewal of the aforementioned provision. On the pretext of an insupportable rise in prices, Piquelin had favoured the resort to alternative sources of supply. His opposition was by no means merely vocal, for he had additionally visited certain of those working by night and attempted to disrupt production by confiscating 'biens, ouvrages et oustils'. Piquelin's action was subsequently opposed by the major guilds, including that of the shoemakers, and by Guillaume Cousinot.

What conclusions, in social and economic terms, may be drawn from this (albeit fragmentary) evidence? It appears, first, that in economic terms the influx of refugees to the major towns of the 'kingdom of Bourges' may have resulted, for certain of the indigenous oligarchies at least, in considerable benefits. For many of the guilds, as for members of the local *bourgeoisie,* the deliberate creation of monopolies on the production and distribution of a range of foodstuffs and domestic products was to some extent assisted both by the greatly-increased demand for these products, and by the lack of competition (occasioned predominantly by the war) from mercantile suppliers.[74] Yet in broader terms — and this seems to have applied, for

---

[74] At Poitiers certain *échevin* families, notably that of Claveurier, appear to have benefited from the diminished resort to external sources of supply (Favreau, *Poitiers,* 305-6 and passim). Similar advantage could accrue to local merchants, the absence of fairs and wider mercantile traffic producing, in effect, a captive market (ibid., 307-9). The profitability of this 'commerce without merchants' led, in some cases, to deliberate attempts to prevent any resort to external sources of supply (see, for instance, A.N. X1ᵃ9197, f.71ᵛ). An attempt by the local *bourgeois* and merchants to monopolise the

instance, at Poitiers — the excessive centralization of the production of various items upon the town itself, allied to the cost of maintaining and defending it, may have resulted in increased fiscal burdens for the population as a whole.[75]

With respect, particularly, to the more powerful guilds, the combined effects of war and immigration may have resulted not only in increased wealth, but also in considerably enhanced power and influence. But these factors, far from combining, as one might naturally assume, to produce an economic effect beneficial to Charles VII's war effort, in many cases worked in precisely the opposite fashion. Increased power and autonomy meant, in many cases, increased resistance to local and royal taxation. The multiplicity of individual interests — social, economic and political — encompassed within a particular town might, when allied to the decentralising and isolating effects of the war in general, go a long way towards explaining why attitudes to the course of the '*grande guerre*' could be conditioned by considerations infinitely more pragmatic and personal than patriotic ones. With these considerations uppermost the *Parlement* worked ceaselessly to impose some measure of control upon the independent aspirations of the major towns loyal to Charles VII. Yet the feeling remains that for many the question as to who were the rightful rulers of France was infinitely less pressing than the matter of the maintenance of individual power and privilege.[76]

## By *Parlementaires*

Many of the individuals or entire families who left Paris in the aftermath of the Burgundian occupation were forced to leave most of

production and sale of certain commodities is also evident at Tours (Chevalier, 157-61). For an attempted monopoly on the sale of wine at La Rochelle see A.N. X1ª9199, f.31ʳ⁻ᵛ. For a remarkable case of opposition to an alien craftsman see A.N. X1ª9200, fos.133ʳ⁻ᵛ, 217ᵛ-218ʳ.

[75] That the poorer inhabitants of the towns suffered from the creation of monopolies by local *bourgeois* and merchants, and by the more powerful guilds, seems undeniable. Disadvantages came in the form of greatly increased prices, and from the sale of under-weight or deficient products. At Poitiers, Jeane Voille, a baker, imprisoned for selling under-weight and over-priced bread was ordered to distribute to each of the mendicant orders in the town 'pain cuit d'un sextier de fromme' (A.N. X2ª21, f.180ᵛ). Other individuals were fined for supplying fish to the mayor and other notables illegally (ibid., fos. 180ᵛ, 230ʳ). The *Parlement* took similar action against the sale of under-weight and over-priced bread at Orléans (A.N. X1ª9200, fos. 228ʳff.; A.N. X1ª9193, f.39ʳ⁻ᵛ); also cloth (A.N. X1ª9200, fos. 11ʳ⁻ᵛff.). In 1422 the consuls of Montpellier complained to the *Parlement* that the prices charged by local fishermen for their fish were such that 'le menu peuple n'en povoit avoir' (A.N. X1ª9200, fos. 112ᵛff.).

[76] No better example of bi-partisan behaviour may be found than that displayed by some of the inhabitants of Bordeaux (M.G.A. Vale, 'The last years of English Gascony, 1451-3', *TRHS* 5th Ser., 19 (1969), 119-38).

their possessions behind, many being later confiscated and redistributed by the Lancastrians. Some, however, as before the siege of Orléans, had foreseen the impending danger and thus managed to evacuate a portion of their valuables to a safer place. Others, though destitute in the immediate aftermath of the occupation managed, nevertheless, to accumulate variable wealth during the period of exile from Paris. In either case, the partition of a man's possessions after his death was frequently the cause of litigation before the *Parlement*. The goods of those who chose to remain in Paris after 1418 were automatically confiscated by the *Parlement* and their distribution made usually according to Charles VII's pleasure.

The early years of the *Parlement*'s operation witnessed a steady flow of cases involving disputes over the wills of individuals murdered by the Burgundians who had possessions in the 'kingdom of Bourges'. A notable proportion came from the town of Orléans.[77] Prominent among the examples of this form of dispute was that arising from the partition of the inheritance of Pierre Lesclat, a former *conseiller* in the Paris *Parlement*. Additionally *maître des requêtes de l'Hôtel du Roi* and *Chancelier* of Charles VI's Queen, Lesclat had accumulated a fortune estimated at 30-40,000 *francs*. In 1417, in anticipation of impending violence in Paris, he moved a large proportion of his valuables and movable possessions into the safekeeping of Étienne l'Amirault at Orléans. In 1418 Lesclat was murdered by the Burgundians, but his widow, Jeanne Porchière, and her children, managed to escape, 'poor and sad', to the safety of Orléans.[78] On 1 April 1427 some years later, the *Parlement* heard Jeanne's complaint against l'Amirault, who had apparently refused to restore Lesclat's possessions. The dispute was not finally resolved until 13 June 1431 when the *Parlement* awarded Jeanne legal custody of her husband's possessions, with the exception of a number of smaller items, which l'Amirault was permitted to keep.[79] Somewhat earlier again, on 23

[77]Many Parisians, non-*parlementaires*, went to Orléans (A.N. X1ª9197, fos. 55ᵛ, 170ᵛff.; A.N. X2ª18, fos. 15ᵛ, 23ᵛ; A.N. X1ª9200, fos. 169ᵛff.; A.N. X1ª9201, fos. 10ᵛff.);others to La Rochelle (A.N. X2ª18, fos. 14ᵛff.) and Saint-Pourcain (ibid., fos. 79ʳff.). Normans went to Orléans (A.N. X1ª9198, f.3ᵛ); Blois (X1ª9191, f.22ʳ); Saumur (X1ª9200, f.133ʳ); Bourges (X1ª9190, fos. 256ᵛff.); Poitiers, Tours, Angers and elsewhere in the Loire valley (above, passim). One inhabitant of Blois, Pierre Godefroy, it was alleged, in 1426, 'migrated' in a reverse manner to Dreux to make money out of localised brigandage (A.N. X2ª18, fos.81ᵛff.).

[78]See A.N. X2ª18, fos. 102ᵛ, 113ʳff., passim. Jean I de Vailly, *premier Président*, was the curator of Lesclat's children, including Pierre II, *licencié-en-lois* (A.N. X1ª9195, f.37ʳ⁻ᵛ).

[79]A.N. X2ª21, f.161ᵛ (ibid., passim, for further details of this affair).

June 1421,[80] the *Parlement* entertained a dispute over the partition of the will of Pierre Boschet, before 1418 *Président* in the Paris *Parlement* . The original execution of Boschet's will had been entrusted to the Poitiers *Parlement.*

In the event of the death of a *conseiller* in the *Parlement*, the preparation of the inventory of his possessions and the execution of his will, were supervised by the *Parlement*. In a number of cases commissioners were actually appointed to inventory not only those possessions located in the 'kingdom of Bourges', but also those in areas under Anglo-Burgundian occupation.[81] The frequent refusal by the commissioners to comply with this directive[82] meant that, if any initiative was ever taken, it was usually only by the heirs of the deceased or by other interested parties. In some cases royal officials who were not *parlementaires* also entrusted the execution of their wills to the *Parlement.*[83] In cases where an individual died intestate his possessions automatically escheated to the crown, and their sale would normally be employed to finance the cost of his funeral, masses and other provisions, including any debts incurred by him during his lifetime. A similar procedure was adopted in instances where a deceased *parlementaire* had surviving relatives who had continued to reside in enemy-occupied areas. The death of the clerical *conseiller* Pierre Paumier in August 1433[84] saw the *Parlement* automatically take possession of his inheritance on the grounds that his only surviving relative, his mother, had remained in Paris after 1418.[85] In this instance the *Parlement*'s action was contested by relatives of the deceased who had left Paris after the Burgundian occupation.[86] After making the usual provision from the will for funeral expenses the *Parlement* was obliged to relinquish a portion of Paumier's possessions to the claimants.[87]

---

[80] A.N. X1ª9190, f.155ᵛ. Concerning the allocation of 4 silver marks by Boschet to the wife of Jean, *seigneur* of Plessis-Bustard.

[81] See, for example, A.N. X2ª21, f.189ᵛ; A.N. X1ª9194, fos. 16ᵛ, 38ʳ.

[82] See A.N. X2ª21, fos. 189ʳ, 223ʳ; A.N. X1ª9194, f.16ᵛ.

[83] A.N. X1ª8604, fos. 91ʳff., 95ᵛff., 97ᵛff.

[84] A.N. X1ª9194, f.53ʳ (14 Aug. 1433).

[85] See A.N. X1ª8604, f.117ʳ (14 Oct. 1433, Tours), where Charles VII ordered one half of Paumier's possessions to be given to the *Parlement* and the *requêtes de l'Hôtel* in part-payment of their wages; the other half was sent to Guillaume Charrier, receiver-general of finances.

[86] Opposition was brought by Paumier's heirs on 19 Jan. 1434 (A.N. X1ª9194, fos. 56ᵛ-57ʳ). This was met by opposition from the *Procureur général du roi* (ibid., fos. 70ᵛff., passim, A.N. X1ª9200, fos. 195ᵛff., passim).

[87] A.N. X1ª9194, f.80ʳ⁻ᵛ (9 Sept. 1434). The final settlement was: one-third of the goods to the *Parlement* to pay for funeral and masses; two-thirds to Paumier's heirs.

In the case of those *conseillers* who opted to remain in Paris and serve the Anglo-Burgundian *Parlement*, yet who retained possessions in the 'kingdom of Bourges', the procedure adopted by the *Parlement* was similar to that followed in respect of those who died intestate, or who had surviving relatives in northern France — that is, their possessions automatically escheated to the crown. Action of this kind taken against Guillaume Aimery, lay *conseiller* in the Paris *Parlement*, resulted in litigation at Poitiers on 15 July 1435.[88] Aimery's failure to appear at Poitiers to answer charges brought some years previously by the *Procureur général du roi*, resulted in the confiscation of that part of his property located below the Loire. Aimery attempted to prevent this course of action by means of an appeal delivered before the Paris *Parlement* in 1428. This proved unsuccessful, and Charles VII subsequently ordered the distribution of Aimery's possessions to Jean Rabateau and Jean Juvénal des Ursins – both *Avocats du roi* at Poitiers — 'pour aucunes causes a ce le mouvans'. Far from relinquishing his appeal, Aimery, in the aftermath of this action, decided to air his complaint at Poitiers, through the medium of his attorney, Jean Gabier. In reply to the charge brought by Jean Barbin, for the *Procureur général du roi*, that in deciding to remain in Paris after the Burgundian occupation he had committed the crime of *lèsemajesté*, Aimery replied that he had been taken prisoner by the Burgundians and compelled to serve in Paris. Furthermore, he went on, 'est tresbien seant pardela par le roy, aussi sont d'autres; et est bien mestier que en la ville de Paris en y ait de bons, car par aventure ils seront, se Dieu plaist, cause de la reduire'. Barbin, little impressed by this argument, pointed out in reply that despite Aimery's claim that he had been forcefully restrained from journeying to Poitiers to answer the original charges brought against him, he had nevertheless in 1427 journeyed into Burgundy and could have easily presented himself on that occasion if he had so wished.

## By foreigners

Besides litigation concerned predominantly with the occupational visits made by foreign merchants to the 'kingdom of Bourges' the registers of the *Parlement* disclose signs of more permanent settlement by foreigners, including merchants, soldiers, *hommes d'affaires* and craftsmen.

On the migration of German workers little is indicated. There is evidence for the presence of a German gunsmith or *fourbisseur* of

---

[88] For what follows see A.N. X1ᵃ9201, fos. 191ʳ-192ʳ.

weapons at Poitiers, [89] and for the presence of German merchants at La Rochelle[90] and at Tours.[91] Further indication of the presence of immigrants, or itinerant labourers of German provenance is, moreover, indicated by litigation before the *Parlement* on 8 May 1430.[92] Cited before the court were Angelin Boursier, Jean Courrant and Henri Lances, called by their opponents in litigation 'gens estrangiers du pais d'Alemeign, ouvries de mines, . . . poueurs gens, joueurs de diz'. Boursier explained that he and his companions had earlier come from Germany 'pour ouvrier en fait des mines' in the Mâconnais (possibly silver mines). He had since married a local woman and settled at Courzieu and had used his house as a base from which to commit numerous robberies in the village by night.

The busy maritime trade at La Rochelle probably led to the growth of a large alien community of merchants in the town. On 2 September 1424,[93] the *Parlement* heard the demand by Guillaume l'Évêque, called *de Montfort*, merchant of La Rochelle, against Jean Boymen, merchant of Flanders and resident of the town, for restitution of the price of three tuns of wine sold at Lecluse in 1410, Boymen being the *homme d'affaires* of Jean d'Estamain, himself the heir of Jourdain Classon, originally responsible for transporting the wine.

In addition to the Flemish at La Rochelle there is evidence for a sizeable Italian presence. I have earlier remarked upon the presence of Genoese merchants at La Rochelle;[94] moreover, on 24 April 1430[95] the *Parlement* heard complaints by the mayor and *échevins* against Guy de Lombars, native of Lombardy, who arrived at La Rochelle in December 1429 'amena une quaraque'. After his arrival it was reported to the *échevins* that Lombars was 'envieux a tuie et passne du peschie'; as a result he was adjourned before their jurisdiction to answer charges. Opposition was lodged by the bishop of Saintes, who alleged that Lombars was Venetian and a cleric. The *Procureur général du roi* nevertheless maintained that Lombars was

[89] See A.N. X2ª21, f.94ʳ⁻ᵛ. For the presence of one Claus Heu, possibly of Metz (cf. Favreau, *Poitiers*, 589, no. 29) at Poitiers, see A.N. X1ª9197, f.146ʳ. See also. A.N. X1ª9198, fos. 33ᵛ-34ʳ.

[90] A.N. X1ª9199, fos. 32ʳff.

[91] A.N. X1ª9197, f. 259ᵛ.

[92] See A.N. X2ª18, fos. 203ᵛff. (also, A.N. X2ª20, f.29ʳ⁻ᵛ).

[93] A.N. X1ª9190, f.307ʳ. For further evidence of trade with Flanders see A.N. X2ª18, fos. 72ʳff.

[94] Above, pp. 127-8.

[95] See A.N. X2ª18, fos. 198ᵛff. For evidence of Lombard merchants at La Rochelle, see Favreau, *Poitiers*, n.1110; and possibly at Poitiers, A.N. X2ª21, f.163ʳ.

lay, and that as such competence in the matter lay with the *Parlement*.

In as much as litigation before the *Parlement* may be interpreted as a convincing guide, the number of Italians at La Rochelle appears to have been considerably inferior to that of Spaniards, and particularly Castilians, resident in the town. The growth of Castilian trade with La Rochelle following the English occupation of the Norman ports was ultimately responsible for the decision by Castilian authorities in 1423 to substitutes the *prévôt* of La Rochelle for the *prévôts* of Harfleur and Leure as the arbitrator of legal disputes involving Castilian merchants and merchandise.[96] Evidence of permanent settlements by Spanish immigrants is indicated by litigation before the *Parlement* on 16 December 1423.[97] Nicolas de Surgiano had complained to the *prévôt* of La Rochelle that another Spaniard, Martinez Donodo (or Doriondo), had earlier been charged with the transport from Saint André in Spain to La Rochelle of five coffers containing domestic effects belonging to Surgiano, valued at 200 *écus d'or*. Failure to deliver the coffers led to Donodo's arrest in June or July 1423 and his eventual appearance before the *prévôt's* jurisdiction. However, Donodo's claim that the passage of the goods had been obstructed by Spanish officials was upheld by the *Parlement* and he was given until 24 June 1424 to complete the delivery. On 7 March 1426[98] the *Parlement* upheld the complaint by another Spaniard, Pierre Peris of Satarro, together with Jean Martines of Vidassoles, against the *échevins* of La Rochelle regarding the partition of the will of another Spaniard, Martin Jehan.

Further evidence of the permanence of Spanish settlement at La Rochelle, even by the late 1420s is displayed by litigation before the *Parlement* on 26 July 1429.[99] Here, Gensalvo Mendes claimed that out of hatred for him, deriving initially from the contested ownership of a certain bed, Jeanne Gauvaigne had fabricated a charge of sexual assault by Mendes against one of her chambermaids called Denise. Gauvaigne maintained to the contrary that Mendes had carnal desires upon Denise, and on the pretext of leading her to meet a certain soldier, Jean de La Ville, to whom she was 'fort tenue', Mendes had drawn Denise into the stables of Jean de La Fons and had 'compagnie charnel contre sa voulente'. However, Rabateau, for the *Procureur général du roi*, judged that as Mendes was sergeant of the mayor of La

[96] Favreau, *Poitiers,* 308 n.1111.
[97] A.N. X1ª9190, fos. 275ᵛ-276ʳ.
[98] A.N. X1ª9198, f.132ʳ.
[99] See A.N. X2ª18, f.169ʳ⁻ᵛ, for what follows. Also A.N. X2ª21, fos. 110ʳ., passim.

Rochelle and *bourgeois* of the town, jurisdiction in the matter lay with the mayor. Similarly indicative of the permanence of Spanish settlement was the appeal by Huguet Bauduceau to the *Parlement* against the governor of La Rochelle on 18 November 1432.[100] Bauduceau alleged that by virtue of his relation to Jean Bauduceau, earlier servant of Loppe Rouys and Tareze Garcie, Spaniards living at La Rochelle in the parish of Saint Sauveur, he was the lawful possessor of a house and other possessions owned by the couple. Bauduceau's claim was, however, denied by the *Procureur général du roi* who maintained that in view of the fact that the couple were aliens, their property automatically escheated to the crown. In addition to the numbers of Spanish concerned mainly with mercantile affairs, these years also witnessed the presence of significant numbers of Aragonese and Castilian mercenaries contracted to fight for Charles VII, both at sea and on land.[101]

La Rochelle was also the disembarking point for large numbers of Scottish mercenaries contracted to serve in the Dauphin's army after 1418. Accompanied in some cases by their families and retainers, the Scots settled, apparently in ephemeral fashion, in Touraine between 1420 and 1424,[102] and in more permanent fashion in Berry and Poitou.[103] Some traces of the movement and settlement of the Scots in the 'kingdom of Bourges' remain in the registers of the Poitiers *Parlement.* On 24 December 1423[104] we have evidence of a robbery, committed two years earlier, upon John Douglas, while he was lodging in the hostelry of Jean Martin, hotelier 'sur les ponts de Saumur', in which 530*l.t.* was stolen in money and valuables. On 23 June 1425 the *Parlement* heard the complaint by Jean Herby and Jean de Moncy against another Scot, Laurent Vernon. The pair alleged that on 1 March 1423 they had lent Vernon 600 *écus d'or* which he promised to repay from the ransom of the duke of Somerset, his prisoner at Baugé in 1421.[105] The money was to be had by recourse to the duchess of Clarence, Somerset's mother, in England. However, the duchess refused to pay and Herby and Moncy subsequently cited

[100] See A.N. X1ª9200, fos. 82rff.

[101] See P. Contamine, *Guerre, État et Société à la fin du Moyen âge,* (Paris, 1972), 253-5.

[102] B. Chevalier, *Tours: ville royale (1356-1520),* (Paris/Louvain, 1975), 179.

[103] Some went much further afield. In 1431 Matthew Hohat was involved in litigation for the office of 'viguier de la court commune du Puy' (A.N. X1ᶜ142, no. 29).

[104] See A.N. X1ª9190, f.267r-v.

[105] A.N. X1ª9190, fos. 348v-349r (also A.N. X1ª9198, f.65v). In May 1423 Vernon received the lordship of Montreuil-Bonin in Poitou in recompense for having relinquished his prisoner to Charles VII (Favreau, *Poitiers,* 274, no. 864).

Vernon before the *Parlement*. The *Parlement* upheld the appeal and ordered Vernon to repay the original 600 *écus d'or*.

On 6 April 1424[106] the *Parlement* was host to the earl of Douglas, recently arrived at La Rochelle with a force of Scottish noblemen and esquires and due to rendez-vous with Charles VII at Bourges on 15 April.[107] Douglas and the constable Buchan were invited by the *Parlement* to witness litigation taking place that day between Jean Rinet, called *Gastart*, and another Scot, John Newton. The case involved the sum of 600 *écus d'or* lent earlier by Newton to Thomas Stone (or Seton).[108] Stone had, allegedly, given the sum to Rinet for safekeeping though the latter had subsequently denied any knowledge of the transaction.

On 4 May 1426[109] another eminent Scot, John Stewart, constable of the Scottish army and *seigneur* of Derval,[110] figured in litigation before the *Parlement* by reason of certain *'vestis et tapiciorum'* sold to him by the late Jean d'Angennes for 800 *écus d'or*. In default of delivery of the articles Stewart demanded the return of the sum of 410 *écus d'or*, which he had already paid. Stewart's complaint was upheld by the *Parlement*.

Something of an ambivalent view towards Scottish military presence in the 'kingdom of Bourges' is evidenced by litigation before the *Parlement* in 1427.[111] The plaintiff, Christy Chamber, captain of Charles VII's bodyguard of Scots archers, explained that he had earlier come to France in the company of the constable Buchan. Buchan later appointed Christy governor and captain of Fontenay-le-Comte.[112] In recognition of his services, furthermore, Charles VII

[106] See A.N. X1ª9197, fos. 302ᵛ-303ᵛ, for what follows.

[107] See L. Caillet, *Étude sur les relations de la commune de Lyon avec Charles VII et Louis XI (1417-1483)* (Lyon, 1909), 342. Douglas received the duchy of Touraine on 19 April 1424 (A.N. X1ª8604, fos. 65ʳff.), and later made a grand entry at Tours (Chevalier, 129 n.79).

[108] For more on Stone see A.N. X1ª9195, fos. 219ʳ, 224ᵛ-225ʳ.

[109] See A.N. X1ª9191, f.20ʳ⁻ᵛ (also A.N. X1ª9198, fos. 109ᵛ-110ʳ).

[110] The Scots, including Buchan, were important allies of Jean V of Brittany in the early 1420s. Following his capture by members of the Penthièvre faction in February 1420 Jean V issued, on 8 October following, collars of his Order of Ermine to 'un chevalier et neuff escuiers d'Escoce, demorans o nostre. . . le comte de Bouquan' (*Lettres et mandements de Jean V, duc de Bretagne* ed. R. Blanchard, *Société des bibliophiles bretons,* vi (Nantes, 1892) no. 1464). Also, G.-A. Lobineau, *Histoire de Bretagne,* i (Paris, 1707), 542-57, passim.

[111] For what follows see A.N. X2ª18, fos. 121ᵛ, 133ᵛ-134ᵛ.

[112] Chamber additionally received the lordship of Villeneuve-la-Comtesse from Charles VII in 1424, in recompense for a loan of 3,000 *réaux d'or*. Opposition to the

152

later promoted him 'capitaine des Escoz de la garde de son corps'.[113] However, Buchan's death, and the heavy defeat suffered by French forces at Verneuil, was followed by a hostile reaction against other Scots who were generally held responsible for the defeat.[114] As a precaution Christy sent his possessions, amounting to the value of over 1,000 *écus d'or*, to the safekeeping of Guillaume de La Roche. La Roche's house was later ransacked by Gauvain de Torigné, servant and captain of Georges de La Trémoïlle, and in the process Christy's valuables were stolen. The *Procureur général du roi* subsequently joined with Chamber in demanding restitution of the goods despite Torigné's counter-allegation that Chamber's enmity toward him had earlier resulted in Chamber's attempt at capture and ransom of his person for the sum of 120 *écus d'or*.

Despite the heavy defeats suffered by Charles VII's armies at Cravant and Verneuil Scottish settlement in the 'kingdom of Bourges' had by the late 1420s begun to take on a more permanent aspect, particularly in the province of Berry.[115] In January 1428[116] the *Parlement* reviewed an appeal from the local assizes of John Stewart, lord of Darnley, at Aubigny-sur-Nère. Conflict derived from the allegation by Stewart's officials that, according to local custom, if 'la femme bat le mari, l'en doit chevaucher l'asne'. Arnoul Durand, victim of this ruling, had earlier become involved in a domestic quarrel with his wife, which culminated with her striking him 'un cop de sa quenoille sur l'ueil'. News of the affair reached John Thomas, Stewart's lieutenant and captain at Aubigny, who confronted Durand about the custom, asking if 'chevaucheroit point l'asne, et se les femmes seroient mestresses'. Durand's rebuttal of Thomas's demand saw the latter nevertheless force him to suffer this humiliating punishment. In the aftermath of the incident Durand, incensed at his treatment retaliated by wounding one of Stewart's officers. The

gift was brought by the *Procureur général du roi* at Poitiers, in 1433 (A.N. X1ª9194, fos. 50ʳff., passim).

[113] For payments to members of the Scots bodyguard for their services see A.N. 1AP 171, nos. 47, 49; A.N. 1AP 172B, no. 20 and B.N. MS. fr.26057, no. 2237.

[114] The defeat at Verneuil may have provoked a general reaction against Scottish presence (Chevalier, 179 n.15). In the short-term it provided the Angevin faction at Charles VII's court with a convenient pretext for the removal of Louvet, Frotier and co., and the installation of Richemont as Constable (ibid., 220).

[115] See, for instance, P.-J. de Bengy-Puyvallée, *Mémoire historique sur le Berry* (Bourges, 1842), esp. 42ff. On the Scottish presence generally, see X. Francisque-Michel, *Les Écossais en France; les Français en Écosse*, i (London, 1862), and E. Cust., *Some account of the Stuarts of Aubigny in France, 1422-1672* (London, 1891).

[116] For what follows see A.N. X2ª18, fos. 136ʳff. (Also, A.N. X2ª21, fos. 87ʳff. and A.N. X2ª20, fos. 18ᵛff.).

*Parlement* subsequently condemned the original indignity forced upon Durand by Thomas, and demanded fines totalling 250*l.t.* on Durand's behalf.

Evidence of a different kind for the entrenchment of Scottish settlement, this time in Poitou, is indicated by litigation before the *Parlement* on 17 January 1429.[117] This concerned the complaint by Laurent Vernon, mentioned earlier, now *seigneur* of Montreuil-Bonin in Poitou, that Antoine, self-styled *seigneur* of Le Pesle, had lately attempted to construct a fortified tower at Le Pesle, which was prejudicial to his own rights in the area. Antoine's opposition followed an earlier attempt by the lieutenant-general of the *sénéchaussée* of Poitou to pull down the tower.

The escalation of conflict in Poitou between the partisans of Richemont and La Trémoïlle after 1429, and the generally diminished interest in the *'grande guerre'* which accompanied it, left mercenary bands in neighbouring provinces in a dangerous state of inactivity. During this period the *Parlement* heard numerous complaints about localised pillaging by soldiery, including Scots, temporarily idle through the lack of conflict with the English. For a *seigneur* 'on the make' redundant mercenary bands could represent convenient 'allies', suitable for employment in conflict of a localised kind against the personal, rather than the common, enemy. Prominent among those who found a convenient use for the mercenaries was Pierre Frotier, *seigneur* of Preuilly-sur-Claise. Frotier's 'banishment' into comfortable circumstances in 1425 following Richemont's reception as constable did not endure for long. Richemont's decline after 1428 in the face of La Trémoïlle's rise to power about Charles VII saw Frotier's attempt at renewed power-building from his old base at Preuilly. On 12 April 1431[118] the *Parlement* heard the complaint by Pierre de Salinhac, with the *Procureur du roi,* that Frotier had recently attempted to force his subjects at Lingé and La Puye to perform watch and guard duties at Azay-le-Ferron. Refusal by the inhabitants of the places to comply saw Frotier destroy Salinhac's fortifications at La Puye, and, in addition, direct an assault on Lingé in which seven people were killed and the place pillaged. Among Frotier's allies in the perpetration of this act were numbers of Scottish mercenaries currently lying idle in Berry in the absence of conflict with the English.

[117] See A.N. X1ᵃ9191, f.111ᵛ. Also A.N. X1ᵃ9192, fos. 312ʳ-313ʳ; A.N. X1ᶜ144, no. 93.
[118] See A.N. X2ᵃ18, fos. 250ᵛff.

This incident was followed, on 23 June 1432,[119] by the *Parlement*'s endorsement of letters of pardon delivered by Charles VII in favour of a Scot and others of his retinue. On 7 July 1433[120] further excesses communicated to the *Parlement* involving Frotier once again indicated Scottish presence among the culprits. In some areas, notably Berry, destruction and pillaging by the Scots was of a serious and enduring kind. On 10 May 1434[121] Raoulin de Vaulx alleged that destruction caused by the Scots at Châtillon-sur-Indre was so great that the captain of the place refused to let him proceed with the levy of a certain *aide*, the inhabitants of the place being too poor to contribute anything.

## The *'Bonnes Villes'*: the Problem of Control

The ability of the *Parlement* to restrict the fiscal and judicial autonomy of a particular town depended largely upon two factors: first, the distance which separated it from the place in question; second, the proximity of the town to alternative forms of political alliance. The regularity with which the *Parlement* conducted litigation relating to the government of Poitiers, La Rochelle or Niort, indicates, not so much that control of these places was considered any more important than that of more distant towns, merely that the likelihood of maintaining a measure of control over their affairs was considerably greater. In the case of towns such as Limoges, Lyon or Tournai, the question of control was infinitely more difficult and delicate, not simply because of their distant location, but because in each case the situation of the town offered convenient recourse to alternative forms of political alliance.[122] Lyon, for instance, is a well-documented example of the way in which a powerful town might employ the war in France, given its important strategic situation, as a deliberate means of increasing its autonomy.[123] Here loyalty was maintained less by deliberate control or coercion than by concession. Even where Charles VII was forced to acknowledge that a town had deliberately abused its enhanced autonomy, as in the case of Limoges,[124] he could,

---

[119] A.N. X2ᵃ21, f.184ᵛ.

[120] A.N. X2ᵃ21, f.217ᵛ.

[121] A.N. X1ᵃ9200, fos. 233ᵛ-234ʳ.

[122] 'Towns on vulnerable frontier lines. . . could not, when those frontier lines were threatened, be too much restricted' (P.S. Lewis, *Later Medieval France. The Polity* (London, 1968), 268).

[123] 'When the war was over, even a town like Lyon. . . began to feel the pinch' (ibid., 269).

[124] See A.N. X2ᵃ20, fos. 43ᵛff.

under the circumstances, do little more than pardon the offenders, however high-handedly the *Parlement* might strive to emphasise the theoretical prerogatives of the sovereign.

In a more important sense, however, the tendency to employ the divisions caused by war with the English for individual advantage — and this was true not only of urban governments but also of Charles VII's more powerful vassals — derived not so much from simple disloyalty or disaffection as from the desire to safeguard individual privileges, fiscal and judicial, against increasing erosion by royal government. During the early decades of the fifteenth century this was by no means a new problem, yet the occupation of Normandy by the English and the formation of an Anglo-Burgundian coalition presented Charles VII's government with the problem of asserting the (predominantly theoretical) rights of the sovereign, not only when there were two claimants to the French throne, but when the opportunity for resistance on the part of those wishing to avoid the implementation of those rights was greatest. After 1418 the war in France was, for Charles VII, a double war: on the one hand a conflict of a proto-national kind with the English; on the other a conflict of a neo-feudal nature with the members of his own nobility. This explains the need to reach a settlement with Burgundy and, in the long term, why the expulsion of the English was so long delayed.

At Poitiers the problem of control was simplified by a number of factors, not least the presence of the *Parlement* at the centre of the town; the links created between *parlementaires* and *échevins;* and the absorption of a significant proportion of the *échevins* into local royal administration. A similar situation may have prevailed at Bourges, home of the *Chambre des comptes,* though we lack evidence for a confident assertion. Elsewhere, notably at La Rochelle, this symbiosis between local royal administration and urban government seems to have been much less pronounced, and the often divergent aspirations of the two authorities provided a regular source of conflict. While it may be accurate to view the recruitment to local royal administration, among individuals who were simultaneously members of urban governments, as an important factor in the crown's eventual ability to impose a measure of control over the towns,[125] it appears, equally, that this progression was both slow and erratic. In the case of towns such as Lyon, Tournai, or Limoges, situated in close proximity to enemy-occupied areas, it was even further inhibited by the political

[125]Lewis, 247. In the more distant towns the period 1418-36 may have witnessed a slackening, if not a reversal, of the drift towards involvement in local royal administration.

156

equivocacy of the governors themselves.[126] At Lyon conflict stemmed
not only from confrontation with the *bailli* and his officials but also
from divisions among the consuls themselves — one party favouring
alliance with the Empire, another with Charles VII.[127] Far from
proving detrimental to the town, the threat of alliance with one party
could easily be employed to exact concessions from the other. It was
in this spirit of self-interest, rather than patriotism that the war was
viewed by many towns.

Confrontation between the *Parlement* and the *échevins* of La
Rochelle derived partly from the proximity of La Rochelle to Poitiers
and partly from the great strategic importance of the town as sole
maritime link for the 'kingdom of Bourges'. Initial confrontation with
the *échevins* came in 1422 soon after the installation of the court. It
followed the complaint by local *bourgeois* and royal officials that the
*échevins* had attempted to create a monopoly on the exercise of fiscal
and judicial authority in the town to the detriment of their own
privileges. In response to an inquiry led by Jean de Vailly, *Premier
Président* and Jean Girard, *maître des requêtes de l'Hôtel du Roi*,
the *Procureur général du roi* in *Parlement* demanded that the
*échevins* be temporarily deprived of the exercise of their authority at
La Rochelle. Restoration of their powers was eventually made on 3
January 1423 by Charles VII, by virtue of letters issued at Bourges,
though under closely defined conditions.[128] Despite the apparent
severity of this edict, however, the importance of La Rochelle's
situation ensured that future dealings with the *échevins* would be
determined more by tact and diplomacy than by strength.

Clearly there were some at La Rochelle who would have been
perfectly happy to countenance the prospect of English presence
within the town. Feelings that the place could easily have become
another Bordeaux must have enhanced the *Parlement*'s concern over
the activities of subversive elements. Prominent among these was
Olivier Chicot. Reprimanded (though not severely punished) by the
*Parlement* in 1420 for spreading rumours in the *Palais* to the effect

[126]At towns such as Tournai, it is difficult to see how the consuls could have acted
otherwise. In 1421 they agreed that, with the town 'environnee des villes et pays de
monseigneur de Bourgogne, ce seroit la desolation de ceste ville d'encourir indignation'
(*Extraits des anciens registres aux délibérations des consaux de la ville de Tournai
(1385-1422)*, ed. H. Vandenbröeck, *Mém. Soc. Hist. Litt. de Tournai* 7 (1861),
225). See also, ibid. 8 (1863), 9-10.

[127]*Reg. consulaires*, ii (Lyon, 1926), 271, 274 and passim. Lyon also maintained
its *procureurs* in the Paris *Parlement* (ibid., 278, 304).

[128]See A.N. X1ª8604, fos. 61ʳff. The *échevins'* privileges were nevertheless restored
by Charles VII in Nov. 1424.

that Montargis had fallen to the English,[129] Chicot was again called before the *Parlement* on 13 December 1423.[130] Here, the *échevins* of La Rochelle and the *Procureur général du roi* heard that Chicot had remained in Paris for some time after the Burgundian occupation in the company of the Veau de Bar. During this time he had somehow contrived that 'Martelet du Mesnil se fist le gouvernement de La Rochelle, ou il fist Chicot son lieutenant; avec ledit. . . Martelet voult estre bailli du grant fief d'Aulnys'. In his capacity as Mesnil's lieutenant, Chicot, it was alleged, had openly abused his self-invested powers. On one occasion news of the advent of an English army at La Rochelle saw the *échevins* appeal to the Dauphin for assistance. The arrival of a relieving force led by Barbazan nevertheless saw Chicot, aided by Jean Meynart, assemble a crowd of some 500 people to prevent Barbazan's force gaining entry to the town. Under cover of the ensuing riot Meynart had additionally incited the crowd to ransack the house of Jean Merichon, a royal official,[131] to the extent of 3,000 *écus d'or* damage. Despite the seriousness of these crimes Chicot, *licencié-en-lois,* was accepted as an *avocat* in the *Parlement* before 1431.[132]

In an attempt to maintain royal authority at La Rochelle the *Parlement* may have followed a deliberate policy of promoting members of reliable Poitevin families into the local royal administration. Jean Merichon, *receveur général de toutes finances* in 1418, and mayor of La Rochelle in 1419 and 1426, was of *échevin* stock, related to the families of Turpin and Guérinet in Poitiers. Étienne Gillier, *Procurer du roi* at Saintonge and La Rochelle by 1420 and mayor in 1427 was linked by marriage to the families of Taunay, Royrand and Guichart. Finally, Jean Mourraut, early *Avocat fiscal du roi* at La Rochelle was related to the most powerful dynasties in Poitiers, including the Claveuriers.

Confrontation between local royal officials and the mayor and *échevins* of La Rochelle was frequent. On 27 November 1424[133] Mourraut appeared before the *Parlement* in response to an allegation by the *échevins* that he had earlier contrived to turn the town over to the

---

[129]*A.H.-G.* MS.59, f.119ʳ⁻ᵛ. For another case of sympathy for the English at La Rochelle see A.N. X1ᵃ9199, f.40ʳ.

[130]For what follows see A.N. X2ᵃ18, fos. 14ᵛff., 19ʳ. Also A.N. X2ᵃ21, fos. 10ᵛff.,; A.N. X2ᵃ20, fos. 3ʳ-4ᵛ.

[131]Merichon, a Poitevin, was an *élu* on the *aides* in Poitou in 1417 (A.N. X1ᵃ9197, f.34ʳ).

[132]See A.N. X1ᵃ9192, f.228ʳ⁻ᵛ.

[133]For what follows see A.N. X2ᵃ18, fos. 46ʳ-58ʳ, passim. Also A.N. X2ᵃ21, fos. 27ʳ, 38ʳ-39ʳ.

English by placing a table beneath the walls to permit the entry of an
armed force. More generally, it was alleged, Mourraut had consistently
attempted to undermine the authority of the mayor and *échevins*. How
far these allegations were true or to what extent they represent an
attempt by the *échevins* to discredit a troublesome opponent is not
clear.[134] In his defence Mourraut claimed that the mayor and *échevins*
bore a grudge against him because he earlier 'fist devant le roy a La
Rochelle la proposition sur le fait du gouvernement de la ville'.
Whatever the truth of these accounts Guillaume I Le Tur, speaking
for the *Procureur général du roi,* stressed the importance of stable
government at La Rochelle in view of the great strategic importance of
the town — a good example of the way in which wider political
considerations could, at times, predominate over purely legal ones.
The affair may have served to debar Mourraut from gaining office in
the *Parlement.* On 15 May 1433[135] he presented letters of election as
*Avocat criminel* in succession to Jean Rabateau, lately promoted lay
*Président* in the *Chambre des comptes.* Despite Rabateau's active
consent (and possibly, through his membership of the *Grand Conseil,*
personal sponsorship) to the election, the *Parlement* refused to accept
Mourraut's nomination, ostensibly because of his involvement in the
earlier case of sedition at La Rochelle. The multiple requests of
ostensibly Charles VII in favour of Mourraut were equally ignored by
the *Parlement.*

Despite its awareness of the need to maintain good relations with
the mayor and *échevins* of La Rochelle, the *Parlement* did not hesitate
to intervene in instances where royal authority might suffer as a
consequence. We have already seen something of this problem in
respect of the mercantile affairs of the town and how, under certain
circumstances, the *Parlement* was compelled to recognise the privileges
of the *échevins.*[136] Confrontation of a different kind resulted in
litigation before the *Parlement* on 26 April 1428.[137] The dispute
originated in the refusal by Rioulet, a member of the guild of
carpenters at La Rochelle, 'alier au May avec autres, qui pour ce sont
accoustumie d'assembler le premier jour de May... ne payer son taux
de la torche de la confrance'. The *échevins* pointed out that it was

---

[134]It is worthy of note that, with regard to the other towns included in our survey,
allegations of sedition directed by the governing bodies against individuals involved to a
marked degree those who were additionally royal officials (below, passim). Such
allegations may have been deliberately employed as a means of loosening irksome
royal control at a local level.

[135]See A.N. X1ᵃ9194, fos. 43ᵛ-44ʳ, 69ʳ.

[136]Above, pp. 127-8.

[137]See A.N. X1ᵃ9199, fos. 48ʳff.

customary for members of each guild to assemble annually on May day under the general supervision of their *maître* or *'roi'* – failure to comply could result in the master of the guild taking appropriate action against the recalcitrant member. Rioulet's refusal to attend the May day conference saw the master of the carpenters' guild, Bonement Gonaut, cite him before jurisdiction of the governor of La Rochelle. This was immediately opposed by the Mayor and *échevins,* who claimed to have authority over the various guilds in the town. This interpretation was in turn countered by Jean Rabateau, for the *Procureur général du roi,* who pointed out that 'le roy est seigneur de La Rochelle... et y a ses officiers, gouverneur, prevost et garde des seaulx... et gouverneur et bailli por le grant fief d'Aulnis'. Gonaut, he went on, was 'maistre ou roy des charpentiers, qui ont certain privilege d'assembler au May et a la confrance, dont la cognoissance appartient aux officiers du roy touteffoiz qu'il y... fist'. Despite the *échevins'* counter allegation that 'les charpentiers n'ont point de privilege royal... et que d'aler au May ils premierement licencier au maierie, et en apparteint la cognoissance au maire', Rabateau maintained that jurisdiction in the matter of Rioulet's refusal to attend the May ceremony lay with royal officials at La Rochelle, this resort being afforded by virtue of specific royal privileges accorded the guild of carpenters. Though originating in a matter of apparently trivial proportions, this incident indicates the degree of concern displayed by the *échevins* for the maintenance of their privileges against encroachment by royal authorities, and the equal determination of the *Parlement* to prevent the abuse of royal prerogatives.

On occasion opposition by the *échevins* to royal authority could assume a more overt form. Contemporaneously with the affair of Rioulet, the *Parlement* reviewed an earlier attempt by the Rochelois authorities to prevent the late Aleaume Cachemarée, *huissier* and *commissaire du roi,* from carrying out an *arrêt* directed against Guillaume Meriau, *bourgeois* and *échevin* of La Rochelle. Cachemarée had been sent by the *Parlement* in 1419 to levy a fine of 800 *l. t.* upon Meriau; failure to first obtain the permission of the mayor and *échevins* for the execution of his writ saw Cachemarée imprisoned at the formers' behest. The mayor's action in ordering Cachemarée's arrest was once again strongly condemned by Rabateau, for the *Procureur général du roi,* who pointed out that the king had supreme authority at La Rochelle and it was not necessary for his officers to seek the permission of the mayor while undertaking a commission on his behalf.[138]

---

[138]See ibid., f.49[r-v]. Also ibid., fos. 142[v], 156[r].

Further evidence of the antipathy displayed by the mayor and *échevins* towards the presence of royal officials at La Rochelle is indicated by litigation before the *Parlement* on 9 July 1426.[139] Here, Martial Vidal and Raymond d'Auvergne, with the *Procureur du roi*, alleged that certain members of the night watch at La Rochelle had, during the course of their duties one night, ransacked the house of Vidal and perpetrated other serious crimes against the plaintiffs. Despite the initial imprisonment of the culprits, the *échevins* had contrived their release. The appeal by Vidal and Auvergne was supported by the *Procureur du roi*, who demanded that one of those responsible for the affair, Perrinet du Pont, should make 'amende honorable en chemise' to Vidal and his wife, and to Auvergne 'a jour de marche, devant l'ostel d'icellui Vidal en la ville de La Rochelle; ... et apres, estre, ce mesmes jour, mene tout nu et batu de urges par les quarrefours de ladite ville. . . et . . . estre bannist. . . des ville et gouvernement de La Rochelle et seneschaucie de Xaintonge' for a period of two years.

Implicated in the crimes against Vidal and Auvergne, royal officials,[140] were prominent *échevins* — among them Antoine Saulx, mayor in 1422, Jean de Treulon, mayor in 1425 and Jean Meriau, sub-mayor. Their indictment in these crimes appears to have further led them to pursue a campaign of violence and intimidation against Auvergne, for on 9 August 1429, he complained of threats against his life by certain at La Rochelle following his return to the town after a journey of pilgrimage.[141]

An important aspect of the *Parlement*'s attempt to maintain sovereign authority at La Rochelle was its constant surveillance of appointments to royal office in the town, and in the related government of Saintonge. On 6 September 1427[142] the *Procureur général du roi* in the *Parlement* upheld the nomination to the office of *Avocat fiscal du roi* at La Rochelle, of Gervaise Martineau. Martineau claimed to have received the office in 1418, in succession to Jean Mourraut, mentioned earlier. In 1422, however, Mourraut had attempted to regain the office, equally claiming to have royal letters of re-

---

[139]See A.N. X2ª18, fos. 97ʳff. Also ibid., fos. 145ᵛff.; A.N. X2ª21, fos. 61ᵛ and 62ʳ.

[140]Auvergne was *maître particulier de la Monnaie* at Poitiers, c. 1419 to 1423 ('Rec. des docs', *Arch. hist. Poitou*, 26 (1896), 351) Vidal was earlier mint official at Villefranche-de-Rouergue (A.N. X1ª9200, fos. 143ʳff).

[141]A.N. X1ª9199, f.192ʳ⁻ᵛ (cf. A.N. X1ª9192, f.334ᵛ).

[142]For what follows see A.N. X1ª9191, fos. 69ʳ-70ʳ.

election.[143] Despite the maintenance of Martineau as *avocat*, Mourraut had, nevertheless, continued to treat the office as his own, and at the request of friends living in Poitiers later sold the charge to Étienne Le Brun for 100 *écus d'or*. In reply to these allegations, Mourraut claimed that the office of *Avocat du roi* was rightfully his, and that the obstruction came from Martineau. Following his simple resignation of the office, Charles VII had given it to Le Brun without any payment being involved. In spite of Mourraut's defence of the legitimacy of Le Brun's election, the *Parlement* maintained Martineau in the office.

Despite this setback, Le Brun refused to relinquish his claim to the office, and on 26 February 1432[144] he was once again before the *Parlement*, this time in opposition to Pierre Bragier, *licencié-en-lois* of Toulouse and formerly *avocat* in the Poitiers Parlement. Bragier claimed to have received the office of *Avocat du roi* at La Rochelle after the death of Gervaise Martineau as the result of a recommendation to Charles VII on his behalf by the *seigneur* d'Albret, member of the *Grand Conseil*. Despite Le Brun's reiteration of his earlier argument against Martineau to the effect that he was the legitimate successor of Jean Mourraut, the *Parlement* dismissed his opposition and maintained Bragier in the office.[145] This protracted affair indicates not only the enduring strength of the *Parlement*'s opposition to Mourraut, but also the way in which it was frequently called upon to regulate disputes over office resulting from Charles VII's willingness, under pressure from patrons within the *Grand Conseil*, to issue letters of election for a particular office to more than one candidate.

Relations of the *Parlement* of Poitiers with the town of Niort were influenced, particularly after 1427, by the great financial necessity of Niort's *seigneur*, Jean II, duke of Alençon following his release from captivity by the English for a ransom of 200,000 *écus d'or* during the same year. Charles VII had originally ceded Niort to Jean II on 28 August 1423 in recompense for large loans made to him.[146] However, capture by the English at the battle of Verneuil in 1424 naturally increased Alençon's concern to confine the revenues of the place to his own exigency. On 14 February 1427[147] this led to a serious confrontation with the *Procureur général du roi* in the *Parlement*,

[143]On the resulting confrontation with Martineau see A.N. X1ᵃ9198, fos. 248ᵛ-260ᵛ (passim). Also A.N. X1ᵃ9199, fos. 180ʳ, 249ᵛ.

[144]See A.N. X1ᵃ9200, fos. 24ᵛ-26ʳ for what follows.

[145]See A.N. X1ᵃ9194, fos. 14ᵛ, 17ᵛ (30 Apr./7 June 1432). Also, A.N. X1ᵃ9192, fos. 287ʳ-288ʳ.

[146]Favreau, *Poitiers,* 285 n.945.

[147]See A.N. X2ᵃ18, fos. 108ᵛff.

owing to the fact that the court had recently received an assignation of its wages on Niort and Saint-Maixent. The attempt by Bertrand de Pontarcher, *huissier* in the *Parlement*, to collect the allotted sum had met with opposition from Alençon's secretary, Jean Aimery, through his refusal to allow the receivers of the particular *aide* to accede to Pontarcher's request. Guillaume I Le Tur, for the *Procureur du roi,* pointed out that: 'tous les subgiez de ce royaulme donnent obeissance a roy et a ses subgiez, et est desobeissance un des plus grans termes qui soit'; as Aimery had no official charge at Niort, nor any specific assignation on the aforesaid sum from the receiver-general, he had not authority to prevent Pontarcher carrying out his brief.

The great financial burdens imposed by the magnitude of Alençon's ransom forced the sale of Fougères to Jean V of Brittany on 9 April 1429. The loss of Fougères, and perhaps equally significantly, the failure by Alençon and others to direct the impetus of the war-effort following the relief of Orléans into English-occupied Normandy, saw Alençon concentrate his attentions more fully upon Niort itself. On 2 March 1430[148] he again faced opposition in the *Parlement* from the *Procureur général du roi,* this time over the appointment and installation of one of his own candidates as mayor of Niort. Alençon had endeavoured to maintain his candidate, Jean Laidet, in spite of the earlier election, sanctioned by Charles VII and the *Parlement,* of Jean l'Amoreux. Jean Juvénal des Ursins, for the *Procureur du roi,* strongly opposed Alençon's initiative, pointing out that: 'quant le roy bailla... Nyort audit d'Alençon, il en fist reservacion; dit que le maire se fist touz les ans, et a on accustume a eslire trois personnes dont le seneschal de Poictou choisist l'un pour maire.' Despite Laidet's recognition of his wrongful election, and the additional prohibition, under pain of a 1,000 silver marks fine not to occupy the office, Laidet had nevertheless ignored the court's warning and complied with Alençon's decision to elect him. Following this confrontation the *Parlement* continued to exercise a careful surveillance over the appointment of mayors at Niort,[149] and at least one of the candidates preferred (Jean Guichard, 1435-6) was by origin of Poitiers itself.

Alençon's constant need of capital in the years following his release led to his appearance again before the *Parlement* on 18 March 1432,[150] this time in respect of 1,000 *francs* allocated to him by

[148] See A.N. X1ª9199, f.242ᵛ.

[149] See *A.H.-G.* MS.59, f.418ʳ⁻ᵛ; A.N. X1ª9194, fos. 10ᵛ, 63ʳ, 94ᵛ.

[150] See A.N. X1ª9200, fos. 34ᵛ-35ʳ. Slightly earlier, in 1431, Alençon's quarrel with Jean V of Brittany over the payment of his mother's dowry saw him imprison the Breton chancellor, Jean de Malestroit. In the resulting siege of Alençon's stronghold at

Charles VII as part of the *aide* levied retrospectively to finance the Reims coronation. Yet the *Parlement*'s determination to restrain his influence at Niort was symptomatic of the more general concern displayed by the court to maintain royal authority even in those areas which, by force of circumstances, had been temporarily relinquished to another authority.

The exposed maritime situation of the Île de Ré was predominantly responsible for the state of political unrest which appears to have persisted on the island in the 1420s and 1430s. On 26 February 1425[151] the *vicomte* de Thouars complained to the *Parlement* about the activities of Guillaume Poupart, an inhabitant of the island, whom he alleged had attempted to undermine the *vicomte*'s seigneurial authority in the area; had conducted a reign of terror against local merchants, and more important, had made slanderous remarks about the *vicomte*'s political credibility. On one occasion, Poupart was at La Rochelle and: 'les habitans d'icelle ville estans sur le cay pour empesche la descendue des Anglois qui estoient sur la mer, Poupart dist a iceulx habitans. . . qu'ilz estoient bien folz, et qu'ils savoient bien que le vicomte ou ses gens et subgiez avoient privilege de devenir trois fois la journee Anglois et trois foiz Francois.' Naturally enough, the *Procureur du roi* in the *Parlement* saw fit to support Thouars's original action in apprehending Poupart.

In May 1430 [152] some of the inhabitants of the Île de Ré were called to answer charges brought by the *Procureur général du roi* in the Poitiers *Parlement* originating in the formers' refusal to contribute to royal taxation on wine. The inhabitants complained that they were too poor to pay the tax, and, in addition, that: 'l'Isle de Re est ouverte et a main des Bretons que d'autres. . . et aucuneffois s'en vont sans paier le droit du roy.' On this occasion the *Parlement* recognised the additional complaint by the inhabitants that they had earlier received royal authorisation freeing them from obligations regarding the tax on wine, and were therefore justified in refusing to pay commissioners delegated to levy the tax. However on 1 November 1433[153] Charles VII personally reversed this decision, ordering the inhabitants to deliver 300 tuns of wine, as arrears accumulated upon the treaty, to

Pouancé, in 1432, Jean V had recourse to English support, collars of Ermine being issued to George Riguemen, the lieutenant of Maine, and to two esquires of lord Scales. A similar issue was made in 1433 to an esquire of Talbot's (G.-A. Lobineau, *Histoire de Bretagne*, ii (Paris, 1707), col. 628).

[151]See A.N. X2ᵃ18, fos. 66ᵛ-67ᵛ (also 84ᵛ-85ʳ).

[152]See A.N. X1ᵃ9199, fos. 272ᵛff. (Also ibid., fos. 279ᵛ-280ʳ).

[153]See A.N. X1ᵃ8604, f.116ᵛ (cf. A.N. X1ᵃ9192, f.205ᵛ).

La Rochelle and elsewhere to be employed in the part payment of the wages of Poitiers *parlementaires*. Following the fall of La Trémoïlle in 1433 Charles VII attempted to reduce the activities of *hobereaux* on the Île de Ré and in the surrounding areas, more especially the marches between Poitou and Brittany, giving orders to the *seigneur* d'Apremont to demolish all non-tenable fortresses and *châteaux* in the area, and to evacuate those worthy of maintenance. One of those responsible for systematic pillaging on the Île de Ré, Jean Josseaume, appeared before the *Parlement* on 10 July 1436.[154] Josseaume's men had operated within a wide area of his base at Commequiers, employing the more general excuse of maintaining order against the Bretons to carry out their depredations.

Evidence for attempts by the Poitiers *Parlement* to restrain the autonomy of the more distant towns loyal to Charles VII, comparable even to the tentative approach adopted towards La Rochelle and Niort, is markedly lacking. We have suggested earlier that the reasons for this might be numerous. As a result the abuses, notably of a fiscal kind, against royal authority, appear to have been serious, particularly during the 1420s, when the degree of monetary and political instability was pronounced.

The *Parlement*'s relations, or, more correctly, its marked lack of relations, with the town of Limoges, exhibit many of the problems characteristic of its dealings with the major towns during the period 1418-36. On 19 February 1428[155] certain of the consuls of Limoges who held office in 1426 were called to Poitiers to answer charges brought by the *Procureur général du roi*, in relation to the murder of Gautier Pradeau, similarly consul of the town, at the behest of Jean Pradeau, son of the deceased. The consuls began their defence in a typical fashion by outlining the importance of the position of Limoges as one of the principal towns of Guyenne, whose 'beaux privileges. . . ont este confermez par le roy'. Pradeau, a native of Lesterps, had apparently come to Limoges and married a local woman, later achieving election to the governing body of the town. Since his election, the consuls alleged, he had, nevertheless, committed numerous crimes, including minting false money, arranging fraudulent contracts with local merchants, and on one occasion, stealing the books from a local convent to sell for cash. More seriously, they alleged, Pradeau had in 1426 conspired with servants of the *seigneur*

---

[154] A.N. X1ª9201, f.209ʳ⁻ᵛ.

[155] For what follows see A.N. X2ª18, fos. 138ᵛ, 142ʳ. Further details on ibid., fos. 128ʳ-145ʳ (passim); A.N. X1ª9198, fos. 291ʳff.; A.N. X1ª9191, fos. 98ᵛ, 115ᵛ, 119ʳ, etc.

of l'Aigle,[156] member of the Penthièvre faction, claimants to the duchy of Brittany, to turn Limoges over to l'Aigle, his personal reward being 20,000 *écus d'or*. In the event the plot was apparently thwarted by the consuls and Pradeau's complicity in the affair, allegedly confirmed by the discovery of correspondence between him and l'Aigle, led to his trial and execution. Pradeau's son told a slightly different story, maintaining that the real motive for his father's death was less one of complicity with l'Aigle than hatred displayed towards him by the consuls. Whatever the truth of the affair, the circumstances of the case bear a certain resemblance to incidents involving royal officials at La Rochelle, where the *échevins* would employ allegations of complicity with the enemy as a means of discrediting troublesome individuals. Jean Rabateau, for the *Procureur général du roi*, took particular execption to the manner of Pradeau's trial and execution, pointing out that it was: 'au roy et... ses officiers... a cognoistre des crimes de lese-majeste; ... dist que Pradeau estoit subgiet du roy et que le cas... estoit directement contre le roy car il s'estoit efforce de mectre la ville en main estrange.' Maintenance of authority over Pradeau's action within their own jurisdiction was thus directly prejudicial to the king's authority in the matter. Rabateau demanded, in conclusion, that the consuls be suspended from the exercise of justice in the town until such time as the matter was resolved, and in addition, that they pay a fine of 20,000 *écus d'or* for their collective misdemeanours.

The aftermath of the affair had unfortunate consequences both for the consuls and for Pradeau's heirs. For the former it marked the beginning of protracted litigation against a succession of claimants to Pradeau's property, among them Robert Le Maçon, *seigneur* of Trèves and formerly *Chancelier* of the Dauphin.[157] In addition, Jean Pradeau was on 23 April 1433[158] ordered by the *Procureur général du roi* to make good a deficiency of 2,000*l.t.* (587*l.* 5*s.t.* current money) in the accounts maintained by his father and Marcial Vidal in 1420 as royal fiscal agents at Villefranche-de-Rouergue.

Later in 1429 or early in 1428[159] the consuls employed the alleged complicity of another royal official, Guillaume Molin, *garde de la*

[156]Jean de Bretagne, *seigneur* of L'Aigle, lieutenant of the comte de Penthièvre and *vicomte* of Limoges. On L'Aigle's attempted power-building in the Limousin see A. Leymarié, *Histoire du Limousin*, ii (Paris, 1846) 340ff.; also, *Chartes, Chroniques et Mémoriaux pour servir à l'histoire de La Marche et du Limousin*, ed. A Leroux and A. Bosvieux (Tulle, 1886), 226ff.

[157]See A.N. X1ª9199, f.181ᵛ (July 1429). Also A.N. X1ª9192, fos. 329ᵛ-330ʳ

[158]See A.N. X1ª9200, f.143ʳ.

[159]See A.N. X2ª18, fos. 166ʳ-167ʳ (also ibid., fos. 169ᵛff.).

*Monnaie* in the town, in the attempt to turn Limoges over to l'Aigle as an excuse for his ejection. Again, these 'partisan' motives may conceal more practical ends, particularly in view of Molin's complaint that the real reason for his expulsion was that he had attempted to prevent certain of his persecutors — Guillaume Disnematin, Jean de Julian, Jean de Quercy and Jean Pavain — from exporting large quantities of bullion from Limoges to Nontron, Geneva and elsewhere. Molin's complaint was upheld by the *Parlement,* and, what is more, supported by others, recently royal officials at Limoges, who confirmed that they had received money bribes from Molin's persecutors in an effort to secure their support of his expulsion.

Considered in relation to events we have already discussed relating to La Rochelle, and particularly to the economic affairs of the major towns of the 'kingdom of Bourges' after 1418, it is difficult to avoid the general conclusion that the various effects of the war produced, for many urban hierarchies, something approaching a monopoly of power in relation to fiscal and judicial matters. This was accompanied in many cases by a marked hostility towards royal officials who attempted to restrict their authority.

In some of the more distant towns corruption extended to royal officials themselves. At Chinon, on 18 January 1432,[160] Charles VII was forced to acknowledge that at Limoges

> noz officiers et autres, ou temps passe, se sont entremis du fait de noz monnoyes et de fait de change; . . . et en ce ont, ou peuvent avoir, mesprins, excede et delinque envers nous, justice et la chose publique en plusieurs et diverses manieres, pour lesquelles choses lesdiz heritans puissent. . . cheoir en danger de justice, et de estre puniz, se sur ce ne leur estoit pourveu de nostre grace.

Specific crimes included the transport of large quantities of bullion outside the kingdom, working in illegal mints at Masseret, Saint Yrieix, Angoulême and elsewhere; also, 'en aloignant de la plusprochaine de noz monnoyes, vendu et achate publiquement et a part, a autre monnoye que de celle a qui nous avons donne course, . . . sans avoir lettre de nous'. Despite the very serious nature of these crimes, Charles VII was forced to acknowledge that under the circumstances a general pardon was, politically speaking, more expedient than prosecution of the culprits. Prominent among his reasons for issuing the pardon was the familiar theme, namely the great strategic importance of Limoges and the services performed by the town 'pour le fait de noz guerres et pour resister aux Anglois, noz anciens

---

[160] See A.N. X2ᵃ20, fos. 43ᵛff., for what follows.

ennemis, mesmement ou pais de Guienne dont ladite ville de Limoges est la'clef principale'. Odious as these letters may have appeared to the *Parlement* they were nevertheless ratified at Poitiers on 14 April 1432. Clearly under certain circumstances royal justice should be seen to be tempered by royal mercy.

The pattern of political unrest at Limoges was visible earlier at Périgueux, situated in even closer proximity to English-occupied Guyenne, and in the neighbouring areas. On 29 March 1424[161] the *Parlement* ordered clerical *conseiller* Jacques Coeur to visit the town and restore order in liaison with the seneschal of Périgord. The *Parlement's* action followed an appeal by the mayor and consuls that subversive elements were attempting to undermine their authority and put the town in enemy hands. Similar allegations were directed in March 1433 against Mathieu Fournier, *prévôt-moine* at La Souterraine.[162]

The *Parlement* took a severe view of abuses against local royal administration when they involved the deaths of royal officials, or clear obstructions of sovereign justice, a fact illustrated by the reprisals ordered against the inhabitants of Saint-Jean-d'Angély following the murder of royal officials Jean I and II Godon.[163]. Similarly heavy penalties were demanded by the *Parlement* against the *capitouls* of Toulouse not long prior to this incident, following the attempt by them to prevent the execution of a female inhabitant of the town, who had been condemned to death by virtue of an *arrêt* delivered by royal officials at Toulouse.[164]

In general terms the union of the *Parlements* of Languedoc and Languedoil into a single body at Poitiers late in 1428 can hardly have been an efficacious move from the point of view of the maintenance of royal authority in Languedoc. The aftermath of the union appears to have led both to a slackening of control over the major towns of the region, and a possible escalation of corruption among royal officials in the Languedocian towns. On 13 November 1430 only months after the *Parlement* had first reviewed the intransigence of the *capitouls* of Toulouse, Guillaume Senet, royal judge at Albi, was called to Poitiers to answer charges brought against him in the conduct of this office.[165] On 24 March 1432 Guillaume de Montjoie, bishop of Béziers,

---

[161] A.N. X1a9195, f.190v.

[162] A.N. X2a21, fos. 204rff.

[163] See A.N. X2a21, fos. 185v, 205v, 234r and passim.

[164] See A.N. X2a18, fos. 217rff. (passim) and A.N. X2a21, fos. 138vff. (passim).

[165] See A.N. X2a21, f.147v.

168

complained about attempts by royal officials in the town to usurp his jurisdiction.[166]

Maintenance of royal authority in fiscal matters at Toulouse was similarly attempted by the *Procureur général du roi* who on 17 July 1432[167] supported a demand by the septuagenarian royal receiver at Rouergue, Arnauld Segnalar, that Deodet Costain, *bachelier-en-décrets* and student at Toulouse in the college of Maguelonne, should be compelled to contribute towards a Tenth recently granted to Charles VII. Costain had claimed exemption by virtue of the fact that members of the university were exempt from such levies.

Problems of control at Toulouse appear to have increased rather than diminished during the years immediately before the return to Paris. The increasing intransigence of the *capitouls* in the face of royal authority was accompanied by a new outbreak of hostilities between the houses of Foix and Armagnac in 1432-3. Some measure of concern over the bellicose activities of Jean I, on the *Parlement*'s behalf, was apparent by March 1434, when the court delegated Gilles Le Lasseur to direct letters to Charles VII and his *Conseil*, and to Foix personally, demonstrating the dangers of this new conflict.[168] By 7 May 1435[169] it appears that royal authority at Toulouse had suffered somewhat as a result of the increasing political instability in the region. In response to a complaint by Jean de Marignac, '*juge des appels des causes civiles de la seneschaussee de Toulouse*', that Arnauld d'Espaigne and others had attempted to usurp his authority, the *Parlement* placed Marignac under the safeconduct of the court, and in addition ordered that one of its own candidates, Jean de Mazac or Guillaume Bernard Bagart, should take Marignac's place until the dispute was resolved. In addition letters were to be sent to the *sénéchal* and *juge ordinaire* at Toulouse, 'sans en faire aucune information au conte de Foix, ne a autre quelconque', ordering the arrest of Bertrand de Nogaret, *viguier* of Toulouse, Fortemer de Ferres, *sénéchal* of Nebouzan, Raymon du Mora, *prévôt* of Pamiers and others, for complicity in the affair of Marignac. If royal officials were unable to execute the orders of the *Parlement* at Toulouse, they were to make 'cri publique en la ville de Grenade. . . et par cedules attaches aux portes de la Sale Noire, ou de la ville de Tholose'. On 19

[166]See A.N. X2ª18, fos. 288ᵛ-335ᵛ, passim; A.N. X2ª21, fos. 180ʳ-195ᵛ, passim.
[167]A.N. X1ª9200, fos. 57ʳ-58ʳ, for what follows.
[168]A.N. X1ª9194, f.62ᵛ.
[169]For what follows see A.N. X2ª21, fos. 271ᵛ, 283ᵛ, 304ᵛ-305ʳ. Also A.N. X1ª9200, f.282ʳ.

November 1435[170] the *Parlement* was forced to take action against those royal officials at Toulouse who had been entrusted with the publication of the earlier *arrêt,* in view of the fact that they had refused to obey this directive unless the letters were initially communicated to Jean I de Foix himself.

The increasing difficulty experienced by the *Parlement* during the 1430s in its relations with the major towns of Languedoc necessitates some amendment to the rather simplistic view that the fall of La Trémoïlle in 1433 witnessed the effective end of Charles VII's political problems. Following the removal of the *Parlement* of Languedoc to Poitiers in 1428 there remained no effective instrument for dispensing sovereign authority, in judicial terms, throughout the vast Languedocian hinterland of the 'kingdom of Bourges'. The recognition of this fact must have helped to persuade Charles VII that the restoration of peace with Burgundy — at whatever price — was essential if royal authority was to be effectively restored in this troublesome and troubled area.

[170]A.N. X2ᵃ21, f.283ᵛ.

# 5

## THE *PARLEMENT,* WAR AND THE NOBILITY
## (1418-1436)

### The *Parlement* and the War in France (1418-1436)

A considerable proportion of the litigation before the *Parlement* dealt with a variety of disputes occasioned directly or indirectly by the war in France. Persons involved in this category can be divided into two groups: combatants and non-combatants. But the effects of the war in France were felt, to a greater or lesser degree, at all levels of society. While some profited others, clearly, did not. In general terms those who suffered most from the effects of the war were consistently to be found among the poorer elements in society, whatever theoretical provision the Laws of War might make for their immunity.[1] The *Parlement,* despite its relative remoteness from the frontier zones or from the immediate theatres of the war, did nevertheless attempt to provide a modicum of protection for these largely defenceless elements through its willingness to entertain the constant stream of complaints arising from the peripheral effects of war or seigneurial depredation.

But the views of many who participated in the war could be more equivocal. For many *seigneurs* as for men of lower estate, the war provided a variety of means legitimate and otherwise to acquire wealth and prestige, not least those related to the immediate profits of war including ransoms and booty.[2] Litigation relating to the legitimate spoils of war was frequently conducted by the *Parlement* by appeal from inferior jurisdictions concerned with this type of dispute, namely those of the *maréchaux* and the *connétable* de France. After 1370 in the Paris *Parlement* the independent tribunals of the *maréchaux* and the *connétable* were frequently located together at the *Table de Marbre,* with the jurisdiction of the *connétable,* by virtue of his position as *chef des maréchaux,* providing, nevertheless, ultimate judicial resort beneath that of the *Parlement* itself.[3] The date of the initial appearance of the *Table de Marbre* at Poitiers is not clear. The

---

[1] See M. H. Keen, *The Laws of War in the Late Middle Ages* (London, 1965), 190-1

[2] See P. S. Lewis, *Later Medieval France. The Polity* (London, 1968), 48-9.

[3] For the early development of these jurisdictions see P. Contamine, *Guerre, État et Société à la fin du Moyen âge* (Paris, 1972), 198-202.

first, and apparently the only reference to this tribunal occurs in litigation conducted on 27 July 1426;[4] however its existence at an earlier date, at least during Buchan's period of office as constable, is certain.[5] The uniform loss of documentation for the *connétable* before 1527 means that the only surviving record of the function of the Tribunal at Poitiers occurs in respect of those cases conducted by it which eventually were transferred on appeal to the *Parlement* proper. These are too few to provide any comprehensive picture of the work of the Tribunal, though some are, nevertheless, of considerable intrinsic interest, predominant among them being those concerned with disputed rights to prisoners of war.

After 1418 the political divisions in France and the need to provide support for those who defected to the Dauphin's cause posed considerable difficulties for the *Parlement* in respect of any attempt at a strict definition of the Laws of War. On 16 December 1423,[6] the court heard the complaint by André Marchand,[7] captain and governor of Orléans, that 'quant aucun est pris en une ville par droit de guerre, . . (il) doit estre prisonnier du capitaine d'icelle ville; . . . aussi qu'il est permis de prandre et ransonner, par maniere de guerre, tous Bourguignons et Anglois et ceulx qui tiennent leur party'. Using this pretext Marchand had taken as his legitimate prisoner Jean Sudré, who had remained in Paris for eight or nine months after the death of Charles VI in 1422 and had allegedly openly fraternised with the enemy and attempted to exact a ransom from him. The money from the ransom was apparently to be employed to facilitate the release of André's son Jean, a prisoner of the English.

While under normal circumstances Marchand's claim might have some foundation, it is equally clear that under the troubled circumstances of the early 1420s, to uphold the complaint could produce an embarrassing dilemma for the *Parlement*. If it pronounced against Sudré, other potential defectors might feel less inclined to come over to

[4] Conduct of a suit before the 'Constabulario francie seu eius locumtenente ad tabulam principalem, aule seu palatii Pictavensis' (A.N. X1ᵃ9191, f.34ᵛ).

[5] For references to the function of the lieutenant or judge of the *Connétable* at Poitiers at an earlier date see A.N. X2ᵃ21, f.26ʳ; A.N. X2ᵃ18, f.185ʳ and A.N. X1ᵃ9198, f.129ᵛ.

[6] For what follows see A.N. X2ᵃ18, fos. 15ᵛ-22ᵛ, passim. Also Y. Lanhers, 'Deux affaires de trahison defendues par Jean Jouvenel des Ursins (1423-1427)'. *Rec. de Mémoires et trav. de la soc. hist. droit écrit*, ed. by the *Soc. Hist. Droit et des Inst. des Anc. Pays de Droit écrit*, Montpellier, 7 (1970), 325-6 (ibid., passim, for the legal problems encountered by the *Parlement* vis-à-vis the reception of defectors).

[7] Probably related to Aimery Marchand, *conseiller* in the *Parlement* at Poitiers (Favreau, *Poitiers*, 281).

Charles VII's cause; yet in upholding Marchand's plea the *Parlement* would be forced to acknowledge that others who left Paris after 1418, including *conseillers* in the *Parlement*, were also enemies, and, as such, eminently ransomable.

On 7 August 1425[8] Marchand was once again involved in litigation at Poitiers, this time with Dunois, for the legitimate ownership of a prisoner-of-war, Robert Parent. The dispute, which came before the *Parlement* on appeal from Jean de Troyes, lieutenant or judge of the *connétable* of France, followed Parent's capture by Sinador de Giresme, Milet Desjardins, Jean de Montcel, Simon de Givry, Thomas Paumard and others, associates, during a skirmish in 1424 between Paris and Luzarchais. Giresme and his companions had originally intended to remove Parent to Saint Benoît-sur-Loire; en route, however, in the forest near Orléans, they were met by an armed force who seized their prisoner and led the entire party before Marchand, governor of Orléans. Marchand subsequently refused to release Parent to his original captors, claiming that Dunois had demanded him as his own prisoner. The affair was brought before the *Table de Marbre* at Poitiers and Marchand was ordered to pay a total of 2,200 *écus d'or* compensation. Attempts to carry out the *arrêt* met with failure, Marchand's house at Orléans containing, allegedly, nothing save 'fuerres-des-liz. . . et avoit messire Andre tout vuidie, dolose'. Marchand's appeal against the sentence was subsequently rejected by the *Parlement* and the original decision of the *connétable*'s jurisdiction upheld.

On 7 December 1430[9] the *Parlement* was confronted by litigation concerned with more technical aspects of the Laws of War. Here, Jean de Tremedern, esquire, pointed out that it was commonplace that

> en fait de guerre, et en la court du Connestable, on print sa cause par iij defaux; en oultre, quelque saufconduit qui soit donne a aucun personne, s'il s'arme et est pris en armes par l'adversaire, le saufconduit ne lui vault riens, selon l'usage; et se le varlet d'aucun. . . qui la arme, prant aucun adversaire ou de parti contraire, le prisonnier est au maistre du varlet qui l'a pris.

[8] On what follows see A.N. X1ª9198, fos. 101ᵛ, 253ᵛ-275ᵛ (passim), 311ʳ-312ʳ; A.N. X1ª9191, fos. 34ᵛ-35ᵛ. The matter was still unresolved in 1432 (A.N. X1ª9200, f.14ᵛ).

[9] See A.N. X1ª9199, f.335ʳ⁻ᵛ (cf., also ibid., fos. 342ʳ, 353ʳ). Litigation between the pair was to be heard at Sablé, in view of Richemont's estrangement from court. La Chapelle's failure to appear led the *Parlement* to call him to defend his case in person at Poitiers. For a similar case see A.N. X1ª9200, fos. 150ʳff.

Tremedern went on to explain that earlier, during the recovery of Laval from the English, members of his company had taken prisoner John Sterre, an English soldier and armed member of the night-watch at Laval. The fact that Sterre was on duty and fully armed rendered him liable to legitimate ransom. Tremedern's attempt to take charge of his prisoner was opposed by Jean de La Chapelle, known as *Chapellois*, who alleged that Sterre was married to one of his relatives and protected by safeconduct from capture. Tremedern's case was upheld, nevertheless, by the tribunal of the *connétable*, and La Chapelle was ordered to restore his prisoner or furnish compensation of 2,000 *écus d'or* — whence La Chapelle's appeal to the *Parlement*.

Disputes over the legitimate ownership of prisoners were frequently lengthy. On 31 July 1432[10] Olivier le Forestier demanded the return of his English prisoner captured at Verneuil in 1424. Forestier had originally sent his captive into the guard of Macium des Molins at Alençon, intending to employ him in part-exchange for a relative, Pierre le Forestier, then a prisoner of the English. In the meantime Pierre secured his release by other means (though was later killed in action); however, Molins had refused to return Olivier's prisoner to him. The prospect of profit from the war in France encouraged certain families to maximise the potential for gain by deliberately maintaining its representatives on both sides of the conflict.[11] Such was the case, it appears, with the Welsh family of Gough. Matthew Gough, a native of Maelor Saesneg, fought on the English side in northern France, his rapacious activities in Perche and Maine in particular arousing considerable resentment among the indigenous population. Prominent in the capture of Le Mans in 1427, he was later, in 1429, forced to surrender Beaugency to French forces, being finally captured and put to ransom in 1432.[12] Philip Gough, relative of Matthew, also figured in the war in northern France, this time however, on the French side, under the banner of the duke of Alençon.

The somewhat perverse nature of the fortunes bestowed by the war upon the Gough family is indicated by their separate involvement in litigation before the Poitiers *Parlement*. On 20 December 1432[13]

[10] A.N. X1a9201, f.94v.

[11] For examples of a territorial kind see A. Bossuat, 'The Re-Establishment of Peace in Society during the reign of Charles VII', in *The Recovery of France in the Fifteenth Century*, ed. P.S. Lewis (London, 1971), pp. 64-6.

[12] See A.D. Carr, 'Welshmen and the Hundred Years War', in *The Welsh History Review*, 4, i (1968), 39-41.

[13] A.N. X2a21, f.197v. For details of what follows see ibid., f.305r-v; A.N. X1a9201, f.145r-v; A.N. X1a9193, fos. 157rff. and A.N. X1a9194, f.144r.

Philip Gough appeared before the *Parlement* in the company of Jean II, duke of Alençon, requiring the registration of default against Jacques de Dinan, *seigneur* of Beaumanoir. Conflict between Gough and Dinan derived from alternative claims to English prisoner-of-war Walter Hungerford, captured at the battle of Patay in June 1429.[14] Alençon alleged that Gough, his associate, had captured Hungerford and four other English soldiers during the course of the battle and, as a result, they had a legitimate claim to the ownership of the prisoner. This followed Dinan's earlier claim that it was not Gough, but one of his own captains, Jean de Mayo, who had initially taken Hungerford. In addition, he alleged that Gough had been perfectly happy to serve under the English, 'jusques a ce qu'il n'a plus eu puissance'. After a lengthy hearing the *Parlement* rejected Dinan's claim on 22 June 1436 ordering him to release Hungerford, 's'il est en vie', to Alençon and Gough: 'et se non, la juste valeur et estimacion d'icellui prisonnier, pour la quelle savoir la court defere le serement ausdiz demandeurs jusques a la somme de xxx^m escuz (d'or); et icellui serement fait, la court extimera icelle somme ainsi qu'elle verra estre a faire par raison.' Dinan was, nevertheless, permitted to conduct his opposition to Alençon and Gough on the specific grounds that it was his own man, not Gough, who had originally taken Hungerford prisoner. Only months after this pronouncement, on 4 August 1436,[15] Matthew Gough, relative of Philip, was himself the object of litigation before the *Parlement,* this time in the less happy respect of conflicting claims by others to the capture and ransom of his person. Gough had been captured earlier during a skirmish between English and French forces near Saint Denis '*in Francia*'. Conflicting claims to his capture later developed between Bos de Commarques, who alleged that one of his archers had taken Gough, and André de Laval, who maintained that it was one of his own men who first received Gough's surrender and oath. The *Parlement* eventually awarded legitimate ownership of the prisoner to Commarques.

The legitimate ownership of English prisoners-of-war was the subject of litigation on 21 July 1434.[16] An interesting feature of this case is the representation in *Parlement* of the captives — Geoffrey and Hubert Wigton (or Witton) and Nicolas de Bosco — as active 'defendants' of

---

[14]Important details relating to the ransoms of Scales and Talbot, also taken prisoner at Patay, may be found on A.N. 1AP 175, nos. 27-8.

[15]See A.N. X1ª9193, fos. 156^v-157^r. On the matter of conflicting claims to prisoners see Keen, *The Laws of War,* 164ff.

[16]See A.N. X2ª20, fos. 72^r-73^r.

their suit. Again, on 28 September 1436,[17] conflict over the ransom of another Englishman, Thomas Aulton, was entertained by the *Parlement* following the demand by one of his captors, Pierre, called *'Le Porc'*, for his legitimate portion of Aulton's ransom of 5,000 *saluts d'or*. Occasionally disputes over rights to English prisoners developed from circumstances occurring far from the original place of capture. On 27 June 1431[18] Pierre Vineu, captain of Grès, complained to the *Parlement* that earlier he had journeyed 'a la couronnement du roy soubz monseigneur d'Alençon. Laissa la garde dudit chastel, et d'un sien prisonniers de guerre Anglois qui leur estoit, a messire Aubert Morin'. On his return from Reims, Vineu was confronted by the refusal by Morin, both to relinquish the captaincy of Grès, and to restore his prisoner, who had since been claimed by a third party.

A certain amount of litigation before the *Parlement* dealt, in converse fashion, with complaints of various kinds deriving from the capture and ransom of supporters of Charles VII by the English. The majority of these disputes came from areas located in the northern frontier zones. However, the vast majority of complaints entertained by the *Parlement* derived from the incidental effects of war with the English — construction of illegal fortifications; disputed captaincy of places; highway brigandage and pillaging of livestock and possessions; disputes over the performance of watch and guard duties and on and on. Problems of this nature came not, for the most part, from the immediate theatres of the war, but from deep within the 'kingdom of Bourges'. Only the most careful scrutiny of the registers of the Poitiers *Parlement* would provide any confirmation that conflict of a proto-national kind was taking place at all. While many *seigneurs* were prepared to confront the common enemy on the battlefield (though their reasons for so doing were usually conditioned by selfish and highly pragmatic motives), others, particularly after 1424, were happy to employ the distraction provided by the war as a cloak for the accumulation of power on a more localised basis. The reluctance of Charles VII's nobility to fight against the English was temporarily suspended following the relief of Orléans in 1429 (though again, as we have argued, for a variety of motives), only to become more firmly entrenched in the ensuing years.

From its inception, the *Parlement* worked hard to impose some sort of check upon the most damaging consequences of seigneurial aggrandisement; however, in Poitou and the neighbouring areas, the

---

[17] A.N. X1ª9193, f.177ʳ⁻ᵛ.
[18] A.N. X1ª9201, f.52ᵛ.

events of 1429 appear to have occasioned a significant break with the preceding years. After this date concern for the *'grande guerre'* assumes a position of remoteness, while the escalation of seigneurial conflict in Poitou occupies page after page of the *Parlement*'s registers. The effects of the private 'war' between the supporters of Richemont and La Trémoïlle gradually spread from Poitou into Saintonge, Anjou, Touraine, Berry and the Limousin. At Poitiers on 28 March 1431[19] only two months before the execution of Joan of Arc at Rouen, Charles VII issued a general directive to the *sénéchaux* of Poitou, Saintonge and the Limousin, and to the *baillis* of Touraine and Berry, indicating his concern about the activities of certain: 'cappitaines et gardes des fortresses et autres... en diverses parties de nostre royaume, hors et loing de la frontiere de nos adversaires et ennemis, compaignees de gens qui se dient gens d'armes et de trait' who, it was clear, had lost all inclination to fight the English, preferring instead to make their profit from the loyal subjects of the 'kingdom'. Merchants, poor labourers and clerics, traditionally immune from the ravages of war, had been systematically robbed, assaulted and imprisoned. Many members of the nobility were similarly treated, having been 'dommaiges en leur corps... et biens... leurs subgiez raenconnez et destruiz', such that they: 'n'osent laissez leurs maisons femmes et enfans, pour eulx emploier en nostre service contre... noz adversaires... pour doubte que, en leur absence, leurs maisons feussent pillees, (leurs) femmes et filles violees.' Excesses committed against merchants and poor labourers had apparently caused many to go and live 'hors de nostre obeissance', this at potentially great damage to Charles VII's cause.

Individual culprits found guilty of these crimes were to be immediately apprehended and punished 'comme crimineux et coupables de crime de leze-mageste'. These letters, ratified by the *Parlement* on 3 April 1431 only weeks before Joan's death at Rouen, authorised the court to proceed 'armee, assemblee de nobles gens de bonnes villes et de peuple, (et) par force d'assault, siege ou autrement... faictes obeir a nous lesdites rebelles'. By dint of these letters Charles VII thus declared war on Frenchmen who were ostensibly his own supporters — clearly any semblance of patriotic spirit inspired by Joan of Arc had been of a highly ephemeral kind.

Often, however, it was more expedient to pardon than to punish; to provide incentive rather than disincentive. Only days after the ratification of these letters, on 16 April 1431,[20] Charles VII issued

---

[19]For what follows see A.N. X2ᵃ20, fos. 31ʳff.
[20]Ibid., fos. 32ᵛff.

general pardons to Jean de La Roche (foucauld), *seigneur* of Barbezieux, and a number of his associates, allies of La Trémoïlle, responsible for a variety of crimes outlined in the letters. The pardon was conditional upon the fact that La Roche would henceforth remove his men from all fortresses, fortified churches and *châteaux* unlawfully occupied by them, to his own places — Barbezieux, Montendre, La Tour Blanche and Puynormant. Additionally La Roche swore to employ his men in conflict with the common enemy rather than in internecine quarrels.

Employment of the general pardon was, however, a dangerous tactic. Regular issue could result in wholesale abuse. In the short term ploys of this kind had little effect on the spread of civil war in Poitou. Most vulnerable in the midst of seigneurial in-fighting were poor labourers and agricultural workers. On 12 June 1433[21] the *Parlement* announced that: 'les lettres qui ont este trouvees, adrecans a la court, de par les pouvres labourers du pais de l'obeissance du roy, et aussi les copies des lettres et requeste envoies de par eulx au roy, comme l'en dit, seront communiquees a. . . . Maurice Claveurier, lieutenant du seneschal de Poitou et maire de Poictiers, et non a autre.' The specific circumstances resulting in the communication of these letters, as their content, is unknown to us. It seems most likely, however, that in view of the earlier allusions by Charles VII to the suffering of the poorer inhabitants of Poitou and the neighbouring areas, the intensity of seigneurial conflict in those areas in the 1430s may have produced unrest bordering upon revolt among those at the lowest economic level of society. For Charles VII, as for the *Parlement*, such developments could only have heightened the conviction that peace with Burgundy — at whatever price — was a fundamental precondition of the restoration of control over an increasingly recalcitrant nobility.


## The *Parlement* and the Nobility of Charles VII (1418-1436)

### The *Parlement* and court politics, 1422-1425:

M. Contamine has remarked upon the tendency, apparent particularly between 1425 and 1440, for many *grands seigneurs* ostensibly faithful to Charles VII to withdraw from the arena of the '*grande guerre*' with the English, and to concentrate on more personal ambitions: on the one hand the extension of territorial power on a localised basis, on the other the accumulation of political power

---

[21] See A.N. X2ª21, f.214ᵛ.

within the court of Charles VII.[22] The accuracy of this observation appears to receive support from a comparison— in terms of territorial strength — of those individuals who successively held sway at court between 1418 and 1436; moreover, there is a marked tendency for litigation before the *Parlement* after 1425, where it concerned the nobility, to feature increasingly those *grands seigneurs* determined to employ their influence at court as a means of increasing their territorial power — a tendency more marked after 1429, as the likelihood of immediate reconquest of northern France receded.

During the years 1418-25 litigation relating to prominent individuals at Charles VII's court was, by comparison with the period 1429-33, scarce. But at the same time the matter of the '*grande guerre*' occupies a much greater prominence in the affairs of the *Parlement.* It was only after initial enthusiasm for the war with the English abated, and the boundaries of the 'kingdom of Bourges' began to be viewed by Charles VII's nobility as the only realistic scenario for the consolidation or extension of seigneurial power, that the importance of the court as an instrument for achieving these ends began to be fully appreciated.

It is within this context that the early exercise of authority by a triumvirate consisting of Jean Louvet, *Président* of Provence, Tanguy du Chastel, *grand maître de l'Hôtel* and Pierre Frotier, *grand écuyer de l'Écurie* should be viewed.[23] With regard to the *Parlement*'s involvement with these men at least, the scant attention prompted by their activities invites marked comparison with the type of domination exercised by La Trémoïlle in the early 1430s. With the exception of Frotier, the exercise of power by the triumvirate, especially between 1422 and 1425, saw, apparently, relatively little attempt at aggrandisement on a territorial basis, their activities, largely confined to the court, being aimed at achieving advantages of a predominantly fiscal kind. Beneath the allegations of a fiscal kind directed particularly at Louvet and Frotier in 1425, lay more fundamental political reasons for their dismissal. The disastrous defeat of Charles VII's military at Verneuil in 1424 left Touraine and Anjou exposed to English attack. Only weeks after this event negotations were begun, under the direction of the Angevin faction, to have Richemont installed as *connétable,*[24] Buchan having died at Verneuil. Richemont's introduction to court was thus a political rather than a purely military manoeuvre, its purpose being to draw Brittany and Burgundy into a closer alliance

[22]P. Contamine, *Guerre, État et Société à la fin du Moyen âge* (Paris, 1972), 260.

[23]See Beaucourt, ii (Paris, 1882), 65-70 on the careers of the triumvirate.

[24]See E. Cosneau, *Le connétable de Richemont* (Paris, 1886), 82ff.

with Charles VII, at the same time relieving the threat of an English invasion of Angevin territory. Richemont's arrival in turn resulted in the expulsion of Louvet, Frotier and Du Chastel. Guillaume Gruel, Richemont's chronicler, informs us that the essential precondition for his patron's acceptance of the *connétable*'s sword was the expulsion from court of those responsible both for the murder of Jean Sans Peur and for the capture of Jean V of Brittany in the following year by Penthièvre claimants to the duchy.[25] The accuracy of Gruel's observation is confirmed, in Burgundy's case, by the fact that Philippe le Bon called for the punishment of his father's murderers during the peace preliminaries with Charles VII at Arras in 1429, and once more prior to the settlement of a formal treaty with the latter in 1435.[26]

This clever political manoeuvre by the Angevins led, in the short term, to a period of considerable political stability between 1425 and 1429. In the long term the plan revealed two serious flaws. In the first place Richemont's credibility at court would henceforth depend heavily upon the political constancy of his secondary patrons, Brittany and Burgundy — always a highly uncertain factor given English presence in northern France and, in the case of Brittany, the alliance of the Penthièvre faction with Charles VII. More important again, the constancy of Richemont's patrons in turn depended upon the willingness of Charles VII to adhere to the conditions of Richemont's acceptance and to co-operate with the banishment and punishment of Louvet, Frotier and their associates. Yet Philippe le Bon's insistence in 1429 that Charles should effect those very conditions,[27] suggests that the latter was unwilling to adhere to this stipulation.[28] We shall examine later the reasons for this reluctance on Charles VII's part. For the moment it will serve to illustrate further the vulnerability of Richemont's position, even at the moment of his election.

The fortunes of one member of the triumvirate which had exercised power at Charles VII's court in the early 1420s, namely Pierre Frotier, *seigneur* of Preuilly and *premier écuyer de l'Écurie*, may be traced in some detail in the registers of the Poitiers *Parlement*. The *Parlement*'s dealings with Frotier additionally provide an indication of the way in which it worked to protect Charles VII, often against his

[25]G. Gruel, *Chronique d'Arthur de Richement*, ed. A Le Vavasseur (*SHF*, Paris, 1890), 36.

[26]See A. Mirot, 'Charles VII et ses conseillers, assassins présumés de Jean sans Peur', *A. Bourgogne* 14 (1942), 197-8.

[27]Ibid.

[28]For confirmation of this fact see ibid., 206-8.

wishes, against the more ambitious members of his entourage. Frotier was the only one among Charles VII's early favourites who appears to have combined power at court with designs of a territorial kind. Confrontation with the *Parlement* was to some extent owing to the fact that Frotier's early power base was located within Poitou itself, at Melle. In July 1423[29] Frotier complained of attempts by the *sénéchal* of Poitou to usurp his own fiscal and judicial prerogatives at Melle. The *Procureur général du roi* dismissed Frotier's complaint pointing out, through the *Avocat du roi*, that the county of Poitou was an integral part of the royal domain, and as such could not be alienated either in part or as a whole except in the form of an appanage. While the *Parlement* was prepared to recognise the king's fallibility in human terms it was unwilling to countenance any diminution of the abstract authority of the sovereign – hence the *Avocat du roi*'s remark that in making the original donation to Frotier the Regent had acted in a purely human capacity, without being aware of the gravity of the act (*'non advisati ad importunam requestam dicti Petri Froterii'*). Frotier's appeal was rejected and the limits of his authority at Melle recognised only in conformity with the terms of the original letters issued on 20 June 1421. Supreme judicial authority at Melle was to continue to reside with the *sénéchal* of Poitou and his officials.

Contemporaneously with the issue of this *arrêt* , on 31 July 1423,[30] the *Parlement* rejected a similar complaint by Frotier, this time in respect of the *château* of La-Prugne-au-Pot in Touraine. Frotier alleged that the *château* had earlier been confiscated from Renier Pot for crimes of *lèse-majesté*, and was later given to him by Charles VII in consideration of the part he had played in the original reduction of the place. Frotier's complaint was once again rejected by the *Procureur général du roi*, who maintained, through the *Avocat du roi*, that the *château* had been taken not by Frotier alone, but by Charles VII's troops with the aid of royal finances (*'per gentes et stipendiarios nostros, ac nostris propriis sumptibus et stipendiis reductum fuerat'*). Furthermore, while the *Parlement* was prepared to acknowledge the fact that Charles VII was empowered to cede the *château* to Frotier, the latter's conduct in attempting to circumvent the *Parlement*'s authority in respect of a slightly earlier 'donation', this time of Gençay, suggested that it would be to the king's advantage to deny Frotier access to La-Prugne-au-Pot. The *Parlement* thus refused to ratify Frotier's letters of gift.

[29] For what follows see A.N. X1ª9190, fos. 241ᵛ-243ᵛ. Also for further details, ibid., f.270ʳ⁻ᵛ; A.N. X1ª9197, fos. 224ʳ, 226ʳff.; *A.H.-G.* MS.59, f.194ʳ.

[30] See A.N. X1ª9190, f.248ʳ⁻ᵛ. Also Beaucourt, ii (Paris, 1882), 66-7, regarding Frotier's acquisition of Gençay.

The animosity harboured by Frotier against local royal officials in Poitou.as a result of these and other confrontations is conveyed by litigation before the *Parlement* on 17 August 1424.[31] Jean Rabateau, speaking on behalf of Maurice Claveurier, *lieutenant-général* of the *sénéchaussée* of Poitou, and for the mayor and *échevins* of Poitiers, explained that: 'a ceste venue et nouvelle entree du roy a Poictiers, les maire et echevins se disposerent d'aler au devant et reverer le roy. Et fist messire Maurice assambler ceulx de la ville au mieulx qu'il pot, et aussi les sergens du roy mectre en ordonnance.' Among the sergeants, Rabateau continued, was one Jean de May, dressed in his official regalia. As the king's party entered Poitiers, Frotier, slightly ahead of the main body, bearing Charles's sword, called out to May:' "Ribaut! Estes vous la?" . . . (jurant. . . qu'il ne mourroit que de ses mains).' May's attempts to pacify Frotier saw the latter reply: ' "je ne vous orray ja, Ribaut; . . . je vous feray mourir mauvaisement et mongier aux chiens" '. Rabateau pointed out that this was 'grant. . . injure et offense, faicte et dicte en presence de son prince a son entree en lieu et assambler publique'. However Frotier, incensed by the confrontation with May, later visited Maurice Claveurier's house in Poitiers, where the *Chancelier* was lodging and drew Claveurier into the garden to question him about the imprisonment of Louis de Blanchefort, one of Frotier's men. A heated quarrel developed which culminated in Frotier grasping Claveurier forcibly by the shoulders; only the intervention of a third party, Rabateau alleged, saved Claveurier's life. Frotier countered these allegations by emphasising the valuable services earlier performed by him for the king, alleging, in addition, that Jean de May, involved in the previous verbal exchange, had earlier committed a serious assault upon his brother at Lusignan. The *Procureur du roi* nevertheless rejected Frotier's defence, at the same time calling, through the *Avocat du roi,* for his imprisonment. Frotier escaped his fate, but was nevertheless soon to fall victim to the more arbitrary forces of court politics.

On 25 May 1425[32] it was broadcast at Lyon that: 'l'on avoit criee a Bourges que tous ceulx qui tindroyent la parti du President, de Frottier et du seigneur de Giach, que l'on disoit publiquement estres traitres au roy, qu'ils vuidassent la ville dedans deux jours apres.' The revolution at the court of Charles VII which followed Richemont's reception displays the complex, and seemingly contradictory, forces which underlay changes in the king's entourage.

---

[31] For what follows see A.N. X1ª9197, fos. 338ʳ-339ᵛ.

[32] *Reg. consulaires,* ii (Lyon, 1926), 135.

If the Angevin faction was primarily responsible for the introduction of Richemont, and for effecting the estrangement of Charles's former favourites, it was equally responsible, with Charles VII, for maintaining certain of them in comfortable conditions.[33] The careers of the triumvirate after 1425 make the continued Burgundian demands for their punishment more comprehensible. Louvet was retired to Saint-André, then to Villeneuve-les-Avignon, where he had earlier served Marie of Anjou as *châtelain* and *viguier*, with wages of 100 *l.t.* per month. In addition he received a royal pension of 3,000 *florins per annum* on the *grenier* at Tarascon. His wife and daughter were also the object of gratifications from Marie of Anjou and Charles VII. With the return of the Angevin faction to prominence in the 1430s, Louvet was re-introduced to the court through the agency of Charles d'Anjou and Yolande. Louvet also participated in negotiations for the release of the duke of Orléans, attempting, at the same time, to negotiate the marriage of the latter to Marguerite of Savoy, widow of Louis III of Anjou. Tanguy du Chastel similarly withdrew into comfortable circumstances at Beaucaire, where he was captain and *châtelain*, and later to Aigues-Mortes, where he held the same functions. In addition to his wages for these offices Du Chastel also received a pension of 2,000 *l.t. per annum* from Charles VII, together with numerous other gratifications. Finally, Pierre Frotier, whose early career we have followed, retired after 1425 in temporary fashion to his seigneurial retreat at Preuilly.

These factors clearly warrant a reassessment of the traditional view of Charles VII's kingship, particularly during the early years of his reign. Clearly Charles was a man to feel gratitude towards his servants – even those he banished. Unlike Louis XI he must also have appreciated early that to display ingratitude was to create opposition; given the difficult circumstances of the early years of his reign Charles was clearly aware that the accumulation of goodwill was of fundamental importance for the very survival of his claim to the French crown. Moreover, the traditional thesis of Charles VII's vulnerability before his 'favourites' appears even more dubious in the face of his repeated unwillingness to punish those who had allegedly exploited him. His protection of those apparently responsible for the murder of Jean Sans Peur, and for the capture of Jean V of Brittany, could stem from a variety of reasons, though it is difficult to view the action as a product of weakness.

Unlike Louvet and Du Chastel, Frotier does not appear to have had close links with the Angevin faction at Charles VII's court; yet, in

---

[33] See Mirot, 199ff., for this, and what follows.

similar fashion, his 'banishment' did not endure for very long after 1425. He appears to have maintained a low profile before 1430, though it is clear that during this period he had taken care to retain the integrity of his central seigneurial base at Preuilly-sur-Claise.[34] After 1430 however, Frotier's career may be traced in some detail in the registers of the *Parlement*. It is clear from a survey of this evidence, that the notion of Frotier's banishment, let alone punishment, for his earlier activities warrants modification. The diversion caused by the escalation of conflict in Poitou between Richemont and La Trémoïlle appears to have provided Frotier with a convenient front for the renewed expansion of his own territorial power. However, the situation of this private 'war' upon Poitou, and the loss of Melle, given to La Trémoïlle on 26 July 1426 by Charles VII as security for a loan of 6,000 *écus d'or*, meant that after 1430 Frotier's activities were more closely confined to places within close proximity of Preuilly-Azay-le-Ferron, La Roche-Posay and Le Blanc — in the duchy of Berry, in addition to smaller holdings at Melzeard and Mizere in neighbouring Poitou.[35] Frotier's renewed attempts at power-building began in earnest in 1430, facilitated by his marriage in 1421 to Marguerite de Preuilly, daughter of Gilles, baron of Preuilly and Marguerite de Naillac. On 2 March 1430[36] Frotier began a protracted legal battle with the heirs of Jean de Naillac, *grand Pannetier,* for the latter's extensive possessions in Poitou, Berry and La Marche. Frotier's misconduct over the suit led to his imprisonment at Poitiers in January 1434.[37] Somewhat earlier on 19 April 1431,[38] he had appeared before the *Parlement* to defend his claim to the ownership of Preuilly itself, in face of competition from Louise de Preuilly, a daughter, like Frotier's wife, of Gilles de Preuilly. Frotier's frustration with the protracted judicial proceedings saw his resort to alternative means of consolidating his territorial power. On 12 April 1431[39] Pierre de Salinhac, with the *Procureur général du roi* complained, in face of Frotier's allegation that, with the consent of other *seigneurs* near Preuilly he had 'pris charge de gens d'armes et de trait, Escotoiz et autres, pour la garde et sehurté dudit pais', that Frotier had instead

[34] See, for instance A.N. X1ᵃ9198, f.309ʳ.

[35] For remarks on Frotier's seigneurial acquisitions, see 'Rec. des docs', *Arch. hist. Poitou,* 26 (1896), 364 n.2.

[36] For details of this affair see A.N. X1ᵃ9199, f.241ᵛ; A.N. X2ᵃ21, fos. 254ᵛff. The final *arrêt* may be found on A.N. X1ᵃ9193, fos. 127ᵛ-128ʳ (3 March 1436).

[37] See A.N. X2ᵃ21, f.231ᵛ.

[38] See A.N. X1ᵃ9199, f. 388ʳ-389ʳ.

[39] For what follows see A.N. X2ᵃ18, fos. 250ᵛff.

184

used this authority in order to terrorise his subjects at Lingé and La Puye from the nearby stronghold of Azay-le-Ferron. In response to Salinhac's appeal the *Parlement* fined Frotier and his associates 4,000 *réaux d'or.*

On 7 July 1433[40] Frotier was again summoned to Poitiers to answer for certain excesses committed by him, together with a Scot, Jean Gerras and others, against a royal sergeant and Philippon Charles, servant of Gilbert de La Fayette. Not long after this, on 19 April 1434,[41] Frotier faced opposition in the *Parlement* from Louis Bonenfant and Louise de Preuilly, his wife, over the matter of the divided succession of La Roche-Posay. Despite the publication of an earlier *arrêt* adjudging half of the revenues of the place to Louise, Frotier had attempted to appropriate by force all the revenues to himself. The *Parlement* called for the restitution of the arrears, and, in addition, imposed fines totalling 1,500 *l.t.* upon Frotier.

It is possible, in view of Frotier's active championship of his seigneurial concerns after 1430, and Philippe le Bon's persistent demand for his punishment, that the 1430s witnessed for him, as for Louvet at a slightly later date, a revival of his fortunes at the court of Charles VII. An *arrêt* of the Poitiers *Parlement* dated 7 June 1432, styles Frotier: 'scutifero nostre scutiferie.'[42] During the 1430s and 1440s his authority at court appears to have steadily increased to the point where by the 1450s he was again a countersignatory to important royal edicts.[43] Some idea of the size of the personal fortune acquired by Frotier during the course of his long career is indicated by his eventual purchase, in 1456, of one half of the *seigneurie* of Le Blanc, in Berry, for the massive sum of 700,000 *écus d'or.*[44]

### Richemont and La Trémoïlle: origins of the conflict

The political intrigues at the court of Charles VII from c. 1422 to 1435 are usually depicted as the consequence of attempts by a succession of 'favourites' to achieve individual political ambitions at the expense of a weak king. While this observation contains an element of truth, the reasons for their being allowed to do so were considerably more

[40] See A.N. X2ª21, f.217ᵛ.

[41] See A.N. X1ª9200, f.225ʳ. Also ibid., fos. 251ᵛff., and A.N. X1ª9193, fos. 79ʳ, 179ʳ⁻ᵛ.

[42] A.N. X1ª9192, f.292ʳ.

[43] See Mirot, 205.

[44] B.N. MS. fr.27739 (Frotier), no. 10.

complex, and may only be understood with regard to the more general and, by this time, more protracted problem of the relations of the French crown with the more powerful feudatories, notably Brittany and Burgundy. Political changes at the court of Charles VII were simultaneously both the reflection of, and, on occasion, the determining factor in the changing political relationships with these quasi-independent powers.

The Lancastrian occupation and settlement of Normandy, and the eventual formation with Burgundy of a governing coalition in northern France, represented not so much an act of political disloyalty by the latter as an attempt to prevent the gradual erosion of Burgundian power by the French crown. This concept of the English role in France could remain a valid one for Burgundy as long as the former's attentions were confined to Normandy, and as long as English political ambitions were confined to maintaining a balance of power in France which could benefit all parties in the war. Cracks in the alliance began to appear particularly after 1429, when it became increasingly apparent that conquest rather than consolidation might be the ambition of certain in the Lancastrian camp. The withdrawal of Burgundian troops from the siege before Orléans and the opening of negotiations leading to the Treaty of Compiègne later in the same year might thus be seen as a natural manifestation of Philippe le Bon's desire to restore the *status quo ante*, and within this a balance of power which would ultimately benefit his own political ambitions. Burgundian suspicions about the unwillingness of the Lancastrians to conform to his own attitude towards power sharing in France were adequately confirmed by the intransigence of the English delegates at Arras in 1435.[45] Yet the breakdown of negotiations at Arras, and Burgundy's decision to sign a separate agreement with Charles VII saw the effective end, not only of the Anglo-Burgundian coalition, but also of the individual political aspirations of both parties.[46]

The very existence of the Anglo-Burgundian alliance inevitably made the question of political relations between Charles VII and the duchy of Brittany more difficult. Yet the importance of maintaining links with Jean V and Philippe le Bon alike was recognised from an early stage by one of the most influential factions at the court of Charles VII, namely the representatives of the House of Anjou. For

[45] On the English attitude at Arras and, more generally, on the conduct of the Congress, see J.G. Dickinson, *The Congress of Arras* (Oxford, 1955).

[46] For the recognition of this by a prominent member of the Lancastrian Council see M.G.A. Vale, 'Sir John Fastolf's "Report": a new interpretation reconsidered', *Nottingham Mediaeval Studies* 17 (1973), 78-84.

while the English presence in France could enhance the independence of certain of the great feudatories it could also threaten that of others. Indeed it is possible to argue that on a political level at least, the survival of Charles VII's kingship during the early years of his reign was only afforded by the determination of one of his most powerful vassals — Yolande of Aragon, governess of the House of Anjou — to resist the disintegration of the Angevin patrimony in the face of encroachment, this time by the English themselves. The situation of the bulk of Angevin territory in close proximity to English-occupied areas meant that the independent political aspirations of the Angevin faction at Charles VII's court were, coincidentally, also those of the crown more generally speaking. Hence the changes which took place in Charles VII's entourage, particularly in 1425 and in 1433, and, beneath this, attempts to create firmer alliances with Brittany and Burgundy, derived, perhaps, not so much from the king's personal initiative as from the Angevin concern to protect its possessions in northern France.

Following the collapse of Charles VII's military at Verneuil it was Angevin initiative which was responsible for the opening of negotiations with Jean V — negotiations that culminated in the Treaty of Saumur on 7 October 1425.[47] The alliance was symbolised, I have argued, by Richemont's acceptance of the *connétable*'s sword at Chinon on 7 March of the same year. M. Pocquet du Haut-Jussé rightly observed that 'l'éppée du connnétable allait moins la consécration de talents militaires. . . que la récompense et l'encouragement d'une tâche diplomatique assidue, et dont on escomptait le ralliement de la Bourgogne et de la Bretagne a la cause française.'[48] In fact the 'cause française', in respect of its attempt to draw Jean V and Philippe le Bon into a closer alliance with Charles VII, is perhaps too anachronistic a view of events. At a different level it was the political concerns of the Angevin faction which predominated in the negotiations. Yolande of Aragon had been the instigator of earlier attempts to woo Brittany and Burgundy,[49] and it appears that it was largely as a result of her personal influence, rather than any determination on the part of Charles VII, that the removal of those responsible, both for the murder of Jean Sans Peur and for the capture of Jean V by members of

[47]On the importance of this treaty see E. Cosneau, *Le connétable de Richemont,* (Paris, 1886), 110-11.

[48]B.A. Pocquet du Haut-Jussé, 'Deux féodaux: Bourgogne et Bretagne, 1363-1491, v, Philippe le Bon et Jean V, 1419-1429', in *Revue des Cours et conférences* 36 (i), (1934-5), 450.

[49]See Cosneau, 75 ff.

the Penthièvre faction, was finally effected.[50] Hence on this occasion the changing political relationships between Charles VII's court and other external powers could affect the composition of the court. Between 1418 and 1425 on the other hand, it had been the activities of Charles VII's 'favourites' which affected relations with external powers. The murder of Jean Sans Peur in 1419 — for whatever motive[51] — inevitably soured relations with Burgundy, and the seeming involvement of certain of the culprits in the attempt to put the duchy of Brittany into Penthièvre hands in 1420[52] inevitably made the prospect of an alliance with Brittany more remote.

It was the interplay of internal and external influences rather than any personal factors, which resulted in Richemont's eclipse at court in 1427-8. Temperamentally, it is true, Richemont appears to have been poorly equipped to deal with the sophisticated intrigues of the court. His preference for the 'voye de fait' is well illustrated in his participation in the brutal elimination of successive 'favourites' Pierre de Giac and Le Camus de Beaulieu.[53] However, as we have argued earlier, Richemont's position as the ambassador at court of Brittany and Burgundy alike could prove to be a mixed blessing, for unlike those who had preceded him, he was directly dependent upon their behaviour for the maintenance of his own authority at court. In this respect it is arguable that Richemont's authority with Charles VII was being eroded even as he made his entry to the court.[54] Only three days before Charles's initial overtures to Richemont, on 17 August 1424, the English won a crushing victory over the French at Verneuil. Irritated by Jean V's attempt to conduct peace negotiations with Charles VII, the English coupled the threat of sponsorship of the Penthièvre claim to the duchy of Brittany with a declaration of war on Jean V on 15 January 1426. As the negotiations with Charles VII continued, Jean V was increasingly confronted with the prospect of isolation, a fact emphasised by his frantic attempts to draw Burgundy into a protective alliance to counter the English threat. Throughout

[50] For a recent survey of the court revolution of 1425 see M.G.A. Vale, *Charles VII* (London, 1974), 35-8. Dr Vale's view (ibid., 35) that 'like Louis XI, Charles was not a man to feel gratitude towards his servants', is perhaps a trifle harsh, particularly when one considers the provisions he made for the banished 'favourites' after 1425 and their later careers (A. Mirot, 'Charles VII et ses conseillers, assassins présumés de Jean sans Peur', *A Bourgogne* 14 (1942), 197-210).

[51] See Vale, *Charles VII*, 28-31, regarding this event.

[52] On the circumstances surrounding Jean V's capture, see Beaucourt, I (Paris, 1881), 202ff.

[53] See Vale, *Charles VII*, 39.

[54] For what follows see Pocquet du Haut-Jussé, 'Deux féodaux', 451ff.

1426 and early 1427, even as the agreement with Charles VII reached its final form, the English began to mount a serious offensive in Brittany. On 8 May 1427 Pontorson capitulated, and the prospect of a full-scale assault upon Rennes seemed likely. Jean V's acceptance of a new agreement with the English on 3 July 1427 meant not only the effective negation of his earlier alliance with Charles VII; it provided, in addition, the context for the emergence of a new 'favourite' at the latter's court in the wake of Richemont's fall from favour.

The private 'war' between Richemont and La Trémoïlle was to endure until the summer of 1433. The situation of the conflict mainly upon Poitou has tended to obscure the broader political perspectives which underlay the affair. While in one sense the events of these years may be viewed simply as a struggle for territorial supremacy in Poitou alone, it is equally possible to view the conflict as a product of differing attitudes towards the conduct of the war in France, manifested at a time when the concept of loyalty to the crown might be conditioned by factors other, and considerably more pragmatic, than the notion of patriotism alone. To understand the differing attitudes of Richemont and La Trémoïlle towards the 'grande guerre' necessitates an examination of their relations with the major powers in opposition to Charles VII, and in particular with Burgundy. Before 1433 at least it is possible to argue that Richemont's attitude towards the question of political relations with Burgundy was governed, in precisely the same fashion as that of La Trémoïlle, by self-interest rather than patriotism. It was in respect of the political role which Burgundy would need to adopt in order to guarantee the satisfaction of these interests that radical differences began to be seen.

Richemont's alliance with the court of Burgundy began at Dijon on 23 September 1423 with his marriage to Marguerite, sister of Philippe le Bon.[55] The importance of this match for Richemont was emphasised by the magnificence of his entourage — a veritable princely household. Through it he made important territorial acquisitions: among them, to the west, in Poitou, Fontenay-le-Comte, which comprised part of Marguerite's dowry; to the east, a string of lordships located between Tonnerre and Montbard in the Armançon valley. More important, however, was the fact that Philippe le Bon had also made provision for Marguerite to receive the duchy of Burgundy in the event of his dying without male heir. In the event, Philippe was not possessed of an heir until 1433. Before that date, as M. Pocquet du Haut-

[55]For what follows see B.-A. Pocquet du Haut-Jussé, 'Le connétable de Richemont, seigneur Bourguignon', A. Bourgogne 7 (1935), 309-36 and 8 (1936), 7-30, 106-38 (passim). Also Cosneau, 70-6 and 113.

Jussé pointed out, Richemont might justifiably entertain the idea that he would one day be duke of Burgundy.

At first sight Richemont's alliance with Charles VII in 1425 might, in view of his Burgundian concerns, seem a rash move. In breaking his earlier vow to the Anglo-Burgundian alliance Richemont might have lost all personal advantage gained by his marriage to Marguerite. Certain factors suggest that this was not the case. Burgundy's reaction to Richemont's election as *connétable* was far from hostile, and Philippe's decision to 'confiscate' his Burgundian possessions *before* his accession to office may have been indicative, less of genuine hostility to the agreement, than of concern to prevent their confiscation by the English under the pretext that Richemont had broken his earlier oath to the coalition.[56] From a personal point of view, Richemont's election as *connétable* could thus prove highly advantageous, for it would enable him to retain the integrity of possessions located in French and Burgundian territory alike.[57] His re-receipt of the lordship of Parthenay from Charles VII in 1427 provided further endorsement of the wisdom of this decision. On a different level, Richemont's appointment could, in theory, have served to strengthen relations between Brittany and Burgundy, and to weaken the Anglo-Burgundian alliance. The weakness in this strategy derived from the fact that in order to guarantee its success, the active co-operation of both Brittany and Burgundy would have to be assured — clearly this could not be guaranteed so long as the Anglo-Burgundian coalition remained in operation. Hence, Richemont's concern to forge closer links between Charles VII and Philippe le Bon could be viewed, in precisely the same manner as the complementary activities of the Angevin faction, as a merger of private interest and public duty.

Yet while for a Richemont public duty and private interest might combine to support the interests of the French crown in general, it is clear that for others the pursuit of private interests could prove, to the contrary, antithetical to the ( arguably still hazy) notion of the public good. Such was the case, arguably, with Georges de La Trémoïlle.

[56]See Pocquet du Haut-Jussé, 'Le connétable de Richemont', 8 (1936), 28-30. (Cf. Vale, *Charles VII*, 36). Jean V's confiscation of Penthièvre possessions in retaliation for the events of 1420 came on 16 Feb. 1425, only one day after Philippe le Bon had 'confiscated' Richemont's Burgundian possessions (Pocquet du Haut-Jussé, 'Le connétable de Richemont', 7 (1935), 324 n.3). Both events therefore appear to have occurred with the certain knowledge that Richemont would accept the *Connétable's* sword.

[57]Richemont's territorial gains from Charles VII were very considerable (Cosneau, 113).

In order to appreciate the differing attitudes of Richemont and La
Trémoïlle towards the conduct of the *'grande guerre'* it is necessary to
move once again outside the confines of Poitou and to examine La
Trémoïlle's relations with external powers, notably Burgundy. The
association of the La Trémoïlle family with the Burgundian court was,
even by 1418, a long-standing one. Georges de La Trémoïlle was
*premier Chambellan* of Jean Sans Peur in 1409, in succession to his
father Guy VI.[58] The events of 1418, far from witnessing a decline of
the family's influence with Burgundy, saw a judicious division of its
members between the French and Burgundian camps — Georges
henceforth electing to serve the Dauphin, while his brother, Jean, lord
of Jonvelle, continued to serve the Burgundians, as *conseiller* and
*chambellan,* under Philippe le Bon.[59] The position of different
members of the family on different sides in the war did not, however,
lead either to conflicting views on general political matters —
Georges and Jean remained on amicable terms throughout the period
1418-35 — or to any diminution of the family's interests in general.
Clearly the position of the La Trémoïlles' patrimony – on the one
hand in Anjou, Poitou and the environs of Orléans, in areas loyal to
Charles VII, on the other in Paris, the Île de France and the
Auxerrois, this time under Anglo-Burgundian domination — meant
that family interests would be better served by maintaining its
representatives in both camps, rather than opting for a single political
alliance.[60] The tendency on the part of other *seigneurs,* as of families
or individuals of lower estate, to maintain their representatives on
both sides in the war is a matter which, as M. Bossuat has shown,
deserves serious study, and might go a long way to explaining why, for
many, the question of political alliances was seldom seen in terms of
black or white, but merely in varying shades of grey.[61]

The advantage of such an equivocal stance by the La Trémoïlle
family was underlined in 1427 when the Lancastrian government
confiscated property belonging to Georges which lay within their
control, and merely transferred it to his brother Jean.[62] Precisely the

[58]P. Héliot and A. Benoît, 'Georges de La Trémoïlle et la mainmise du duc de
Bourgogne sur les Boulonnais', *R. Nord* 24 (1938), 31 n.7.

[59]Ibid., 32.

[60]See A. Bossuat, 'The Re-Establishment of Peace in Society during the Reign of
Charles VII', in *The Receovery of France in the Fifteenth Century,* ed P.S. Lewis
(London, 1971), p. 65.

[61]See P.S. Lewis, *Later Medieval France. The Polity* (London, 1968), 66.

[62]Bossuat, p. 65 n.18. La Trémoïlle seems to have likewise been obliged to cede
control of the county of Boulogne to his brother after 1418 as a means of avoiding
Burgundian confiscation (Héliot and Benoît, 35-6).

same step was taken by Georges de La Trémoïlle in May 1431 following the confiscation of property belonging to Louis d'Amboise, *vicomte* of Thouars.[63] All those places within the *vicomté* formerly the property of Jean de La Trémoïlle were carefully reserved by Georges, thus preventing any erosion of the family's overall holdings. There are signs — and future research may confirm this view — that by 1431 Georges was favourably disposed towards some sort of agreement with the English, aimed, perhaps, at achieving a balance of power between the major parties in the war. Such a strategy may have found support with many in the English camp; here, again, we need to know much about differing attitudes within the Lancastrian Council with regard to the conduct of the war in France. Some within the Council were earlier strongly opposed to the attack on Orléans, preferring instead to consolidate English presence in Normandy. It is possible that, in respect of the decision to attack Orléans, as in the later decision to abandon the negotiations at Arras, the extremist party won the day. But the possibility of an agreement between those Lancastrians more concerned to restrict their ambitions to Normandy, and certain of Charles VII's *Conseil*, may not have been entirely out of the question between 1430 and 1435.

The successful perpetuation of La Trémoïlle's strategy might thus, unlike Richemont's, depend less upon the achievement of a formal alliance with Burgundy, than upon a careful maintenance of a balance of power between the major parties in the war, including the English. In this respect, the 'war' between Richemont and La Trémoïlle in Poitou was not merely a battle for local supremacy. At a deeper level it was a conflict over the way in which the '*grande guerre*' should be conducted. In reality, the wider concerns of the French crown may thus have played only a small part in what was at root a conflict of individual interests. It was merely the compatibility of the individual interests of Richemont with those of Charles VII that admitted the posthumous (and perhaps peripheral) question of 'patriotism' into the conflict.

## The 'War' in Poitou between Richemont and La Trémoïlle[64] (1427-1433)

By 1427, even as he entered the court of Charles VII, La Trémoïlle was already firmly entrenched, territorially, in Poitou. In addition to

---

[63]'Rec. des docs', *Arch. hist. Poitou* 29 (1898), xxx. Jean de La Trémoïlle had earlier married Jacqueline d'Amboise, Louis' sister.

[64]For details of the conflict between Richemont and La Trémoïlle in the late 1420s and early 1430s, I have relied largely upon the researches of Guérin ('Rec. des docs',

his patrimonial possessions the new 'favourite' also controlled, by inheritance from his mother, Marie de Sully, an important group of lordships situated to the north-west of the county — the Île de Noirmoutier, Mareuil-sur-Lay, Saint-Hermine, Prahecq and Le Bois - Pouvreau. The most important of these places were, additionally, situated in uncomfortably close proximity to Richemont's lordship of Fontenay-le-Comte. During 1427 the pattern of future conflict continued to be delineated, Richemont obtaining Parthenay and its dependencies in October-November of that year, following the death of Jean l'Archêveque,[65] while La Trémoïlle, by virtue of a judicious marriage to Catherine, dame de l'Île Bouchard, widow of the murdered 'favourite' Pierre de Giac, added Gençay, situated to the south of Poitiers, to his own Poitevin possessions. In addition the obtaining of Melle in 1426, and Lusignan, in 1428, from Charles VII in return for large personal loans, provided La Trémoïlle, by the beginning of 1429, with a string of lordships, ranged in the form of a great arc running to the south and west of Richemont's territories, and broken only by the town of Niort, ceded earlier by Charles VII to Jean II duke of Alençon in recompense for large loans.

The spread of the conflict between Richemont and La Trémoïlle more widely in Poitou, and also into neighbouring areas — Saintonge, the Limousin and Berry — derived from the attempt by both men to strengthen their positions by contracting alliance with other *seigneurs*. Richemont initially attempted to compensate for his vulnerability at Fontenay-le-Comte by forming a coalition of interests to the north of Poitou involving his younger brother, Richard de Bretagne, *seigneur* of Châteaumur, Aizenay, Pallau and Les Essarts, Louis d'Amboise, *vicomte* of Thouars, André de Beaumont, *seigneur* of Lezay, and Antoine de Vivonne. This alliance of a mainly territorial kind was supplemented along more broadly political lines by means of an agreement with Jacques de Bourbon, and with the counts of Clermont, Pardiac and Armagnac. In spite of these arrangements, however, the weakness of Richemont's position at court was emphasised by Jean V's decision to enter into a new alliance with the English on 8 September 1427. Jean V's behaviour left Richemont dangerously isolated as the ambassador of a hostile power. At the same time, to

*Arch. hist. Poitou* 29 (1898), i-lxiii), based upon the registers of the Poitiers *Parlement*. My interpretation of the evidence differs from Guérin's in the sense that it sees the origins of the conflict not so much in the weakness of the French crown under Charles VII (though this was undoubtedly a short-term contributing factor), as in the natural desire on the part of Charles VII's nobles to resist the gradual tendency by the crown to usurp their territorial and judicial powers.

[65] See ibid., v-viii for Richemont's enduring attempt to procure Parthenay.

relinquish his personal authority at court might mean, for Richemont, the abandonment of all hope of a Breton-Burgundian alliance with Charles VII, and, in turn, the loss of favour with Burgundy. Hence during 1427 and early 1428, Richemont resorted to more forceful methods to maintain his authority. The attempt during early 1428 at capture and ransom of La Trémoïlle, was followed in the summer of that year by a rash attempt to take control of Charles VII's government by force. The collapse of this enterprise at Bourges on 17 July merely alienated Richemont further from Charles VII.

A more serious result of the capture of La Trémoïlle at Gençay was La Trémoïlle's decision to retaliate by strengthening his own position through protective alliances with, on the one hand, Jean de La Roche (foucauld), *seigneur* of Barbezieux and Mussidan, and captain of Angoulême for Jean d'Orléans; on the other, and with damaging consequences for Richemont's relations with Jean V, as for Charles VII's war-effort in more general terms, Jean de Blois, called *de Bretagne, comte* de Penthièvre et de Périgord, *vicomte* de Limoges. With the English invasion of Anjou imminent, the 'kingdom of Bourges' was thus approaching a state of civil war.

It was possibly English awareness of the increasing internal disorder of the 'kingdom of Bourges' during the summer of 1428 which prompted certain in the Lancastrian camp to reject an earlier plan for the invasion of Anjou in favour of penetration, *via* Orléans, into the heart of the 'kingdom'. Quite a different interpretation has, however, been offered by M. Harmand, who suggests that:

> d'après des sources administratives,[66] Bedford, au début de 1428, s'attend à un gros effort de Charles VII. Devant cette toile de fond, l'expédition conduite sur Orléans par Salisbury, à quelques mois de là, prend sa véritable signification; ce ne fut point le dernier pas d'un conquérant vers l'achèvement de la victoire, mais l'ultime sursaut de quelque envergure d'une puissance qui perdait pied.[67]

Whatever the truth of this observation, it seems clear that from the outset strong reservations were displayed by many prominent members of the Lancastrian Council about the wisdom of an attack upon Orléans. The siege proved, in the event, to be protracted and costly, both in financial and psychological terms; the decision by Philippe le

---

[66] Harmand does not make it convincingly clear what these sources are. For a contrary view see M.H. Keen, *England in the Later Middle Ages* (London, 1975), 386.

[67] J. Harmand, 'Un document de 1435 concernant Houdan et la fin de l'occupation Anglaise dans l'ouest de l'Ile de France', in *B. Soc. Antiq. France*, 1975, 208.

Bon to withdraw his troops from the siege at a late stage could thus be seen as a vital blow to the morale of the besieging army[68] and the appearance of a French relieving force with Joan of Arc among its numbers saw a complete disintegration of residual Lancastrian commitment to the enterprise.

The sources of concern for the relief of Orléans on the French side, and in particular those responsible for the decision to employ Joan of Arc against the English, are not difficult to discern: it was perhaps the immediate territorial concerns of the House of Anjou which provided the fundamental impetus. The likelihood of an English invasion of Anjou had remained the determining factor in Angevin political policy around Charles VII for some years before 1428. The initial decision by the Lancastrian council in the summer of 1428 to strike at Angers might have confirmed this view; yet the decision to attack Orléans could not have entirely averted Angevin fears — loss of the town might have permitted instead the complete encirclement of Touraine and Anjou by way of Tours and Angers. The introduction of Joan of Arc into the conflict has been suggested as a possible political move by the representatives of Anjou;[69] it is also easy to discern the involvement of this faction at every subsequent stage of Joan's career up to the coronation at Reims.

The attitude of La Trémoïlle to the prospect of English success at Orléans appears to have been considerably more equivocal. The Herald, Berry, tells us that at an early stage, Salisbury sent as captain of nearby Sully: 'un chevalier de Nivernois, nomme messire Guillaume de Rochefort, lequel tenoit le party des Anglois, et estoit parent du... seigneur de La Trimouille, seigneur dudit Sully;... or, le siege d'Orleans durant, ceux dudit Sully avitailloient lesdits Anglois, de ce qui leur estoit possible.'[70] If the relief of Orléans and the Reims coronation represented, at root, a triumph for Angevin diplomacy, La Trémoïlle was alleged (perhaps unfairly) by some of the more partisan chroniclers to have been primarily responsible for preventing the initiative gained from these events being employed in a major offensive against the English in northern France.[71] Such a view ignored, arguably, the political realities of the moment. An initial

---

[68] For a discussion of the reasons for the departure of Burgundian troops from the siege see above, pp. 92ff.

[69] M.G.A. Vale, *Charles VII* (London, 1974), 49-51. For remarks on the early stages of Joan's career see above, Chapter 3.

[70] Ed. D. Godefroy (Paris, 1661), 376.

[71] See for example, Chartier (ed. D. Godefroy (Paris, 1661), 28); Berry (ibid., 381) and Cagny (ed. H. Moranvillé (*SHF*, Paris, 1902),170-1).

agreement with Burgundy was under the circumstances a far more practical step; yet, in the short term, the Treaty of Compiègne in August 1429 permitted the restoration of a *status quo ante*, which, in allowing La Trémoïlle to concentrate upon the expansion of his own territorial interests in Poitou, simultaneously prevented Charles VII from consolidating his temporary advantage over Burgundy.

The years 1430-3 witnessed the zenith of La Trémoïlle's power. During 1430 Charles VII appears ostensibly to have attempted a reconciliation between Richemont and La Trémoïlle by offering letters of remission to their principal allies. La Trémoïlle's attempt to arrange a meeting between himself and the *connétable* between Parthenay and Poitiers saw Richemont, possibly fearful of reprisals for his earlier behaviour towards La Trémoïlle, send, instead, his confederates, Louis d'Amboise, André de Beaumont and Antoine de Vivonne. The conference, which took place at Gien between July and October 1430, witnessed instead an attempt by Richemont's allies to take La Trémoïlle by force. The failure of the plot saw the unfortunate Beaumont and Vivonne condemned to death at Poitiers, on 8 May 1431 for crimes of *lèse-majesté*. Louis d'Amboise escaped death, but his imprisonment was preceded by La Trémoïlle's appropriation of his possessions. The aftermath of the plot thus provided La Trémoïlle with considerable moral and territorial advantage. Richemont's desperate attempt to recover his position saw him try to occupy Marans, Benon and the Île de Ré, property of the *vicomte* of Thouars, but a fresh offensive led by La Trémoille forced him to retire to Fontenay in September 1431. By the beginning of 1432 La Trémoïlle's possessions stretched in the form of a great almost unbroken arc from the Île de Noirmoutier and Mareuil-sur-Lay to the north and west, to Chauvigny, situated to the east of Poitiers. From Chauvigny the line continues northward, through the possessions of the recently-'returned' Pierre Frotier, and, by virtue of patrimonial and marital possessions, round in another great sweep to join the recently-confiscated territories of the *vicomte* of Thouars. This expansion in Poitou was coupled during 1431 with an accompanying domination of Saintonge and the Île de Ré, and was extended, by virtue of alliances with Jean de La Roche and the Penthièvre faction, into areas of Angoulême and Périgord.

But even as the summit of La Trémoïlle's power was reached, his authority at the court of Charles VII was increasingly exposed to the play of external politics. The withdrawal of Charles's forces below the Loire after the abortive attack on Paris allowed a reaffirmation of the Anglo-Burgundian alliance on terms more favourable to Burgundy. By 1432 the coalition sought to draw Jean V and his principal allies into its orbit, this time by playing the game of incentives which was to be later emulated by Charles VII himself in the reconquest of Normandy and Guyenne. On 7 January Henry VI 'ceded' the county of Poitou to Jean V. Richemont was offered the yet more tempting bribe of Touraine, Saintonge, Aunis and La Rochelle, together with all the possessions of La Trémoïlle located in Poitou. The implications of this strategy were immediately recognised by La Trémoïlle, for, between 5-25 March, at Rennes, counter-negotiations took place to try to heal the rift between himself and Richemont by offering the latter new concessions. La Trémoïlle's removal from court followed speedily in the wake of these events. In June 1433 he was ousted and replaced by a new 'favourite', Charles d'Anjou.

The view of La Trémoïlle's eclipse as a triumph for patriotic forces is, however, an anachronism. As M. Guérin observed: 'les nouveaux maîtres du pouvoir userent de la plus extrême moderation vis-à-vis des créatures et des amis de l'ancien favori. Aucun ne fut inquiété.'[72] In this sense La Trémoïlle's treatment differed little from that of Charles VII's earlier 'favourites'. Whether this should be taken as an index of the king's personal weakness is a matter for debate. In the troubled conditions of the 1430s Charles clearly needed every ally he could get. The emergence of an Angevin favourite permitted a 'change' in his character not because the personal ambitions of a Charles d'Anjou were necessarily any weaker than those of a Georges de La Trémoïlle but because the broader political concerns of the House of Anjou coincided more closely with those of the crown. Without the consistent support of the Angevin faction during the 1420s and 1430s it is arguable that, on a political level at least, Charles's kingship might never have survived. It was perhaps fitting that the territorial possessions of the House of Anjou should be among the last to be absorbed into the royal domain under Louis XI. In the short term the symbiosis of Angevin and royal interests afforded Charles VII, following the negotiation of a peace with Burgundy, the opportunity to turn his full attention to the subjugation of those of his allies who had earlier worked to exploit his 'weakness'. The principal cause of the *Praguerie* was to be, as Professor Favreau has remarked, 'la reprise en main du royaume par Charles VII, sous l'impulsion du parti Angevin'.[73] Stability in the kingdom of France thus represented, at root, for the House of Anjou, a perfect coincidence of private interest and public duty.

[72]'Rec. des docs', *Arch. hist. Poitou,* 29 (1898), xliii.

[73]R. Favreau, 'La Praguerie en Poitou', *Bibl. Éc. Chartes* 129 (1971), 283.

# The War in Poitou: Attempts at Control by the *Parlement*

## Internal organisation:

The early years of the *Parlement* of Poitiers' operation from 1418-29, displayed an energy, and a facility for organisation which belies the traditional picture of the poverty of the resources of the 'king of Bourges'. Yet between 1429 and 1436, the escalation of internal warfare and brigandage in the centre and west of France undoubtedly made the question of control by the *Parlement* considerably more difficult. The negative aspect of this problem has been amply described by Didier Neuville, particularly in respect of the problems engendered by the escalation of seigneurial conflict within Poitou and its environs.[74]

One of the most serious obstacles to the *Parlement's* efficient operation was the irregular, or non-payment of its wages. Repercussions were felt in two respects; first, and most obviously, *conseillers* of lower rank having no supplementary income may have been reduced to a situation of considerable hardship; second, and more seriously in the long term, obstruction of the assignations from different *bailliages* and *sénéchaussées,* upon which wages were normally distributed, meant that the *Parlement* was obliged to resort to extraordinary sources of finance to pay its members. Most convenient of these resorts was the *Recette des amendes* of the *Parlement;* yet the danger inherent in taking this course of action stemmed from the fact that the *amendes* also provided a source of ready capital from which all the ancillary operations related to the central judicial function of the *Parlement* were financed. The increasing concern, during the later period of the *Parlement's* operation, carefully to regulate the outflow of capital from this source was thus both a recognition of the need to pay the wages of *conseillers* in the absence of other finance and also of the importance of maintaining the ancillary functions of the *Parlement* which were essential to its efficient operation.

The inability of the *Parlement* to guarantee the prompt arrival of various assignations, particularly after 1429, produced more serious problems of internal control. The need for resort to the *amendes* had been apparent before 1429 but it had remained strictly an extraordinary recourse. After 1429 this course was followed with increasing frequency. Scarcity of finance multiplied the problem of control by the *Parlement* over its members in various ways; some of the

---

[74]D. Neuville, 'Le Parlement royal à Poitiers (1418-1436)', *R. hist.* 6 (1878), 291ff.

*conseillers* attempted to take their wages from particular assignations at their source to the detriment of others; some, if we are to believe complaints by the *Parlement,* were even compelled to leave Poitiers and live off their benefices or in their native regions; some had recourse to more lucrative commissions as royal agents in a variety of fiscal matters; finally there was the additional resort to bribery, and the willingness to accept illicit payments to guarantee a particular litigant's case. By early 1433 these problems had reached serious proportions, and the *Parlement* was obliged to issue a series of prohibitions which provide an echo of the earlier *Cabochien* ordinance.[75]

The flexibility of the *Parlement* in finding ways to surmount these problems, coupled with the determination to retain strict control of its members' activities, bears witness to the long years of corporate organistion developed at Paris during the previous century. In this respect it is unwise to view the 'crisis' faced by the *Parlement* of Poitiers during these years as an isolated event of unusual proportions; the study by M. Aubert of the *Parlement* of Paris during this period shows clearly that difficulties of a similar kind were being experienced contemporaneously at Paris, and the degree of hardship which they engendered was arguably of greater proportions.[76] Problems of this nature had been recurrent at Paris particularly during the last half-century or so, and they persisted, to a greater or lesser extent, after the return to Paris in 1436. It is thus possible that the degree of severity with which the *Parlement* of Poitiers was judged in respect of this 'crisis' represented, for many French historians, an attempt to explain Charles VII's apparently 'illogical' inability to proceed to the reconquest of France, following the relief of Orléans by Joan of Arc.[77] Such a simplistic view hardly does credit to the complex reality of political events during this period; it also unjustifiably diminishes the prominent role played by the *Parlement* in maintaining a degree of order in the aftermath of these events.

Some indication of the trend of later years was already apparent in 1427. In January, March and July of that year payments were made from the *Recette des amendes* to Jean de Maine, called *de Blois,* *greffier civil,* and to Jean d'Asnières, *greffier criminel* in the *Parlement.*[78] Furthermore on 13 September 1427 the court announced

[75] See A.N. X1ᵃ9194, fos. 35ʳff. (Feb. 1433).

[76] F. Aubert, *Histoire du Parlement de Paris de l'origine à François Iᵉʳ (1250-1515),* i (Paris, 1894), especially 101-3.

[77] See the remarks by J. Harmand (207 n.1.) on the damaging effect of the Joan of Arc legend on the work of Beaucourt and others.

[78] See A.N. X2ᵃ21, f.68ᵛ and *A.H.-G.* MS.59, f.301ʳ.

that a fine of 800 *l.t.* imposed upon Jean Patharin, lieutenant of the *bailli* of Mâcon, would be employed to pay the wages of *conseillers*.[79] Late in 1428 these problems were temporarily surmounted by the *Parlement*'s receipt of a formal assignation. However the escalation of seigneurial conflict in the centre-west following the Reims coronation saw the difficulty of guaranteeing assignations become once more a serious factor; the aftermath of this event obliged the *Parlement* to engage in an often futile battle with the receivers of various assignations in an effort to guarantee payment of the sums allotted for their wages. Coupled with this came more serious supervision of the *receveur des amendes et exploits* of the court. On 27 April 1430 the clerical *conseiller,* Pierre Paumier, was delegated to supervise the accounts of Miles Chaligant, receiver; Chaligant was also ordered to allow no delay to debtors of the court.[80] On 12 September of the same year the wages of the *greffiers* of the *Parlement* and their clerks were also paid from the *amendes*.[81] Finally on 13 November *conseillers* Nicole Géhée and Aimery Marchand were ordered once more to examine the state of the *Recette*: 'tant au regard des amendes de la court comme au regard des assignations faites pour gages d'icelle court, et de adjuster et pourveoir a la poursuite qui est a faire pour la court au regard des assignations, et de ce qui en depend.'[82] Employment of the *amendes* for payment of the *conseillers'* wages continued beyond this period, almost until the return to Paris in 1436. On 2 August 1432 François de La Grange, who had lately been engaged 'raporter et visiter en ladite court certain grant proces', between the *Procureur du roi* and the *capitouls* of Toulouse, was promised 20 *réaux d'or* for his pains and expenses, which was to come from the first sums received from the resulting fine of 10,000 *réaux d'or* imposed on the *capitouls*.[83] In November 1432 distribution of the wages of the *parlementaires* was made from a fine imposed on the minters of Lyon.[84] Again, in March 1434, Guillaume II Le Tur and Pierre de Tuillières were ordered by the court to ensure that sums coming into the *recette* were employed

[79] A.N. X2ª21, f.80ᵛ. If the *A.H.-G.* MS.59 is used as a guide to the financial difficulties of the *Parlement* in the later 1420s and 1430s, it seems that the years 1424-5, 1427-8 and 1430-1 produced the most serious problems. Here, the correlation between corruption and the non-payment of wages is abundantly clear. Thereafter, the problem became most acute in 1433, and regular resort to *ad hoc* sources of payment was made until 1436.

[80] *A.H.-G.* MS.59, f.365ʳ⁻ᵛ.

[81] Ibid., f.398ʳ.

[82] Ibid., f.400ᵛ.

[83] A.N. X2ª21, f.186ᵛ.

[84] A.N. X1ª9194, f.30ᵛ

in the correct fashion.[85] Finally, on 16 July 1435, the court repaid Miles Chaligant the sum of 100 *réaux d'or* which had been earlier borrowed from his *Recette* to pay the wages of *conseillers.*[86]

Clearly the *Parlement* was aware of the potentially damaging consequences of this form of resort for the smooth operation of the court, and some attempt was made to devise other ways of paying the wages of the *conseillers.* On 11 January 1430 it was suggested that the sum of 2,000*l. t.* should be taken from the revenues of the *vicomté* of Polignac, currently contested in the *Parlement* by the families of Chalençon and Montlaur, to pay 'gages a ceux qui seront a juger le proces'.[87] Another more temporary solution was to employ the wages and *'espices'* of absent *conseillers* to pay those present in Poitiers. However in the long term these measures were bound to be inadequate, and the resulting attempts by *conseillers* to apply individual remedies to the problem led, during the period 1429-33, to a serious escalation of absenteeism and corruption, countered by persistent attempts by the *Parlement* to maintain a semblance of control.

Individual *conseillers* could find various ways of overcoming problems brought about by the increasing unreliability of assignations on their wages. For the geographically mobile members of the court it was relatively easy to approach a particular receiver of finances and simply take the sums due to them before the assignation reached Poitiers. This course of action was followed early in 1427 by Arnaud de Marle and Jean de Montmorin, *maîtres des requêtes de l'Hôtel du Roi.* The *Parlement* was, however, quick to take action against the culprits and on 4 April and 5 July of the same year, the greater proportion of the wages due to these individuals was withheld until the sums they had already taken from the receiver were restored to the main bulk of the assignation.[88]

Another more serious aspect of the non-payment of *conseillers'* wages was the resort to bribery as an alternative source of income. The practice of offering *'douceurs'* to magistrates was a common enough occurence, and the acceptance of these payments by no means constituted an illegal activity; however, successive *Parlements* had attempted to restrict the size and frequency of these payments to

[85] Ibid., f.62[v]

[86] A.N. X2[a]21, f.277[r].

[87] *A.H.-G.* MS.59, f.350[v]. For another *ad hoc* solution, see A.N. X1[a]8604, f.117[r].

[88] See *A.H.-G.* MS.59, fos. 290[v]-291[r], 305[r]ff.

reasonable proportions. During the period 1429-33, there are numerous indications that at Poitiers these attempts were increasingly unsuccessful. On 3 April 1430 Guillaume de Laillier, Jean Mauloué and Guillaume de Lannoy were ordered to inquire into the 'abbus touchant ladite court'.[89] Shortly before this, on 2 June 1428, the *Parlement* had ordered an inquiry into the behaviour of *conseillers,* Geoffroy Vassal and Thibaud de Vitry, in their conduct of a particular case, following a complaint by one of the litigants.[90] Similar action was taken at a later date against Pierre Cousinot, *Procureur général du roi* in the *Parlement,* following his receipt of certain money payments in the course of litigation following the discovery at La Souterraine of a considerable quantity of treasure-trove.[91]

A final means of avoiding the worst aspects of penury may be grouped under the general rubric of absenteeism. While in part this may have been promoted by individual hardship, the general tone of the *Parlement*'s directives against absent *conseillers* suggests that in many cases absenteeism had a more practical end — namely that of seeking more lucrative employment as *commissaires du roi* within a wider range of administrative matters. The *Parlement* had been alert to this tendency in the 1420s, for the *ad hoc* fiscal administration of the 'kingdom of Bourges' provided numerous opportunities for *conseillers* to undertake quasi-judicial missions for the king, often of a highly lucrative kind. Clearly this type of activity could seriously diminish the authority of the court, particularly in a time of crisis; this recognition seems to have underlain the increasing attempts by the *Parlement,* from 1430 onwards, to compel absent *conseillers* to come and serve at Poitiers — a tendency which remained prominent until the return to Paris in 1436. Thus the *Parlement*'s demand, on 13 November 1430 addressed to absent *Présidents* and *conseillers,* 'qu'ils viengnent et soient devers la cour dedans le premier jour de Janvier. . . pour deservir et faire le deu de leur charge et office',[92] was immediately qualified by the understanding that in future, 's'aucun officier ou conseiller veut aller hors, soit *par commission du roy* ou de la court, ou que ce soit. . . il en prendra congie de la court'.[93] The date of the departure and return of each

[89] Ibid., f.363$^v$.

[90] Ibid., fos. 322$^r$-323$^v$.

[91] Namely a hoard of 'monnaie d'or, nobles et florances', found in the course of repairs made to a wall dividing two houses (see A.N. X2$^a$18, fos. 158$^r$ff.).

[92] *A. H.-G.* MS.59, fos. 400$^v$-401$^r$.

[93] Ibid., f.401$^v$.

*conseiller* was also in future to be communicated to Miles Chaligant, *receveur des amendes et exploits.*

One of the most obvious ways of preventing absenteeism was to withhold the wages of absentees, giving preference to those present at Poitiers. On 29 November 1430 the *Parlement* instructed that any *conseillers* 'qui pour commissions de reformacion, ou de leur volente, sans authorite ou licence de ladite cour sont absens, ne prendront aucun paiement de gages avec les presens'.[94] But despite this measure, the problem of absenteeism continued, so much so that on 23 February 1431 the court entertained the complaint by Bureau Boucher, that as he was the only lay *maître des requêtes* present in Poitiers he could not 'bonnement entendre a l'expedicion de certaine cause criminelle pendant en la court desdit requestes'. The *Parlement* was subsequently compelled to evoke the case before its own competence.[95] By the early months of 1433 the dual problems of corruption and absenteeism, coupled with the difficulties posed by irregular, or non-payment of wages, forced the *Parlement* to take more severe measures to prevent further loss of integrity. The issue of these reforms came only weeks before the fall of La Trémoïlle in June 1433. Preoccupation with problems of this kind and the ravages of the nobility in Poitou should not necessarily persuade us, as M. Neuville has argued, that this period witnessed a complete negation of the *Parlement*'s activities; at a less exalted level, justice continued to be done, and by 26 January 1435 the amount of litigation reaching the *Parlement* was so much that the court decided that 'de cy en avant, il y ait establi de mois en mois, en la chambre derriere la Grant chambre, nombre. . . de messires de la court, lesquelx vacqueront. . . et juger proces, ainsi que on souloit faire en la Chambre des enquestes a Paris, pour le temps que le Parlement de France y seoit'.[96]

The reforms attempted by the *Parlement* were introduced in February and March 1433.[97] Their main object was the prevention of

---

[94] Ibid., f.403$^r$.

[95] A.N. X2$^a$21, f.156$^r$. It is important to emphasise that absenteeism among the *parlementaires* (except, perhaps, at the very lowest level) was not necessarily directly linked to their 'poverty'. Absence from Poitiers in the service of the *Conseil* or *Grand Conseil* was common among the *maîtres des requêtes* and the *Avocats du roi* (*Écrits politiques de Jean Juvénal des Ursins*, ed. P.S. Lewis, i (*SHF*, Paris, 1978), 324 n.1; H. Daniel-Lacombe, 'L'hôte de Jeanne d'Arc à Poitiers: maître Jean Rabateau, président au Parlement de Paris', *R. Bas-Poitou* 6 (1893), 166).

[96] A.N. X1$^a$9194, f.88$^v$ (cf. Favreau, *Poitiers*, 279 n.895).

[97] A.N. X1$^a$9194, fos. 35$^r$ff., for what follows. Neuville (23ff.) has misinterpreted the sense of these 'reforms', giving them an unwarranted originality (E. Maugis, *Histoire du Parlement de Paris de l'avènement des rois Valois à la mort d'Henri IV*, i (Paris, 1913), 55 n.4).

corruption of *conseillers* by limitation of incidental payments 'soit d'or ou d'argent, pain ou vin ou vitaille ne autre chose', which they received from litigants. All *conseillers* and practitioners in the court were obliged to swear that in future they would adhere to the *Parlement*'s ruling on the distribution of incidental payments. In addition a commission was formed to ascertain the identities of those who had revealed that 'secrez de la court. . . pardevers le roy ou les seigneurs et autres qui sont entour lui'. Underlying these reforms was an awareness of the need to maintain a certain regularity in the payment of *conseillers'* wages. Additional supervision of the *receveur des amendes et exploits* was provided in the form of a coadjutor, Jean Chasteignier, *greffier* of the *Cour des aides,* and on 18 February 1433 the *Parlement* decided to communicate to Charles VII and his *Conseil* 'la povrete de la court, et l'indigence particuliere de plusieurs; . . . la grant some que on leur en doit de plusieurs parlemens; . . . et que longtemps ils ont supporte la necessite, laquele ilz ne peuent plus supporter'.

The determination to implement these reforms was sustained until the return to Paris three years later despite a serious outbreak of plague in Poitou during the summer of 1433 which forced the *Parlement* to suspend its normal business at the premature date of 27 July.[98]

In addition, in April 1433 the *Parlement* strongly resisted the registration of royal letters attempting to prevent appeals to its jurisdiction from the *Chambre des comptes* at Bourges.[99] This was followed by deliberate measures to regulate the numbers of *conseillers* and to reduce the preponderance of clerical *conseillers* over lay members.[100] Absentees were compelled to return to Poitiers under threat of privation of office and the wages of those absent on royal commissions were withheld in favour of those serving in Poitiers.[101]

### External Control, 1429-1436

The considerable difficulties encountered by the *Parlement* in attempting to maintain royal authority in Poitou and the surrounding areas during the years following the Reims coronation have been

[98]A.N. X1ᵃ9194, f.52ʳ. This epidemic was particularly severe, causing the deaths of several *parlementaires.*

[99]Ibid., f.42ʳ (cf. Neuville, 13-14).

[100]Ibid., fos. 54ᵛ, 93ᵛ.

[101]Ibid., fos. 123ᵛ and 124ʳ.

frequently related, often in great detail.[102] But the effects of this 'war', and indeed of the Hundred Years War generally, upon the mentalities of civil-servants embroiled in the conflict have received scant attention. With regard to the *parlementaires* in particular, the traumatic events of 1418, the long period of exile at Poitiers, and, above all, the political divisions in France during the years 1418-35, must have contributed, in private and occupational terms, to a much closer identification of their individual interests with the broader political concerns of the crown. The additional (and indeed closely related) fact that during this period the recruitment of *parlementaires* was made predominantly along dynastic and Parisian lines suggests that these years may have resulted, at Poitiers, in a rapid hardening of the separate caste identity of this group of servants. At a judicial level however, the *Parlement*'s determination to maintain the theoretical prerogatives of the sovereign was confronted by practical difficulties of a kind that would preoccupy lawyers for many years after the return to Paris in 1436.[103]

The politicising effects of the 'war' in Poitou upon the various levels of local royal administration are difficult to assess in quantitative terms. At Poitiers, where a high proportion of the *échevins* were simultaneously royal fiscal and judicial agents, the escalation of seigneurial conflict, coupled with the decline of the *Parlement*'s authority, saw many families compelled to take a more active (and, on occasion, forceful) role in maintaining individual and royal authority.

It was argued earlier that for a variety of reasons the war in France after 1418 may have resulted in a considerable increase in political and economic power for the members of governing families in the major towns of the 'kingdom of Bourges'.[104] A notable example at Poitiers was the family of Claveurier; moreover, the *Parlement*'s concern over the activities of members of this powerful clan after 1429 suggests that for them, the 'war' in Poitou may have provided a pretext for the enhancement of personal authority in Poitiers while ostensibly working for royal or public good. On 15 October 1429 the *Parlement* issued stern warnings to Guillaume Claveurier, the son of Maurice

---

[102]See, especially, D. Neuville, 'Le Parlement royal à Poitiers (1418-1436)', in *R. hist.* 6 (1878), 291ff. and 'Rec. des docs', *Arch. hist. Poitou* 29 (1898), xxii-lv.

[103]For some early problems see above, pp. 171-2. For the period post-1436 see A. Bossuat, 'The Re-Establishment of Peace in Society during the reign of Charles VII', in P.S. Lewis (ed.) *The Recovery of France in the Fifteenth Century* (London, 1971), 60-81 and C.T. Allmand, 'The Aftermath of War in Fifteenth-Century France', in *History* 61 (1976), 344-57.

[104]Above, Chapter 4, passim.

Claveurier, lieutenant-general of the *sénéchaussé* of Poitou, and Hilaire Larcher, not to carry 'harnoiz, ne voisent de nuyt riblant par la ville de Poictiers'.[105] In the summer of 1432[106] a serious incident occurred, in the form of a street attack by Guillaume and Pierre Claveurier upon a member of the merchant family of Bernard, natives of Riom, at that time based in Poitiers. The attack followed complaints by the Bernards against the activities of royal *commissaires-réformateurs* in respect of money changers. The affair was heard before the criminal court in the *Parlement*, with the result that fifteen of the heads of local families were ordered not to attempt any reprisals against the relatives of the Bernards. Maurice Claveurier's demand for an armed guard to protect him against reprisals by the Bernards was granted by the *Parlement*, in the shape of an escort including an *huissier* and a royal sergeant.[107] A similar provision was made by the *Parlement* following an identical demand by the Bernards.[108] Maurice Claveurier was additionally obliged to swear that he would not interfere further with the Bernards. Residual bitterness from the confrontation seems to have persisted in spite of these warnings, for on 19 June 1433[109] Guillaume Claveurier and Jean Bernard the younger, their fathers in attendance, were warned by Jean I de Vailly, *premier Président*, that the earlier prohibition issued by the *Parlement* in order to curtail the feud included slanderous remarks as well as physical confrontation, within its compass. Vailly additionally warned that contravention of this new order would render Guillaume and Jean liable to prosecution as 'traitors and rebels' against king and government alike.

Not many months prior to this fresh confrontation, on 3 January,[110] another of Maurice Claveurier's sons, Pierre, a cleric, was imprisoned along with Alain Trignian and Guillaume Touchebeuf, following the violation of Guillemette Petit. On 2 July 1435[111] the bishop of Poitiers

---

[105] A.N. X2ª21, f.116ᵛ.

[106] For details of this affair see ibid., fos. 183ᵛff., passim.

[107] This provision followed Claveurier's allegation, on 14 June 1432, that Jean I and II Bernard had threatened to kill him (ibid., f.184ʳ⁻ᵛ) in spite of earlier warnings by the *Parlement* to Claveurier and Bernard not to carry 'armeures, ne espees ou autres bastons ou harnoiz de guerre' in Poitiers (ibid., f.184ʳ).

[108] Ibid., f.184ᵛ.

[109] Ibid., fos. 215ʳ-216ʳ for what follows. On the sociological context for vendettas of this kind see J. Heers, *Le clan familial au Moyen âge* (Paris, 1974), especially 81-100, 115-20, 145-6, 157-66 and 175-7. So far as Poitiers is concerned displays of aggression by powerful clans seem to have coincided with periods of marked political disorder.

[110] Ibid., fos. 199ᵛ and 200ʳ.

[111] Ibid., fos. 275ᵛ and 176ʳ.

demanded that Pierre be handed over to his jurisdiction, by virtue of his being a cleric; however, the *Parlement* refused and Pierre was eventually released on bail of 500*l. t.* provided by his father, Maurice. Not long after this, in August 1435,[112] the *Parlement* released Guillaume Boutin, implicated in the earlier 'ribliz' of the Claveuriers, from the *conciergerie.* So far as the registers of the *Parlement* are a reliable guide, this behaviour specifically by the Claveurier family does not seem characteristic of the earlier period of the *Parlement*'s stay at Poitiers. But it is worthy of note that a certain amount of violence and intimidation of townspeople occurred in Poitiers during the siege of Parthenay.[113]

As the 1430s progressed, and seigneurial conflict in Poitou grew worse, the fundamental impulse of the *Parlement*'s attempts at amelioration of the situation appears to have come from the *échevins* of Poitiers. Their property, and, by virtue of their functions as royal administrators, their persons, were frequently exposed to the depredations of local *seigneurs.*[114] The situation of Maurice Claveurier in the midst of the conflict provides some illustration of this point. In the years before the return to Paris, Claveurier was, like other *échevins,* frequently employed by the *Parlement* in its dealings with recalcitrant *seigneurs;* this frequently exposed them to considerable danger and discomfort.[115] The function of Claveurier and others as royal fiscal agents occasionally made them the objects of arbitrary behaviour by those in need of liquid capital. On 25 February 1434[116] Claveurier complained to the *Parlement* that, following a request by the *Chancelier,* Regnault de Chartres, by La Trémoïlle and others of the *Conseil,* for a loan of 600*l. t.,* it was threatened that refusal to pay would see the money taken from him by force. Hence for many of the *échevins* the determination to uphold royal authority could stem from a combination of public duty and private interest.

Outside Poitou, the disintegration of royal authority appears to have reached serious proportions by the 1430s. On 21 May 1432[117]

[112] Ibid., f.278ᵛ.

[113] *A. H.-G.* MS.59, fos.33ᵛ, 44ʳff. (passim).

[114] See for instance, A.N. X2ᵃ18, fos. 242ʳff. and A.N. X2ᵃ21, fos. 137ᵛ, 138ᵛ, 141ʳ, 152ʳ-162ᵛ (passim), 233ʳ, concerning the family of Eschalart.

[115] See for instance, A.N. X2ᵃ21, f.244ᵛ(Claveurier) and 'Rec. des docs', *Arch. hist. Poitou* 29 (1898), ix-x (Mourraut).

[116] See A.N. X1ᵃ9200, f.209ʳ (cf. ibid., f.204ʳ and A.N. X1ᵃ9194, f.63ʳ).

[117] See A.N. X2ᵃ21, fos. 180ᵛ-181ʳ (also ibid., fos. 188ʳ-189ᵛ (passim); A.N. X2ᵃ18, f.320ᵛ).

the *Parlement* heard complaints by Yolande of Aragon about the actitivies of 'plusieurs sergens royaulx demourans ou pais d'Anjou'. The *Parlement* subsequently ordered the sergeants: 'en leurs personnes, a la peine chacun de dix marcs d'argent, que doresnavant ils n'adiornent nulz ne aucuns des subgez de ladite royne de Sicile. . . sans mandement expres. . . du roy nostre seigneur.' The patterns of the breakdown of royal authority, or the corruption of royal officials, appears with monotonous regularity in the registers of the criminal *Conseil* up to the return to Paris.

In its efforts to maintain royal authority the *Parlement* combined traditional forms of opposition with *ad hoc* techniques. Prominent in the former category was the *Parlement*'s consistent refusal to ratify royal letters of gift consenting to the alienation of the king's domain. On 18 January 1436,[118] shortly before the return to Paris, the *Procureur général du roi* declared his official opposition to 'toutes les alienations que le roy a fait, des terres et seigneuries, chasteaulx et chastellenies du temps passe, et que on dit qu'il fait de jour en jour'. The king, it was pointed out, was frequently persuaded to consent to these gifts against his better judgement, 'la quelle chose ne se doit faire'. Specific opposition was brought to the alienation of the 'terres et seigneuries de Montferrant et d'Usson[119] et leurs appartenances'; in addition, 'a quelxconques seigneurs ou personnes et pour quelque cause que ce soit, ou puisse estre, et aux expedicions d'icelui'. The terms of the *Procureur général*'s opposition were to be bound within the registers of the *Parlement* 'pour la conservation des droiz et prerogatives du roy. . . et pour lui valor et proufites en lieu et en temps ce que raison donna'. Though in a theoretical sense far-sighted, this provision probably appeared under the prevailing political conditions as little more than legal rhetoric. Other methods employed by the *Parlement* to combat the political unrest in Poitou were both practical and highly partisan. For while it might deliberately drag its heels over the ratification of letters of donation relating to places within the 'kingdom of Bourges', the *Parlement* was quick to lend support to Charles VII's game of incentives, as witnessed by the marked lack of

---

[118] For what follows see A.N. X1ª9194, f.122$^v$ and the separate leaf inserted between ibid., fos. 122$^v$ and 123$^r$.

[119] See A. Bossuat, *Le Bailliage royal de Montferrand (1425-1556)* (Paris, 1957), 41-57. Early in 1430 the duke of Orléans complained, *in absentia*, of attempts by the *Parlement* to usurp his fiscal and judicial authority in the county of Blois and its appurtenances, this despite Orléans' claim that: 'des l'an 1429 fut octroye (by Charles VII) a tenir icelle conte en pairie' (A.N. X1ª9199, f.214$^v$).

resistance to Charles d'Anjou's 'gift' of the county of Mortain, still in enemy-occupied territory, in February 1434.[120]

Various kinds of incentives were employed by the *Parlement* as a deliberate means of reducing the worst forms of seigneurial excess. Suspension of litigation was provided to enable individuals to take part in campaigns against the English. Letters of remission were ratified on the express condition that the recipients would in future serve Charles VII against the common enemy. A more remarkable bribe, offered with increasing frequency by the *Parlement* in the 1430s, was that of the ratification of royal letters of remission offered to ostensibly loyal *seigneurs,* on the condition that they direct their forces against other *seigneurs, routiers* and brigands currently terrorising Poitou and its environs. On 22 April 1434[121] for example the *Parlement* released Geoffroy de Taveau, *seigneur* of Mortemar, orginally imprisoned for his pillaging activities, with a commission enabling him to take others perpetrating similar crimes and bring them to justice.

In the short term at least, these measures appear to have had little effect on the situation in Poitou. The fall of La Trémoïlle in 1433 witnessed, if anything, a deepening of internecine conflict, with La Trémoïlle himself among the major culprits. In 1434 a number of *échevins* of Poitiers begged Jean Rabateau to go and remonstrate with the newly-deposed 'favourite' about the harm he and his associates were causing in Poitou.[122] On 24 July 1434 a similar commission was given by the *Parlement* to Guillaume I Le Tur, *président,* this time involving Antoine de Levis, *seigneur* of Vauvert.[123] On 4 January 1435 Jean I de Vailly, *premier Président,* was sent, despite his infirmity, to remonstrate 'au long' with Charles VII about the capture of Alain Moreau by the men of Charles d'Anjou, and in addition about the excesses perpetrated by the counts of Foix and Harcourt.[124]

[120] A.N. X1ª9200, f.307ᵛ (cf. A.N. X1ª9194, f.90ʳ). Letters ratified and published by express mandate of the king.

[121] A.N. X2ª21, fos. 239ᵛ-240ʳ. For similar examples see ibid., fos. 136ᵛ and 175ʳ-letters issued under the seal of the *chancellerie* at Poitiers.

[122] A.N. X1ª9194, f.56ᵛ. (Cf. 'Rec. des docs', *Arch. hist. Poitou* 29 (1898), lii-liii). After 1433 besides being allowed by Charles VII to recoup losses incurred through earlier loans, La Trémoïlle continued to be one of the king's principal creditors (see A.N. 1AP 172B, 1AP 173 and 1AP 175, pieces relating to period post-1433).

[123] A.N. X2ª21, f.248ᵛ (cf. ibid., f.254ʳ).

[124] Ibid., f.262ʳ (cf. ibif., god. 262ᵛ-263ʳ). For a note on Moreau, see B. Chevalier, *Tours: ville royale, 1356-1520,* 159 n.206.

The seriousness of the decline of royal authority in the centre-west of France, and particularly in areas of the Languedoc, must have emphasised the need for a positive settlement with Burgundy.[125] It may also have contributed in great measure to Charles VII's willingness to negotiate with Burgundy on terms which might have appeared, in the short term, to be damaging to his own cause and immensely favourable to Burgundy. The long delay which followed Arras before the English were finally driven from France may, in this light, be seen to derive less from the strength of the English occupation than from Charles VII's enervating battle with his own nobility. It was only in the late 1440s, when Charles had resolved these fundamental problems, that he could turn to the possibly less pressing matter of English presence in Normandy and Guyenne.

[125]That reconciliation with Burgundy was viewed by Charles VII not, primarily, as the prelude to an offensive against the English, but rather as a way of providing a breathing-space to enable him to bring his own nobility to heel, is convincingly illustrated by the fact that the issue of the edict in December 1438 revoking all alienations of parts of the royal domain since 1418, came only three years after Arras and two years after the return to Paris. The location of the *Praguerie* mainly in Poitou bore witness to the fact that this county had suffered a far greater percentage of alienations than any other (see R. Favreau, 'La Praguerie en Poitou', *Bibl. Éc. Chartes* 129 (1971), 277-301).

# CONCLUSION

The chief aim of this book has been an attempt to provide a reassessment of Charles VII's government and kingship during the years 1418 to 1436, using new material from the registers of the Poitiers *Parlement,* and within this the need to explain how, given the popular view of the weakness of Charles's regime during this period, the 'recovery' of France was finally effected.

Charles's position as Dauphin of France was perhaps most vulnerable in the years between the Burgundian occupation of Paris in 1418 and Charles VI's death four years later. Even here however events of the last decade or so of Charles VI's reign presented his son with certain ironical advantages in his attempt to form an opposition government. The domination exercised over Charles VI by the princes of the blood saw the princes establish quasi-independent administrations modelled closely upon the royal archetype. The earlier death of the duke of Berry provided the Dauphin, by 1418, both with ready-made bases for his judicial and fiscal administrations, in the shape of the *Grands jours* at Poitiers and the *Chambre des comptes* at Bourges, and a corpus of ducal servants easily assimilated into the local royal administration. The absence of the duke of Orléans, taken prisoner at Agincourt in 1415, presented the Dauphin with a similar advantage, a large proportion of the *parlementaires* after 1418 being former servants of Orléans, both at Paris or in the duchy of Orléans.

The extraordinary rapidity and efficiency of the *Parlement's* foundation and organisation at Poitiers bore witness, above all, to traditions developed at Paris since the middle of the thirteenth century. On the other hand, it was precisely the air of uncertainty produced by the political upheavals of the years between 1418 and 1422 which provided the essential dynamic for the Dauphin's administration. These years were characterised not by weakness and apathy but by great industry and flexibility. Innovations such as the creation of a *petite chancellerie* at Poitiers — after 1436 the *Chancellerie du Palais* — or the substitution of the *requêtes du Palais* by the *requêtes de l'Hôtel,* albeit of an *ad hoc* nature, convey an acute awareness on the part of the Dauphin's administration of the need for greater flexibility in the face of political instability. It is too often forgotten that this assiduousness, this capacity for change, derived from a fundamental human impulse. Many of the *parlementaires* and other civil servants who left Paris in the summer of 1418 left as refugees, deprived of livelihoods, possessions and property. For them the maintenance of the Dauphin's cause was indissolubly linked with the question of their own survival. This concept of survival is a factor which the historian must constantly bear in mind in any realistic assessment of the early years of Charles VII's reign. The desire for political survival explains to a large extent Charles's 'weakness' as king (though in the long run it was arguably this 'weakness' which ensured his very survival) as it does the compensatory theoretical 'tyranny' conducted on his behalf by the *Parlement* and other branches of the royal administration.

With regard to this 'tyranny', the creation of sovereign *Parlements* first at Poitiers, then, in 1420, at Toulouse were acts of the greatest importance for the extension not only of the Dauphin's judicial authority but also of that of the French crown generally speaking into areas formerly only lightly touched by sovereign jurisdictions. Throughout this period the *Parlement* of Paris, while nominally serving the English, continued nevertheless to uphold the abstract authority of the French crown in northern France with the result that, following the return to Paris and the eventual expulsion of English forces, Charles VII was invested with a greater measure of real judicial authority than any of his predecessors. In this and other respects the war brought Charles VII and the French crown surprising benefits.

The notion of the feebleness of the Poitiers *Parlement* and the poverty of its magistrates — a view consciously or unconsciously perpetrated by nineteenth century historians in keeping with the view of a weak and hapless king only stirred to action by the appearance of Joan of Arc — owes little to fact. Throughout the years of exile from Paris the *Parlement* strove to maintain Charles VII's judicial authority in the face of 'war' in Poitou between Richemont and La Trémoïlle in the 1430s and, possibly more seriously from the point of view of the *Parlement*'s institutional structure and autonomy, the increasing demands made upon its members to meet the needs of the royal administration generally speaking. In this respect it is arguable that constant complaints by *parlementaires* over the non-payment of wages (which on account of the numerous commissions provided by the king no longer bore any real relationship to the wealth of a *conseiller*) derived not so much from 'poverty', but from the desire to protect the structure of what was essentially a body of equals with a professional rather than a social or material hierarchy from erosion by distinctions of a material or social kind.

The desire for survival, at both the occupational and the material level, applied not only to members of Charles VII's administration.

The years after the English invasion and settlement of Normandy witnessed the departure from the duchy, and from northern France in general, of several thousand refugees, including a high percentage of artisans. Many of the refugees eventually settled among the indigenous populations in the larger towns of the Loire valley, others in the smaller towns and villages of Poitou, Touraine and Saintonge. Quite apart from the social revolution engendered by this influx of aliens, the economic consequences in the form of the creation of new industries and the expansion of existing ones were of the greatest importance, both for the towns receiving them and for the economy of the 'kingdom of Bourges' in general. For the English the departure of so many artisans south of the Loire may have dealt a severe blow to the economic infrastructure of a duchy which badly needed to be self-supporting if the burden of occupation was not to fall increasingly upon the English people.

In terms of trade and mercantile resources, the occupation of Normandy by the English was probably less damaging for Charles VII's 'kingdom of Bourges' than is generally reckoned. Bourges was ideally situated for overland trade with Geneva and the Empire; with Avignon, Marseille and Montpellier, and beyond this, the Italian seaports. Sole maritime outpost for the 'kingdom of Bourges' after 1418, La Rochelle's importance as a trading centre with Spain, Brittany and northern Europe increased dramatically in the ensuing years.

Apart from government and trade, it is in Charles VII's early handling of his nobility that allegations of his early weakness and apathy are most commonly founded. Such views arguably derive both from serious underestimations of the gravity of Charles's political situation after 1418 and from an equal misunderstanding of the difference between fifteenth-century and nineteenth-century views of the authority of the French crown. Contrary to the ideas of many nineteenth-century French historians Charles VII's inheritance in 1422 was not that of a nation fallen into anarchy. In fact Charles's reign constituted one of the last phases in the centuries-old attempt by the French crown to control the independent ambitions of its greater vassals and to bring them more closely into its own orbit — a battle not finally won, in the case of Brittany, until the early years of the sixteenth century. To ignore this fact is to underestimate Charles VII's problems and belittle his very real achievements.

Of fundamental importance to the maintenance of Charles VII's authority during the troubled early years was his recognition of the need to retain the support of those members of the nobility who remained faithful to his cause after 1418. Thus, far from exhibiting weakness, Charles's lavish concessions to the nobility in the form of pensions and grants of land arguably displayed great foresight. In the highly unstable political circumstances of these years Charles needed every ally he could get, and his policy of maintaining deposed 'favourites' in conditions of great comfort shows both his awareness of this fact and an understanding of the problems that callous treatment of a former servant might produce. The weakness of this policy in the short term, however, was apparent by 1435, when Charles sought peace with Burgundy at any price as a means of quelling the increasingly intransigent behaviour of his own nobles forced, after 1429, to pursue their independent territorial ambitions within the narrow confines of the 'kingdom of Bourges'. In the event a desperate manoeuvre became an astute one, with the final rupture of the Anglo-Burgundian coalition and the effective end of both parties' political aspirations.

Hence conciliation and concession rather than punishment and alienation, are themes which occur again and again during Charles VII's reign: in his treatment of those who had supported the Anglo-Burgundian regime in Paris, of those who participated in the Praguerie, or of those who figured in the treason trials of the 1450s. Only in a limited sense could such a policy be seen to derive from weakness; instead, it portrays Charles VII as a monarch with an acute grasp of the political realities of his time. The war conducted by Charles VII during the early years of his reign was thus, increasingly, one of a proto-national kind with the English, and, on the other hand, one of a neo-feudal kind with the major vassals of the French crown — including the English and Burgundians — and, particularly after 1429, with members of his own nobility.

Ironically again, it could be argued that the survival of Charles VII's kingship during the early years owed much to the determination of one of his major vassals — namely the House of Anjou — to retain the integrity of its own possessions in the face of threats of English invasion. For the Angevin faction at Charles's court, private interest thus coincided with public duty. The impact of Angevin policy may be seen at work during every major change in Charles VII's entourage, and the root cause of the Praguerie, early in the 1440s, was Charles's revocation of all previous alienations of land in favour of the nobility, under Angevin impulsion. Fittingly, the possessions of the House of Anjou were among the last to be incorporated into the royal domain by Louis XI.

The view of the 'weakness' of Charles VII's kingship during the years 1418-36 may thus owe relatively little to an objective understanding of fifteenth-century politics, rather more to nineteenth-century inability to grasp the slow development of the reality, as opposed to the theory, of a French nation during this period. The idea of the 'recovery of France' under Charles VII is a beguiling one; yet arguably it owes more to the work of lawyers and propagandists than to concrete fact. Charles's achievement appears all the more impressive if we view the accomplishment of his reign not as the 'recovery' of a nation, but of its creation.

# NOTE ON TECHNICAL TERMS

A glossary of all the terms employed in this book, if it were not to be misleading, would be prohibitively long. Readers are therefore advised to consult the following works:

(1) On officials in the *Parlement* and in the royal administration in general: 'Dictionnaires des charges, emplois et métiers relevant des institutions monarchiques en France au xiv⁰ et xv⁰ siècles', ed. M. Ornato, *Centre d'Histoire des Sciences et des Doctrines: Équipe de Recherche sur l'humanisme français des xiv⁰ et xv⁰ siècles. Travaux méthodologiques et répertoires,* 1 (*CNRS,* Paris, 1975).

(2) On the tribunals within the *Parlement* and the royal *Conseil* and their respective areas of judicial competence: 'Guide des recherches dans les fonds judiciaries by l'Ancien Régime', various editors, with an introduction by C. Braibant (*Archives Nationales,* Paris, 1958).

(3) On the coinage: A. Blanchet and A. Dieudonné, *Manuel de numismatique française*, ii (Paris, 1916), iv and 270-97 (Paris, 1936), passim.

P. Spufford and W. Wilkinson, *Interim Listing of the Exchange Rates of Medieval Europe* (Keele, 1977), 207-46.

# BIBLIOGRAPHY

Readers who wish to pursue aspects of the subject in greater depth will find a much fuller bibliography in my doctoral thesis, a copy of which is deposited in the Bodleian Library, Oxford.

I. Manuscript Sources

    (A)   Archives of the Poitiers *Parlement*

    (B)   Related Sources

    (C)   General Manuscript Sources

II. Published Sources, Including Chronicles

III. Secondary Works, Including Unpublished Theses

## I   MANUSCRIPT SOURCES

(A)   Archives of the Poitiers *Parlement* (1418-1436)

(1)   *Archives Nationales, Paris*

(i)   **Sub-series X¹: *Parlement Civil***

### X1ᵃ9195-9196:

Two volumes of *Lettres, Commissions* and *Appointements,* which cover the period from December 1418 to July 1436. The first volume (X1ᵃ9195) runs from 1418-29 and contains 446 folios; at f.303$^v$ the pagination moves, on the succeeding folio, to f.434$^r$, apparently without loss of documentation. This volume therefore contains only 316 folios in all. A number of folios also appear to be missing from the end of this volume as f.446$^v$, the 'last' folio, finishes in mid-sentence. The succeeding volume (X1ᵃ9196) only begins on 6 April 1430. It runs from April 1430 to July 1436, and contains 160 folios. Both volumes are written on parchment, in Latin.

### X1ᵃ9197-9200:

Four volumes of *plaidoiries 'matinées',* which cover the period from November 1421 to November 1435. An additional volume, covering the period 1418-21, is now lost.[1] The loss of

---

[1] See A. Grün's remarks in 'Notice sur les archives du Parlement de Paris', in *Actes du Parlement de Paris*, ed. E. Boutaric, i (Paris, 1863), ccxv.

this volume, together with an accompanying volume of '*après-dinées*', [2] is particularly regrettable as it probably contained a great deal of material relating to the flight from Paris in 1418 and also to the early organization and personnel of the *Parlement.* I have compensated in some measure for this loss by utilising the copy of the first register of the *Conseil* of the *Parlement (A.H.-G.* MS.59), the first volume of *arrêts* and *jugés* (X1ᵃ9190), and the first volume of *lettres* (X1ᵃ9195).

The *plaidoiries 'matinées'* are written on parchment, in French.

### X1ᵃ9201:

Sole surviving volume of *plaidoiries 'après-dinées'* of the *Parlement,* which covers the period from May 1430 to October 1436. It begins: 'Istud est registrum causarum seu litigiorum post prandium, in Parlamento Regis Pictavis anno Domini 1430 agitatorum par Johannem Cheneteau, clericum magistri Johannis de Maisne, dicti de Blesis, grapharii civilis Parlamenti predicti, receptorum.' Possibly two volumes of *'après-dinées'* are therefore missing from this series, covering the period from 1418 to 1430. The surviving register is of 225 folios written on parchment, in French.

### X1ᵃ9194:

Sole surviving register of the civil *Conseil* of the Poitiers *Parlement.* It begins: 'In nomine Patris et Filii et Spiritus Sancti. Incipit registrum Consilii seu consultacionum Curie Parlamenti regii Pictavis, quod incepit die lune xij novembris anno Domini 1431.' The register covers the period from November 1431 to November 1436. It contains 156 folios of parchment written in French.

### X1ᵃ9190-9193:

Four volumes of *arrêts* and *jugés* which cover the period from December 1418 to September 1436. The first volume begins: 'Arresta et judicata in Curia Parlamenti domini nostri regis Pictavis prolata. . . '. At Poitiers the *arrêts* were not separated from the *jugés,* as at Paris during the same period. All volumes are written on parchment, in Latin.

[2] Ibid.

The first volume of this series (X1ᵃ9190), contains 365 folios. Volumes two and three (X1ᵃ9191-2) may have been contained within a single volume as the folios run consecutively from f.1ʳ in X1ᵃ9191, to f.352ᵛ in X1ᵃ9192. However they are now kept in separate volumes, with X1ᵃ9191 running from f.1 to f.165, and X1ᵃ9192 from f.166 to f.352. The fourth volume in the series (X1ᵃ9193) contains 185 folios.

### X1ᵃ8604:

The 'Liber accordorum et ordinacionum Pictavis'.[3] So termed as, in addition to transcriptions of ordinances, letters patent, etc., it contains (fos. 1-23) a list of the *accords* of the Poitiers *Parlement*, 1418-36. The documents in this volume cover the period 1418 to 1436. Written in Latin and French it comprises 148 folios of parchment.

(Note: Folios 130-45 contain a number of *arrêts* seemingly detached from X2ᵃ20, covering the period 3 Sept, 1429 to 5 Apr. 1430).

### X1ᶜ116-152:

The *accords* of the Poitiers *Parlement*, which cover the period from 1418 to 1436. The Poitiers *accords* (many of which are now lost) are mixed with those of the *Parlement* of Paris for the same period. The number of the Poitiers *accords* is greatly inferior to those of Paris. A list of the *accords* may be found in X1ᵃ8604 (fos. 1-23). The originals are on paper and, for the most part, in French.

(ii) **Sub-series X²:**

*Parlement criminel* **X²18**: Sole surviving register of *arrêts criminels d'audience* at Poitiers which covers the period from March 1423 (n.st.) to September 1432. The first page of this volume, which now carries the folio number 1, is without a formal title or introduction, and begins on 18 March 1423 (n.st.). This suggests that a number of folios, or a separate volume, covering the period from 1418 to March 1423, are now missing. A further volume covering the period 1432-6 is also missing from this series.

The surviving exemplar is of 335 folios of parchment, written in French.

[3] See the remarks on the contents of this volume by Grün, cxlviii.

**X2ª21:**

Sole surviving volume of *arrêts criminels du Conseil* which covers the period from July 1423 to November 1436.

It begins: 'Registrum consiliorum judicatorum et appunctamentorum secretorum Curie Parlamenti domini nostri Karoli Francorum regis in causis criminalibus.' A second volume of *arrêts criminels du Conseil,* covering the period from 1418 to July 1423 is now lost. The surviving volume is of 319 folios written on parchment, in French.

**X2ª20:**

Volume entitled: 'Registrum arrestorum in causis criminalibus.' The *arrêts criminals* of the Poitiers *Parlement,* which may be found on folios 1-110ᵛ of this volume, cover the period from July 1423 to September 1436. Folios 111-209 contain the *arrêts criminels* of the Paris *Parlement.* Probably one volume, covering the period 1418 - July 1423, is now lost. The surviving folios are of parchment, written in Latin.

(Note: A number of folios belonging to this series, which run from 3 Sept. 1429 - 5 Apr. 1430, are now in X1ª8604 (fos. 130-145).)

**X2ª19:**

'Registre des arrests criminelz et autres exploiz de la court du Parlement.' It contains a number of criminal *arrêts* and some *lettres* of the *Parlement* covering the period from May 1422 to February 1431 (n.st.), without distinction between sessions. Folios 3-50 appear to be a rough copy of X2ª20. The register contains 51 folios of paper written in Latin.

(iii) *Lacunae:*

*Minutes*

The *minutes* of the Poitiers *Parlement* are lacking in their entirety. An interesting example of a part of an early *minute* may have survived on the reverse of *accord* no. X1ᶜ118 (pièce 12, dated 11 July 1419). The *minute* itself is undated and struck through in ink. It begins: 'A Nosseigneurs de la court souverayne'. The blank side of the *minute* appears to have been utilised within a short time to make the *accord* mentioned above, and its survival is therefore accidental. I have been able to find no other similar specimens.

### Enquêtes

Although we possess evidence for the function of the *enquêtes* at Poitiers, both during the early period of its operation, and in the period immediately before the return to Paris in 1436, no documentation survives relating to the function of this tribunal.

### Requêtes du Palais

At Poitiers after 1418 the function of the *requêtes du Palais* was absorbed by the *requêtes de l'Hôtel.* No documentation survives for the operation of the latter tribunal.

### The Table de Marbre

The tribunal of the *connétable* of France functioned at Poitiers at least from Buchan's inception as *connétable* in 1421. No documentation survives, however.

### The petite chancellerie

Founded at Poitiers in 1418; after 1436, in the Paris *Parlement,* it was styled the *Chancellerie du Palais.* No documentation survives. Documentation for the *Grande Chancellerie* under Charles VII is also scarce before the 1450s.

(2) **Bibliothèque Nationale, Paris**

(i) **Nouv. acq. lat. no. 1968:**

The first and only surviving register of *présentations* of the Poitiers *Parlement.* The preamble is dated 16 September 1418. It contains a list of *présentations* to the *greffe* for the period from November 1418 to September 1419. Written in Latin, it contains 176 folios of parchment.

A. Thomas (*Documents relatifs au comté de La Marche, extraits des archives du Parlement de Poitiers (1418-1436), Bibl. Éc. Hautes-Études* 174 (Paris, 1910) 1-10) printed extracts from this document relating to the *comté* of La Marche.

(3) **Archives départementales de la Haute-Garonne (Toulouse)**

(i) **MS.59 (F.49):**

A valuable eighteenth-century copy of the first register of the *Conseil civil* of the Poitiers *Parlement,* which covers the period

1418-31. Its survival is of great importance in view of the loss of the original first register of the *Conseil* between 1733 and 1791.[4] The existence of this document was indicated in 1953 by A. Viala.[5] Though in appearance a very full copy, this document probably represents a series of extracts from what must have been a voluminous original, rather than a complete transcript. Extensively employed in the compilation of this book, the MS.59 comprises 440 folios of paper and is written in French.

A copy similar, though seemingly less full, to the MS.59 was compiled, likewise in the eighteenth century, by Lenain. Originally part of the library of the *Chambre des Députés* in Paris it is today kept at the *Archives Nationales* (no. U2224), together with a smaller volume of extracts compiled by the same author (U2225). The MS.U2224 has 277 folios and covers the same period (1418-31) as the MS.59. The existence of Lenain's copy, as of the MS.59, was unknown to the historian of the Poitiers *Parlement,* D. Neuville.[6] The existence of U2224 was indicated in 1914 by A. Thomas,[7] though it had already been utilised by Valois[8] and Guérin[9], contemporaries of Neuville. In addition to these copies of the first *Conseil* register, the *Bibliothèque Nationale* also possesses a number of smaller copies of extracts (seemingly also eighteenth-century), from the various registers of the *Parlement.*[10]

---

[4]Grün, ccxiv.

[5]*Le Parlement de Toulouse et l'administration royale laïque, 1420-1525 environ,* i (Albi, 1953), 10.

[6]D. Neuville, 'Le Parlement royal à Poitiers (1418-1436)', *R. hist.* 6 (1878), 20-1. Strangely Neuville referred (21 n. 1) to Grün's description of the Poitiers archives, yet failed to notice that Grün ( cclxxxi), had elsewhere alluded to the existence of Lenain' transcript of the first register of the *Conseil* of the Poitiers *Parlement,* covering the period 1418-31.

[7]Le Parlement de Poitiers et l'Église de France', *Journal des Savants* 7 (1914), 315-17.

[8]See N. Valois, *Étude historique sur le Conseil du roi* (Paris, 1886), xiii n. 12 and xiv nn. 2, 5. Thomas's assertion that Valois was unaware of the existence of Lenain's copy (315) was therefore incorrect.

[9]See 'Recueil des documents concernant le Poitou contenus dans les registres de la Chancellerie de France', ed. P. Guérin, *Arch hist. Poitou* 26 (1896), 337 n. 1 and 377 n. 1.

[10]See for instance, B.N.MS.fr. no. 21302; Nouv. acq. fr. nos. 2377 and 23705 (fos. 81-144$^v$).

222

(B)   Related Sources

(1)   *Archives Nationales, Paris*

Z1ᵃ8:

Sole surviving register of the *Chambre des généraux sur le fait de la justice des aides,* established at Poitiers on 22 October 1425. It covers the period from August 1428 to June 1434 and comprises 127 folios of papers, written in French.

X1ᵃ9808:

Register of *appointements* and *arrêts* of the *Parlement* of Toulouse, which covers the period from November 1422 to August 1423. It comprises 394 folios of paper, and is written in Latin.

X1ᵃ9809-9810:

Two registers of *présentations* of the *Parlement* of the Languedoc, which cover the period from 1425 to 1427, and are of 152 folios and 245 folios respectively. They are both written on paper, in Latin.

X1ᵃ1480, X1ᵃ4792-3:

Various registers of the Paris *Parlement* which cover the period 1418-36.

(2)   *Bibliothèque Nationale, Paris*

Nouv. acq. lat. no. 2615, fos. 6ʳ-11ʳ:

Memoir (incomplete) compiled by Nicole Aymar on the transmission of offices of *notaire et secrétaire* under Charles VII, from April 1418 to c. 1450.[11] It gives important information on the successions to office in the *Grande Chancellerie,* especially during the early part of Charles VII's reign. The chronology of the various successions to office is difficult to interpret successfully.

---

[11] This document has been printed and analysed by G. Tessier and G. Ouy ('Notaires et secrétaires du roi dans la première moitié du xvᵉ siècle, d'après un document inédit', *B. philol.,* 1963, 861-90).

(3) *Archives départementales de la Haute-Garonne, Toulouse*

**MS.51, B1:**

'Sextum registrum curie Parlamenti Tholose. . . '. It covers the period from November 1424 to November 1425 and comprises 352 folios of paper, in Latin.

**MS 51, B2:**

'Secundum registrum curie Parlamenti Bicterris. . . '. It covers the period from November 1426 to August 1427 and contains, in all, 543 folios of paper, in Latin.

(C) General Manuscript Sources

(1) *Archives Nationales, Paris*

**Chartrier de Thouars:**

Nos: 1 AP 171, 1 AP 172B, 1 AP 173, 1 AP 174, 1 AP 175, 1 AP 176 and 1 AP 571.

(Inventory to this series by C. Samaran, *Archives de la maison de La Trémoïlle* (Paris, 1928), 1-129).

**Series K (monuments historiques): Carton des rois:**

K62 and K63

(2) *Bibliothèque Nationale, Paris*

**Manuscrits français:**

Nos: 20417, 20583, 21302, 23878, 25968, 25970, 26053, 26054, 26057, 27739, 28342, 29380, 29416, 29516, 32137, 32514.

**Nouvelles acquisitions français:**

Nos: 2377, 7626-7, 21291, 23705.

**Pièces Originales:**

Nos: 693, 1787, 2419.

**Collection Clairambault:**

Vol. 85.

## II PUBLISHED SOURCES, INCLUDING CHRONICLES

*Actes du Parlement de Paris,* ed. E. Boutaric, vol. i (Paris, 1863).

Barbot, A., 'Histoire de La Rochelle', ed. D. Joly d'Aussy *AHSA* 14 (1886).

Cagny, Perceval de, *Chroniques,* ed. H. Moranvillé (*SHF,* Paris, 1902).

*Chartes, chroniques et mémoriaux pour servir à l'histoire de la Marche et du Limousin,* ed. A. Leroux and A. Bosvieux, Tulle/Limoges, 1886.

*Chartularium Universitatis Parisiensis* vol. iv (1394-1452), ed. H.S. Denifle and É. Chatelain, Paris, 1897.

*Chronique de la Pucelle ou chronique de Cousinot suivie de la chronique normande de P. Cochon relatives aux règnes de Charles VI et de Charles VII,* ed. A. Vallet de Viriville, Paris, 1859.

*Chronique du religieux de Saint-Denys, contenant le règne de Charles VI, de 1380 à 1422,* ed. L. Bellaguet, 6 vols (*Coll. des docs. inédits sur l'histoire de France, 1st. Ser. Histoire politique),* Paris, 1839-52.

Devic, C. and Vaissètte, J., *Histoire générale de Languedoc,* 15 vols, Toulouse, 1872-92.

'Documents relatifs à l'histoire maritime du XVe siècle', ed. P. Marchegay, *R. Soc. Savantes,* 6th Ser. 2 (1875), 160-70.

*Documents relatifs au comté de la Marche extraits des archives du Parlement de Poitiers (1418-1436),* ed. A. Thomas, *Bibl. Éc. Hautes-Études* 174, Paris, 1910.

*Documents sur les États généraux de Poitiers de 1424 et 1425,* ed. R. Lacour, *Arch. hist. Poitou* 48 (1934), 91-117.

*Écrits politiques de Jean Juvénal des Ursins,* ed. P.S. Lewis, i (*SHF,* Paris, 1978).

*Extraits des anciens registres aux delibérations des consaux de la ville de Tournai,* ed. H. Vandenbröeck, *Mém. Soc. Hist. et Litt. de Tournai* 7 (1981) and 8 (1863) (which cover the period from 1385-1430). A third volume, ed. A. de La Grange, same series, vol. 23 (1893), covers the period from 1431-76.

Fauquembergue, Clement de, *Journal,* ed. A. Tuetey, 3 vols (*SHF,* Paris, 1903-15).

*Foedera, conventiones, litterae, etc.,* ed. T. Rymer, vols ix and x, London, 1709-10.

Godefroy, D., ed., *Histoire de Charles VII. . . ,* Paris, 1661.

Gruel, Guillaume, *Chronique d'Arthur de Richemont, connétable de*

*France, duc de Bretagne (1393-1458)*, ed. A. Le Vavasseur (*SHF,* Paris, 1890).

*Journal d'un bourgeois de Paris, 1405-1449*, ed. A. Tuetey (*Soc. Hist. Paris),* Paris, 1881.

*Journal du siège d'Orléans, 1428-1429...*, ed. P. Charpentier and C. Cuissard, Orléans, 1896.

Juvénal des Ursins, Jean, *Histoire de Charles VI, Roy de France, in* J.A.C Buchon, *Choix de Chroniques et Mémoires sur l'Hist. de France avec notices littéraires,* V, Paris, 1838, 323-573.

*Les relations commercials entre Gênes, la Belgique et l'Outremont d'après les archives notariales gênoises...*, ed. R. Doehard and C. Kerremarns, vol. iv (1400-40), Brussels, 1952

*Lettres et mandements de Jean V, duc de Bretagne,* ed. R. Blanchard, *Société des bibliophiles bretons,* vols iv-viii, Nantes, 1889-95.

Longnon, A., *Paris pendant l'occupation anglaise, 1420-1436,* Paris, 1878.

Monstrelet, Enguerrand de, *Chronique,* ed. L. Douët-d'Arcq, 6 vols. (*SHF,* Paris, 1857-62).

Morosini, Antonio, *Chronique,* ed. G. Lefèvre-Pontalis, 4 vols (*SHF,* Paris, 1898-1902).

*Ordonnances des roys de France de la troisième race,* 21 vols, Paris, 1723-1849.

*Procès en nullité de la condamnation de Jeanne d'Arc,* ed. P. Duparc, vols i and ii (*SHF,* Paris, 1977-9).

*Procès de condamnation et de réhabilitation de Jeanne d'Arc, dite la Pucelle,* ed. J. Quicherat, 5 vols (*SHF,* Paris, 1841-9).

*Procès de condamnation de Jeanne d'Arc,* ed. P. Tisset and Y. Lanhers, 3 vols (*SHF,* Paris, 1960 and 1970-1).

'Recueil des documents concernant le Poitou, contenus dans les registres de la chancellerie de France', ed. P. Guérin, vols 7-8 (1403-47), vols. 26 (1896) and 29 (1898) of the series of the *Arch. hist. Poitou.*

*Registres consulaires de la ville de Lyon...*, ed. M.-C. and G. Guigue, 2 vols (1416-50), Lyon, 1882 and 1926.


## III SECONDARY WORKS, INCLUDING UNPUBLISHED THESES

Allmand, C.T., 'L'Évêché de Sées sous la domination anglaise au XVe siècle', *A. Normandie* 11 (1961), 301-7.

———, 'The Aftermath of War in Fifteenth-Century France', *History* 61 (1976), 344-57

Armstrong, C.A.J., 'La double monarchie France-Angleterre et la maison de Bourgogne (1420-1435)', *A. Bourgogne* 37 (1965), 81-112

———, 'La politique matrimoniale des ducs de Bourgogne de la maison de Valois', *A. Bourgogne* 40 (1968), 5-58, 89-139.

Aubert, F., 'Les huissiers du Parlement de Paris (1300-1420)', *Bibl. Éc. Chartes* 47 (1886), 370-93.

———, *Histoire du Parlement de Paris de l'origine à François I*er *(1250-1515)*, 2 vols, Paris, 1894

———, 'Les Requêtes du Palais (xiiie-xvie siècle). Style des Requêtes du Palais, *Bibl. Éc. Chartes* 69 (1908), 581-642

Audinet, E., 'Les origines de la Faculté de droit de l'Université de Poitiers', *BSAO,* 3rd Ser. 6 (1922-4), 17-46.

Autrand, F., 'Offices et officiers royaux en France sous Charles VI', *R. hist.* 242 (1969), 285-338

———, 'Les librairies des gens du Parlement au temps de Charles VI', *Annales* 28 (1973), 1219-44

———, *Naissance d'un grand corps d'État: les gens du Parlement de Paris, 1345-1454* (thèse d'État), Paris, 1978 (forthcoming)

Bailhache, G., 'Les Maîtres des Requêtes de l'Hôtel du Roi depuis l'avènement de Jean le Bon jusqu'à l'édit de Compiègne (1350-1553)', in *Éc. nat. des Chartes. Pos. des thèses soutenues par les élèves de la Promotion de 1924,* Paris, 1924, 27-32.

Bengy-Puyvallée, P.-J. de, *Mémoire historique sur le Berry,* Bourges, 1842.

Blanchard, F., *Les Présidents au mortier du Parlement de Paris,* Paris, 1647.

———, *Les généalogies des Maîtres des Requestes ordinaires de l'Hostel du Roy,* Paris, 1670

M. De Boismarmin, 'Mémoire sur la date de l'arrivée de Jeanne d'Arc à Chinon', *B. philol.* 1892, 350-9.

Boissonnade, P., 'Une étape capitale de la mission de Jeanne d'Arc: Le séjour de la Pucelle à Poitiers. La quadruple enquête et ses résultats (1er mars - 10 avril 1429)', in *R. Quest. Hist.* 113 (1930), 12-67.

———, *Histoire de l'Université de Poitiers, passé et présent (1432-1932),* Poitiers, 1932.

Bonney, F., 'Autour de Jean Gerson: opinions de théologiens sur les superstitions et la sorcellerie au début du xve siècle', *Moyen Age* 77 (1971), 85-98.

Bossuat, A., 'Un manifeste des comtes de Richemont, de Clermont et de Pardiac contre Georges de la Trémoïlle (1428)', *B. Philol.* 1944-5, 87-97.

————, 'L'idée de nation et la jurisprudence du Parlement de Paris au xvᵉ siècle', *R. hist.* 204 (1950), 54-61

————, *Le bailliage royal de Montferrand (1425-1556),* Paris, 1957.

————, 'La formule, "Le Roi est empéreur en son royaume". Son emploi au xvᵉ siècle devant le Parlement de Paris', *R. hist. Droit,* 4th Ser. 39 (1961), 371-81.

————, 'Le Parlement de Paris pendant l'occupation Anglaise', *R. hist.* 229 (1963), 19-40

————, 'The Re-establishment of Peace in Society during the reign of Charles VII', in P.S. Lewis (ed.), *The Recovery of France in the Fifteenth Century* (London, 1971), 60-81

Caillet, L., *Étude sur les relations de la commune de Lyon avec Charles VII et Louis XI (1417-1483),* Lyon, 1909

Carr, A.D., 'Welshmen and the Hundred Years War', *The Welsh History Review* 4, i (1968), 21-46

Cazelles, R., 'Un problème d'évolution et d'intégration: les grands officiers de la couronne de France dans l'administration nouvelle au Moyen âge', *Annali della Fondazione Italiana per la Storia Amministrativa* 1 (1964), 183-9

Chaludet, M.-D., 'Robert de Rouvres, évêque nommé de Saint-Flour', *R. Haute-Auvergne* 7 (1905), 86-90

Champion, P., *Vie de Charles d'Orléans (1394-1465),* Paris, 1911

Chevalier, B., 'The Policy of Louis XI towards the *Bonnes Villes:* The Case of Tours', in *The Recovery of France in the Fifteenth Century,* ed. P.S. Lewis (London, 1971), 265-93

————, 'Pouvoir urbain et pouvoir royal à Tours pendant la guerre de Cent ans', *Annales de Bretagne et des pays de l'Ouest* (Maine, Anjou, Touraine) 81 (1974), 365-92

————, *Tours: ville royale, 1356-1520,* Paris/Louvain, 1975

Cheyette, F.L., 'La justice et le pouvoir royal à la fin du Moyen âge français', *R. hist. Droit,* 4th Ser. 40 (1962), 373-94

Contamine, P., *Guerre, État et Société à la fin du Moyen âge,* Paris, 1972

Cosneau, E., *Le Connétable de Richemont, Artur de Bretagne, 1393-1458,* Paris, 1886

Coville, A., *Jean Petit: la question du tyrannicide au commencement du xvᵉ siècle,* Paris, 1932

————, 'Pierre de Versailles (1380?-1446)', *Bibl. Éc. Chartes* 93 (1932), 208-66

Cuissard, C., 'Notes chronologiques sur Jean de Mâcon', *B. Soc. archéol. et hist. de l'Orléanais* 11 (1895-7), 529-45

Cust, E., *Some Account of the Stuarts of Aubigny in France, 1422-*

*1672,* London, 1891

Daniel-Lacombe, H., 'L'Hôte de Jeanne d'Arc à Poitiers: maître Jean Rabateau, président du Parlement de Paris', *R. Bas-Poitou* 4 (1891), 48-66; 5 (1892), 22-51, 297-328; 6 (1893), 158-87; 7 (1894), 272-98

Delachenal, R., *Histoire des avocats au Parlement de Paris (1300-1600),* Paris, 1885

————, 'Une clause de la paix d'Arras. Les conseillers bourguignons dans le Parlement de Charles VII', *B. Soc. Hist. Paris* 18 (1891), 76-83

Delisle, L., 'Nouveau témoignage relatif à la mission de Jeanne d'Arc', *Bibl. Éc. Chartes* 46 (1885), 649-68

————, 'Jean de Mâcon, Professeur d'Orléans', *Bibl. Éc. Chartes* 56 (1895), 223-6

Deman, T., 'Jeanne d'Arc et les Dominicains', *Arch. Frat. Pred.* 1 (1931), 366-90

Desama, C., 'Jeanne d'Arc et Charles VII: l'entrevue du signe (mars-avril 1429)', *R. Hist. Religions* 169-70 (1966), 29-46

————, 'La Première Entrevue de Jeanne d'Arc et de Charles VII à Chinon (mars, 1429)', *Analecta bollandiana* 84 (1966), 113-26

————, 'Jeanne d'Arc et la diplomatie de Charles VII: l'ambassade française auprès de Philippe le Bon en 1429', *A Bourgogne* 40 (1968), 290-9

Dickinson, J.G.D., *The Congress of Arras,* Oxford, 1955

Ditcham, B.G.H., *The Employment of Foreign Mercenary Troops in the French Royal Armies, 1415-1470,* Edinburgh Ph.D. thesis, Edinburgh, 1979

Dodu, G., 'Le Roi de Bourges', *R. hist.* 159 (1928), 38-78

Dondaine, A., 'Le Frère Prêcheur Jean Dupuy, évêque de Cahors et son témoinage sur Jeanne d'Arc', *Arch. Frat. Pred.* 12 (1942), 118-84

————, 'Le témoinage de Jean Dupuy sur Jeanne d'Arc. Note additionnelle à A.F.P., 12 (1942) 167-84', *Arch. Frat. Pred.* 38 (1968), 31-41

Du Cange, *Glossarium ad scriptores mediae et infimae Latinitatis,* ed. G.A.L. Henschel, 7 vols (with suppl.), Paris, 1840-57

Du Fresne de Beaucourt, G., *Histoire de Charles VII,* 6 vols, Paris, 1881-91

Dujardin, J., 'Les débuts de la carrière de Jeanne d'Arc', *Séminaire d'Histoire moderne, Université de Liège,* Liège, 1962

Du Motey, H.J., *Jeanne d'Arc à Chinon et Robert de Rouvres,* Paris 1927

Dupont-Ferrier, G., 'Le rôle des commissaires dans le gouvernement de la France spécialement du xiv<sup>e</sup> au xvi<sup>e</sup> siècle', *Mélanges Paul Fournier,* Paris, 1929, 171-84

————, *Gallia regia ou état des officiers royaux des bailliages et des sénéchaussées de 1328 à 1515,* 6 vols, Paris, 1942-64

Favreau, R., 'La condition sociale des maires de Poitiers au xv<sup>e</sup> siècle', *B. philol.* 1961, 161-77

————, 'Guillaume Gouge de Charpaignes, évêque de Poitiers (1441-1448)', *BSAO,* 4th Ser. 8 (1965-6), 89-100

————, 'Épidémies à Poitiers et dans le Centre-Ouest à la fin du Moyen âge', *Bibl. Éc. Chartes* 125 (1967), 349-98

————, 'La boucherie en Poitou à la fin du Moyen âge, *B. philol.* 1968, 1, 295-318

————, 'La Praguerie en Poitou', *Bibl. Éc. Chartes* 129 (1971), 277-301

————, 'Le palais de Poitiers au Moyen âge. Étude historique', *BSAO,* 4th Ser. 11 (1971-2), 35-65

————, 'Voyages et messageries en Poitou à la fin du Moyen âge', *BSAO*, 4th Ser. 13 (1975-6), 31-53

————, 'La Ville de Poitiers à la fin du Moyen âge: une capitale régionale', *MSAO,* 4th Ser. 14-15 (1977-8), Poitiers, 1978

Fédou, R., 'A Popular Revolt in Lyons in the Fifteenth Century: The *Rebeyne* of 1436', in *The Recovery of France in the Fifteenth Century,* ed. P.S. Lewis (London, 1971), 242-64

Francisque-Michel, X., *Les Écossais en France, les Français en Écosse,* 1 (London, 1862)

Gazzaniga, J.L., *L'Église de Midi à la fin du règne de Charles VII (1444-1461), d'après la jurisprudence du parlement du Toulouse,* Toulouse, 1973

Gilles, H., 'Autorité royale et résistances urbaines, un exemple languedocien: l'échec de la réformation générale de 1434-1435', *B. philol.* (1961), 115-46

Guenée B., 'La géographie administrative de la France à la fin du Moyen âge: élections et bailliages', *Moyen Age* 67 (1961), 293-323

————, *Tribunaux et gens de justice dans le bailliage de Senlis à la fin du Moyen âge (vers 1380 - vers 1550),* Paris, 1963

————, 'État et nation en France au Moyen âge', *R. hist.* 237 (1967), 17-30

*Guide des recherches dans les fonds judiciaires de l'Ancien Régime,* Archives Nationales, Paris, 1958 (Introduction by C. Braibant)

Guillois, A., *Recherches sur les Maîtres des Requêtes de l'Hôtel, des origines à 1350,* Paris, 1909

Hardy, M., 'La Mission de Jeanne d'Arc prêchée à Périgueux en

1429', *B. Soc. Hist. et archéol. du Périgord* 14 (Jan.-Feb. 1887), 50-5

Harmand, J., 'Un document de 1435 concernant Houdan et la fin de l'occupation anglaise dans l'ouest de l'Île de France', *B. Soc. Antiq. France* 1975, 25-47

Heers, J., *Le Clan familial du Moyen âge,* Paris, 1974

Héliot, P., and Benoît, A., 'Georges de la Trémoïlle et la mainmise du duc de Bourgogne sur les Boulonnais', *R. Nord.* 24 (1938), 29-45 and 182-6

Jusselin, M., 'Remontrances du Parlement au roi sur la situation de l'église de France (1430) a. st.', *Bibl. Éc. Chartes* 74 (1913), 516-24

Keen, M.H., *The Laws of War in the Late Middle Ages,* London, 1965

———, *England in the Later Middle Ages: A Political History,* London, 1975 (paperback ed.)

Lacaze, Y., 'Philippe le Bon et le problème hussite: un projet de croisade bourguignon en 1428-1429', *R. hist.* 241 (1969), 69-98

———, 'Le Rôle des traditions dans la genèse d'un sentiment national au xv<sup>e</sup> siècle: la bourgogne de Philippe le Bon', *Bibl. Éc. Chartes* 129 (1971), 303-85

Lacour, R., *Le gouvernement de l'apanage de Jean, duc de Berry*

La Martinière, J. de, 'Frère Richard et Jeanne d'Arc à Orléans, mars-juillet 1430', *Moyen Age* 44 (1934), 189-98

Lanhers, Y., 'Deux affaires de trahison défendues par Jean Jouvenel des Ursins (1423-1427)', *Rec. de mémoires et trav. de la soc. hist. droit écrit,* ed. by the *Soc. Hist. Droit et des Inst. des Anc. Pays de Droit écrit,* Montpellier, 7 (1970), 317-28

Launay, L'Abbé J. de, 'Pierre de Versailles, examinateur de Jeanne d'Arc (1375?-1446)', *R. Hist. Versailles* 1923, 11-18, 160-9

Lavergne, G., 'Quelques étudiants en l'Étude et Université d'Orléans (juin 1412 - juin 1414)', *B. philol.* 1938-9, 137-46

Le Feron, J., *Histoire des connestables, chanceliers et gardes des sceaux,* ed. D. Godefroy, Paris, 1658

Lefèvre, E., *Les avocats du roi depuis les origines jusqu'à la Révolution,* Paris, 1912 (thèse droit)

Lefèvre-Pontalis, G., 'La Panique anglaise en mai 1429', *Moyen Age* 7 (1894), 81-96

———, *Les sources allemandes de l'histoire de Jeanne d'Arc. Eberhard Windecke,* Paris, 1903

Leguai, A., *Les Ducs de Bourbon pendant la crise monarchique du xv<sup>e</sup> siècle,* Paris, 1962

Le Verdier, P., 'Guillaume de Quiefdeville, ambassadeur de Charles VI et Charles VII', *B. Soc. Hist Normandie* 15 (1931-9), 2-16

Lewis, P.S., 'The failure of the French Medieval Estates', *Past and Present* 23 (1964), 3-24

———, *Later Medieval France. The Polity,* London, 1968

———, (ed.), *The Recovery of France in the Fifteenth Century,* London, 1971

Leymarié, A., *Histoire du Limousin,* 2 vols, Paris/Limoges, 1846

Lobineau, G.-A., *Histoire de Bretagne,* 2 vols, Paris, 1707

Longnon, A., 'Les limites de la France et l'étendue de la domination anglaise à l'époque de la mission de Jeanne d'Arc', *R. Quest. Hist.* 18 (1875), 444-546

Lot, F., and Fawtier, R., *Histoire des institutions françaises au Moyen âge,* ii *(Institutions royales),* Paris, 1958

Luce, S., *Jeanne d'Arc à Domrémy,* Paris, 1886

Magne, L., *Le palais de justice de Poitiers. Étude sur l'art français au xiv^e et au xv^e siècles,* Paris, 1904

Major, J.R., *Representative Institutions in Renaissance France, 1421-1559,* Madison, 1960

Maugis, E., *Histoire du Parlement de Paris de l'avènement des rois Valois à la mort d'Henri IV,* 3 vols, Paris, 1913-16

Meunier, R.A., 'Charles VII et la genèse du culte de Jeanne d'Arc (Poitiers, mars-avril, 1429)', in *Faculté des Lettres de l'Université de Poitiers. Mélanges littéraires et historiques publiés à l'occasion du centenaire de sa restauration (8 oct. 1845),* Ligugé, 1946

———, 'Les traditions parlementaires à Poitiers et la grande ordonnance d'avril 1454 pour la réformation de la justice dans le royaume de France', *BSAO,* 4th Ser. 1 (1949-51), 97-106

———, 'Une des sources de l'histoire politique et sociale de la France du xv^e siècle: les registres du Parlement de Poitiers de 1418 à 1436', *BSAO,* 4th Ser. 2 (1952-4), 344-55

Mirot, A., 'Lettres de provision de lieutenant général et sénéchal de Provence délivrées en faveur de Tanguy du Chastel', *B. philol.* 1938-9, 95-109

———, 'Charles VII et ses conseillers, assasins présumés de Jean Sans Peur', *A. Bourgogne* 14 (1942), 197-210

Mollat, M., *Le commerce maritime normand à la fin du Moyen âge,* Paris, 1952

———, 'De la Piraterie sauvage à la course réglementée (xiv^e-xv^e siècle)', *Mél. Ecole franç. Rome. Moyen Age, Temps modernes* 87 (1975), 7-25

Morel, O., *La Grande Chancellerie royale,* Paris, 1900

Neuville, D., 'Le Parlement royal à Poitiers (1418-1436)', *R. hist.* 6 (1878), 1-28 and 272-314

Ornato, M., ed., 'Dictionnaire des charges, emplois et métiers relevant des institutions monarchiques en France au xiv^e et xv^e siècle', *Centre d'Histoire des Sciences et des Doctrines: équipe de recherche sur l'humanisme français des xiv^e et xv siècles. Travaux méthodologiques et répertoires,* 1 (publ. C.N.R.S., Paris, 1975)

Ouy, G., 'Histoire "visible" et histoire "cachée" d'un manuscript', *Moyen Age* 64 (1958), 115-38

————, ' "La Deploratio super civitatem aut regionem que gladium evaginavit super se", Gerson, est-il l'auteur de ce texte anonyme sur les massacres de juin 1418 à Paris?', in *Miscallanea André Combes,* 2 (Rome, 1967), 351-87

————, 'In Search of the Earliest Traces of French Humanism: the Evidence from Codicology', offprint from *The Library Chronicle University of Pennsylvania* 43 (Number i), Spring, 1978

Perroy, É., 'Feudalism or Principalities in Fifteenth-Century France', *BIHR* 20 (1947), 181-5

Petracchi, A., 'I "Maîtres des requêtes", Genesi dell'amministrazione periferica di tipo moderno nella monarchia francese tardo-medioevale e rinascimentale', *A. Fondazione ital. Stor. amministrativa,* 1 (1964), 190- 241

Pocquet Du Haut-Jussé, B.A., 'Deux féodaux: Bourgogne et Bretagne, 1363-1491': v and vi. 'Philippe le Bon et Jean V', *Revue des Cours et Conférences* 36 (1) (1934-5), 439-57 and 641-56

————, 'Le connétable de Richemont, seigneur bourguignon', *A. Bourgogne,* 7 (1935), 309-36; 8 (1936), 7-30, 106-38

Rémy, C., 'Jeanne d'Arc et les Dominicains. La commision de Poitiers et les Dominicains (février-mars, 1429)', *Annales Dominicains* 1 (1904), 207-15

Renouard, Y., 'Les hommes d'affaires italiens à La Rochelle au Moyen âge', in *Studi in onore di Armando Sapori,* 1 (Milan, 1957), 403-16

Robin, P., *La compagnie des secrétaires du roi (1351-1791),* Paris, 1933

Rowe, B.J.H., 'The Grand Conseil under the Duke of Bedford 1422-35', in *Essays. . . H.E. Salter* (Oxford, 1934), 207-34

Samaran, C., *Archives de la maison de La Trémoïlle,* Paris, 1928

Santoni, P., 'Gérard Machet, Confesseur de Charles VII et ses lettres', *Pos. des thèses de l'Éc. nat. des Chartes soutenues par les élèves de la promotion de 1968* (Paris, 1968), 175-82 (publication pending)

Salvini, J., 'Un évêque de Poitiers, Jacques Jouvenel des Ursins (1410-1457)', *BSAO*, 4th Ser. 6 (1961-2), 85-107

Shennan, J.H., *The Parlement of Paris*, London, 1968

Souty, P., 'Jean Barbin, riche et influent seigneur de Touraine et Poitou sous Charles VII', *B. trimest. Soc. archéol. Touraine* 37 (1974), 383-7

Tessereau, A., *Histoire chronologique de la Grande Chancellerie de France*, Paris, 1676 (in two vols. Paris, 1706-10)

Tessier, G., *Diplomatique royale française*, Paris, 1962

———, and Ouy, G., 'Notaires et secrétaires du roi dans la première moitié du xv$^e$ siècle d'après un document indédit', *B. philol.* 1963, 861-90

Thomas, A., '*Les États provinciaux de la France centrale sous Charles VII*, 2 vols, Paris, 1879

———, 'Le siège d'Orléans, Jeanne d'Arc et les capitouls de Toulouse', *A. Midi* 1 (1889), 232-7

———, 'Nouveaux documents sur les États provinciaux de la Haute-Marche (1418-1446)', *A. Midi* 25 (1913), 429-52

———, 'Le Parlement de Poitiers et l'église de France', *Journal des savants* 7 (1914), 315-21

Trocmé, E., and Delafosse, M., *Le commerce rochelais de la fin du xv$^e$ siècle au début de xvii$^e$ siècle*, Paris, 1952

Tyrrell, J.M., 'Financial Activities of the Estates of Poitou', in *Medieval Studies*, 26 (1964), 186-209

———, *A History of the Estates of Poitou*, Paris - La Haye, 1968

Vaesen, M.J., 'Un projet de translation du Concile de Bale à Lyon en 1436', *R. Quest. Hist.* 30 (1881), 561-8

Vale, M.G., 'The Last years of English Gascony, 1451-3', *TRHS*, 5th Ser. 19 (1969), 119-38

———, 'Sir John Fastolf's "Report" of 1435: a New Interpretation Reconsidered', *Nottingham Medieval Studies* 17 (1973), 78-84

———, *Charles VII*, London, 1974

Vallet De Viriville, A., 'Charles VII, roi de France, et ses conseillers', in *L'Investigateur* 8 (1858), 5-20, 110-18, 167-81, 245-53, 278-86, 332-71

———, 'L'Avènement de Charles VII, roi de France, à la couronne', *Bibl. Éc. Chartes*, 5th Ser. 3 (1862), 54-60

Valois, N., *Étude historique sur le Conseil du Roi*, Paris, 1886

———, *Le conseil du roi aux xiv$^e$, xv$^e$ et xvi$^e$ siècles*, Paris, 1888

Viala, A., *Le Parlement de Toulouse et l'administration royale laïque, 1420-1525 environ*, 2 vols, Albi, 1953

234

Voltaire, F.M.A. De, *Histoire du Parlement de Paris,* London, 1773

Waugh, W.T., 'Joan of Arc in English sources of the Fifteenth-Century', in *Historical Essays in Honour of James Tait,* ed. J.G. Edwards, V.H. Galbraith, and E.F. Jacob (Manchester, 1933), 387-98

Wayman, D.G., 'The Chancellor and Jeanne d'Arc, February-July 1429', *Francisc. Stud.* 17 (1957), 273-305

Weigert, P.A., *La tapisserie française,* Paris, 1956

Wolff, P., *Commerces et marchands de Toulouse (vers 1350-vers 1450),* Paris, 1954

———, 'Le théologien Pierre Cauchon de sinistre mémoire', *Mélanges. . . Édouard Perroy* (Paris, 1973), 553-70

# INDEX

# List of volumes in this series

250

Copies obtainable on order from
Watmoughs (City Print) Ltd, 1-7 Albion Place, Britton Street, London EC1M 5RE